EMPORARY BRITISH
JSTRIAL RELATIONS

1

Also by Sid Kessler

CONFLICT AT WORK (with B. Weekes)

Also by Fred Bayliss

BRITISH WAGES COUNCILS

CONTEMPORARY BRITISH INDUSTRIAL RELATIONS

Third Edition

Sid Kessler

and

Fred Bayliss

MACMILLAN
Business

First edition 1992
Reprinted twice
Second edition 1995
Reprinted three times
Third edition 1998

Published by
MACMILLAN PRESS LTD
Houndmills, Basingstoke, Hampshire RG21 2XS
and London
Companies and representatives
throughout the world

ISBN 0–333–73187–5

A catalogue record for this book is available from the British Library.

10 9 8 7 6 5 4 3 2 1
07 06 05 04 03 02 01 00 99 98

Copy-edited and typeset by Povey–Edmondson
Tavistock and Rochdale, England

Printed and bound in Great Britain by
Antony Rowe Ltd
Chippenham, Wiltshire

Contents

List of tables

List of abbreviations

ACAS	Advisory, Conciliation and Arbitration Service
AEU	Amalgamated Engineering Union (previously AUEW)
AEEU	Amalgamated Engineering and Electrical Union formed by merger of AEU and EETPU
AMMA	Assistant Masters' and Mistresses' Association
APEX	Association of Professional, Executive, Clerical and Computer Staff
APT&C	Administrative, Professional, Technical and Clerical grades in local government
ASLEF	Association of Locomotive Engineers and Firemen
ASTMS	Association of Scientific, Technical and Managerial Staff
ATL	Association of Teachers and Lecturers (formerly AMMA)
AUEW	Amalgamated Union of Engineering Workers
BEC	Building Employers Confederation
BIFU	Banking, Insurance and Finance Union
BMA	British Medical Association
BPIF	British Printing Industries Federation
BT	British Telecom
CAB	Citizens Advice Bureau
CAC	Central Arbitration Committee
CBI	Confederation of British Industry
CIR	Commission on Industrial Relations
COHSE	Confederation of Health Service Employees
CPSA	Civil and Public Services Association
CWU	Communication Workers Union
DATA	Draughtsmen's and Allied Technicians' Association
DE	Department of Employment
DTI	Department of Trade and Industry
EC	European Community
EAT	Employment Appeal Tribunal
ECJ	European Court of Justice
ECSC	European Coal and Steel Community
EEF	Engineering Employers' Federation
EETPU	Electrical, Electronic, Telecommunication and Plumbing Union

EMU	European Monetary Union
EOC	Equal Opportunities Commission
EPA	Employment Protection Act 1975
ERM	Exchange Rate Mechanism
ETUC	European Trade Union Confederation
EU	European Union
EWC	European Works Council
FWR	Fair Wages Resolution
FIET	International Federation of Commercial, Clerical, Professional and Technical Employees
GCHQ	Government Communications Headquarters
GDP	Gross Domestic Product
GMB	General, Municipal and Boilermakers' Union
GNP	Gross National Product
GPMU	Graphical Paper and Media Union
HRM	Human Resource Management
ICFTU	International Confederation of Free Trade Unions
ILO	International Labour Organisation
IMF	International Monetary Fund
IMS	Institute of Manpower Studies
IPCS	Institution of Professional Civil Servants
IPMS	Institute of Professionals, Managers and Specialists (formerly IPCS)
IRSF	Inland Revenue Staff Federation
ITB	Industrial Training Board
ITWF	International Transport Workers' Federation
JIC	Joint Industrial Council
JRC	Joint Representation Committee
LAs	Local Authorities
LFS	Labour Force Survey
MLC	Meat and Livestock Commission
MSC	Manpower Services Commission
MSF	Management Science and Finance Union (formerly ASTMS and TASS)
MTFS	Medium Term Financial Strategy
NALGO	National and Local Government Officers' Association (now part of UNISON)
NAS/UWT	National Association of Schoolmasters/Union of Women Teachers
NATFHE	National Association of Teachers in Further and Higher Education
NBPI	National Board for Prices and Incomes
NCB	National Coal Board
NCU	National Communications Union (formerly POEU)
NEDC	National Economic Development Council
NEDO	National Economic Development Office
NES	New Earnings Survey
NGA	National Graphical Association (now part of GPMU)
NHS	National Health Service
NIC	National Incomes Commission
NIRC	National Industrial Relations Court

NJAC	National Joint Advisory Council to the Ministry of Labour
NMW	National Minimum Wage
NUBE	National Union of Bank Employees (now BIFU)
NUCPS	National Union of Civil and Public Services
NUGMW	National Union of General and Municipal Workers (now GMB)
NUJ	National Union of Journalists
NUM	National Union of Mineworkers
NUPE	National Union of Public Employees (now part of UNISON)
NUR	National Union of Railwaymen (now part of RMT)
NUS	National Union of Seamen (now part of RMT)
NUT	National Union of Teachers
OECD	Organisation for Economic Cooperation and Development
OFTEL	Office of Telecommunications
OPEC	Organisation of Petroleum Exporting Countries
POA	Prison Officers' Association
POEU	Post Office Engineering Union (now NCU)
PSBR	Public Sector Borrowing Requirement
PSTCH	Public Services Tax and Commerce Union (previously IRS and NUCPS).
PRP	Performance-Related Pay
RCN	Royal College of Nursing
RMT	National Union of Rail, Maritime and Transport Workers
RPI	Retail Prices Index
SCPS	Society of Civil and Public Servants (now part of NUCPS)
SOGAT	Society of Graphical and Allied Trades '82
STE	Society of Telecom Executives
TASS	Technical, Administrative and Supervisory Staffs of AUEW (previously DATA)
TBF	T. Bailey Forman
TECs	Training and Enterprise Councils
TGWU	Transport and General Workers Union
TINALEA	'This is not a legally enforceable agreement'
TUC	Trades Union Congress
TULRA	Trade Union and Labour Relations Acts 1974 and 1976
TUPE	Transfer of Undertakings (Protection of Employment) Regulations
UCW	Union of Communication Workers
UDM	Union of Democratic Workers
UMA	Union Membership Agreement
USDAW	Union of Shop, Distributive and Allied Workers
WIRS	Workplace Industrial Relations Survey

List of cases

Acknowledgements

In bringing our material up-to-date for the third edition of this book we interviewed, as we did for the first and second editions, 40 or so industrial relations practitioners: mainly union general secretaries and personnel directors of major companies. They are all busy and eminent people and we would like to thank them for devoting their time and for answering our questions with great frankness.

When we were first considering and planning the book we received encouragement and constructive comments from Bill McCarthy, George Bain, Bill Daniel and Pat Lowry, to whom we are most grateful. We are also greatly indebted to the late Hugh Clegg, William Brown, Pat Lowry and Ian Kessler for reading our draft manuscript of the first edition in its entirety, and to Roy Lewis for reading the legal chapters. They all made invaluable and helpful suggestions.

We would also like to thank Anne Stewart, secretary of the Department of Human Resource Management and Organisational Behaviour at the City University Business School, for her hard work, efficiency and good humour in undertaking the administrative and secretarial work involved in the preparation of all editions of this book.

Finally, we are both grateful for the support and encouragement of our wives, Irene and Mary.

SID KESSLER
FRED BAYLISS

The authors and publishers are grateful to the following for permission to reproduce tabular material: The Organisation for Economic Cooperation and Development's *Unemployment 1979–97: International Comparisons*; and Blackwell Publishers Ltd and the London School of Economics for material in the *British Journal of Industrial Relations* in 1983. Every effort has been made to contact all the copyright-holders, but if any have been inadvertently omitted the publishers will be pleased to make the necessary arrangement at the earliest opportunity.

Introduction to the third edition

Since 1979 British industrial relations have been affected by powerful forces of a kind previously unknown in the post-war period. Compared with the previous decades, the 1980s and 1990s were years of new departures. These were the result of three major influences.

The first was political. During the whole period up to 1997 there were 'radical' Conservative Governments which, by a series of legislative steps, and in other ways, sought to limit the scope of trade union action, set new rules for trade union operations and enhance the role of management.

The second was economic. Unemployment rose to levels previously thought politically intolerable, reaching over 3 million in 1987. There was a subsequent decline to 1.5 million in the short-lived boom of the late 1980s before the second great post-war recession which raised unemployment to nearly 3 million in 1992. The slow economic recovery which followed eventually reduced unemployment significantly to 1.5 million in the summer of 1997. In effect, for most of the last two decades there has been high unemployment compared to the full employment of the early post-war decades. The decline in manufacturing industry was a main reason for the high levels of unemployment but there were other significant changes taking place in the labour market. In particular, there was the continued growth of the private service sector and the increase in the proportion of the labour force which was female and part-time. In addition to labour market changes there were profound product market changes as a result of growing world competition, deregulation and the effects of new technology.

The third was change in management policies. As a result of product market competition and the swing in bargaining power, the initiative was firmly with management, who sought to achieve far greater cost effectiveness than they had in the past. There was also the growth of human resource management with its individualistic undertones as against collectivism. It is against this background that the changes in industrial relations have to be considered.

Moreover, if the changes are to be fully understood, they must also be considered against the background of the traditional system of British industrial relations.

The first edition concentrated on the period from 1979 to 1990; the second edition came up to mid-1994; this edition comes up to mid-1997. There was no break in the continuity of developments between 1991 and 1997 so this edition takes the period 1979 to 1997 as being subject to the same influences throughout. There is one major exception to this continuity and that is the election of a Labour Government in May 1997. It is too early to say how far this political change will affect industrial relations. Nevertheless, we do discuss likely changes at some length. Is it the beginning of a new era or not?

We commence in Chapters 1 and 2 with a description of industrial relations in the early post-war decades. At least until the 1970s industrial relations were conducted against a background of full employment and steady economic growth, even if the latter was eventually seen as inadequate compared with that of our main industrial competitors. The post-war 'consensus' – shattered by Mrs Thatcher – included commitment by all political parties to the maintenance of full employment, the welfare state and a mixed economy: that is to say, an acceptance that the public sector as well as the private sector had a significant role to play. It was also accepted that trade unions had an important and legitimate role in industry and in society as a whole, even if there was a growing belief that the balance of power had swung too strongly in their favour.

In retrospect, industrial relations developments in the early post-war years appear to have been relatively unspectacular. But change was constantly taking place, and above all in the growth in certain industries of the power of the shop floor. However, the 1970s saw dramatic events including the re-emergence of major national strikes, the imposition of incomes policies and a determined, but unsuccessful, attempt to change the law. All this took place against an economic background of rapidly rising inflation and a marked slowing down in economic growth which was primarily the consequence of the quadrupling of oil prices by the Organisation of Petroleum Exporting Countries in 1973 and the economic reaction to that event by the leading industrial countries.

If industrial relations developments appeared dramatic in the 1970s, they paled almost into insignificance compared with developments since 1979. We commence our analysis of the period since 1979 with the changing environment. In Chapter 3 we consider the economic background, in Chapter 4 government values and policies, and in Chapter 5 changes in the law, including developments in the European Union. While we do not devote a separate chapter to technological change, we are conscious of its rapid development and application; reference is made to its important effects in a number of places in the text.

We then move on to consider the parties themselves. Thus Chapter 6 examines management strategies in the private sector, Chapter 7 examines the role of government as an employer and quasi-employer, while Chapter 8 looks at the trade unions, which have basically been at the receiving end of change and have had to struggle to adapt in adverse circumstances.

Having considered the changing political, economic and legal environment and the changes in employers and unions, we move on to examine the effects of these changes and their implications for the conduct of industrial relations in the future. Thus in Chapter 9 we consider the institutions of industrial relations, in Chapter 10 pay and productivity and in Chapter 11 strikes. Finally, in Chapter 12 we make an assessment of the changes which have taken place and their causes, and we look forward to what are likely to be the developments in future. This is the chapter which differs most from the first two editions.

An important part of the preparation of the first two editions was the holding of semi-structured interviews on a confidential basis with over 40 key industrial relations practitioners; for this third edition we have again conducted a similar series of interviews. Our interviewees again consisted on the trade union side of general secretaries and senior officials of most of the major unions and the Trades Union Congress. On the employers' side they included personnel directors of leading companies in both the manufacturing and services sectors, the public sector, former public corporations, and major employers' associations, including the Confederation of British Industries. We would in no way claim that this was a scientific sample, but we do believe that we have interviewed most of the key participants.

Our interviews were based on three simple, but major questions. What has happened since 1979? Why did it happen? What are the implications for the future? The answers to these questions are woven into our assessment. The differences of judgement and emphasis in the responses are brought out as well as the areas of agreement. The book is a combination of academic description and analysis with the reporting of the opinions of those who have shaped the years since 1979 and will be in the driving seat for some years to come.

To the memory of Allen Flanders

CHAPTER 1

The early post-war decades, 1945–70

Introduction

Britain's post-war industrial relations system was determined in large part by the economic, political and social environment then prevailing. The immediate post-war economic environment was one of scarcity and shortages of most goods and raw materials. There was no need therefore to fear for full employment (particularly given Marshall Aid) or acute overseas competition, with most of Europe devastated by the war.

Politically, the scene had been set in many respects by the wartime Coalition Government and in particular by the White Papers on Employment and on Social Insurance in 1944. The election of a Labour Government in 1945 ensured that the pledges made by the Coalition Government would be fulfilled. In a truly radical programme that government pursued, first, a policy of full employment; second, it nationalised certain basic industries, such as coal, gas, electricity, railways, air transport and water, a number of which required massive investment if they were to be modernised and made more efficient. Such investment, given the prevailing circumstances, was most unlikely to have been forthcoming from the private sector. Third, the Government introduced what became known as the 'welfare state', the crown piece of which was the National Health Service (NHS), but which also included comprehensive Social Security covering unemployment benefit, old age pensions, sickness and industrial injuries benefit. Fourth, a massive housing programme was undertaken and, fifth, sweeping changes were made in the education system as a result of the 1944 Education Act. All these changes had the support of the Trades Union Congress (TUC). Socially they were in line with public opinion as evidenced by the overwhelming Labour victory in the general election of 1945, despite the personal popularity of Winston Churchill.

1

There was a widespread determination that the nation's wartime sacrifices should not have been in vain and that a better Britain should be built in contrast to the inequities of inter-war Britain and its mass unemployment, poverty and many declining industries and regions.

In terms of the industrial relations system itself, the ground had again been laid during the War. Trade union membership had grown from 6.01 million in 1938 to 7.88 million in 1945. Recognition of unions had grown during the war, strongly encouraged by government: for example, in the engineering industry and at the Ford Motor Company. In a sense, recognition and negotiating machinery were pushed forward as the complement to the direction of labour. The great expansion of union recognition was not so much built on unions steadily acquiring members, as on the fiat of the Ministry of Labour with Ernest Bevin, General Secretary of the Transport and General Workers Union (TGWU), at its head. Moreover, during the War, the TUC learnt about Whitehall and penetrated into its system of consultation so that the National Joint Advisory Council (NJAC) to the Ministry of Labour was only the tip of the iceberg.

Unions had ceased to be 'the Opposition' but had become almost partners both at governmental level and within industry: 'the Fourth Estate'. At national level, early in the war, the government considerably extended its control over labour matters, mainly through Orders under the Defence Regulations. The most important of these was the Conditions of Employment and National Arbitration Order, 1940, familiarly known as Order 1305, which made strikes and lock-outs illegal and provided for binding arbitration. It lasted until 1951 when it was replaced by Order 1376, which ended the illegality of strikes but still provided for unilateral arbitration until 1959. Meanwhile, early in 1939, the NJAC had been established under the chairmanship of the Minister of Labour and National Service. It consisted of fifteen representatives each of the TUC and British Employers' Confederation, and was intended to discuss matters of common interest and assist the Minister in formulating policy. It was largely superseded in wartime by a smaller constituent body known at the Joint Consultative Committee, and this was important in getting cooperation for the main changes in working arrangements necessitated by the war. The NJAC was reconstituted in 1946, representatives of the newly nationalised industries were given seats on the council in 1949, and it continued to function into the 1960s (ACAS 1980b).

Union cooperation in the war effort had been readily forthcoming, helped when Ernest Bevin became Minister of Labour in the 1940 Coalition Government. In industry, the setting-up of Joint Production Committees during the war enhanced the number and influence of shop stewards and greatly extended the practice of joint consultation. This was further enhanced in the immediate post-war years by imposing on the nationalised industries the duty to consult with and, indeed, to recognise representative unions and negotiate with them. The latter obligation considerably extended, in particular, the development of white-collar unionism. Despite the growth in importance of shop stewards, collective bargaining in most sectors of the economy was firmly at industry or regional level and conducted primarily by full-time union officials and employers' associations. The procedures for collective bargaining had been largely left undisturbed during the war, with the exception of Order 1305, and they continued as such in the immediate post-war period.

Indeed, there was a considerable extension of collective bargaining machinery with the establishment of many new Joint Industrial Councils (JICs) and new Wages Councils – the machinery for legal minimum remuneration – for most of retailing and catering and also for a number of smaller trades.

Account should also be taken of Bevin's successful plan to demobilise some 4–5 million servicemen between 1945 and 1947 without causing unemployment, as unemployment remained below 2 per cent between 1945 and 1948. While helped by the high level of demand, the relative ease of the transition from war to peace in the labour market was an important part of the compact between unions and both the wartime Coalition Government and the post-war Labour Government.

Finally, it is worth noting that in the period 1948–50 Britain's first prices and incomes policy was introduced (*Personal Incomes, Costs and Prices*, 1948). It was introduced unilaterally by the Labour Government and subsequently endorsed by the TUC. There was no doubt that the government – the political wing of the labour movement – was in charge and felt entitled to decide that there should be an incomes policy and that the unions – the industrial wing – must acquiesce. Arguably, this was to prove to be the most successful of British incomes policies until it was overwhelmed by inflation as a result of the Korean War and the subsequent upsurge of raw material prices.

1951–64

The year 1951 saw the electoral defeat of the Labour Government and the Conservative Party won the two following elections as well (in 1955 and 1959), so that Conservative Governments were in power from 1951 to 1964. However, the basic post-war consensus continued. There were no major changes in economic policy and full employment was maintained. Unemployment stayed well below 2 per cent throughout this period. There were no concerted attacks on the welfare state or on trade unions.

During the 1950s, national income continued to increase, as did productivity, at a fairly steady rate. Money earnings increased at a moderate rate, as did real earnings and inflation. However, inflationary warning signals emerged in the mid-1950s and became stronger in the early 1960s. In 1956 the Government published a White Paper (*The Economic Implications of Full Employment*, 1956) which called for wage and price restraint. In the following year, the Government established the Council on Prices, Productivity and Incomes which became known as 'The Three Wise Men'. Its task was to publish reports from time to time on the economy, which it was hoped would influence attitudes and ultimately behaviour. In total the Council published four reports during its four years of existence. The first report argued that wage and price increases were primarily caused by excess demand and that the Government should act to reduce demand. This report was attacked by the TUC and others. It was argued that the Council's task was to reconcile full employment with reasonable price stability, whereas the measures proposed meant the abandonment of full employment. In its fourth and final report, the Council changed its approach considerably (perhaps not unassociated with a change in the composition of 'The Three Wise Men'), and explored the possibilities of 'cost-push' inflation as well as 'demand-induced' inflation, and tentatively considered the question of prices and incomes policy.

Although increases in wages and prices continued at a moderate pace, compared with later periods, as did increases in economic growth and productivity, concern became increasingly expressed with regard to Britain's economic performance compared with that of her competitors. Thus while Britain's economic growth and productivity growth were high compared with her own historical record, they were seen as inadequate compared with those of her competitors. France and Germany, for example, as well as Japan, had recovered from wartime destruction and were all showing much faster rates of growth and greater productivity than Britain. International competition was increasing and Britain's share of world export markets was decreasing. Inflation was rising faster than that of Britain's main competitors. There was also concern at what became known as 'stop-go', whereby periods of economic growth led to balance of payments crises which led government to restrict demand and hence slow down growth.

The Macmillan Government's response to these problems was twofold: first, it introduced a prices and incomes policy (*Incomes Policy: The Next Step*, 1962), and second it sought to increase economic growth and productivity. Its incomes policy started with a pay pause in 1961 and was followed by a 'pay norm' or 'guiding light', as it was then called. This was originally set at 2.5 per cent – the estimated growth in national output – the argument being that if income increases were kept to the increase in national output and overall productivity, such increases would be non-inflationary. 'The guiding light' was subsequently increased to 3.5 per cent as the date of the next general election approached. Furthermore, the government established the National Incomes Commission (NIC) in 1962, which was chaired by an eminent barrister and consisted of other independent figures rather than direct representatives of unions and employers. Its terms of reference were very limited and it depended on issues being referred to it by the Government. In its two or so years of existence, it issued only five reports. The one report which had a significant and practical effect was that on university teachers' pay; it resulted in a significant pay increase. The NIC tended to adopt an inquisitorial approach through public hearings; it relied primarily on the evidence of the parties, rather than on building up its own staff to carry out its own enquiries; and it took a year or so to publish reports. Its real importance was that it was the first body to be created which examined the pay of specific groups.

The second creation was the National Economic Development Council (NEDC) in 1962. This was a tripartite body, with the council consisting of members drawn from the TUC, employers' organisations, government and independents; the Council had its own quite considerable staff. Its task was to examine and report on factors which would encourage faster economic growth. Its model was to a considerable extent the French Commissariat du Plan, for the success of French economic planning in achieving rapid growth was much admired at the time.

In terms of industrial relations there were no apparent major changes. Trade union membership grew slowly, from 9.54 million in 1951 to 10.08 million in 1964. However, this growth was virtually no more than proportionate to that of employment, so that union density did not increase significantly over the period (see Table 1.1).

Industry-wide bargaining continued to be the norm, helped by strong central union leadership in the 1940s and 1950s, although towards the end of the period there was increased awareness of the growth in the number and importance of shop stewards and the negotiations in which they engaged with plant managers. This appeared to be mainly in the engineering industry and above all in the motor car industry. The officially recorded number of disputes and the working days lost through disputes continued to be low (see Table 1.2); so much so that some academics were writing of 'the withering away' of the strike (Ross and Hartman 1960). For most of the period the coal-mining industry accounted for well over half the total number of disputes. These disputes characteristically were unofficial and unconstitutional, involved few men and were of very short duration. Consequently, although they accounted for over half the total number of disputes, they accounted for only 5 or 6 per cent of days lost in most years. They were overwhelmingly the result of the piecework system then prevailing in the industry. Outside mining the average number of disputes rose significantly in the 1960s. However, again towards the end of the period, public awareness of small-scale unofficial strikes grew, and much publicity was given to some of these, particularly in the docks, in shipbuilding and the motor car industry, where a stoppage by relatively few people could have major repercussions. Irrespective of the statistics, such unofficial wild-cat strikes had a major impact on public opinion.

Public concern about industrial relations thus grew at this time, partly through the rising number of disputes (many of which were given extra

TABLE 1.1   **Union membership and density, 1945–69 (UK)**

Year	Union membership (000s)	Potential union membership (000s)	Union density
1945	7 875	20 400	38.6
1948	9 363	20 732	45.2
1949	9 318	20 782	44.8
1950	9 289	21 055	44.1
1951	9 530	21 177	45.0
1952	9 588	21 252	45.1
1953	9 527	21 352	44.6
1954	9 566	21 658	44.2
1955	9 741	21 913	44.5
1956	9 778	22 180	44.1
1957	9 829	22 334	44.0
1958	9 639	22 290	43.2
1959	9 623	21 866	44.0
1960	9 835	22 229	44.2
1961	9 916	22 527	44.0
1962	10 014	22 879	43.8
1963	10 067	23 021	43.7
1964	10 218	23 166	44.1
1965	10 325	23 385	44.2
1966	10 259	23 545	43.6
1967	10 194	23 347	43.7
1968	10 200	23 203	44.0
1969	10 479	23 153	45.3

Source: Price, R and Bain, G. S. 'Union Growth in Britain: Retrospect and Prospect', *British Journal of Industrial Relations*, March (1983), Table 1.
Potential union membership = employees in employment (seasonally unadjusted figures for June) plus the number of unemployed in June.

publicity through public enquiries: Scamp, 1968), and partly as a result of the *Rookes* v. *Barnard* case (1964), and to a lesser extent the *Stratford* v. *Lindley* case (1965). The former concerned the dismissal of Rookes by BOAC because Rookes had left his union and a closed shop agreement was in existence. The union – DATA (Draughtsmen's and Allied Technicians' Association: the forerunner of the Technical, Administrative and Supervisory Staffs, or TASS and now the Management Science and Finance Union, or MSF) – threatened industrial action and BOAC thereupon dismissed Rookes. Rookes brought the case against the union officials involved for causing his dismissal and he was ultimately successful in the House of Lords, with damages awarded against

TABLE 1.2   Industrial disputes 1945–68

Year	Number of stoppages beginning in year		Number of workers involved in stoppages beginning in year (000s)		Aggregate number of working days lost in stoppages in progress in year (000s)	
	All industries and services	Outside mining	All industries and services	Outside mining	All	Outside mining
1945	2 293	987	447	204	2 835	2 194
1946	2 205	876	405	188	2 158	1 736
1947	1 721	668	489	181	2 433	1 321
1948	1 759	643	324	135	1 944	1 480
1949	1 426	552	313	65	1 807	1 053
1950	1 339	459	269	127	1 389	958
1951	1 719	661	336	201	1 694	1 344
1952	1 714	493	303	29	1 792	1 132
1953	1 746	439	1 329	1 161	2 184	1 791
1954	1 989	525	402	198	2 457	2 008
1955	2 419	636	599	235	3 781	2 669
1956	2 648	572	464	223	2 083	2 031
1957	2 859	635	1 275	1 010	8 412	7 898
1958	2 629	666	450	201	3 462	3 012
1959	2 093	786	522	331	5 270	4 907
1960	2 832	1 166	698	461	3 024	2 530
1961	2 686	1 228	673	424	3 046	2 309
1962	2 449	1 244	4 297	4 143	6 798	6 490
1963	2 068	1 081	455	303	1 755	1 429
1964	2 524	1 466	700	528	2 277	1 975
1965	2 354	1 614	673	555	2 925	2 513
1966	1 937	1 384	414	364	2 398	2 280
1967	2 116	1 722	551	510	2 787	2 682
1968	2 378	2 157	2 073	2 043	4 690	4 636

Source: Adopted from various Ministry of Labour and Department of Employment and Productivity *Gazettes*.

the union officials. This was considered a disastrous judgment by the trade union movement who, together with most labour law experts, had considered that trade union officials were protected from such an action, as were trade unions themselves, by the 1906 Trade Disputes Act. The trade union movement believed that unless the new legal position was rectified through legislation, union officials would not be able to carry out their essential functions.

Industrial relations thus became an issue between the major political parties in the 1964 election. The apparent difference between them was not, however, great although Conservative Party pressure groups were arguing for greater legal constraints on unions (Inns of Court Conservative and Unionist Society 1958). The Labour Party stated that if elected it would immediately pass legislation reversing the decision in *Rookes* v. *Barnard* and restore the position to what it was thought to have been under the 1906 Trades Dispute Act. It did, however, pledge that it would set up a Royal Commission to investigate the state of industrial relations, thus acknowledging the growth of public concern. The Conservative Party also pledged itself to set up a Royal Commission, the only difference being that a Conservative Government would not take action on the *Rookes* v. *Barnard* decision until the Royal Commission had reported, and that *Rookes* v. *Barnard* would be part of the terms of reference for such a Royal Commission.

1964–1970

The 1964 Labour Government had a tiny majority, which was converted to a substantial majority at the 1966 election. A major theme of the Labour Party during the 1964 election campaign was that Britain had suffered from 'thirteen wasted years' under Conservative governments. However, living standards had increased substantially in those years, hence the Conservative Party's slogan: 'you've never had it so good'. The Labour Party's thrust, however, was that the country had suffered from repeated 'stop-go' economic policies and that Britain's growth had been far smaller than that of her major competitors, with adverse consequences for relative living standards and for the future efficiency of British industry. The Labour Party's electoral programme was therefore based on the need for faster economic growth which would be helped by economic planning and by more capital investment, particularly by the greater use of new technology. It was feared, however, that faster growth would lead to increased inflationary pressures, and so there was a need for a prices and incomes policy. Further, there was a need for improved industrial relations, specific measures for which would depend on the report of the proposed Royal Commission.

In order to further its plans for faster economic growth, the Labour Government created the Department of Economic Affairs, transferring to it a large part of the NEDC's functions and staff. The new Department was given the task of producing a plan for economic growth.

At the same time, the government sought agreement with the TUC and the Confederation of British Industry (CBI) on a prices and incomes policy. This proceeded in three steps. First, in December 1964, the government, TUC and employers agreed the objectives of such a policy in a tripartite 'Declaration of Intent', namely:

1. To ensure that the British economy is dynamic and that its prices are competitive
2. To raise productivity and efficiency so that real national output can increase and to keep increases in wages, salaries and other incomes in line with the increase
3. To keep the general level of prices stable.

Second, in February 1965 (*Machinery of Prices and Incomes Policy*, 1965), the three parties agreed on the mechanism for implementing the policy. NEDC would keep under review the general movement of prices and of money incomes of all kinds, and a National Board for Prices and Incomes (NBPI) would be set up to examine particular cases in order to advise whether or not the behaviour of prices or of wages, salaries or other money incomes was in the national interest as defined by the government after consultation with management and unions.

Third, in April 1965 (*Prices and Incomes Policy*, 1965), the criteria were agreed namely a 3.5 per cent norm and four possible exceptions:

1. Where the employees concerned, for example, by accepting more exacting work or a major change in working practices, had made a direct contribution towards increasing productivity;
2. Where it was essential in the national interest to secure a change in the distribution of manpower and a pay increase would be both necessary and effective for this purpose;
3. Where there was a general recognition that existing levels of remuneration were too low to maintain a reasonable standard of living;
4. Where there was widespread recognition that the pay of a certain group of workers had fallen seriously out of line with the level of remuneration for similar work and needed in the national interest to be improved.

Much was to depend upon how the NBPI interpreted these exceptions. In practice, the NBPI strongly favoured the productivity exception and was extremely restrictive in its interpretation of the other three. For example, even where the NBPI found that low pay existed, it sought to link improvements in pay to measures to increase productivity, as it did in its report on manual workers in local government, the NHS, gas and electricity (NBPI, 1967a), where it argued that the solution to low pay was to increase productivity and hence earnings, to which end it advocated the introduction of payment by results schemes.

Where it found labour shortages, as in the case of the London busmen (NBPI, 1966a), it sought ways of economising on the use of labour and raising labour productivity – for example, one-man bus operation – rather than advocating a straightforward pay increase above the norm in order to attract labour from elsewhere. It made the valid point that in conditions of full employment when one organisation raised pay to attract labour from other organisations, this would only result in labour shortages elsewhere or in the other organisations raising wages in order to maintain their labour forces. As a main part of its approach, the NBPI actively promoted the concept of productivity agreements. Early on it sought (and obtained) from the Government a general reference on productivity bargaining with specific reference to a number of well-known cases: for example Esso Fawley, Esso Milford Haven, Esso Distribution, British Oxygen, ICI and Alcan's Rogerstone Plant. From a study of these and other productivity agreements, the NBPI in its reports (NBPI, 1966b and 1967b), produced a set of guidelines which were embodied by the Government in its subsequent White Paper on the next stages of incomes policy.

The NBPI had a number of notable achievements to its credit (Fells, 1972; Mitchell, 1972). Although firms and industries were only referred to the Board if their proposed pay or price increases were not in accord with the policy, the Board invariably took the opportunity to examine the whole range of firms' operations on the grounds that these affected their prices and the wages they could afford to pay. One example was the Board's persistent recommendation of the tachograph in road haulage. Apart from references on specific firms and industries the Board received a number of general references: for example, on payment by results, job evaluation, hours of work, overtime and shiftworking (NBPI, 1968a, 1968b, 1969), which produced guidelines which were widely considered by industry. Moreover, the Board encouraged the widening of the agenda of collective bargaining through its championing of productivity bargaining.

The Board was never negative in its approach and considered that in addition to its function as interpreter of the guidelines of incomes policy, it had an advisory and consultancy function to improve efficiency and to improve industrial relations in British industry. There was widespread agreement that credit should be given to the Board for adopting a creative and constructive approach, rather than a purely negative and restrictive one. The Board consisted of senior representatives of unions, employers and independent academics, as well as ex-Ministers of both political parties. Its chairman for most of its life, Aubrey Jones, and its first secretary, Alex Jarratt, set the tone for its positive role, and in the field of industrial relations in its early years it had the benefit of Hugh Clegg as a Board member and Allan Flanders as its adviser.

Apart from its substantive achievements, it pioneered new methods of enquiry. The NBPI built up a substantial staff with seconded civil servants forming the admininstrative basis and specialist teams, consisting originally of economists, industrial relations experts and statisticians, who were soon to be joined by accountants and management consultants. Each reference was headed by a Board member and working parties were formed, normally with a civil servant as Chairman, another as Secretary, and members of appropriate specialist groups. These working parties conducted their own research and enquiries as well as taking evidence from the parties. One notable feature of most pay references was the carrying-out of earnings surveys to discover the composition and distribution of pay and hours of work, instead of relying on average earnings figures or basic rates of pay. Indeed, the NBPI, by exposing the inadequacy of government statistics on pay and earnings, was instrumental in the introduction of the annual *New Earnings Survey* in 1968.

However, incomes policy soon ran into difficulties with pay increasing faster than the norm. In 1965 the Government announced (*Prices and Incomes Policy: An Early Warning System*, 1965) its intention of introducing compulsory notification of pay and prices increases. In 1966, a severe sterling crisis led the Government to abandon its voluntary incomes policy, to introduce a six-month freeze (*Prices and Incomes Standstill*, 1966) and to introduce a statutory basis for the policy, backed by legal sanctions (Prices and Incomes Act, 1966). The six months freeze on incomes and prices was followed by a period of 'severe restraint' when there was a nil norm and a tightening of the original productivity exceptions (Period of Severe Restraint, 1966). Subsequently further easements were made (*Prices and Incomes Policy after 30 June, 1967* and *Productivity, Prices and Incomes in 1968 and 1969*). Indeed, with a general election looming there was a considerable loosening of controls (*Productivity, Prices and Incomes Policy after 1969*). In January 1970, statutory controls were lifted, although negotiators were urged to restrict settlements to between 2.5 per cent and 4.5 per cent, with exceptions for productivity agreements and where settlements included moves towards equal pay.

Although the policy had a number of achievements to its credit, there was also a debit side. Too much had been expected and in too short a time: trade union cooperation (which had been readily given at the beginning of the policy) was eroded, partly as a result of the statutory interference with free collective bargaining, and partly because the administration of the policy almost inevitably bred anomalies. Such anomalies were increased by the fact that pay settlements were vetted by the Ministry of Labour and (from 1968 to 1970) the Department of Employment and Productivity, rather than the NBPI. The parties learned a lesson which was to lead to problems with all successive incomes policies: if the parties could find ways round the policy, the vetters were either too overburdened to challenge them or were pleased to find that a confrontation could be avoided. The application of the policy became an extension of bargaining, with managers and trade unionists going to the Department to explain how what they had agreed met one or other of the criteria for exceptional treatment. In such a bargaining atmosphere, the professional negotiators had a great advantage. The Department was indeed completely inadequately staffed for this task. Also it had to take account of political realities and was more inclined to let powerful groups through the vetting process, greatly stretching the criteria in the process. In contrast, if a reference was made to the NBPI, it on the whole abided by the criteria, partly because they provided its *raison d'être* and partly because it had to publish a public report to justify its conclusions in the light of the criteria.

The relaxation of criteria by the government meant rising expectations on the part of unions and employees, while management was conscious of the need to deal with anomalies. Real pay had been curtailed as a consequence of incomes policy and as a result of the devaluation of sterling in 1967 and the severe budgets which followed in an attempt to deal with balance of payments problems.

The Donovan Commission

Meanwhile the Royal Commission on Trade Unions and Employers' Associations (subsequently known as 'The Donovan Commission' after its chairman, Lord Donovan, a judge) had been established in 1965 with the following terms of reference:

> To consider relations between managements and employees and the role of trade unions and employers' associations in promoting the interests of their members and in accelerating the social and economic advance of the nation with particular reference to the law affecting the activities of these bodies.

The Commision was noteworthy not only for the contents of its Report (it was, after all, the first Royal Commission on industrial relations for 60 years), but for the research which it commissioned and published in a series of papers. It was, like the NBPI, not content simply to hear the formal evidence of the interested parties, but sought its own information in a systematic and coordinated manner.

The Commission's Report was published in 1968. Among its central conclusions was that collective bargaining was the best and most democratic means of conducting industrial relations, and that the role of the law in collective relations should be a very limited one. It rejected various proposals for legal restraints: for example, to ban closed shops, to make collective agreements legally enforceable, to restrict the right to strike, to interfere in union rule books, and to impose 'cooling-off' periods and ballots before industrial action. Donovan did not say that the law should never be introduced to industrial relations; it said that it would be inadvisable to do so on practical grounds, and that voluntary reform, if it could be achieved, was preferable.

Central to the Donovan analysis was that Britain had 'two systems' of industrial relations. One was the 'formal system', embodied in the official institutions of collective bargaining at industry level. The other was the 'informal system', based on the actual behaviour of managers, shop stewards and work groups at the place of work. The two systems were often in conflict, with the informal system undermining the formal system. One symptom of this was the growing gap between actual earnings and industry-wide rates of pay, called 'wage drift'. Domestic bargaining had also led to fragmented bargaining and fragmented pay structures. Moreover, the growth of workplace bargaining had put industry-wide disputes procedures under pressure at a time when plant and company level procedures were virtually non-existent.

The Donovan Report related to the growing importance of workplace representatives as a result of the needs of managers and trade union members to have negotiators at the point where disputes over pay, overtime, discipline and recruitment occurred. Its recommendations brought the shop stewards into the official fold. Trade unions had to come to terms with them and employers had to accept them 'officially' in settled procedures. Indeed, Donovan's remedy was not the use of law, but the reform and reconstruction of industrial relations procedures by voluntary means. It was neither desirable nor possible to suppress plant and company bargaining. Industry-level agreements should be confined to those matters which they could effectively determine, while plant and company bargaining should be recognised and formalised. The objective was the development of authoritative collective bargaining machinery and comprehensive procedural agreements at plant and company level. The responsibility for this should rest with the parties themselves, although the prime responsibility lay with top management since they had the final power. However, to help the process the Donovan Commission proposed that larger organisations should register their agreements with the Department of Employment and Productivity, and that an independent Standing Commission should be established to facilitate the voluntary reform of collective bargaining.

The Donovan Commission's recommendations had a mixed reception. There were academic attacks which claimed, for example, that the Commission had concentrated too much on procedural instead of on substantive matters and that the Commission had generalised too much from the situation in the engineering industry (*British Journal of Industrial Relations*, 1968). Those who had wanted substantial legal changes, such as restrictions on unofficial strikes and the legal enforcement of collective agreements, were disappointed. Unions were not on the whole dissatisfied (particularly as restrictive legal measures had not been proposed), whilst employers' reactions were somewhat mixed.

The Government's response was contained in its White Paper, *In Place of Strife* (1969). It accepted most of the analysis of the Commission and its conclusions, including the immediate establishment of a reforming Commission on Industrial Relations (CIR) as a body to promote collective bargaining and good industrial relations on a voluntary basis. However, it felt that this was not sufficient to deal with Britain's industrial relations problems and thus it put forward some legal changes which went well beyond what Donovan considered practicable. It proposed reserve powers for the Secretary of State to enforce a conciliation pause in unconstitutional strikes and other stoppages where adequate joint discussions had not taken place; compulsory ballots in certain severe strikes; and measures to deal with inter-union disputes.

The proposed legal changes aroused strong opposition from the TUC and led to prolonged and often bitter discussions between the TUC and the Government (Jenkins, 1970). These culminated in an agreement whereby the Government withdrew its proposed 'penal' clauses in exchange for the TUC's promise to alter its rules so that more control could be exercised by the TUC over unofficial strikes, inter-union disputes and disputes which affected workers outside the company or industry directly involved. Within the Parliamentary Labour Party, James Callaghan had successfully argued that the 'penal' clauses would wreck the interdependence of the unions and the Party to the disadvantage of both; the unions would be weaker in collective bargaining, and voters would be driven away from the Party.

Although the TUC did amend its rules – to little practical effect – the dispute between government and the TUC did great harm to the standing of the government, which was perceived by the public to have backed down. Also, while it enhanced the power of the TUC, it added weight to the perception of those who already thought that the unions were overpowerful and needed to be curtailed.

The Commission on Industrial Relations

Meanwhile the CIR started work early in 1969 with the support of unions and employers. The Commission itself was headed by George Woodcock, who retired early from the General Secretaryship of the TUC in order to become Chairman. Other members with a trade union background were Will Paynter (full-time), recently retired General Secretary of the National Union of Mineworkers (NUM), and Alf Allen (part-time), General Secretary of the Union of Shop, Distributive and Allied Workers (USDAW); those with an employers' background were Leslie Blakeman (full-time), former industrial relations director of Ford, and J. R. Edwards (part-time), former managing director of the British Motor Corporation. The final full-time member was a noted industrial relations academic, Allan Flanders, whose publications and evidence had had a significant effect on the thinking and conclusions of the Donovan Commission. The staff was headed by the Secretary of the Commission, a seconded senior civil servant, Norman Singleton, and consisted of a number of other civil servants, mainly in administrative roles, and operational staff who were recruited from industry, trade unions and academia.

In its first General Report (CIR, 1970b), the CIR stated that its broad purpose, which was derived from the Donovan Commission, was:

> that collective bargaining was the best method of regulating questions of pay and conditions of employment and of providing a means for orderly and constructive change and of conducting industrial relations generally. The practice of collective bargaining was, however, held to be deficient in many respects. Over large areas of employment it did not exist at all and where it did exist, its scope and subject matter was often narrowly limited. In many, including some of the most important, industries, actual pay and conditions, which were nominally the subject of industry-wide agreements, were often in practice effectively settled informally by local managements and workgroups. One of the principal measures of reform recommended by the Donovan Commission was the creation of an agency specifically devoted to developing and improving collective bargaining and the general conduct of industrial relations.

The Report noted that *In Place of Strife* had elaborated on the functions of the CIR and that, under the Royal Warrant which had established the CIR, its role was the examination and improvement of 'the institutions and procedures for the conduct of industrial relations'. Such examination was carried out on the basis of references made to it by the Secretary of State for Employment and Productivity. These references were of four main types. The first was general references, which were not restricted to a particular company or industry, but were of general industrial relations application. Early examples were *Facilities afforded to Shop Stewards* (CIR, 1971a) and *The Disclosure of Information* (CIR, 1972b). Second, there were references concerned with industrial relations questions throughout a whole industry. Early examples were the *Shipbuilding and Ship Repairing Industry* (CIR, 1971b) and the *Hotel and Catering Industry* (CIR, 1971c). Third, there were company procedural cases where the purpose was to examine the conduct of industrial relations within a particular company or within selected establishments: for example, *Birmid Qualcast* (CIR, 1970a). Fourth, and finally, there were recognition cases where one or more unions sought recognition which the employer was unwilling to grant, early examples of which were the *Associated Octel Company Ltd* (CIR, 1969a) and the *General Accident Fire and Life Assurance Company Ltd* (CIR, 1969b).

The CIR defined its role as that of a third party, the prime responsibility for the conduct of industrial relations resting with unions and managements. However, it sought to distinguish its role from that of traditional third-party intervention – conciliation, arbitration and enquiry – by stating that it was not a 'fire-fighting' organisation but rather a 'fire-prevention' agency, and that it was not concerned with attributing blame but to help with problems and to try to achieve practical solutions.

With regard to the CIR's methods of work (CIR, 1970b), there were close similarities between its approach and that of the NBPI. This was not altogether surprising as a number of the key staff at the CIR, as well as one of the Commissioners, had worked at the NBPI and had played a vital role in establishing its enquiry methods in its early days. When a CIR reference was received from the Secretary of State, it was normally assigned to a Commissioner supported by a small group of staff. A difference here with the NBPI was that whereas the CIR's operational staff were all essentially industrial relations experts, the NBPI's staff had necessarily come from a variety of disciplines.

At an early stage there were discussions with the parties about the reference, the information that would be required, and the best method of obtaining such information. When the main enquiries had been completed, there were further discussions with the parties about the issues that had arisen and the CIR's ideas for dealing with them. A draft report was prepared and discussed with the parties, and their agreement sought on a course of action before the final report was published. Indeed, the whole process sought to carry the parties along with the CIR from beginning to end and, to that extent, took the consultative process further than had the NBPI. This was explicable, apart from its inherent desirability, by the fact that the CIR at this stage in its history had no compulsory powers, so its success depended on persuasion and achieving a voluntary agreement with, and between, the parties. With an emphasis on ascertaining the facts for itself, the CIR made use not only of documentary records and evidence from the parties, but conducted attitude, and often earnings, surveys of its own. To quote again from the CIR's *First General Report*:

> Much crucial information is, however, concerned with attitudes and beliefs of which there is no record and about which there can be serious misconceptions. We are concerned with how things work in practice and with what people actually think, as distinct from what it is assumed that they think. (For this type of information we have found structured interviews and attitude surveys to be useful working methods.)

Conclusion

At the end of the 1960s, the trade unions had emerged from the Donovan Commission and from the battle over *In Place of Strife* relatively unscathed and in an apparent position of enhanced power. Legal constraints had been rejected by Donovan, and the restrictive legislative proposals contained in

In Place of Strife had been withdrawn. The CIR had been established, and had commenced work with the remit of extending and improving collective bargaining and its institutions and procedures, but on a purely voluntary basis. Formal incomes policies had run their course and the unions' objective of the restoration of 'free' collective bargaining had been virtually achieved.

Employers, for their part, were more ready to accept union recognition – particularly for white-collar employees – and tended to regard the extension of collective bargaining as inevitable. Some employers were prepared to engage in reform, as witnessed by some of the productivity agreements. Unfortunately, making productivity agreements the major exception to incomes policy constraints had led to the 'debasing of the currency', and much of the good in the early comprehensive productivity agreements became forgotten as a consequence of numerous 'phoney deals', but not entirely so. The educational effect of NBPI reports was not completely wasted and, for example, its constant emphasis on the link between real pay improvements and efficiency, and its attempts to improve pay structures through job evaluation and the reappraisal of payments systems continued to have an effect long after the demise of NBPI. Similarly, the recommendations of the Donovan Report and the continuation of its themes through the work of the CIR stimulated some companies to rethink their industrial relations practices and to seek to improve their workplace arrangements: in particular to try to reduce fragmented bargaining, to introduce more rational and formalised procedures in order to deal with grievances and bargaining matters and to acknowledge and formalise the role of shop stewards.

In conclusion, during the whole span of the post-war period up to 1970 the consensus underlying industrial relations had proved remarkably durable. Employers and unions, together with successive governments, had jointly supported collective bargaining as the means for determining pay and settling disputes. But there were signs of strain; the fabric was wearing thin in several places. Two were paramount. First, full employment tended to make negotiated settlements and the working of the labour market generate pay increases which exceeded what was compatible with low inflation, or inflation as low as that of our competitors. Incomes policies had become progressively more complicated and more draconian; the fiercer they were, the more difficult they were to relax without them running out of control.

Second, the paramountcy of the industry agreement had been sapped by the spontaneous growth of negotiations in the place of work. This was of great significance for incomes policies which had to strive to restrain pay wherever it was determined, and it was obviously far harder to affect multitudinous local bargains than a limited number of industry agreements. But it had a profound long-term significance for both employers and unions. Local negotiations meant that senior managers had to consider how local managers' bargaining decisions could be fitted into company objectives. In trade unions, the balance of power between workshop organisation and representatives and

CHAPTER 2

The 1970s

Introduction

The 1970s was a decade of considerable economic and political upheaval. In the political field, the 1970 general election resulted in the return of a Conservative Government under Edward Heath. The Conservative Party had moved somewhat to the right while in opposition and its programme envisaged much greater emphasis on free market forces, the abolition of the prices and incomes policy and a strong new industrial relations law. After a tumultuous four years, during which it had done a U-turn on prices and incomes policy, the Government went to the electorate in the midst of a national mineworkers' strike in 1974 on the issue of 'Who governs Britain?' and was defeated. The new Labour Government had only a very small majority, and a second election in 1974 still did not provide a significant Labour majority in the House of Commons. The Government was ultimately dependent on the support of the Liberals and the Scottish and Welsh Nationalist Parties. It had been elected at least partly on the basis that it knew how to get on with the trade unions and this indeed appeared to be the case in its early days when the Social Contract was in force.

However, with startling price and wage inflation, the Social Contract came under severe pressures, although for two years a voluntarily agreed incomes policy with the TUC was remarkably successful in bringing down the rate of wage and price inflation through a reduction in real pay. Such a situation could not continue indefinitely, and after two years of trade union restraint, pressure mounted, culminating eventually in the so-called 'Winter of Discontent' in 1978/79 which resulted in the general election of 1979 and the return of a Conservative Government under Mrs Thatcher.

The economic background to those political events was equally dramatic. In 1973 the Organisation of Petroleum Exporting Counties (OPEC) quadrupled the price of oil with devastating effect. The Western world reacted to what it feared would be a major inflationary force by restrictive economic and monetary policies. World economic growth slowed markedly and indeed in some countries there was actually recession and a fall in Gross National Product (GNP). Unemployment increased and some economists considered this the period when the consistent and high economic growth of the industrialised Western world since the Second World War ended. Equally it was considered by many to mark the end of the post-war era of full employment. The new phenomenon of rapidly rising prices, combined with an absence of significant economic growth, became known as 'stagflation'.

Britain's record was among the worst and consequently in 1976 the sterling exchange rate came under great pressure, resulting in the need for drastic action and in the Government having to apply for a major International Monetary Fund (IMF) loan. This was granted, but, as was normal practice, it was accompanied by a number of restrictive conditions, paramount among which was that public expenditure should be reduced and a strict monetary policy adopted. These measures killed what little hope there was of a successful continuation of the 'Social Contract'. With very low economic growth and consequently low growth in real incomes, with cuts in public expenditure and rising unemployment, antagonism between unions and government grew, culminating in the Winter of Discontent.

1970–4

Incomes policy

The Heath Government ended incomes policy and abolished the NBPI (although a small number of staff were transferred to a new organisation called the Office of Manpower Economics whose main task was to service the Pay Review Bodies and to study any general matters referred to it by the Government). In place of incomes policy, there was 'free collective bargaining'. Collective bargaining does not, however, take place in a vacuum, and the fact that the Government did not have an overt incomes policy did not mean that it did not have a policy for pay. The Government indeed sought to bring down the level of wage settlements in the private sector by persuasion, by creating more competitive labour and product markets, by more restrictive economic policies, and by the example of what could be achieved in the public sector. In the public sector, the Government sought to reduce progressively the level of settlements by a policy which was dubbed by the press as 'N−1'. This policy provoked a national postmen's strike in 1970 as well as other disputes in certain parts of the public sector, including local authority manual workers, electricity and coal-mining. The postal strike lasted several weeks, but in the end was defeated. The policy indeed in its early days had some degree of success.

However, in the end it came to grief with the national coal-mining strike of 1972 (the first such miners' national strike since 1926). Miners' earnings during the 1960s had slipped markedly down the earnings ladder from the top position which they had held during the 1950s. The industrial action began with an overtime ban at the end of 1971 and escalated into an all-out strike early in 1972. Coal production ceased, and successful picketing reduced the movement of fuel supplies, in particular to power stations. There were power cuts, as there were to be again during the 1974 miners' strike. Thus industrial relations reached right into people's homes – their lights went out – and that raised the significance of industrial action in pursuit of pay claims to a new political level. With the position becoming critical, the government set up a Court of Inquiry under Lord Wilberforce who reported with great speed, recommending a very substantial pay increase and improvements in other terms and conditions (Court of Inquiry, 1972). The NUM did not accept the Wilberforce Report immediately, although the government did. Further negotiations took place with the government which resulted in a settlement in which the NUM won further concessions. The NUM's success meant the end of the government's N−1 policy.

Other unions sought to emulate the NUM by seeking very substantial pay increases, while the government reversed its position by seeking to obtain an agreed incomes policy. Talks with the TUC and CBI took place in the second half of 1972 and continued for several months. The government offered the TUC a place in the formulation of economic policy, based on NEDC, which went further than anything offered by any previous Government, in exchange for active support of an incomes policy. In the end the TUC drew back and, on the failure of the talks, the government proceeded to implement a unilaterally determined statutory policy in November 1972 (Counter Inflation Act). The policy was implemented in three stages. Stage 1 – up to April 1973 – consisted of a complete freeze on pay, prices, dividends and rents. Stage 2 – from April to November 1973 – permitted maximum pay increases of £1 a week plus 4 per cent up to a maximum of £250 per year for any individual worker (the only exception being equal pay). Stage 3 – from November 1973 – permitted maximum increases of 7 per cent on total pay bills (the 'kitty' principle) or £2.25 a week up to a maximum of £350 per annum for an individual employee. An extra 1 per cent of the pay bill was allowed for restructuring, and exceptions existed for equal pay, proven 'efficiency' schemes, the working of 'unsocial hours' and to deal with major 'anomalies' which had arisen as a result of the freeze. Finally, there was provision for 'threshold' payments at a flat-rate payment of 40 pence for each 1 per cent point increase in the Retail Prices Index (RPI), to be triggered if the Index increased by more than 7 per cent. The government's expectation was, of course, that the Index would not reach that level, but it had reckoned without the oil price increase and the escalation of other raw material prices.

The Counter Inflation Act 1973 established the machinery to operate the policy – a Pay Board and a Price Commission – and there were detailed and precise codes for the regulation of pay and prices. Pay settlements covering over 1000 workers had to be approved by the Pay Board, while settlements involving smaller numbers had to be notified to the Board. The institutions and guidelines of the Heath Government's attempt at an incomes policy thus differed from those of the Wilson Government 1964–70. The machinery set up somewhat earlier by the Nixon administration in the USA to run its pay and prices policy was consciously imitated, especially on the prices side. First, two bodies were established – one for pay and one for prices – instead of a single body to deal with both as with the NBPI. Second, detailed rules were established for pay and price increases with the Pay Board and Price Commission having little scope for interpretation, unlike the 1960s when the exceptions to the norm were phrased in fairly general terms leaving the NBPI wide scope for interpretation and for acting in a constructive manner. Third, having established precise rules, vetting of pay increases was in the hands of the Pay Board and not as previously in those of the Department of Employment (DE), with the NBPI as a long stop. In some respects it might be argued that the new arrangements were an improvement on the old for there was only one interpreter of the policy but, in other respects, they were clearly less flexible and hence provided less scope for a constructive and reforming role, although there were some signs that the Pay Board would be used to give general guidance (for example, in its references on pay anomalies and on London weighting).

The policy appeared to be working reasonably well until a dispute over the annual pay negotiations developed in the coal-mining industry. The NUM had received an enormous boost from its successful strike in 1972 and its bargaining power was enhanced by OPEC's quadrupling of oil prices; a remarkable contrast with the decline in its power and status in the 1960s, when it had acquiesced in, and indeed peacefully cooperated with, a major reduction in the size of the coal industry (and hence in its membership), and a relative decline in miners' real earnings. The government believed that it could accommodate the miners' pay demands within its incomes policy guidelines through its provision for unsocial hours payments. This proved not to be the case and, after an initial ban on overtime in November 1973, a national strike was called in February 1974. Coal shortages soon developed, and the electricity industry in particular was badly affected. Flying pickets of miners were organised to prevent the movement of coal – it was in connection with these pickets that Arthur Scargill first came to national notice – and at Saltley coke depot the police were unable to control the large numbers involved, an event which had important repercussions when the use of legislation against trade unions was being considered by the next Conservative Government. The Government introduced emergency measures, including a three-day week for industry and restrictions on domestic supply. It also referred the miners' case to the Pay Board, but this did not lead the NUM to call off its industrial action. Eventually, after many talks, including attempted conciliation by the TUC, the Government decided to call a general election in February 1974 on the issue of 'Who runs the country?'

Industrial relations inevitably was a major feature of the election campaign. Indeed Mr Heath attributed his defeat to two industrial relations matters: first, the statement during the campaign, attributed to the Deputy Chairman of the Pay Board, that the miners' earnings figures as officially recorded and used by the government were inaccurate, or at least misleading to the miners' disadvantage when used for comparisons with earnings in other industries; second, the statement during the campaign by the then Director General of the CBI that the government's 1971 Industrial Relations Act had been a disaster. When the Pay Board reported at the end of the general election, it found in favour of the miners.

Industrial relations and the law

The Heath Government had included in its election manifesto proposals for major changes in industrial relations law and these were embodied in the Industrial Relations Act 1971 (Weekes *et al.*, 1975; Arbitration, Conciliation and Advisory Service, ACAS, 1980b). The Act established a new industrial relations institution, called the National Industrial Relations Court (NIRC); put the CIR on a statutory basis; revised and extended the jurisdiction of industrial tribunals and that of the Industrial Court (renaming the Court the Industrial Arbitration Board); and replaced the Registrar of Friendly Societies with a Registrar of Trade Unions and Employers' Associations, with whom independent trade unions and employers' associations could be registered if their rules and procedures, particularly those relating to the rights of the members and the holding of ballots, conformed to certain standards laid down in the Act.

NIRC was made part of the High Court and consisted of both judges and lay members with industrial relations expertise from both sides of industry. The Act removed from the jurisdiction of the ordinary courts most legal proceedings arising out of industrial disputes and partly replaced traditional common law by a new ground for legal proceedings: a complaint of 'unfair industrial practice'. The traditional immunities were in general limited to unions which registered under the Act. In addition, registered unions were given special facilities, notably over access to the NIRC, and one major new immunity over breach of commercial contracts.

The CIR was given statutory powers to deal with union recognition disputes. However, the Act made post-entry 'closed shop' agreements void and sought to make pre-entry closed shop agreements unenforceable by giving workers the right to belong or not to belong to any union, and by making it an 'unfair industrial practice' to prevent anyone from exercising this choice. As an alternative, an 'agency shop' could be established under which employees had to join the union, or pay the union the equivalent of its subscription in lieu of membership, or pay the equivalent sum to charity (CIR, 1973a). The Act also allowed in exceptional circumstances for an 'approved' closed shop on application to NIRC and after reference, enquiry and recommendation, by the CIR (CIR, 1972a, 1973b).

The Act contained a number of other provisions: for example, the Secretary of State was given the power to order a 'cooling-off period' of up to 60 days where an industrial dispute threatened the economy or public health or safety, and to restrain industrial action in certain circumstances while a compulsory ballot was conducted (CIR, 1973a). This power was used only once – in 1972 – and involved a major railway dispute. The unions obeyed the Court Order and suspended industrial action while the CIR conducted a ballot among the membership. The ballot resulted in an overwhelming majority for union action. Picketing at a person's home (unless it was also that person's place of work) was exempted from statutory immunity for 'peaceful picketing'. Written collective agreements were presumed to be legally enforceable contracts unless they expressly contained a disclaimer. A code of practice was issued giving guidance on good industrial relations practice, and while failure to observe the Code did not render anyone liable to legal proceedings, it could be used in evidence before industrial tribunals or the NIRC. The Act also extended individual employees' rights in a major way to include a right not to be unfairly dismissed.

As can be seen by this brief summary of the contents of the Act, it was an attempt to deal with everything at one fell swoop, and much of it was based on American law. It sought to control by legislation the status of collective agreements, the rights of individuals *vis-à-vis* trade unions and the closed shop, picketing, industrial disputes in essential services, and the registration of unions eligible for immunity from legal action. Overarching it all was NIRC, to which all breaches of the Act's provisions would be directed. It was naive in its scope and its intention. Its originator and the master of its detail was Geoffrey Howe, the Solicitor General, who to all intents and purposes became a DE Minister until the Bill reached the statute book. It was the lawyers' solution to politically defined industrial relations problems. It marked the end of the Conservative Party's acceptance of the 1906 Act's definition of trade union immunities and the Labour Government's repeal in 1946 of the 1927 Trade Disputes Act. From this point on, the use of law by all governments to bring about changes in industrial relations was permanently on the agenda.

Consequences of the 1971 Act

The Act was bitterly opposed by the trade union movement. Member unions were advised by the TUC to boycott it, not to cooperate with the CIR and NIRC, not to enter into binding collective agreements and not to serve on industrial tribunals. The major plank of TUC opposition, however, was to advise (and eventually to instruct) affiliated unions not to register with the new Registrar. The government sought to counter this policy by automatically transferring to the new register unions who were already registered with the Registrar of Friendly Societies. TUC unions therefore had to actively de-register, which caused special problems for some who were required to be registered under their rules. The overwhelming majority of unions including all of the largest, followed TUC policy and de-registered, even though they lost tax advantages in the process, as well as legal protection for most forms of industrial action. Some 30 unions did not de-register, including a few medium-sized unions such as the National Graphical Association (NGA) and the National Union of Bank Employees (NUBE). They were all consequently expelled from the TUC (to be readmitted a few years later, after the repeal of the 1971 Act by the next Labour Government).

Employers, whose bargaining power the legislation was intended to strengthen, generally did not seek to enforce the provisions of the Act. They readily accepted the insertion of a clause in collective agreements, initiated by the unions, that 'This is not a legally enforceable agreement' (TINALEA), and most closed shops were undisturbed. Trouble did, however, develop with the dockers, whose employment opportunities were being threatened by containerisation, especially when the loading and unloading of containers was carried out at inland depots. The dockers demanded that this work should be carried out only by dockers and, in seeking to enforce this demand, depots were picketed and the movement of goods blacked. One firm – Heatons – applied for, and was granted, an order from NIRC that the blacking should stop. The TGWU refused to appear in court, in line with TUC policy, and was fined £5000 for contempt followed by a further fine of £50 000 and a warning that all its assets would be frozen. The TGWU thereupon appeared before the Court, with TUC approval, in order to defend itself. Its defence was that the union could not be held responsible for the actions of its stewards. NIRC rejected this defence, but at the Court of Appeal the decision was reversed, only to be restored by the House of Lords (*Heatons Transport Ltd* v. *TGWU*, 1973).

In the meanwhile, before the first appeal, a number of dockers' stewards were on the point of being sent to prison by NIRC for contempt when they were rescued (rather against their will) by the appearance of the Official Solicitor, who argued that the evidence was insufficient to prove that these particular stewards had been engaged in blacking. Soon after, NIRC ordered five stewards to prison at Pentonville for refusing to end their picketing of another depot. Sympathy strikes broke out and the TUC set a date for a one-day general strike. The situation was saved, however, by the House of Lords' decision to make the Union liable for the actions of its stewards and 'The Pentonville Five', as they had become known, were released, although the union was heavily fined.

The other major union which was significantly involved in the operation of the Act was the Amalgamated Union of Engineering Workers (AUEW). Its first involvement was in 1972 when Mr Goad (*Goad* v. *AUEW*, 1972) obtained an order from NIRC instructing the union to accept him into membership despite the opposition of the local branch. The union was fined £5000 for refusing to comply and then a further £50 000 for still refusing, with assets sequestered in order to obtain payment. Its second involvement related to a closed shop agreement at Chryslers where Mr Langston, who had resigned from the union, was dismissed by the employer. NIRC had reaffirmed his right not to belong to the union but, faced with union opposition and the employer's unwillingness to re-engage Langston, NIRC deemed that it would be impractical to order his reinstatement, and so the closed shop was preserved (*Langston* v. *AUEW*, 1973).

The third and final case concerned a small engineering company, Con Mech (*Con Mech Ltd* v. *AUEW*, 1973), where the AUEW was on strike in order to obtain recognition. Con Mech obtained an order from NIRC that the strike should be called off while the recognition issue was referred to the CIR. To take industrial action while there was such a reference was an 'unfair industrial practice'. The AUEW refused to obey the Order and had some of its assets sequestered, in order to pay a fine of £75 000. The CIR's report (CIR, 1973c) recommended recognition, but this was ignored by the company and could not be enforced by the union because it was not a registered union. The strike at Con Mech continued, and there was a series of one-day strikes in the engineering industry in support. NIRC awarded £47 000 in damages to Con Mech and, when again the AUEW refused to pay, its assets were sequestered. An indefinite national engineering strike was called in protest and there were sympathy strikes in other parts of industry, including the national newspaper industry. The dispute was ended by an anonymous group of businessmen offering to pay the AUEW's fine, an offer which NIRC accepted.

The Act was largely a failure (Weekes *et al.*, 1975). It was ignored by most employers, used by only a few small ones, and the government itself invoked its cooling-off powers only once when the ballot in the railway industry, required under the law, showed a very large majority in favour of industrial action. The government conspicuously failed to use it in the major strike by the NUM in 1974. The Act was the cause of several major disputes and was almost certainly a factor in the failure of the Heath Government to obtain an agreed incomes policy. To some degree, it had also brought the law into disrepute. Indeed, its failure led to a widespread belief that such laws could not succeed unless they had widespread acceptance among trade unionists.

The campaign of demonstrations called by the TUC and the resistance by the unions to the application of the Act showed that there was widespread hostility to the government's policy among trade unionists.

1974–9

Incomes policy

The Labour Government came to office in February 1974 with the miners' strike still in progress. The claim had been referred to the Heath Government's Pay Board whose Report recommended very substantial increases. The Report was readily accepted by the new government and the dispute settled. The scene was not, however, a happy one: prices were rising rapidly due primarily to the oil crisis; threshold clauses were being triggered by price increases; and wage settlements were being concluded at very high levels, mainly to recompense for rapidly rising prices and to make good the restraints and anomalies of the Heath incomes policy, particularly in the public sector. Thus executive and administrative civil servants obtained increases ranging from 24 per cent to 36 per cent, the Houghton Committee recommended teachers should receive average increases of 27 per cent and the Halsbury Committee recommended average increases of 30 per cent for nurses.

The government had already renounced the Conservative Government's incomes policy, abolishing the Pay Board but retaining the Prices Commission. However, in order to control the situation, the Government and TUC concluded a Social Contract whereby the TUC agreed that wage increases should be limited to compensation for the rise in the cost of living and should be restricted to annual claims, while the government agreed to restrain prices, increase public expenditure and take other measures to reduce unemployment.

With soaring inflation and wages, the agreement did nothing to halt their upward spiral (between July 1974 and July 1975, average earnings rose by 26 per cent and so did the cost of living). An initiative came in the form of a proposal from Jack Jones, General Secretary of the TGWU, adopted by the TUC, and accepted by the government (*The Attack on Inflation*, 1975) with only minor amendments – the Social Contract phase 1 – whereby for the 1975/76 wage round settlements would be limited to a £6 per week maximum flat rate increase with nothing for those earning over £8500 per annum. The limits were generally followed and in the period July 1975 to July 1976, the increase in average earnings was reduced to 14 per cent and the cost of living to an increase of 13 per cent. This was followed by a further agreement between the

TUC and the government – Social Contract Phase 2 (*The Attack on Inflation: The Second Year*, 1976) – whereby for the wage round 1976/77 limits were set for pay increases of 5 per cent of total earnings, with a minimum of £2.50 per week and a maximum of £4.00. As part of the agreement, the government introduced certain tax reductions. Phase 2 resulted in a further reduction in the rate of increase in earnings to 9 per cent between July 1976 and July 1977, although the cost of living rose by 17.6 per cent in the same period. In the third year – Phase 3 – the government failed to get TUC support for a further formal agreement, although it got 'reluctant acquiescence' for its unilaterally determined limit of 10 per cent plus self-financing productivity agreements (*The Attack on Inflation after 31 July* ,1977). The result of this government policy was a substantial reduction in the increase in the cost of living to 7.8 per cent, although earnings rose by 14 per cent, thus making good some of the fall in real earnings which had taken place in the previous round.

For Phase 4 – the wage round 1978/79 – the government again failed to get TUC agreement and went ahead alone with a wage limit as low as 5 per cent (*The Attack on Inflation after 31 July*, 1978), plus self-financing productivity agreements, in spite of being warned by the TUC that such a figure was impossibly low. The government knew from the previous year's experience that earnings were likely to increase by about half as much again as the 5 per cent norm, so it was an increase in earnings of 7.5 per cent which the TUC was warning against, despite the prospect of lower prices. But it was by no means certain that TUC agreement could have been secured for any level of wage norm. The government had no statutory powers to enforce its policy and there was no machinery, such as the NBPI, to deal with exceptions. There was however the Central Arbitration Committee (CAC) whose awards were exempt from pay policy limits. Consequently, unions made great use of the Fair Wages Resolution (FWR) and Schedule 11 of the Employment Protection Act, 1975 (EPA), which broadly extended the principles of the FWR to all of industry, as a means round pay policy. In this there was often a form of collusion with employers, and indeed in some instances employers initiated the procedure. Thus the number of FWR references increased from 35 in 1976 to 414 in 1978 and the number of Schedule 11 references reached 742 in 1977 (CAC 1976, 1977, 1978).

In the absence of power, the government sought to enforce its policy in the public sector through strict cash limits and in the private sector by threats in the form of the loss of export credit guarantees and the withdrawal of government contracts. One celebrated example of the latter sanction involved the Ford Motor Company, but the government's threatened sanction of withdrawing contracts was defeated by a vote in the House of Commons towards the end of 1978, which resulted in the end of such threatened sanctions.

Meanwhile resistance in both the public and private sectors to the 5 per cent limit was increasing, and culminated in the Winter of Discontent which was particularly marked by industrial action by local authority manual workers and by ancillary workers in the NHS. Since the government was the pay-master it had to stand by its policy. But the strikes in such services were bound to hit ordinary citizens hard, and many of them were trade unionists. The conduct of the strikes gave the impression that local trade union representatives were more in control of services like refuse collection and hospitals than were the government and the managers of these services. The impact on the public of these strikes was to go beyond industrial relations and to have long-term political effects.

To try to deal with such discontent in the public sector the government belatedly established in March 1979 the Standing Commission on Pay Comparability, chaired by Professor Hugh Clegg. The Commission produced some notable reports – for example on the pay of nurses, teachers and local authority and NHS manual workers (Standing Commission, 1980) – but it was overtaken by events and the general election of 1979. Even so, the new Conservative Government allowed it to complete all the cases which had been referred to it before abolishing it early in 1981. The Clegg Commission might have provided a sound long-term solution to the problem of pay comparability between the public services and other employment, but it did not have a chance to do so.

Industrial relations and the law

The Labour Government came to power with pledges to repeal the 1971 Industrial Relations Act, to introduce certain new rights for unions and employees, and to introduce a measure of industrial democracy. The first pledge was fulfilled by the Trade Union and Labour Relations Acts 1974 and 1976 (TULRA). TULRA repealed the 1971 Act and essentially restored trade union immunities to what they were believed to have been under the 1906 Trade Disputes Act. In addition, the Acts abolished the CIR, the NIRC and the Registrar of Trade Unions and Employers' Associations, the Registrar being subsequently replaced by the Certification Officer. They retained the unfair dismissal provisions introduced in 1971 (although amended to remove restrictions on the closed shop). They redefined the law on the status and regulation of trade unions, employers' associations and collective agreements and on behaviour in disputes.

The second pledge was achieved by the Employment Protection Act, 1975. The provisions of the EPA divide into those relating to collective matters and those relating to individual rights. On collective matters the EPA had six provisions.

ACAS was established on a statutory basis, it having started work in the previous year. ACAS was given the general duty of promoting the improvement of industrial relations, and in particular of encouraging the extension of collective bargaining and the development (and, where necessary, the reform) of collective bargaining machinery. Its main functions were as set out below:

1. To provide facilities for conciliation, mediation, arbitration and enquiry.
2. To provide a free advisory service on industrial relations and personnel practice.
3. To examine and make recommendations on applications for trade union recognition under a statutory recognition procedure. If ACAS recommended recognition and the employer failed to comply, the union concerned could apply to the CAC to award by means of unilateral arbitration specified improvements in terms and conditions of employment.
4. To publish Codes of Practice.
5. To provide conciliation where individuals considered that their rights under employment legislation had been infringed (for example, by unfair dismissal) where ACAS had a duty to conciliate before a tribunal hearing.

ACAS was governed by a council consisting of a full-time chairman and nine other members appointed by the Secretary of State for Employment, three after consultation with the TUC, three after consultation with the CBI, and three independents. The EPA stated that 'The service shall not be subject to directions of any kind from any Minister of the Crown as to the manner in which it is to exercise any of the functions under any enactment.' The rationale behind the setting-up of an independent service, instead of as hitherto having it as part of the DE, was trade union fears that a Departmental service would not be fully independent of ministerial interference as, for example, in the refusal of Mr Heath to refer the dustmen's strike of 1970 to the conciliation service because the employer's offer already exceeded the government's unofficial norm. ACAS has continued to function as the EPA specified, with the exception of the statutory recognition procedure which was abolished by the Employment Act of 1980, albeit on the recommendation of ACAS itself. The hiving-off of conciliation, arbitration and the advisory services from the Department has had strong support from both trade unions and employers' organisations, and there has been no political reason for overriding that joint commitment.

The CAC was established by the EPA, replacing the Industrial Arbitration Board which had itself replaced the Industrial Court in 1971. The provision of a standing national arbitration body – the Industrial Court – dated back to the Industrial Courts Act, 1919, and had been recommended by the Whitley Committee. The constitution and proceedings of the CAC were set out in Schedule 1 of the EPA. There was an independent chairman and deputy chairmen, with two panels of side members consisting respectively of experienced representatives of employers and trade unions. The CAC had a number of functions under the EPA, some inherited from the old Industrial Court (such as the application of the FWR and voluntary arbitration), and some new functions relating, for example, to Schedule 11 of the EPA, disclosure of information, the Equal Pay Act, and unilateral arbitration under the recognition procedures of the EPA (CAC, 1976). These have all been abolished by the Conservative Governments of the 1980s, with the exception of voluntary arbitration and the disclosure of information.

The Certification Officer was established by the EPA in February 1976 in place of the Registrar who, in trade union eyes, had been tainted by his association with the 1971 Act. The Certification Officer was made responsible for:

(a) maintaining lists of trade unions and employers' associations;
(b) determining the independence of trade unions;
(c) seeing that trade unions and employers' associations kept accounting records, had their accounts properly audited and submitted annual returns;
(d) ensuring the periodical examination of superannuation schemes;
(e) securing observance of the statutory procedures for transfers of engagements, amalgamations and changes of name;
(f) supervising the statutory requirements as to the setting-up and operation of political funds and dealing with complaints by members about breaches of political fund rules (Certification Officer, 1977).

This, too, was a sound long-term development and the Conservative Governments of the 1980s have given additional responsibilities to the Certification Officer.

Disclosure of information to recognised independent unions for purposes of collective bargaining is an obligation placed on employers. Any information, without which unions would be 'materially handicapped' in collective bargaining and which it would be in accordance with good industrial practice to disclose, must be given on request. The Act does, however, provide employers with certain defences against such requests: for example, if it is harmful to the employers' undertaking or to national security, if it would be in breach of an enactment or confidence, or if it related to an individual without his consent. If an employer refuses, the union may bring a complaint to the CAC who, at an informal meeting, will try to conciliate with the assistance of ACAS. If conciliation fails or appears hopeless the CAC will proceed to a formal hearing where if it finds the complaint well-founded, it will make a declaration to that effect and specify what information is to be disclosed and the date by which disclosure should take place. If the employer refuses to comply, the union may make a further complaint accompanied by or followed by a claim for improved terms and conditions; that is to say, a right to unilateral arbitration. Any award on such a claim is binding on the employer. These provisions continue in force.

Consultation on redundancies with an independent recognised union was required by s.99 of the EPA. Consultation had to begin at least 90 days in advance of the dismissals if the employer was proposing that 100 or more employees were to be made redundant at one establishment, and at least 30 days in advance if 10–99 employees were to be dismissed at one establishment. The employer had to give similar notice to the Secretary of State for Employment. The reasons for the proposals, the number and description of employees involved, the total number of such employees at the establishment in question, the proposed method of selection for redundancy and the proposed method of timing of the dismissals had to be given to the union in writing. The employer had to further consider any representations made by the union and reply, stating reasons, if rejecting them. These, too, continue to be in force although with certain modifications.

Schedule 11 of the EPA replaced s.8 of the 1959 Terms and Conditions of Employment Act and indeed extended it, so that employers or independent trade unions, representing a substantial proportion of the employers or employees in the trade or industry, could bring a claim to the CAC that an employer was not observing the recognised terms and conditions of employment, or was paying less than 'the general level' in the trade or industry where there were no recognised terms and conditions. The CAC was empowered to make an award which was legally binding on the employer. However, Schedule 11 was abolished by the new Conservative Government in its Employment Act, 1980.

On individual rights, the EPA provided for maternity pay and for the right to return to work after maternity leave; for the right to guaranteed pay for employees who were put on short-time working or laid-off by their employers, for reasonable time off work for industrial relations and trade union duties, and for public duties. The various individual rights in the EPA and those contained in earlier legislation (such as the Redundancy Payments Act, 1965, and the Contracts of Employment Act, 1972, and TULRA, 1974 and 1976) were subsequently consolidated in the Employment Protection (Consolidated) Act, 1978. Other rights and protections were provided by the Sex Discrimination Act, 1975 and the Race Relations Act, 1976.

Finally, there was the enactment in 1974 of the Health and Safety at Work Act, which established the Health and Safety Commission and the Health and Safety Executive. The Act extended the protection of the law to some 8 million workers who were not previously covered by health and safety legislation. It placed statutory general duties on employers, the self-employed and employees in achieving acceptable safety standards at work. Subsequent regulations provided for the appointment of safety representatives, with considerable rights and powers, by independent recognised trade unions. In addition, at the written request of any two union-appointed safety representatives, an employer was obliged to form a safety committee.

The third pledge was legislation to further industrial democracy. As a first step the government established a Committee of Inquiry under the chairmanship of Lord Bullock, with terms of reference to report on how representation of trade unions on boards of directors could best be achieved. The Bullock Committee's Majority Report (Bullock, 1977) recommended that companies with more than 2000 employees should have worker directors, provided that any recognised trade union which represented 20 per cent or more of a company's employees requested a secret ballot of all the company's employees to see if they supported the introduction of employee directors. If a majority, totalling at least one-third of the electorate, agreed, then employee directors would be chosen through the trade unions and the Board would be constituted on a $2X + Y$ formula: employees and shareholders would have equal representation $(2X)$ and there would be a small uneven number of independents (Y) who would be jointly chosen. If employees chose to adopt worker directors, then all the unions in the company would establish a Joint Representation Committee (JRC) to decide how to allocate employee directorships and to coordinate the employee side.

The three CBI representatives on the Committee did not accept the majority report and issued their own minority report, while the CBI itself engaged in an energetic campaign against the Bullock proposals. The TUC was divided in its views and, although the majority view favoured worker directors, many unions (including large and important ones like the NUGMW and the AEU), feared that trade union independence and collective bargaining freedom might be adversely affected by their having representatives on company boards. In the event the government issued a White Paper (*Industrial Democracy*, 1978) which considerably watered down the Bullock proposals, but even this version did not reach the statute book before the 1979 election and the defeat of the Labour Government.

In this period an experiment on 'worker directors' was carried out in the Post Office (Batstone, Ferner and Terry, 1983). It lasted for only two years (1978–80) for, when the time came to consider whether it should be renewed, there was not only an unsympathetic Conservative Government but opposition from the Board of the Post Office who considered that the experiment had been a failure.

The main legislation affecting industrial relations was presented at the height of the Social Contract when the trade unions were at the summit of their ability to influence the government. That being so, it is important to notice how much was not interfered with by the Conservative Government after 1979. ACAS, the Certification Officer, disclosure of information, consultation on redundancies, health and safety representatives and committees, and most of the individual rights have turned out to be permanent legal changes.

Trade unions and employers

This chapter has so far been primarily concerned with the economic and political environment of the 1970s, the impact at macro level of incomes policy, and legal changes. What was happening within this context to the primary actors in our industrial relations system and to their joint procedures and relationships?

It could be argued that in the 1970s the trade unions reached the pinnacle of their power in terms of membership and influence. First, there was a large increase in total trade union membership, from 10.5 million at the end of 1969 to 13.3 million at the end of 1979, and in union density from 45.3 per cent to 54.8 per cent, while TUC membership over the same period increased from 10.0 million to 12.2 million (see Table 2.1).

Growth was particularly marked among white-collar employees, and certain unions showed remarkable increases in numbers (see Table 8.2).

Second, trade union influence with government reached its peak with the Social Contract. The repeal of the 1971 Industrial Relations Act was rapidly achieved and further legislation followed, giving support and additional rights to trade unions and individual employees. Third, at company level, union recognition became more widespread, not just horizontally, but in

TABLE 2.1   Union membership and density 1970–9

Year	Membership	Potential membership	Union density
1969	10 479	23 153	45.3
1970	11 187	23 050	48.5
1971	11 135	22 884	48.7
1972	11 359	22 961	49.5
1973	11 456	23 224	49.3
1974	11 764	23 339	50.4
1975	12 026	23 587	51.0
1976	12 386	23 871	51.9
1977	12 846	24 069	53.4
1978	13 112	24 203	54.2
1979	13 289	24 264	54.8

Source: Price, R. and Bain, G. S. in *British Journal of Industrial Relations* March (1983), Table I.
Figures for UK. Potential union membership = employees in employment (seasonally unadjusted figures for June) plus the number of unemployed in June.

many cases also vertically so that recognition and collective bargaining were extended to many groups of white-collar workers, going beyond clerical workers to supervisory, technical and lower managerial levels as well. The number of shop stewards and office representatives increased, in particular the number of full-time shop stewards. There was greater formal recognition of their role, and that role itself was expanded with the widening of the scope of collective bargaining. This growth in steward numbers and influence was partly the result of employer policy, but it was also the deliberate result of decisions taken by certain unions. Whereas the gradual extension in the post-war years of steward numbers and influence had been largely an informal process, unions such as the TGWU, National Union of Public Employees (NUPE) and the National and Local Government Officers' Association (NAL-GO) made it a deliberate part of their policy in the 1970s to decentralise power, to increase steward numbers and to strengthen their role in the unions.

Union power could, however, be overstated. While the exercise of union power (for example, through strikes) is highly visible and much publicised in the media, the exercise of employer power is much less visible and less publicised. Employers' power to determine what products and services to provide is largely unquestioned, as are their decisions on capital expenditure, on location of production (whether at home or overseas) on technology, and indeed their power to make all major strategic decisions. Attempts in the second half of the 1970s to affect some of these powers (through planning agreements, for example) came to nought, as did attempts to achieve greater industrial democracy. Even *vis-à-vis* the Labour Government, at the height of the Social Contract, unions were unable to prevent higher unemployment and restrictions on public expenditure; and while money incomes rose fast in the 1970s, real pay increases were markedly lower than those achieved in the 1950s and 1960s. Again, the favourable legislation on union rights did little more than restore union rights to what they were pre-1971, and the improvement in individual rights did no more than move towards a position which had been common practice in most of Western Europe for many years. Yet the trade unions had been in a position without parallel to influence the Labour Government. The Social Contract was unique. But the incomes policy which was at its heart was the cause of its collapse. The trade unions had seemed to be part of the government – one poll showed that a majority considered Jack Jones, the general secretary of the TGWU, more powerful than the Prime Minister – but in the winter of 1978/9 the exercise of that power helped to bring down the Labour Government (as the miners' strike had been instrumental in bringing down Heath's Conservative Government). If the trade unions had got above themselves, they could not be said to have consolidated their position.

Employers in the 1970s, as has been seen, faced a difficult economic environment. The growth in international trade suffered from the oil crisis, and the resultant restrictive economic responses of governments dampened world economic growth at the same time as it increased inflation. International competition increased, and the relative decline in British manufacturing intensified. At home, there was increasing concentration in British industry, increasing intervention by government and the increased power of trade unions. Industrial relations assumed greater importance for most companies, partly as a result of the growth of trade unionism and its impact, particularly at workplace level, and partly because of greater government intervention; not just through incomes policies but through laws enhancing the individual rights of employees, in particular unfair dismissal, but also laws on equal pay and equal opportunities, and safety and health legislation. Traditionally, in many industries, companies had left industrial relations to be dealt with by their employers' associations, which had the alleged advantage from the employers' viewpoint of keeping trade unions out of the workplace. For historical reasons this had never been completely true in Britain and certainly was no longer a valid policy in the 1970s for the reasons mentioned above, and as shown by the Donovan Report.

Many employers indeed accepted the Donovan analysis and its core recommendations, and proceeded to seek to reform their industrial relations policies and their internal procedures. Industrial relations and personnel management specialists grew in number and in importance. Many large companies enlarged their recognition of stewards, accepted joint shop steward committees and indeed encouraged a marked growth in the number of full-time stewards. The check-off became widely accepted, and there was an expansion of the closed shop. There was also the development of disciplinary and grievance procedures, formalised negotiating and consultative committees at workplace and company level. This wider acceptance of, and greater role for, unions at workplace level was partly the acceptance of the inevitable, in the light of greater union power, but it was also a policy whereby management sought to bring greater order out of relative chaos, as in Flanders' often quoted statement 'Management . . . can only regain control by sharing it' (Flanders, 1967). It was also a means of legitimising management's decision-making authority through the involvement of stewards, particularly senior stewards.

This process of establishing order and control was not confined to the procedural side of industrial relations, but embraced the substantive side, through, for example, the reform of payments systems, in particular a reduction in the incidence of individual payment by result schemes, the growth of measured day work and work study, the extension of job evaluation, and the reform of pay structures. The success of such reforms at workplace level is difficult to evaluate, but it was not insignificant. However, in public perception, such reforms were lost among the dramatic general developments which have been described in this chapter.

Conclusion

If the 1960s ended on a note of strain in the consensus, the 1970s ended with the most ambitious exercise in the consensus lying in ruins. The decade had seen a Conservative Government committed to working through market forces and using legislation to catch the union tiger by the tail. But the government did an about-turn and offered the unions a partnership in economic policy in return for the delivery of an incomes policy. Failing to secure that it embarked on the most detailed of all prices and incomes policies. The Labour Government in the second half of the decade had swung from the intimacy of the Social Contract to the bitter disagreements of the Winter of Discontent. Both political parties had practised consensus and both had become the object of union hostility.

The general election of 1979 is now seen as having turned on the votes of trade unionists. The experience of the 1970s caused more of them than ever before to vote Conservative. What happened in the 1980s and 1990s to industrial relations was in large part the product of the 1970s. It was the trade unionists' reaction to the events of that decade which put the Conservative Government of 1979 in power.

CHAPTER 3

The economic background

Introduction

It is not the purpose of this chapter to delve into a detailed analysis of the British economy during the 1980s and 1990s. The intent is rather to record very briefly the main changes in the leading economic indicators insofar as they are relevant to industrial relations. The Conservative Government that came to power in 1979 was wedded to a firm belief in monetarism and a free market economy. Mrs Thatcher held to these beliefs as articles of faith, along with a conviction that Britain's problems in the post-war decades (whether under a Labour or a Conservative Government) were the result of a departure from this faith. Thus any form of corporatism or tripartism was anathema to her as was Keynesian economics and most forms of public enterprise and public expenditure.

The era can be divided broadly into five periods. First, there was the severe recession of 1979–81; second, a period of slow recovery between 1982 and 1986; third, the boom period of 1987–9; fourth, the severe recession of 1990–2; and fifth, from 1993 there were mixed signs suggesting the beginning of a slow upturn, and in the following years there was indeed a sustained recovery.

The first Thatcher Government inherited in 1979 an economy with unemployment at 1 million which, although high by post-war standards, had fallen somewhat in the previous two years. Inflation was at 10 per cent and had begun to move upwards as had wage settlements, accelerated by the Winter of Discontent after the relative success of Stages 1 and 2 of the Labour Government's Social Contract in greatly reducing the rises in wages and the cost of living. The inflationary spiral was soon to be given a further boost by another large increase in OPEC oil prices in 1979/80 and by the Thatcher Government's first budget, which doubled the rate of VAT and thereby added 4 percentage points to the RPI. The current balance of payments had shown a surplus of £964 million in 1978 but a deficit of £496 million in 1979. However,

Britain's North Sea oil was beginning to flow, providing during the 1980s substantial tax revenues and eliminating for the first time in the post-war decades balance of payments' constraints on Britain's economic growth.

The early 1980s saw the worst economic recession of the post-war years. Gross Domestic Product (GDP) at constant prices declined by over 3 per cent between 1979 and 1981 before beginning to grow again, while manufacturing output over the same period fell by 14 per cent. Unemployment increased from 1 million in 1979 to 2.1 million at the end of 1980, to 2.8 million at the end of 1981 and to 3.1 million at the end of 1982. Thereafter, unemployment increased more slowly but stayed at over 3 million until 1987. This was despite the numerous changes in the definition of unemployment made by the Government over the years in order to make unemployment appear lower than it actually was. It would be more correct to describe the figures as those unemployed and claiming benefit. Thereupon, with economic growth, it declined significantly to under 1.6 million by 1989. However, during 1990 the country entered into its second major post-war recession and unemployment started to move up again, reaching almost 3 million by early 1993. Thereafter, with the slow recovery, official unemployment figures came down to close to 1.5 million in mid-1997.

The cause of Britain's recession in 1979/82 was partly the worldwide recession and partly the government's economic policy. The government in its battle against inflation, which it saw as the greatest economic evil, pursued a tight monetary policy, raised interest rates to a peak of 17 per cent, sought reductions in public expenditure and removed all exchange controls. The effect of high interest rates and an emerging balance of payments surplus (as a result of North Sea oil) boosted the exchange rate of the pound against the dollar to an unrealistic level for British exporters. The effect on British manufacturing industry was catastrophic, causing a 14 per cent fall in output between 1979 and 1981 and consequent redundancies.

Once growth began again from the low point of 1981 it was fairly steady until 1986, averaging over 3 per cent per annum. Employment started to grow, although most of the increase was in female part-time employment, and there were marked differences between the North and the South. Full-time male employment did not increase. By 1987/8 labour shortages had emerged in certain parts of the country, particularly London, the South-East and East Anglia, and in certain occupations.

The RPI, after a dramatic increase of over 20 per cent between 1979 and 1980 (an increase in the post-war years second only to that of 1974/5) fell markedly by 1983 and then stabilised at around 5 per cent until 1988. By the end of 1988 it started to accelerate again reaching over 9 per cent early in 1990. It then fell steadily during the second recession to a low point of about 1.5 per cent in mid-1993. It thereafter increased somewhat but remained around or below 3 per cent in the following few years. This was indeed low by recent UK standards, but most of Britain's competitors did even better.

The increase in average earnings also rose dramatically in 1979/80 to its second highest post-war level of over 20 per cent. During the next two years the annual increase in earnings fell significantly before levelling out at around 8 per cent per annum for several years. Towards the end of the 1980s, the increase in earnings started to move up again, reaching about 10 per cent per annum in each of the years 1988-90. In every year in the 1980s the rise in average earnings exceeded the rise in RPI. Thereafter, with the second recession, the rate of increase fell in the years 1991–4, reaching a low of about 3 per cent and remaining at approximately 3–4 per cent for the following few years, despite economic recovery.

The cause of Britain's second major economic recession beginning in 1990 was largely the result of the government's own policies, although it is true that the USA was also suffering a recessionary period. There was, however, no recession at that time in Western Europe and Japan, where expansion continued until 1992. Their recession came later.

In Britain, the government in reaction to the Lawson financial boom increased interest rates, so that by the end of 1989 they had been increased from 7.5 per cent to 15 per cent. The problems of the economy were intensified when the government decided to join the European Exchange Rate Mechanism (ERM) in October 1990 at a rate of exchange which most observers considered far too high. It was a rate which appeared sustainable only by keeping interest rates high, even though the state of the domestic economy required a drastic lowering of interest rates as well as a fall in the rate of exchange of sterling. On 16 September 1992 – a day referred to as 'Black Wednesday' – the pound was driven out of the ERM, after attempts to keep it in at the cost of billions of pounds. Forced departure from the ERM meant that it was no longer necessary to keep interest rates at a high level to defend the pound. Over the next few months there were substantial cuts in interest rates which together with the fall in the value of sterling, helped to lead to the beginning of a patchy upturn. The fall in GDP between 1990 and 1992 had been some 3 per cent, and the fall in manufacturing output over 6 per cent. Unemployment during the recession (on government figures) nearly doubled from 1.6 million to virtually 3 million. In the subsequent recovery there was a moderate increase in output and a fall in unemployment. The recovery eventually gathered pace and, by mid-1997, unemployment had fallen to 1.5 million.

Output and productivity

Britain's GDP fell between 1979 and 1981 by over 3 per cent: thereafter there was a gradual recovery which accelerated markedly in the mid to late 1980s but slowed down in 1989 and 1990 and then declined over the period 1990–2.

TABLE 3.1   Output and productivity 1980–96 (UK) – per cent change on previous year

Year	Whole economy		Manufacturing	
	Output	*Output per person employed*	*Output*	*Output per person employed*
1980	−2.8	−2.1	−9.1	−3.9
1981	−1.3	1.8	−5.9	3.4
1982	2.0	3.8	0.2	6.7
1983	3.3	4.4	2.7	8.6
1984	2.8	0.7	3.8	5.7
1985	3.4	2.7	2.7	3.1
1986	3.5	3.3	1.3	3.6
1987	4.6	2.8	4.6	5.5
1988	5.0	1.5	5.6	5.8
1989	2.5	0.0	4.5	4.1
1990	0.6	0.0	−0.2	1.9
1991	−2.4	0.4	−5.3	1.3
1992	−0.6	2.2	−0.8	4.9
1993	2.0	3.0	1.8	4.6
1994	4.0	4.0	4.3	5.4
1995	2.4	1.8	1.9	1.2
1996	2.4	1.7	0.3	0.2
1996 level (1980=100)	139.2	138.8	124.7	195.4

Source: Adapted from *National Institute Economic Review's* Statistical Appendices (average estimates) and *Monthly Digest of Statistics*.

There was then a slow recovery (Table 3.1). The decline in manufacturing output between 1979 and 1981 was much more drastic with a fall of 14 per cent: thereafter there was some recovery, although it was not until 1987 that the 1979 level of manufacturing output was exceeded. Between 1987 and 1989 the rate of increase in manufacturing output speeded up considerably, but then declined markedly between 1990 and 1992 as Britain entered into another recession. From 1993 output started to recover and economic growth continued in the following years.

Output per person employed, both for the economy as a whole and for manufacturing industry, after an original fall in 1980, followed an upward path until towards the end of the decade, when the rate of increase fell markedly. There was then some improvement after 1992. The rate of increase in manufacturing was much greater than that of the economy as a whole, with a productivity increase in 1980–96 of 95 per cent (compared with 39 per cent). Nevertheless, manufacturing output in 1996 was only 25 per cent above its 1980 level. The overall growth in GDP of 40 per cent during 1980–96 was similar to that of France, but markedly less than Germany, USA, Japan and the average of OECD countries (Table 3.2). None of the other countries experienced as sharp a recession in 1979/81 as did Britain, and neither did they suffer the same decline in the rate of growth in 1989/90; or, indeed, Britain's absolute decline in 1990/2. However, between 1993 and 1996 Britain's growth was faster than the OECD average.

Employment and unemployment

The deep recession of 1979/81 brought about a large increase in unemployment. It doubled between June 1979 and June 1981 from 1.14 million (or 4.7

TABLE 3.2   Gross Domestic Product 1980–96: international comparisons (% increase on previous year)

Year	UK	USA	Japan	France	Germany*	OECD
1980	−2.0	−0.2	3.5	1.6	1.5	1.1
1981	−1.0	1.8	3.6	1.2	0.2	1.4
1982	1.3	−2.2	3.2	2.5	−1.0	0.0
1983	3.7	3.8	2.7	0.8	1.5	2.8
1984	1.9	6.3	4.3	1.2	2.8	4.4
1985	4.0	3.1	4.9	1.9	2.1	3.2
1986	4.3	2.9	2.7	2.6	2.3	2.9
1987	4.8	2.9	4.1	2.2	1.3	3.2
1988	5.0	3.8	6.3	4.5	3.6	4.4
1989	2.2	3.4	4.7	4.2	3.7	3.3
1990	0.4	1.3	5.2	2.6	6.3	2.3
1991	−2.0	−1.0	3.9	0.7	4.6	1.3
1992	−0.6	2.8	1.1	1.4	1.9	1.8
1993	2.3	2.2	0.2	−1.5	−1.2	0.9
1994	3.8	3.5	0.5	2.8	3.0	2.8
1995	2.4	2.1	1.0	2.4	2.1	1.9
1996	2.4	2.5	3.7	1.5	1.4	2.6
1996 (1980=100)	139.8	145.4	165.6	135.9	150.3	146.9

Source: Adapted from *National Institute Economic Review's* Statistical Appendices.
* West Germany until 1990; all Germany thereafter.

per cent of civil employment) to 2.3 million (or 9.4 per cent). Thereafter, unemployment continued to rise to over 3 million (or 11.4 per cent) of the labour force, reaching its peak in 1986: it then began to fall and there was a steady reduction in unemployment to nearly 1.5 million by the end of 1989. There were further small reductions in the early months of 1990 but, during the second half of that year, unemployment resumed its upward movement; by early 1991 it had exceeded 2 million and by early 1993 it had reached almost 3 million. After this second major post-war recession, unemployment started to fall and was officially close to 1.5 million in mid-1997. During the 1980s and the first half of 1990s unemployment in the UK exceeded the OECD average in every single year (Table 3.3). Thereafter the UK did better than either France or Germany.

The number of employees in employment in all industries and services in June 1996 at 21.5 million was over 1 million less than it had been in June 1979. Between 1979 and 1983 it declined by over 2 million, while during the rest of the decade it increased by nearly 2 million. Between 1990 and 1993 there was a

TABLE 3.3 Unemployment, 1979-96: international comparisons*
(% of total labour force)

Year	UK	USA	Japan	France	Germany	OECD
1979	5.0	5.8	2.1	5.9	3.2	5.0
1980	6.4	7.0	2.0	6.3	3.0	5.7
1981	9.8	7.5	2.2	7.4	4.4	6.6
1982	11.3	9.5	2.4	8.1	6.1	8.0
1983	12.5	9.5	2.6	8.3	8.0	8.5
1984	11.7	7.4	2.7	9.7	7.0	8.0
1985	11.2	7.1	2.6	10.2	7.2	7.8
1986	11.2	6.9	2.8	10.4	6.5	7.7
1987	10.3	6.1	2.8	10.5	6.2	7.3
1988	8.4	5.4	2.5	10.0	6.1	6.7
1989	6.9	5.2	2.2	9.4	5.6	6.2
1990	6.9	5.4	2.1	8.9	5.0	6.0
1991	8.8	6.7	2.1	9.4	4.3	6.8
1992	9.9	7.3	2.1	10.2	4.8	7.5
1993	10.3	6.8	2.5	11.7	5.8	7.8
1994	9.6	6.0	2.9	12.3	7.2	7.8
1995	8.7	5.6	3.1	11.6	8.2	7.5
1996	8.2	5.4	3.3	12.4	9.0	7.5

Source: OECD.

* Standardised according to international definitions by the OECD.

further decline of over 1 million followed by an increase of 0.5 million between 1993 and 1996 (Table 3.4). However, it is not only movements in total employment which are significant. Changes in structure are crucial to an understanding of labour markets and the implications for industrial relations. Thus, between June 1979 and June 1996, male employment declined by nearly 2.3 million, while total female employment grew by over 1 million. Part-time employment of women increased by over 1 million. Self-employment during the period grew substantially, from 1.8 million in 1979 to 3.2 million in 1996.

Not only was the experience of men and women very different, but so was the experience of manufacturing industry on the one hand and the service sector on the other. Employment in manufacturing between 1979 and 1996 declined by over 3 million, or by nearly 50 per cent, while employment in services rose by 3 million, or over 20 per cent.

Inflation

The annual average RPI rose between 1980 and 1996 by 129 per cent. There was an increase of 18 per cent in 1979/80, 12 per cent in 1980/1 and nearly 9 per cent in 1981/2. Thereafter, there was much greater stability, with the annual inflation rate staying at about 5 per cent until towards the end of the decade, when there was a rise of nearly 8 per cent between 1988 and 1989 and of 9.5 per cent between 1989 and 1990 (Table 3.5). The increase in the RPI peaked in October 1990 at 10.9 per cent and thereafter there was a decline in the rate of increase. With the onset of the recession and the eventual decline in interest rates, the rate of increase in inflation declined markedly reaching below 2 per cent in 1993. Thereafter it stayed at relatively low levels, mainly between 2.5 per cent and 3.5 per cent (although higher than that of Britain's main industrial competitors).

In terms of international comparison, Britain's record has not been a good one. The increase in the UK's cost of living between 1980 and 1996 was 129 per cent, compared with the OECD average of 92 per cent. France had an increase of 110 per cent but her record improved very markedly in the second half of the period and was better than that of the UK, although the UK also improved considerably. The USA had an increase of 89 per cent, but also improved markedly in the second half of the period, while Japan and Germany had increases respectively of only 31 and 54 per cent.

TABLE 3.4 Employment 1979–96 (Great Britain)

	Employees in employment						Self-employed	HM Forces	Work-related govt training programmes	Workforce in employment	Workforce
	Male	Female All	Part-time	Total	Manufacturing	Services					
	(000s)	(000s)	(000s)	(000s)	(000s)	(000s)	(000s)	(000s)	(000s)	(000s)	(000s)
June											
1979	13 183	9 455	3 870	22 638	7 107	13 260	1 842	314	–	24 794	25 969
1980	13 018	9 440	3 941	22 458	6 801	13 384	1 950	323	–	24 731	26 176
1981	12 278	9 107	3 817	21 386	6 099	13 142	2 058	334	–	23 777	26 077
1982	11 930	8 985	3 783	20 916	5 751	13 117	2 109	324	–	23 348	26 012
1983	11 670	8 901	3 776	20 572	5 418	13 169	2 160	322	8	23 061	25 932
1984	11 619	9 123	3 889	20 741	5 302	13 503	2 435	326	168	23 671	26 582
1985	11 632	9 228	3 976	20 920	5 254	13 769	2 550	326	168	23 964	27 021
1986	11 477	9 409	4 081	20 886	5 122	13 954	2 567	322	218	23 992	27 095
1987	11 431	9 650	4 169	21 080	5 049	14 247	2 801	319	303	24 502	27 282
1988	11 702	10 057	4 232	21 740	5 089	14 860	2 926	316	335	25 336	27 561
1989	11 718	10 416	4 494	22 134	5 080	15 261	3 182	308	452	26 076	27 714
1990	11 776	10 550	4 604	22 370	4 994	15 574	3 222	303	412	26 263	27 723
1991	11 327	10 383	4 691	21 710	4 599	15 377	3 066	297	333	25 406	27 549
1992	10 937	10 359	4 689	21 310	4 396	15 374	2 914	290	320	24 819	27 436
1993	10 676	10 390	4 713	21 066	3 808	15 822	3 108	271	295	24 740	27 502
1994	10 642	10 462	4 812	21 104	3 789	15 912	3 216	250	286	24 856	27 345
1995	10 771	10 590	4 944	21 361	3 840	16 179	3 269	230	210	25 070	27 239
1996	10 856	10 684	4 994	21 540	3 810	16 395	3 205	221	184	25 151	27 162

Source: Adapted from *Labour Market Trends*, *Employment Gazette*, *Historical Supplement*, *No.2*, and *Monthly Digest of Statistics*.
Figures for June each year unadjusted for seasonal variation.

TABLE 3.5   Consumer prices, 1980–96: international comparisons (% increase on previous year)

Year	UK	USA	Japan	France	Germany	OECD
1980	17.9	13.5	8.1	13.8	5.4	12.9
1981	11.9	10.3	4.8	12.9	6.3	10.8
1982	8.6	6.2	2.7	11.4	5.3	8.0
1983	4.6	3.2	2.0	9.5	3.3	5.7
1984	5.0	4.3	2.2	7.3	2.4	5.6
1985	6.1	3.6	2.1	6.0	2.2	4.9
1986	3.4	2.0	0.6	2.1	−0.2	3.0
1987	4.2	3.7	0.2	3.4	0.2	3.6
1988	4.9	4.1	0.6	2.8	1.3	4.3
1989	7.8	4.8	2.3	3.2	2.8	5.3
1990	9.5	5.4	3.0	3.1	2.7	5.8
1991	5.9	4.3	3.3	3.1	3.5	4.5
1992	3.7	3.1	1.7	2.7	4.0	3.5
1993	1.6	2.9	1.3	2.6	4.1	2.8
1994	2.5	2.6	0.7	1.9	2.6	3.0
1995	3.4	2.8	0.1	1.9	1.8	2.4
1996	2.7	2.1	0.2	1.8	2.0	2.0
1996 level (1980=100)	228.8	188.8	131.1	209.6	154.2	192.2

Source: Adapted from *National Institute Economic Review's* Statistical Appendices. Figures are annual averages.

Earnings

The movements in earnings are analysed in depth in Chapter 10. Here only a few brief points are made. Average earnings for men rose between April 1979 and April 1996 by 286 per cent, and for women by 349 per cent (Table 10.1). This increase compared with an increase in the RPI of 180 per cent over the same period so that there was an increase in real average earnings of 38 per cent for men and 60 per cent for women.

The rate of increase in average earnings was not spread evenly throughout the period. In the first year of the Conservative Government 1979/80, the increase was over 20 per cent (Table 10.1). In the following two years the government was markedly successful in bringing down the rate of increase in earnings although this was perhaps not surprising given the recession, mass unemployment and redundancies, falling profits and a falling rate of increase in the RPI. In the following six years the rate of increase was remarkably stable at between 7 and 8 per cent. However in 1989 and 1990 there was a substantial rise in the rate of increase followed by substantial decreases in 1991–3 as unemployment rose and the recession deepened. The subsequent slow economic recovery saw a relative stability in the rate of increase in earnings: basically between 3 per cent and 4 per cent.

Compared with the other main industrial countries, Britain's record was not good. Table 3.6 shows figures for movements in average earnings in a number of leading countries. Britain's increase was 191 per cent between 1980 and 1996. The only other country with an increase approaching this order of magnitude was France, with an increase of 152 per cent. Again, the crucial difference between the two was that whereas Britain's performance got worse towards the end of the 1980s, France's performance improved markedly. Among other major countries, the USA had an increase of 105 per cent, Japan 83 per cent and Germany 81 per cent.

TABLE 3.6   Average earnings, 1980–96: international comparisons
(% increase on previous year)

Year	UK	USA	Japan	France	Germany
1980	19.6	9.1	7.9	15.9	7.4
1981	13.2	8.9	7.3	14.5	4.9
1982	8.9	6.0	4.6	14.1	4.3
1983	8.3	4.2	3.5	10.1	3.7
1984	5.9	5.3	4.7	8.2	3.3
1985	7.7	5.3	4.5	6.5	3.1
1986	8.0	3.6	3.9	4.4	3.8
1987	7.1	5.2	2.9	3.9	3.4
1988	8.1	5.6	4.0	4.5	3.2
1989	8.9	3.8	5.4	4.7	2.9
1990	9.6	5.7	6.6	5.6	4.9
1991	7.8	3.6	5.8	4.9	5.9
1992	6.5	4.9	3.1	4.2	5.4
1993	3.7	2.2	2.0	3.1	3.0
1994	3.0	1.9	1.9	1.8	2.6
1995	3.2	3.0	1.1	2.4	3.5
1996	3.8	3.7	0.8	2.9	2.6
1996 level (1980=100)	291.4	204.8	182.8	251.8	181.0

Source: Adapted from *National Institute Economic Review's* Statistical Appendices.

Monetary and fiscal policy

As stated in the introduction to this chapter, the Thatcher Government which took office in 1979 was wedded to monetarism. In its extreme form this meant that if there was sufficient control over monetary supply, all other economic variables would fall into place: inflation in particular would not occur, and excess wage demands would cease or, if granted, would increase unemployment which would in turn drive down wages. The government also believed that for monetarism to work there needed to be first, free labour, product and financial markets. Second, public expenditure had to be greatly reduced – certainly as a proportion of the GDP – and the budget had at least to be balanced or else the Public Sector Borrowing Requirement (PSBR) would increase and that would add to the money supply. Third, the public sector also had to be greatly reduced, for by definition there was not a free market in the supply of public services.

Accordingly in its early years the Thatcher Government put great weight on seeking to reduce the monetary supply. In his 1979 Budget Statement the Chancellor said that 'We are committed to the progressive reduction of the money supply.' The selected monetary target was 'M3': that is, currency in circulation and bank deposits. The following year saw the introduction of the Medium Term Financial Strategy (MTFS). This set out the government's projections for both the money supply and the PSBR over the next four years. When the government failed to meet its targets for M3, it used other monetary measures which it thought would be easier to control (Robinson, 1986, p. 417). The government also put great emphasis on interest rates, the Chancellor stating that 'No government that is interested in controlling the quantity of money can be indifferent to its price.' The government accordingly raised the bank rate in 1979 from 12 per cent to 14 per cent and then to 17 per cent, and through most of 1980 it stayed between 16 and 17 per cent.

The first Thatcher Budget in 1979 introduced a cut in the standard rate of income tax from 33 per cent to 30 per cent, and in the top rate from 83 per cent to 60 per cent. To pay for these cuts and to reduce the PSBR, VAT was doubled to a single rate of 15 per cent, and there were big increases in the prices of nationalised industries. The 1981 Budget was also deflationary, in the midst of the severest depression since 1929–31.

Indeed throughout the decade the Conservative Government sought to reduce public expenditure and the PSBR, but its efforts with regard to the former were thwarted for many years because of the greater cost of social security through the increase in the number of unemployed and in the number of old-age pensioners, as well as increases in expenditure on defence and law and order. The government was, however, more successful in reducing the PSBR and indeed for a short period the PSBR was negative thanks to the boost to government revenue from North Sea Oil and the proceeds of privatisation.

Towards the end of the decade much less was heard of monetarism. However, a budget deficit re-emerged and was defended in the early 1990s by the Conservative Government as being reasonable in the midst of a recession. But the budget deficit continued in the mid-1990s despite economic recovery and sharp public expenditure restrictions.

In 1987, there had been the deregulation of financial markets and 'Big Bang' on the Stock Exchange. There was also a massive 'give-away' budget which reduced the top rate of income tax by one-third to 40 per cent and further reduced the standard rate. What followed was an upsurge in consumer expenditure fuelled by the tax concessions and a credit boom, which in turn led to falling unemployment, rising inflation, rising wages and a large balance of payments deficit. To control inflation, interest rates were raised drastically from 7.5 per cent in May 1988 to 15 per cent in October 1989 (the only weapon acceptable to the Conservative Government). By late 1990 inflation had started to fall at the cost of a new recession and with unemployment rising again and manufacturing output and GDP falling.

As mentioned earlier, the Conservative Government had entered the ERM in October 1990 at a high sterling exchange rate. In order to maintain the exchange rate, interest rates had to be kept at a penal level and this added to deflationary pressure, as did the unrealistic high exchange rate. When the pound was driven out of the ERM in September 1992, it made possible successive cuts in interest rates which were reduced to a low of 5.25 per cent early in 1994 and continued at a low level for the following three years.

Meanwhile the tax base had been eroded by the earlier Lawson concessions, while the near-doubling of unemployment, together with increased public expenditure prior to the 1992 election, resulted in a large budgetary deficit. This in turn after the 1992 election led to severe cuts in public expenditure and to heavy increases in taxation, albeit not in the basic and higher rates of income tax. These measures did not succeed in correcting the budget deficit, and the PSBR continued to be a major problem for the Conservative Government in the following years despite economic recovery.

The Labour Government introduced a slightly deflationary budget in the summer of 1997, and there were a number of small interest rate increases by the Bank of England.

Balance of payments

Britain in 1979 had a current balance of payments deficit of £661 million, which consisted of a deficit in visible trade of £3349 million, largely offset by a surplus on invisible trade of £2788 million. The next six years saw significant surpluses on the current balance, and indeed in the first three of these years there was also a surplus on visible trade, largely the consequence of a relatively depressed demand for imports due to recession and the large boost to exports provided by North Sea oil.

From 1983 onwards, there was a steadily increasing deficit on visible trade, which reached a peak of £24 billion in 1989. Indeed, in 1983, Britain for the first time since the Industrial Revolution imported more manufactured goods than she exported. By 1986, the invisible surplus was no longer sufficient to offset the deficit on visible trade, so that the current balance from 1986 onwards also showed steadily increasing deficits, reaching £20 billion in 1989.

During the 1990s the deficit on visible trade continued, virtually never falling below £10 billion a year. However, there were improvements in the surplus on invisible trade so that the overall current balance did come down significantly in the mid-1990s.

Nevertheless, it is a sad commentary that the era of North Sea oil (which, it was originally thought, would provide Britain with a lengthy period free of balance of payments difficulties) lasted for no more than six yetars, and the country has run a current deficit balance from that time.

Conclusion

The main significant features of the changing economic environment for industrial relations were, first, the drastic cutbacks in manufacturing industry in 1979–81, and again in 1990–2, where unions had traditionally been strongly organised, and the resultant large-scale redundancies.

Second, after three post-war decades of virtually full employment, there was the near trebling of unemployment to well over 3 million between 1979 and 1987. There then came the brief Lawson boom and a fall in unemployment to under 1.6 million. This was followed by the second major recession of 1990–2 with unemployment almost doubling to virtually 3 million. The subsequent recovery still left the number of unemployed and claiming benefit at 1.5 million in mid-1997 on official figures, and real unemployment considerably higher. The virtually persistent high unemployment throughout the last 18 years has meant a more competitive labour market.

Third, there was the changing structure of the economy and consequently of the labour force, in particular the decline of manufacturing; the growth of the private service sector; the growth of female employment (much of it part-time) and the decline of male employment; the growth of white-collar employment and the decline of blue-collar employment; and the growth in self-employment.

Fourth, there was the growth of international competition in product markets. International competition meant (among other things) attempts by employers to reduce labour costs, certainly in the first instance by the large-scale shedding of labour and the closure of plants, and subsequently by the speeding up of technological change, organisational change, a fall in the average size of manufacturing units, increased take-over and merger activity, and very substantial investment abroad, including the transfer of manufacturing capacity.

One remarkable fact, in view of all the above features, was that throughout the 1980s average money earnings (and indeed real earnings) continued to increase significantly, albeit the increase was very unevenly distributed in favour of the better-paid. In the recession of the early 1990s the average rate of increase in money earnings fell substantially, although average real earnings continued to increase but at a much slower rate than previously. This trend continued during the economic recovery of the mid-1990s. We will return to the issue of pay in subsequent chapters, particularly in Chapter 10.

What effect the election of the Labour Government in May 1997 will have on economic policy remains to be seen. As the economic recovery has proceeded apace, there was a slightly deflationary budget in the summer of 1997, and interest rate increases. The Labour Government is pledged neither to increase income tax rates nor the total of public expenditure, so its room for manoeuvre (at least in the short-run) might well be limited. A long-term inflation target has been set and interest rates are now the responsibility of the Bank of England. The value of sterling has been very high in 1997, leading to more pressure on manufacturing industry. In the near future there is also the question of the European Monetary Union (EMU) to be considered.

CHAPTER 4

Government values and policies

Introduction

At the general election of 1979 a Conservative Government was returned with a majority of 43 seats over all other parties, with the support of 44 per cent of those who voted. The manifesto on which the government was elected heralded major changes in industrial relations and, in particular, steps to curb the power of trade unions.

The Conservatives were returned again on three successive occasions in 1983, 1987 and 1992, every time with 42 per cent of the votes cast. Their seat majorities over all other parties were 144, 100 and 21, even the last being a working majority. (Appendix I).

Throughout the 1980s the government rarely felt under any threat at a general election. In 1983 the improvement in their popularity as a result of the Falklands War played an important part in their victory, and unemployment at over 3 million turned out not to be the political disadvantage it had widely been believed to be in the 1970s by many Conservatives, a belief which lingered on into the 1980s among those who were called 'wets'. In all three general elections – 1983, 1987 and 1992 – the opposition was divided, Labour taking 28, 31 and 34 per cent of the vote, and the Alliance/Liberal Democrats 25, 23 and 18 per cent. Many of the trade unionists who had voted for Conservative candidates in 1979 continued to be loyal to them right through to the 1992 general election.

As for many other areas of policy, the significance for industrial relations of the command of the Commons which the government possessed throughout the 1980s without effective electoral challenge was that a whole sequence of legislative steps could be confidently taken. There was a sharpening of the government's intervention later in the decade which continued into the 1990s when the legislation, and plans for legislation, became more extreme than the first steps taken in the 1979–83 Parliament. Contrary to the usual rhythm of politics, continued power was not associated with a tempering of the attack on trade unions, but with yet deeper interference.

Of course, industrial relations were part of a wider canvas in 1979, and more general objectives set the scene for the government's action in that field. There were two particular, related, general ideas which had profound implications for industrial relations, and both marked departures from the assumptions which had underlain successive governments' policies for over 30 years.

These were a belief that the results of the freest possible play of economic forces were almost always to be preferred, and that consensus between the two sides of industry and the government was almost always malign. It followed that impediments to the operation of market forces were in the government's sights. The workings of the labour market are not easily left to unimpeded market pressures because those who labour are not tins of beans: they have votes and a capacity to organise and act collectively. But the activities of trade unions and the processes of collective bargaining, perhaps even their very existence, were plainly at odds with the free play of market forces. The consensus of the post-war period, which had varied in intensity, was erected on the widely-held belief that the determination of pay was bound to be dominated by organised action resulting in collective agreements which were major modifications of market forces. The consensus had been that those agreements would need from time to time to be subjected to an overall framework of restraint put together with the parties on the initiative of governments. That could not be reconciled with a free market approach.

A concerted attempt to weaken the fabric of collective bargaining in order to allow market forces much greater impact on pay and conditions of employment was one of the radical changes which the government inaugurated and pursued until it fell.

The Labour Government which was returned to office at the general election of May 1997 with a majority of 189 secured 44 per cent of the votes cast, a similar proportion to that obtained by the Conservatives in 1983, 1987 and 1992. In 1997 the Conservatives received 32 per cent of the votes, compared with Labour's 31 and 34 per cent in 1987 and 1992. So the electorate reversed the fortunes of the two main parties at the ballot box although the impact on the composition of the House of Commons in 1997 with its large Labour majority was almost unprecedented.

The advent of a Labour Government meant that government policy on industrial relations was no longer dominated by hostility to the trade unions as it had been under the Conservatives and, indeed, involved drawing trade unions and employers into advising Ministers on a wide variety of policies. But on economic policy the new government continued its predecessor's emphasis on the importance of market forces and, in particular, the need for a flexible labour market. Moreover, apart from minor changes, the Government was not committed to a repeal of the Conservatives' legislation on industrial relations.

There were three policy developments which had implications for industrial relations. First, the government was committed to introducing a national minimum wage (NMW) which would be a significant intervention in the operation of the labour market, especially in service industries among mainly unskilled and part-time female employees, few of whom were trade union members. Second, the adoption of the Social Chapter of the Maastricht Treaty recognised that the regulation of conditions of work would be increased and would owe something to the European Union's (EU) ideas of social partnership. Third, a statutory procedure to govern the recognition of unions by employers, with the object of ensuring that where employees showed that they wished to be represented by a trade union employers could not refuse to negotiate, would help the unions to get established in new firms.

Important as these three promised policy initiatives are likely to be during the life of the present Parliament, the elements of continuity in the new Government's approach leads to the likelihood of limited change in industrial relations.

This chapter shows how the Conservative Government from 1979 to 1997 sought to transform British industrial relations and the legal framework within which they are conducted. In each policy area it estimates the likely extent to which the Labour Government may seek to conserve what it inherited, or to take new initiatives.

Full employment

A commitment to the maintenance of full employment had been the centrepiece of the consensus across the political spectrum from 1945 to the end of the 1970s. It had two sources. Out of the Second World War had come a universal hostility to mass unemployment and a general assumption that no party could win a general election unless it was committed to full employment. The second source was Keynesian economics; the means were available for managing the economy in such a way that full employment was maintained.

A central question of economic policy up to the end of the 1970s was how to manage elements other than employment in the performance of the economy – consumption, investment, taxation, savings, incomes – so that full employment could be preserved. It became progressively more difficult to do so on two fronts. The putting together of an effective incomes policy (usually covering prices as well as incomes, and unearned as well as earned income) ran into more and more snags and collapsed in the most thoroughgoing way in the Winter of Discontent in 1978/9. But, more importantly, the policies which kept the demand for labour at the full employment level came increasingly to be seen as standing in the way of the long-term adjustment of the British economy to its international position. So not only did governments find it increasingly difficult to prevent unemployment rising but productivity, unit labour costs, prices, investment and profitability were getting increasingly out of line with Britain's major competitors in Europe and the rising economies of the Far East. The oil and gas of the North Sea were a bonus but, under the pressure of short-term political demands, they ended up being used to protect the weaknesses of the economy instead of being the means of their reform. As early as 1976, soon after he became Prime Minister, James Callaghan bluntly told the Labour Party Conference that full employment could not be guaranteed: 'it used to be thought that a nation could just spend its way out of recession and increase employment by cutting taxes and boosting government spending. I tell you in all candour that that option no longer exists' (Labour Party, 1976, p. 188).

The new Conservative Government was divided on whether action should be taken to prevent unemployment rising, but the Prime Minister and her supporters succeeded in adopting policies which left the level of employment to be determined by the competitiveness of producers with unemployment coming out as a residual. More jobs would be created, it was argued, by greater success in competitive product markets, than by macro-economic management by the government. It was on this issue that the term 'wets' was most accurately used to describe unreformed ministers. It was the rising level of unemployment and the acceptance of it by the government as an adjustment which should be allowed to run its course which caused such alarm among them. They saw political penalties ahead but they were proved wrong by the result of the 1983 general election.

The dropping of the commitment to full employment and the swift rise of unemployment between 1979 and 1982 from 5 to over 11 per cent on the OECD definition pulled away a major assumption on which collective bargaining had been conducted for over 30 years. It was seen most clearly not in pay, but on the employment front. Trade unions and employers were precipitated into major redundancies in manufacturing industry as the rising value of the pound made exports dearer and imports cheaper, and the government stood back from the consequential reductions in employment. Employment in manufacturing had fallen by about 0.75 million in the 1970s but between 1979 and 1984 it fell by 1.8 million (over 25 per cent). The negotiators had to deal with the direct effects of the inability of British manufacturers to cope with foreign competition. The shock was as great for managers as for trade unionists; as factories closed the government did not accept that it should act to moderate the increase in unemployment.

For several years unemployment ran at about 3–3.25 million, and then fell between 1987 and 1990 to 1.5 million. Inflation picked up again, and the economy was put back into recession with unemployment rising to nearly 3 million. A slow recovery began in 1992 but the fall in unemployment was halting, and 2.75 million were still unemployed in the spring of 1994. High levels of unemployment, even after a period of expansion, had become endemic and acceptable to many. For most of the period, high unemployment had replaced full employment as the normal background to government economic policy, although it is true that by mid-1997 unemployment was down to 1.5 million and inflation was still relatively low.

Although the TUC and others endeavoured in the run-up to the general election of 1997 to get full employment back on to the political agenda (see Britton, 1997), the Labour Party steered clear of it. It was impressed by the dependence of the British economy on its global performance; the level of employment could not be internally managed or guaranteed. A 'high and stable level of employment', to use the words of the 1944 Employment Policy White Paper (Cmnd 6527), could only be achieved if Britain's performance in the world economy justified it. The pressure to have an employment objective was weakened by the continued fall in unemployment during the long recovery after 1992, and unemployment reached its lowest level since 1979 two months after the Labour Government took office. But at the 1997 Labour Party Conference, Gordon Brown, the Chancellor of the Exchequer, made 'full employment for the 21st century' a goal of Labour Party policy, defining it as 'employment opportunities for all'.

Inflation

The Conservative Government's commitment which replaced full employment was the reduction (and, if possible, the elimination) of inflation. The implication was that if unemployment helped to reduce inflation, unemployment there would have to be; or, if measures to reduce unemployment would be inflationary, they would not be taken. They came together in the belief that if inflation could be removed, non-inflationary growth would occur, and that would bring growing employment and falling unemployment.

Stemming inflation, which had risen to over 20 per cent in the spring of 1980, required monetary policies as opposed to demand management; the government would concentrate on controlling the money supply and using the rate of interest, thus making otiose the apparatus of incomes policies, regional grants, investment subsidies and all the other forms of intervention which had been used in attempts to prevent low levels of unemployment causing inflation.

The effect was to push industrial relations to the periphery of political concern. It had previously been at its centre with successive governments constructing policies, at varying levels of detail, in consultation with the CBI and TUC in order to retain a consensus. A monetarist attack on inflation treated collective bargaining as one of the mechanisms for settling prices, albeit shot through with imperfections. Instead of being coopted members of the ruling circle, leading employers and trade unionists were no longer needed in the corridors of Whitehall. Negotiators in the private sector were left to get on with pay settlements against the background of unemployment, interest rates and exchange rates which prevailed at the time. It was assumed that the levels of pay arrived at would be compatible with the government's objectives and, even if they were not, the government would not presume to know better than employers what they should pay their employees.

On inflation, too, the Labour Government displayed continuity in its policy: avoidance of inflation was at the top of its economic agenda. It adopted a target for prices which was similar to the previous Government's. It came to power after several years of low inflation and quickly took action to temper the rate of recovery as the economy approached full capacity. Indeed, by giving the Bank of England responsibility for interest rates, having itself set the inflation target, it let go of a major instrument of economic management, a move which had been contemplated by Conservative Chancellors of the Exchequer such as Nigel Lawson. It brought us closer to the practice in other EU countries, notably Germany.

Public expenditure and the welfare state

It had been a major theme of the 1979 general election that the Conservative Party was in favour of people paying less in taxation, keeping more of their incomes, and deciding for themselves how to spend them. It continued throughout the decade to be a politically attractive theme to many wage and salary earners, and was a strong element in the government's popular appeal.

Reductions in direct taxes helped to reduce inflation. Trade unionists who were paying less in income tax (although they could well be paying more in National Insurance contributions as their incomes rose) could be more relaxed about the size of their pay claims. In the 1970s the level of personal taxation and increases in it had played an important part in stoking up pressure for pay claims, and when Denis Healey was Chancellor of the Exchequer in 1976 he made attempts to trade off tax reductions against the size of pay increases.

From 1979 there was a drastic change in the approach to public expenditure; from being the engine of the economy, changing speed as required to maintain full employment, it was cast for the role of wrecker. The more it could be reduced, the better the economy would perform. Although it was not reduced as a proportion of national income until the end of the decade and resumed its upward course with the new recession in the early 1990s, downward pressure was exerted from the time the government came into office. Activities which were financed or subsidised out of public funds were suspect either in principle (and ought to be privatised), or in terms of their assumed inefficiency. Cash limits were used to set ceilings on what could be spent. If wages and salaries were settled at levels which put up the pay bill by more than the cash limit allowed, there would usually be no more money. The excess expenditure on pay had to be met by increased efficiency or by a reduction in the scale and quality of the service, both of which would reduce the number of jobs.

The settlement of pay and the negotiations about working practices in all activities financed out of public funds were powerfully affected. Trade union membership was high in the public sector and the government's approach to public expenditure was a direct challenge to the unions (the managers being, in most cases, bound by the Government's policy).

Nowhere was continuity from the previous government closer than in taxation and public expenditure policy. The Labour Party gave a firm commitment both that it would not increase personal rates of tax and that it would keep to the levels of public expenditure planned by the Conservatives for 1997/8 and 1998/9. It was a touchstone of New Labour that the Party could only win at the general election if it gave those undertakings which, in its first months of office, it showed every intention of keeping. Additional expenditure on programmes would be financed either by specific reductions in expenditure (paying for reductions in class sizes to a maximum of 30 in primary schools by ending the assisted places scheme) or by new taxes (paying for the new deal on welfare to work for the long-term unemployed by a levy on certain privatised industries).

Holding the Conservatives' line on public expenditure meant little relief of pressure on pay in the public sector. At the time of the 1996 TUC it was reported that trade union leaders had warned Tony Blair that the Labour Government might well face difficulties over pay among public service workers in his third year of office unless something were done to improve their relative pay.

Deregulation

The freer play of all markets which the Conservative Government favoured required a direct attack on the accretions of rules, regulations, limits, customs and practices which had been tolerated in the belief that if people had their interests protected in this way they would be more amenable to government proposals that they should exert their bargaining power moderately.

The approach touched many established interests, including the obvious candidates in the industrial relations field. In industrial relations, practices like the closed shop and restrictive practices came under the heading of deregulation. It was not only the Monopolies and Mergers Commission which was brought to bear. In disputes, like those in the newspaper industry, the removal of the regulations controlling entry to employment fitted in closely with the government's objectives.

Regulations in the labour market which had been introduced to protect individuals from the exploitation of unregulated employment were attacked as barriers to the efficient operation of market forces. Limits on the maximum hours which women and young people could work were generally removed. Wages Councils which provided legal minimum wages for 2 million employees (mainly women), were abolished in 1993 after they had been confined in 1986 to fixing one rate of pay for all employees aged 21 and over, with the consequence that the relative pay of some of the lowest paid workers worsened (Machin and Manning, 1993).

The Labour Government was committed to introducing a NMW, as it had been at the general election of 1992. Although it had been adopted to some extent as a replacement for Wages Councils, it was a quite different measure. Instead of dealing with low pay industry by industry, it proposed setting a single level of average hourly earnings to which all adult employees would be entitled universally; it would put a floor into every firm's wage structure. A Low Pay Commission was set up in July 1997 to recommend the level of the NMW, with the government reserving to itself the power to accept the recommendation or to determine the level itself.

The NMW would be a major intervention in the labour market. In 1996, 7.6 per cent of all employees had average hourly earnings of less than £3.50: that is, about 1.4 million people. But among part-time employees the proportion was 20.6 per cent, or about 1.2 million. At average hourly earnings of £4.00 the numbers paid less are 3 million, of whom 2.1 million are part-timers (*New Earnings Survey*, April 1996, which tends to underestimate the number of part-time low paid employees).

Service trades such as catering, retailing, hairdressing, private health care and contract cleaning, which employ large numbers of part-time women employees, would be heavily affected. Obviously trades employing mainly male workers and people in white-collar and professional occupations would not be affected. Large numbers of mainly small employers would have to increase the earnings of most of their employees if the NMW were set at a level like £3.70 which is well below trade union expectations. There would be impacts on internal and external pay differentials. The regular up-dating of the NMW on recommendations of the Low Pay Commission would inevitably be referred to in pay negotiations.

A major change instituted by the Conservative Government in July 1995, when a reshuffle of Ministers required a reduction in their number by one, was the abolition of the DE. The Department had by that date become a shadow of its former self with the creation of agencies for the Employment Service and the Health and Safety Executive, the abolition of Wages Councils, the completion of the programme of legislation on industrial relations, the decline of strikes, and the abandonment of intervention in the labour market.

Training and employment policies went to the Department for Education and Employment; industrial relations, individual employment rights and redundancies to the Department of Trade and Industry (DTI); Health and Safety to the Department of the Environment; and employment and training statistics to the Office of National Statistics. it marked the end of labour issues as a central preoccupation of government for there had been a Cabinet Minister for labour or employment since 1916 (see Employment Policy Institute, 1996).

The main significance of the change was the integration of training with education. The DE had seen training as mainly focused on employers, whereas the new arrangements put the emphasis on the links between vocational training and educational institutions. Industrial relations had become so low key from the government's point of view that the DTI could absorb the subject as an additional minor activity. The Labour Government left the departmental arrangements unchanged, with the DTI taking on the new responsibility for the NMW.

The role of the individual

Emphasis on the obligation of the individual citizen to look after his or her own interests, such as getting on your bike to find a job as Norman Tebbit advised the Conservative Party Conference in 1983, was complementary to a preference for market forces. But impediments to individual action prevented citizens from doing things for themselves and so reducing their dependence on the state. The government had, therefore, to be interventionist in order not only to create space for individuals, but also to create an environment in which individuals could be pressed by government to be more self-reliant.

This had a direct link with government action on industrial relations. On matters like the closed shop, picketing and balloting before strikes, the key idea was that collective action and its restraints on individual choice should be made to give way to wider individual preferences on whether or not to join a trade union, or cross a picket line, or join a strike even if a majority had voted in favour of it. Legislative action of a detailed kind on these matters was based on the belief that if individuals could choose, they would tend to reject collective action and the government's objective of reducing impediments to the working of the labour market would be served.

This emphasis on the individual got stronger as the decade passed, and by the general election of 1987 the legislative commitments of the Conservative Party gave the leading place to the right of individual members to challenge their unions in the Courts with the aid of the Commissioner for the Rights of Trade Union Members 'with the power to help individual trade unionists to enforce their fundamental rights' (Conservative Party Manifesto, 1987). This shift from concern with the legal status of unions and their internal government to subsidised access to the courts for individual members had a number of sources, not least the unwillingness of many employers to resort to the law.

However, it drew on a much broader change lying behind industrial relations and going much deeper than specific legislative changes. The Government rode on a wave of 'acquisitive individualism [which] tended to supersede both social solidarity and social service' (Phelps Brown, 1990, p. 8) in a range of policy areas including industrial relations. The same change lay behind the substantial shift of manual worker voters from Labour to Conservative at the 1979 general election which was sustained in the elections of 1983 and 1987. Enabling individual union members to challenge their collective leaders fitted in with the belief that 'the loyalty that sprang from the individual worker's sense of common interest . . . had ebbed away' (Phelps Brown, 1990, p. 11).

In terms of general objectives the Labour Government favoured community action and emphasised the responsibilities of individuals as a complement to their rights. But it did not propose amending, for example, those provisions of the legislation on trade unions and individuals which prevented unions from taking action against members who refused to strike when there was a majority in favour.

Reducing the public sector

The public sector presents a major problem to those who believe in the efficiency of markets as allocators of goods and services because a number of public services are either not capable of being sold at a price (defence), or are kept in the public sector by a political decision (the NHS). But others could be put into the private sector. The government's desire to inject the discipline of the market took several forms: privatisation of monopolies subject to controls and limited competition (for example, British Telecom, Mercury and the Office of Telecommunications), contracting-out of services after competitive bids (for example, local authority refuse collection and the cleaning of hospitals), and the creation of internal markets with pseudo-prices (for example, general practitioners' purchase of hospital services and the opting-out of schools from local authority control).

The privatisation programme did not get going until the mid-1980s, but by 1991 the main nationalised industries had been sold into private ownership: telecommunications, gas, buses, airlines and airports, steel, water and electricity. After the general election of 1992 the railways, coal-mining and parts of nuclear energy were privatised, but not the Post Office.

What could not be privatised could be decentralised and encouraged to imitate the private sector. Major government activities, such as tax collecting and the payment of benefits, were put into agencies so that by April 1994 half of all civil servants were covered by delegated pay agreements in agencies and by 1997 virtually all of them. All hospitals had become trusts by 1994, with a high degree of independence on questions of employment and pay. In what was left of central government, market testing was extensively applied after the 1992 general election in order to determine what functions could be put out to contract with the private sector.

All of these changes had major implications for industrial relations. As managers were encouraged to behave like independent employers, central agreements on pay and conditions were replaced or supplemented by locally negotiated agreements. One purpose was to put managers in a stronger position in their bargaining with unions. Against a background of high levels of unemployment and possible redundancies, decentralisation of the management of the public sector reduced the unions' bargaining power.

The Labour Government, returned in 1997, did not propose reversing any privatisation. But it did make some changes in the NHS by ending the internal market and restoring the national pay agreements. It also ended compulsory contracting-out with an obligation to secure best value. In this area of policy the new government broadly accepted the position left to it by its predecessor.

The trade unions

It was of crucial importance to the confidence with which the Conservative Government took steps to curb the power of trade unions that it had the support of trade unionists. Until the early 1970s trade union membership itself worked in favour of Labour. By 1979 it was no longer an independent determinant of voting preference, and by the 1983 general election more trade unionists than non-trade unionists voted Conservative (Himmelweit *et al.*, 1985, p. 208). This positive attraction which the Conservative Party had for trade unionists can be seen in the decline of Labour voting among the growing number of owner-occupiers who were trade unionists; in 1974, 45 per cent had voted labour, but by 1983 the proportion was down to 28 per cent (Rose and McAllister, 1986, p. 97). In the 1987 general election 30 per cent of trade union members voted Conservative and 26 per cent Liberal Democrat, and even in

1992 when the pressure on trade unionists to vote Labour was strong, 30 per cent still voted Conservative but only 19 per cent voted Liberal Democrat. The proportion of trade union members voting Labour, which had been 42 per cent in 1987, was still less than half at 47 per cent in 1992 (*Sunday Times*, 12 April 1992, reporting a MORI poll). It is widely recognised by trade union leaders that the defection of more of their members from Labour to Conservative in 1979, especially in the south of England, was a major reason, if not *the* major reason as some would acknowledge, for the return of a Conservative Government in 1979 and Tory victories in 1983, 1987 and 1992.

It was a major objective of the Labour Party's campaign before the 1997 general election to regain the votes of those who had left it for the Conservative Party in the general elections of 1979, 1983, 1987 and 1992, including many trade unionists. But this did not involve any major commitment to strengthening trade unions or to repealing the limitations which the Conservative legislation had placed upon them, although it did mean that trade unions would again be involved with employers in advising the Government. The strategy worked: 59 per cent of trade unionists voted Labour in May 1997 (NOP/BBC exit poll).

The unions' power had five objectionable aspects for the Conservative Government. First, unions were too powerful in the system of pay determination; they pushed up pay beyond what was compatible with effective performance in the international economy. They protected practices which prevented increases in productivity. They stood out against changes which managers proposed in the interests of efficiency. They usurped managerial authority where they could, especially in the public services. The unions' defence was that they were legitimate organisations which existed to bargain about pay, productivity and working practices. Their right to bargain was mirrored by the employers' right to bargain. If there were cases where they were strong enough to reap the rewards of strength, there were many other cases where the boot was on the other foot and managers were able to make their proposals prevail.

However, the Conservative Government's position was not only that the balance of power had swung too far towards the unions, which was probably what had electoral appeal, but also that their very existence was at odds with an efficient labour market. The same legislative and other actions were appropriate to both positions to a considerable extent, so that differences between them were not of political importance at the beginning of the decade. Even so, there was no doubt that the government believed that firms which did not recognise unions fitted in better with their approach than those which did; IBM was more popular with them than ICI. So the second basis for hostility to unions was that they existed, and it followed that the government wanted employers without unions to resist granting recognition, and managers of new plants to avoid unions or to limit the degree of recognition.

The question of derecognition was fraught with practical difficulties. After all, the government was the direct employer of about 600 000 civil servants, most of whom were in trade unions and who even had their union subscriptions deducted from their pay by their employer under a check-off agreement. But a government which saw trade unions as organisations seeking to develop their position as monopolists in a labour market which needed to be made freer was clearly on the side of any employers who wanted to derecognise unions. The banning of trade unions at Government Communications Headquarters (GCHQ) Cheltenham in 1984, though brought about for other reasons, showed that the government was prepared to practise what it preached. But it was not extended to other parts of the civil service and so it acquired a symbolic significance for the trade union movement. One of the first actions of the Labour Government in 1997 was to restore to the staff of GCHQ the right to belong to a trade union.

The third source of hostility to trade unions was their place in consensus politics and industrial relations. In the post-war period the consensus approach had been based on the belief that if trade unions were incorporated in the apparatus of government along with employers they would use their power and influence reasonably, meaning with restraint. If they were kept outside the circle of government they were sufficiently powerful to wreck any government's policies, especially any policy of full employment. So not only was there a succession of incomes policies of varying degrees of complexity and bite but the TUC, as the national body speaking to governments on behalf of trade unions, and embodied most strikingly in George Woodcock (assistant general secretary and general secretary of the TUC from 1947 to 1969), had a finger in every aspect of government affairs in the economic and social fields. There were formal bodies such as the NEDC (1963) and the Manpower Services Commission (MSC) (1974) to which the TUC had, in effect, powers of nomination. Almost every public board from the Bank of England to the BBC had at least one TUC nominee. In the Woodcock era the TUC regarded the list of organisations for which it was invited to submit nominations as proof of its position as the fourth estate of the realm.

Incomes policies in the 1960s and 1970s depended on specially close tripartite arrangements which tended to go deeper and be more far-reaching as time passed. In long and detailed discussions with ministers and employers, trade unions were party to schemes which limited the use of their bargaining power. They were represented on the bodies set up to administer prices and incomes policies. They entered into compacts with governments in which they traded restraint on pay for benefits in other areas of policy. Although it was a common feature of incomes policies that unions became less able to deliver their side of the bargain as the incomes policy progressed, the idea that the economy could only be successful if the unions were closely connected with policy had a powerful hold across the political spectrum.

The Conservative Government of 1979 saw trade union involvement with governments in all these ways as giving them an unfair advantage and not as taming them. As part of the change in economic policy, trade unions had to be expelled from the places where the decisions of government were discussed. As opportunities arose, institutions which linked the unions with employers and government were abolished. Training Boards, with a few exceptions, were abolished in the early 1980s. The MSC was wound up in 1984. The NEDC, after being cut back in staff and activities, was eventually abolished in 1992.

The unions' area of activity had to be confined to that of bargaining with employers. If they could not negotiate agreed settlements, strikes should be faced with the intention of defeating them. Arbitration should be refused because it always split the difference and gave unions more than they would get if their threats of action were resisted. As things turned out, in the early 1980s, the extensive redundancies in manufacturing provided a helpful context for this approach. The unions' bluff was to be called; they should get no more than they could extract by their bargaining power alone.

Fourth, with the emphasis on the role of the individual in economic affairs, the government was sharp to notice any sign that collective action was bought at the cost of undue subjugation of individual members. At the root of this source of hostility to unions was the belief that sturdy individuals pursuing their own self-interest would not wish to join a union if they could avoid it. Since they plainly did join in large numbers, it must be either because they were misguided in believing it was in their interests to do so, or they were being coerced to some degree, perhaps even compelled, to join in order to keep their jobs. On this view the poll results, showing that while there was support from trade unionists for curbing the unions, respondents thought their own unions were doing a good job, could be interpreted as indicating a widespread wish to escape from tyranny combined with a reluctance to admit that it existed.

The Government held that trade unionists would come to see the advantages of not being members of trade unions when their unions' power was clipped and when employers treated them as valued individuals and not as undifferentiated parts of a trade union lump. The coercion to which they were subjected could be removed by putting an end to the closed shop, by limiting picketing and lawful strike action, and by the introduction of ballots which would enable individuals to assert themselves against the small groups of activists who dominated the affairs of unions.

The idea that union leaders held power independently of their members was a central feature of the belief that individual citizens would not readily support what trade unions did. The overmighty trade union barons with immediate access to ministers, or the jumped-up hospital shop steward who thought he ran the hospital, were important figures in the doctrine that if only the unions were in the hands of their members they would not behave so badly. So 'handing the unions back to their members' became a companion expression to 'get on your bike'.

The fifth reason for hostility to the unions, arising out of the period of the Labour Government from 1974 to 1979 and reinforcing the other four, was the legislative protection given in that period to certain union aspirations. The Conservative Party manifesto of 1979 had two themes on the unions: they had fallen into the hands of a minority of extremists, and the Labour Government had 'heaped privileges without responsibility' on them. They came together in the key sentence, 'Labour enacted a "militants' charter" of trade union legislation.' These privileges, such as the right to have claims for recognition looked at by ACAS, and unilateral arbitration, were the first candidates for legislative repeal.

Lying behind these five sources of hostility to trade unions was the memory of events in the early 1970s which reinforced the desire to cut the unions down to size. The Conservative Government returned in 1970 had made the transformation of the role of the unions through legislation a major feature of its policies. Sir Geoffrey Howe, as Solicitor General, was given special charge of the Industrial Relations Bill on the basis of his long association with proposals to reduce the legal privileges of trade unions as set out in the Inns of Court Conservative and Unionist Society's influential pamphlet, *A Giant's Strength* (1958). But the Industrial Relations Act of 1971 was for the most part a failure. It gave employers opportunities to take legal proceedings which would check union action but they failed to do so, mainly because they believed they would be more trouble than they were worth. To the extent that it was used, the NIRC, and cases which went before it, led to confrontations or to legal fiascos (see Chapter 2). That Conservative Government got it wrong, the new one was determined to get it right.

It did get it right in the sense that the step by step approach to legislation, which was made possible by winning four general elections in a row, was widely accepted despite opposition at the time of each Bill from the unions and some employers. It was also aided by the fact that developments in the world economy were working in the same direction.

It also got it right in another sense, however. The subject ceased to be a political football because the Labour Party at the general election of 1997 proposed hardly any changes to the legal position of the unions. The Conservative Government's legislation on industrial relations had, as far as could be foreseen, become the long-term settlement of issues such as strikes, picketing, secondary action, the closed shop, and the election of union leaders.

The employers

Since the Conservative Government wished to end consensus and unleash market forces, it was bound to be critical of many employers on some of the same grounds as it was critical of trade unions. A willingness to operate incomes policies and to discuss economic policy jointly with government and the unions was what prevented employers adopting the economic policies for which the Conservative Party stood in 1979.

The new government distanced itself from the CBI, preferring the Institute of Directors, and also from the major firms which for decades had helped to make the consensus work. The government's preferred employers tended to be companies which were independent and not large; the managers it appointed to turn state enterprises round and take them into the private sector were often 'outsiders' like Michael Edwardes (breaker of the unions at the Longbridge plant of British Leyland), Ian McGregor (leader of the British Steel Corporation and British Coal during the strikes which the unions lost), and Graham Day (in charge of British Shipbuilders during the industry's rundown), who were untainted by consensus and who wanted to put industrial relations on the sort of new footing of which the government approved. The personnel directors of large companies were particularly suspect because of their close association with the old ways. Small firms with managers who were owners stood especially high in the government's estimation.

The manner of the Labour Government's end in 1979 clinched the Conservative Party's conviction that private employers had to be reformed and that public employers had to be brought firmly under the government's control. The Social Contract was at one and the same time the closest collaboration ever instituted between a Labour Government and the trade unions and, after some initial success, in the end the least effective. This was partly because of external forces like the oil price shock of 1973 and the IMF intervention of 1976, but it was also because, when it mattered, neither side could deliver what mattered most to the other side.

The problem of public sector pay, which was always the most acute problem under all incomes policies, had been hived off very late in the day in March 1979 to the Comparability Commission under Professor Hugh Clegg. The Conservative Party committed itself to honouring Clegg's awards when it came to power, and the cost of doing so served to reinforce its hostility to a solution of that type. The public sector strikes which led to the Commission being set up marked the end of the claim that only a Labour Government could deal successfully with the unions. The Conservative Government adopted a pay policy towards public sector employees which was the opposite of that represented by the Commission. Public sector pay was to be governed by cash limits, not by comparisons with the private sector. Disputes were to be settled by trials of strength, which the Government intended to win. There was to be the minimum of arbitration. Only those who repudiated strike action, such as the nurses, were allowed to join the select band with Review Bodies (the armed forces, doctors, dentists, judges, and senior civil servants), although an exception was made for teachers in 1991. Improvements in efficiency and reductions in numbers, whether in their own right or as a means of living within cash limits, were largely separated from pay settlements. There was, therefore, a clear and coordinated policy on pay for the public sector and the Government believed that as an employer it was a model which private employers would do well to imitate.

Yet the Government's approach made it impossible for Ministers to tell private employers within what limits they should settle, although from time to time Chancellors of the Exchequer in particular would warn that high pay settlements endangered competitive ability and threatened jobs. In a freer labour market it was for employers to settle pay without interference because they alone were the best judges of their own interests. Yet, as the Government knew, many large employers after the redundancies of the early 1980s were not inclined to resist pay claims as robustly as the Government's objectives indicated was desirable. Employers persistently settled for increases which kept earnings moving up faster than prices; between 1979 and 1996 average weekly earnings for the whole economy rose by 286 per cent for men and 349 per cent for women, while prices rose by 180 per cent. In manufacturing the fast increases in productivity – 95 per cent between 1980 and 1996 – covered increases in pay in excess of prices to a considerable extent, but over the whole economy the increase in average productivity was much lower at 39 per cent, well behind the rate of increase in earnings. As a result, labour costs per unit of output rose faster over the 17 years for the whole economy (113 per cent) than for manufacturing (77 per cent). Such increases in unit labour costs, particularly outside manufacturing, marked many private employers as 'wet'. There were few strikes over pay in the private sector by contrast with the large strikes over pay in the public sector, where the Government usually succeeded in defeating the unions. A change in private sector employees' attitudes to the unions and to collective bargaining was an essential part of the Government's strategy. Whatever changes may have occurred, they did not include a willingness to wield the hammer against the unions on pay with the verve which the Government itself displayed as an employer.

In the latter part of John Major's administration prices, earnings and productivity were more in line than in the 1980s. Between 1993 and 1996 prices rose by 9 per cent, average earnings for men by 11 per cent and for women by 12 per cent, and overall productivity by 10 per cent. There was a wide dispersion of pay increases around the average. Many employees, especially the low paid, received increases in pay which were no more, and often less, than the increase in prices. The Labour Government inherited a position which indicated that little inflationary pressure was coming from pay increases, despite the fall in unemployment since 1994. But further tightening of the labour market could be expected to cause employers to bid up increases in earnings.

Before and after the general election, on a wide range of matters the Labour Party indicated that the advice of employers would play a major part in Government decision-making.

Conclusion

The Conservative Government took pride in its convictions; pragmatism, fudging and nudging were what it rejected. But industrial relations is about bargaining between organised groups. The successful achievement of compromises, where the parties at first take their stands some distance apart, is the hallmark of its quality; back-up systems of conciliation and arbitration, often provided by government, are there to make good the failures of negotiators, not to inject new standards. As a method of regulating divergent interests in the workplace, industrial relations were based on a principle (compromise is superior to conflict) which was the opposite of that adopted by the Government (the market rules). The Government was bound, therefore, to attempt major reforms in industrial relations. They were a prominent feature of Mrs Thatcher's programme. They continued under Mr Major with extensive restrictions on trade unions in the Trade Union Reform and Employment Rights Act of 1993, further privatisation and contracting-out, the creation of public sector agencies, and fundamental changes in the NHS, all of which had significant implications for the conduct of industrial relations.

Under the Conservative Government the unions found the environment in which they operated to be unfavourable, with high unemployment, insecurity associated with redundancies, and economic policies which strengthened the hands of employers. These factors were reinforced by the legislation which regulated both their internal government and their bargaining options.

The election of a Labour Government in May 1997 did not herald significant changes in the legislative position of trade unions; the Government was committed to much less than the unions sought. But commitments to a NMW, the Social Chapter of the Maastricht Treaty, and a statutory basis for union recognition by employers met some of the unions' desires. Even so, it would appear that the new government intended to make no major alteration to the basic balance of power in industrial relations which in most places of work (in both the public and the private sectors) gave the employers the upper hand.

CHAPTER 5

The law and industrial relations

Introduction

Under common law employment rights and duties are based on the individual's contract of employment. The contract of employment is supposedly a contract between equals and one which is freely entered into. In fact, the individual employee is almost invariably in a weaker position than the employer. Hence the need and right for individuals to be able to organise in free and effective trade unions and the need for protective legislation in some areas.

Legislation from the 1870s onwards, culminating in the 1906 Trade Disputes Act, sought to protect workers and counteract the inequality of bargaining power inherent in the employment relationship. The 1906 Act enhanced the characteristic feature of British industrial relations – 'voluntarism' – by providing trade unions with immunity from liability for civil wrongs (torts) and individuals, including union officials, with immunity from certain torts (conspiracy, inducing a breach of contract of employment, and interference with a person's freedom to use his capital or labour), as long as they were acting 'in contemplation or furtherance of a trade dispute'.

This remained broadly the position until the introduction of the 1971 Industrial Relations Act. The repeal of this Act by TULRA (as described in Chapter 2), and the new provisions of TULRA, broadly restored the position to what it had been under the 1906 Act.

The new Conservative Government of 1979 had pledged itself to restrict what it considered to be excessive trade union power, and this it proceeded to do in a series of Acts: the Employment Acts of 1980 and 1982, the Trade Union Act 1984, and the Employment Acts of 1988 and 1990. Also relevant to industrial relations were the 1986 Wages Act, the 1986 Sex Discrimination

Act and the 1989 Employment Act. The Conservative Governments pursued a step-by-step approach, rather than one large all-embracing Act, such as the 1971 Industrial Relations Act. These Acts were consolidated in the Trade Union and Labour Relations (Consolidation) Act 1992. In 1993 there was yet further legislation: the Trade Union Reform and Employment Rights Act.

In this chapter we first outline the most important provisions of the main Acts and then proceed to consider the use made of the new laws and some of the leading cases. We concentrate on collective labour law and not on individual employment law although, of course, there is an important overlap between the two. It might be argued that as far as the legislation is concerned, it would be sufficient to summarise the 1992 Consolidation Act and the 1993 Act. This would, however, prevent understanding of how and why the law developed in the way it did. Such an understanding is vitally important when one comes to consider the future. The Acts are therefore dealt with in the order in which they became law.

Employment Act 1980

The provisions of the 1980 Act fell into three main categories:

1. Limitations of trade union immunities in industrial action so that peaceful picketing was limited to the workers' own place of work (s.16(i)) and secondary action was made unlawful except in certain limited circumstances (s.17). Thus, s.13 of TULRA only provided protection for secondary action where the contract concerned was a contract of employment, and where:
   (a) the employer was a supplier or customer providing goods or services under contract to the employer in dispute;
   (b) the principal purpose was directly to prevent the supply of goods or services during the dispute between their employer and the employer in dispute;
   (c) the action was likely to achieve that purpose.
2. A strengthening of individual rights against trade unions by providing legal remedies for unreasonable exclusion or expulsion from a trade union (ss.4 and 5) and extending the grounds on which an individual could refuse to join a union where there was the practice of a Union Membership Agreement (UMA or closed shop). Thus instead of protection only on account of religious belief was substituted protection from unfair dismissal:
   (a) 'If he genuinely objects on grounds of conscience or other deeply-held personal conviction to being a member of any trade union whatsoever or of a particular trade union';
   (b) if he was not a union member before the closed shop came into agreement.

In addition, for any new closed shop agreement, there had to be a ballot in which 80 per cent of those entitled to vote, voted in favour (s.7).

3. A weakening of individual employee protection: for example, the burden of proof that he had acted reasonably in unfair dismissal cases was removed from the employer. Above all, in a number of steps, the individual was prevented from bringing a case of unfair dismissal unless he or she had been employed for two years.

The Act also removed the limited legal channel whereby unions might be able to obtain recognition by abolishing the recognition procedures contained in the 1975 EPA (ss.11–16). Furthermore, it abolished Schedule 11 of the 1975 EPA whereby a case could be brought for unilateral arbitration to the CAC that a firm was paying less than the recognised terms and conditions or, if no such terms and conditions existed, less than the general level.

Employment Act 1982

The 1982 Act continued the attack on the closed shop. Thus whereas the 1980 Act required a ballot for any new closed shop (with a majority of 80 per cent of those entitled to vote), the 1982 Act extended the ballot requirement to existing closed shops where there had not been a secret ballot in the preceding five years (although in such cases a majority of 85 per cent of those voting was required). If these requirements were not met an individual could bring a claim for unfair dismissal against the employer and the union, with new provisions for punitive damages. In addition, a further exemption was made to membership where a closed shop existed, namely where an employee was bound because of his qualifications to observe a written code of conduct (ss.3–8).

Second, the Act made void any term in a commercial contract which required a person to use only union labour (or only non-union labour) in fulfilling a contract. It also made it unlawful to exclude someone from a tender list or to fail to award a contract to him or to terminate a contract with him on the grounds that anyone employed or likely to be employed on work connected with the contract was or was not a union member (s.12). Further, the Act made void any term in a commercial contract which required the contractor to recognise, negotiate or consult with trade unions or trade union officials. It also made it unlawful to exclude someone from a tender list or to fail to award him a contract or to terminate a contract with him on the grounds that he did not negotiate or consult with trade unions or trade union officials (s.13). Finally, the Act removed immunity from trade unions and other persons who organised industrial action to put pressure on an employer to act contrary to the above. It also removed immunity from those who organised or threatened industrial action which interfered with the supply of goods or services on the grounds that:

(a) work done in connection with the supply of goods or services had been or was likely to be done by non-union (or union) members;
(b) the supplier of the goods or services in question did not recognise or consult with trade unions or trade union officials (s.14).

Third, and of even greater significance, was the repeal of s.14 of TULRA which had restored the immunity of trade unions from actions in tort (s.15). The effect of this was to restrict their immunities to those given to persons by s.13 of TULRA. It thus abolished the special and wider immunities for trade unions and brought them into line with those given to other persons (for instance, individuals and union officials). As a result, those who suffered a loss because of unlawful action (for example, action which was not in contemplation or furtherance of a trade dispute; unlawful secondary action; and secondary picketing), would be able to sue a union for damages and seek injunctions (s.15). While it was true that s.16 set upper limits to damages awarded against a union ranging from £10 000 for a union with less than 5000 members to £250 000 for a union with 100 000 or more members, the real threat to a union's power and financial stability (as a number of subsequent cases showed), was not damages but injunctions, which if not obeyed could lead to unlimited fines for contempt of court and to sequestration of all the union's assets. S.15 also set out the circumstances in which a union would be liable for unlawful action organised by its officials. The union was to be liable for unlawful action which was authorised or endorsed by its Executive Committee, its President, its General Secretary, or any of its officials with authority to call industrial action under the union's own rules. It was also to be held liable for unlawful action authorised or endorsed by its employed officials or any committees to which they reported, except where the authorisation was overruled by the Executive Committee, President or General Secretary or the union rules prohibited the official from calling industrial action. As we shall see later, the courts have interpreted the 'vicarious liability' of unions very strictly indeed.

Finally, the Act substantially narrowed the definition of a trade dispute in s.29 of TULRA in that:

(a) in place of the words 'between employers and workers' it substituted 'between workers and their employer';
(b) the words 'or between workers and workers' were omitted;
(c) in place of the words 'is connected with' was substituted 'relates wholly or mainly to'.

The first part of s.29 now reads a 'trade dispute means a dispute between workers and their employer which relates wholly to . . .', instead of 'a dispute between employers and workers, or between workers and workers which is connected with . . .'.

In addition, industrial action relating to matters overseas ceased to be protected unless the persons taking the industrial action in Great Britain were likely to be affected by the outcome of the dispute as regards their own employment (s.18).

Trade Union Act 1984

The Trade Union Act 1984 had three stated purposes. The first was to provide for secret ballots for election to union executive committees. Thus all voting members of union executive committees had to be directly elected at least once every five years. The Act laid down requirements for such elections: for example, entitlement to vote had to be accorded equally to all members (with certain exceptions); voting had to be secret, without interference, and by the marking of a voting paper; and so far as reasonably practical, voting had to be by post, although a union was allowed to hold a workplace, rather than a postal, ballot where it was satisfied that there were no reasonable grounds for believing that a workplace ballot would not meet the necessary requirements. In addition a duty was placed on unions to compile and maintain a register of names and addresses of its members. Finally, a member of a union could apply to the Certification Officer or the High Court for a declaration that the union had failed to comply with the necessary provisions for a ballot and for an enforcement order.

The second purpose was to provide for a secret ballot before a union organised industrial action. S.10 removed immunity from legal action (as provided in s.13 of TULRA) where unions did not hold a ballot before authorising or endorsing a call for a strike or any other form of industrial action which broke or interfered with the contracts of employment of those taking part in it. It also made it a condition of immunity that a majority of those voting had voted in favour of the action; that the ballot was held no more than four weeks before the industrial action began; and that the ballot satisfied certain requirements, as laid down in s.11 of the Act. These requirements were that entitlement to vote had to be given to those, and only those, whom it was reasonable for the union to believe would be called upon to take or continue to take strike or other industrial action. Immunity would be lost if any member was called on to strike after being denied entitlement to vote. The question on the ballot papers had to invite a 'yes' or 'no' answer and specify whether the action involved a strike or other type of industrial action involving the voter in a breach of his contract of employment. So far as was reasonably practical, every person entitled to vote had:

(a)   to be supplied with a ballot paper or have one made available to him during his working hours (or immediately before or after his working hours) either at his place of work or at a place more convenient to him;

(b)   to be given a convenient opportunity to vote by post *or* an opportunity to vote during his working hours (or immediately before or after his working hours) at his workplace or at a place more convenient to him *or* a choice between these two methods of voting. Finally, the detailed results of the ballot had to be made known to those entitled to vote.

The third purpose was to provide secret ballots for union political funds. Trade unions which had in the past balloted their members under the Trade Union Act 1913 to enable them to have political funds in order to spend money on 'political objects' had to ballot their members at least every ten years if they wished to continue to do so (s.10). Any of these trade unions which had not held a ballot in the nine years before 31 March 1985 had to do so before 31 March 1986. Further, the Act updated the provisions of the 1913 Act and required the approval of the Certification Officer for political fund ballot rules. In particular, it provided that the Certification Officer had to satisfy himself that the rules provided for ballots either by post or at the workplace; ballots had to be secret; ballots had to be conducted by the marking of a voting paper; and there had to be equal entitlement to vote. It was also made clear that the Certification Officer had to approve the ballot rules before each ballot (s.13). The Act also contained an updated definition of 'political objects' on which trade unions were only allowed to spend money if they had authority from their members to do so. Most of these related to the financing of a political party, but s.17 (f) also included: 'the production, publication or distribution of any literature, document, film, sound recording or advertisement, the main purpose of which is to persuade people to vote for a political party or candidate or to persuade them not to vote for a political party or candidate'.

This particular provision so alarmed a number of unions, particularly in the public sector (for example, NALGO), that although hitherto they had not had political funds, they balloted their members (successfully) to establish such funds (Leopold, 1988).

Finally, the Act placed a duty on employers, who had 'check-off' arrangements for deducting trade union subscriptions from their employees' pay, to vary the level of check-off deductions by the amount of the political levy if they were informed by a trade union member in writing that he was exempt from paying the levy, or had put in a request to be exempt to his union.

Wages Act 1986

This Act was in three parts: the first, entitled 'Protection of Workers in relation to the Payment of Wages', ss.1–11, repealed the Truck Acts and associated legislation, thereby leaving the method of wage payment to the employer or (if unions were recognised) to negotiations. As a result, manual workers no longer had a statutory right to insist on being paid in cash, although existing rights under their employment contracts were not affected. In addition, certain protection was given against unlawful deductions from wages: for example, workers in retail distribution were given special protection against deductions from wages because of cash or stock shortages, these being limited to 10 per cent of the employee's pay.

Part II, ss.12–16, related to Wages Councils, the main provisions being, first, that Wage Council Orders no longer applied to workers under 21 years of age; second, Wage Councils were limited to setting one basic hourly rate of pay and one premium rate: third, Councils must consider the impact on jobs of the minimum rate they set: and fourth, a simplified procedure for abolishing or changing the scope of Wage Councils was introduced (namely, the power was given to the Secretary of State who was required only 'to consult such persons or organisations as he considers appropriate').

Finally, in Part III, Redundancy Rebates, ss.27–9, employers with 10 or more employees were no longer to get rebates (of 35 per cent) from government for any redundancy payments they had to make.

Sex Discrimination Act 1986

In s.1 the Act removed the exemption for small firms with five or fewer employees, which had been given in the 1975 Sex Discrimination Act, from complying with that Act's employment provisions: that is to say, small firms must not discriminate against employees or prospective employees on grounds of their sex or because they were married, in recruitment, treatment during their employment or in dismissing them. S.2 brought within the scope of the 1975 Act any provision made by an employer in relation to retirement, dismissal, demotion, promotion, transfer or training. Discriminatory retirement ages in state authorities were already unlawful under European law which was directly effective in the UK. Private employers were no longer able to have policies which set different compulsory retirement ages for men and women in comparable positions, and neither were they able to refuse promotion or training. S.2 also amended the 1970 Equal Pay Act in a similar way so that such discriminatory terms in a contract of employment were contrary to the Act. Finally, s.3 amended the unfair dismissal provisions of the 1978 Employment Protection (Consolidation) Act to ensure that men and women in the same position had the right to complain to an industrial tribunal of unfair dismissal up to the same age. Where the employment had no non-discriminatory normal retirement age, employees whether men or women could complain up to the age of 65.

Employment Act 1988

This Act contained a number of miscellaneous provisions, the most important of which were as follows:

1. A member of a union who claimed that the union had, without the support of a ballot, taken industrial action, could apply to the court for an Order (s.1.). Under the 1984 Trade Union Act, it was effectively employers only who had been given the right to apply for an injunction. A union member, or ex-member, was also entitled to take the union to court on an issue, despite any provision in the union rules preventing such action: for example, by saying that the Union's decision or arbitration was final (s.2).
2. An individual had the right not to be unjustifiably disciplined by his union for failure to take part in industrial action, even where there had been a majority in favour in a secret ballot. He was also given the right not to be disciplined for encouraging others to do the same; for consulting the Trade Union Commissioner or the Certification Officer; or for asserting that the union or any official was contravening union rules on the law (s.3).
3. It was made unlawful for the property of a trade union to be applied to indemnify any individual for any penalty imposed on him for any relevant offence or for contempt of court. An individual member could bring an action for the union to recover any such payment if the union itself failed to do so (s.8). Also any union member could bring an action where the trustees proposed to use the union's property unlawfully. The Court could order the trustees to recover any such property, could dismiss the trustees and could appoint a receiver (s.9).
4. Protection from actions in tort was removed in respect of industrial action to enforce membership of a UMA (s.10).
5. With regard to ballots, s.1. of the 1984 Trade Union Act was amended so that:
    (a) non-voting members of union executive committees had to be elected;
    (b) presidents and general secretaries had to be elected (s.12).
    In addition, ballots for political funds had to be postal (amending the 1913 Act), and ballots for the election of certain officials had to be postal (deleting s.3. of the 1984 Trade Union Act: see s.14). Also for elections and political fund ballots, there had to be appointed an independent scrutineer, who would be responsible for supervising the production and distribution of voting papers, be the person to whom ballot papers were returned and be responsible for reporting the result (s.15). Any member was given the right to complain, with regard to political ballots, to the Certification Officer or the Court, that the necessary requirements had not been met (s.l6).
6. With regard to ballots on industrial action, certain conditions were specified which had to be satisfied if a union intended to organise industrial action as a result of an aggregated ballot covering different places of work. These conditions were that the union must reasonably believe that each union member whose votes

were to be aggregated had a factor, relating to his terms and conditions of employment, or occupational description, in common with one or more of the other members entitled to vote. This factor must not be one which those employed by the same employer had in common as a consequence of working at the same place. Where these conditions were not satisfied, a union had to conduct separate ballots for each place of work (s.17).

7.   A Commissioner for the Rights of Trade Union Members was established, with power to support individual union members (for example, by giving advice and by paying legal costs) in complaints against their union.

A number of the above provisions were opposed at the consultative stage by leading employer and professional organisations, such as the CBI and the Institute of Personnel Management, particularly the provision preventing unions taking disciplinary action against members who failed to take part in industrial action after a democratically conducted ballot. Their fear was that ballots would be brought into disrepute and also that social action by work-mates against the transgressing member could be more disruptive than official union discipline. Some also queried the necessity for the establishment of a Trade Union Commissioner, particularly bearing in mind other areas of national life, where it could be argued that the need to help individuals to secure their rights was far greater and far more important (for example, in the field of social security entitlements). Indeed, since the proposals for this Act were produced shortly before the 1987 general election, it is hard to believe that their purpose was other than to provide a further stick with which to beat the unions during the campaign in the belief that many voters, including trade union members, approved.

Employment Act 1989

The stated purposes of the Act were, first, to remove many restrictions on the employment of women and young people; second, to help employers create jobs and become more competitive by easing the burden of regulation on them; and third, to take forward the Government's training strategy for the 1990s.

With regard to the first objective, most legislation that still discriminated between women and men in employment and training matters was repealed or amended to remove the discrimination. This included the ban on women working underground in mines and some restrictions on their working with machinery in factories. Protection was, however, retained in some special cases, such as work which (through exposure to radiation or lead) might endanger the health of an unborn child. Restrictions on the hours of young people were removed, including the prohibition of night work. Certain other restrictions on young people's employment were also removed, such as that on street trading. The Act did not remove restrictions on working with dangerous machinery, and neither did it remove any restrictions on the employment of children under school-leaving age.

With regard to the second objective, burdens on employers were reduced by a number of deregulatory amendments to the Employment Protection (Consolidation) Act of 1978. Thus, under s.13, employers with fewer that 20 employees were exempted from the requirements to provide employees with a separate note of particulars of disciplinary rules which applied to them. S.14 amended s.27 of the 1978 Act to limit the duties in respect of which an employer was required to allow officials of a recognised trade union time off with pay to carry out duties which were concerned with matters in respect of which the employer recognised the union, or with the performance of functions for which the union was not recognised but which the employer had agreed the union might perform. It similarly limited the duty to allow such officials to take time off with pay to undertake training which was relevant to those duties. S.15 amended s 53 of the 1978 Act to increase from six months to two years the qualifying period of continuous employment after which employees were entitled to be given, on request, a written statement of the reasons for their dismissal.

With regard to the third objective, the Act dissolved the Training Commission and transferred its property rights and liabilities to the Secretary of State for Employment. Ss.23–25 amended the Industrial Training Act in order to facilitate the transition of the remaining Industrial Training Boards (ITBs) from statutory to non-statutory status. The amendments also made possible the creation of employer-led statutory bodies for training. In addition, the amendments meant that in future the Secretary of State needed to consult only employer organisations before making an order affecting the operation or existence of an ITB, and that the Secretary of State needed to consult only employer representatives before appointments were made to an ITB. A majority of the members of an ITB had to be employer representatives.

There were a number of other provisions which did not fall under the three stated purposes of the Act but which were nevertheless of considerable significance. One such was s.16 which removed the difference whereby men might receive statutory redundancy payments up to the age of 65 and women up to only age 60. Where there was a 'normal retiring age' for the job in question which was below 65 and was non-discriminatory, the entitlement of both sexes was to be restricted to that age. In all other cases women's entitlement was extended to the age of 65, in line with that of men. This provision was made necessary by the EEC's 'Equal Treatment' Directive (No.76/207) and Article 119 of the Treaty of Rome. A second provision, contained in s.17, abolished the scheme entitling employers with less than 10 employees to rebates on their statutory redundancy payments. Rebates to all other employers had been abolished in 1986. A third provision, contained in s.20, provided for regulations to be made to give an industrial tribunal chairman sitting alone, or a full tribunal, discretion at the pre-hearing stage to require a deposit of up to £150 as a condition of proceeding further, if it was considered that case had no reasonable prospect of success or that pursuit of it would be frivolous, vexatious or otherwise unreasonable.

Employment Act 1990

The Act had three main objectives: the abolition of the pre-entry closed shop, the removal of immunity from virtually all forms of secondary action, and the regulation of unofficial industrial action. In addition, the Act increased the powers of the Commissioner for the Rights of Trade Union Members, made minor amendments to the rules for industrial action ballots, and provided for the revision or revocation of Codes of Practice.

With regard to closed shops, the 1988 Employment Act had made post-entry closed shops wholly unenforceable, removed immunity from any industrial action taken to impose or enforce a closed shop and made dismissal or discrimination of an employee who refused to belong to a union auto-matically unfair. The 1990 Act made it unlawful to refuse employment to a person because he was or was not a member of a trade union or because he would not agree to become a member or because he ceased to be a member (s.1).

With regard to the second objective, the right to take secondary action had been severely limited by the 1980 Act. Under the 1990 Act, it was virtually outlawed. Indeed, outlawed secondary action now included action organised among those doing work or performing services under any contract, including contracts other than contracts of employment.

The third objective related to union liability for unofficial action. The provisions of the Act (ss.6 and 7) substantially extended the potential liability of unions and imposed stringent conditions over the steps that had to be taken if a union was to repudiate industrial action. This was done by largely rewriting s.15 of the 1982 Act, which first made trade unions themselves liable in actions in tort arising out of industrial action not covered by immunity.

A union was now responsible (and liable) for the organisation of industrial action by any of its officials, including shop stewards, any of its committees or any group whose purposes included organising or coordinating industrial action and to which any of its officials belonged. The section also modified and extended the requirements which had to be satisfied if a union was to avoid liability. Thus the action had to be repudiated as soon as reasonably practical after coming to the knowledge of the executive committee, or the President or General Secretary. Written notice of the repudiation had to be given to the committee or official in question, and the union had to do its best to give written notice to every member who had taken (or might take) industrial action and to every employer of any such member. The written notice of repudiation had to contain the following statement:

> Your union has repudiated the call (or calls) for industrial action to which this notice relates, and will give no support to unofficial action taken in response to it (or them). If you are dismissed while taking unofficial action, you will have no right to complain of unfair dismissal.

The union had also to respond to any requests for confirmation of the union's repudiation made within three months by a party to a commercial contract which had been or might be interfered with by the industrial action.

S.9 permitted an employer to dismiss selectively employees who took part in unofficial action, and such employees had no right to complain to an industrial tribunal of unfair dismissal. Where an action became unofficial because of union repudiation, a full working day was allowed following the day of repudiation before the union's members taking unofficial action became liable to selective dismissal. Industrial action because of such selective dismissal was deprived of immunity.

Finally, the Act extended the power of the Commissioner to cover assistance to union members in proceedings arising out of an alleged breach or threatened breach of the union's rules, relating (for example) to the appointment or election of a person to, or the removal of a person from, any office, disciplinary proceedings by the union, the authorising or endorsing of industrial action, the balloting of members and the application of the union's funds or property (s.10).

Trade Union and Labour Relations (Consolidation) Act 1992

As stated at the beginning of this chapter, this legislation was consolidated in the 1992 Act which is now the main statutory basis of collective employment law, subject to one further Act in 1993.

Trade Union Reform and Employment Rights Act 1993

This Act had two main purposes: first, to impose further restrictions on trade unions and trade union activity; second, to enact certain employment rights as a result of EU directives and case law. Of other matters, the most significant by far was the complete abolition of Wage Councils, thus ending a mechanism for protecting the very low paid which had existed since 1909.

Part I of the Act relates to trade union matters, with ss.1–7 dealing further with union elections and ballots. Additional duties are required of the independent scrutineer appointed to oversee a ballot, including a right of access to the union's membership register so that he can check its accuracy; the storage and distribution of voting papers; and the counting of votes by an independent person. The new requirements for election and political ballots also apply to merger ballots. S.7 phases out the scheme whereby unions could get financial help for balloting and removes the obligation of employers to make premises available.

Ss.8–12 make further provisions regarding the financial affairs of unions. These include the requirement to provide each member with a statement of its financial affairs. This statement must now include details of the salary and other benefits provided to the president, general secretary and each member of the executive. They also give the Certification Officer power at any time to investigate a union's finances if he thinks there is good reason to do so.

Ss.13–16 concern rights in relation to union membership. S.13 permits employers to provide inducements to employees to opt out of collective bargaining or to leave a union. Such inducements are not to be considered unlawful 'action short of dismissal' on grounds related to union membership or activities. This section was put into the Bill when it was due for its Third Reading in the House of Lords. It was done within days of the decision of the Court of Appeal in two cases: *Palmer* v. *Associated British Ports (1993)* and *Wilson* v. *Associated Newspapers Ltd (1993)*. In these cases the Court held that where an employer pays extra money to individuals who accept 'personal' contracts which contain no reference to collective bargaining, and does not pay money to individuals who refuse to sign these contracts on the grounds that they still wish to have their terms and conditions determined by collective bargaining, this constituted action short of dismissal on the grounds of trade union membership contrary to s.146 of the Trade Union and Labour Relations (Consolidation) Act 1992. S.13 therefore nullifies the decision of the Court of Appeal. In the event, in 1995 the House of Lords in its judicial capacity overruled the decision of the Court of Appeal so that from the then government's point of view there had been no need for the addition to the 1993 Act deciding that withholding increases offered under personal contracts did not prevent or deter trade union membership.

S.14 limits further the right of a union to exclude or expel an individual from membership. The effect of this section is to undermine the TUC's Bridlington Principles which sought to prevent inter-union rivalry and the poaching of members.

S.15 provides that if an employer is lawfully to make check-off deductions from a worker's pay there must be prior written consent from the worker and renewed consent at least every three years. Additionally, if there is an increase in the amount to be deducted, the employer may only deduct the increased amount if he has given the worker at least one month's advance notice of that increase, with a reminder that the worker may withdraw his consent to the arrangement at any time.

S.16 extends the conduct for which discipline imposed by a trade union is unjustifiable.

Ss.17–22 relate to industrial action. Thus s.17 introduces a requirement for industrial action ballots to be conducted fully by postal voting. S.18 requires a union to provide employers with written notice of its intent to ballot its members on industrial action at least seven days before the opening day of the ballot, and with sample voting papers at least three days before. S.19 requires a union to take steps to provide the employers of members balloted with details of the ballot result. S.20 requires industrial action ballots involving 50 or more members to be subject to independent scrutiny. S.21 requires a union to give the employer at least seven days notice in writing of its intention to take official industrial action. Finally, s.22 provides that any individual who is deprived of goods or services as a result of unlawfully organised industrial act. In addition, an individual contemplating or taking proceedings under this provision can apply to a new Commissioner for Protection against Unlawful Industrial Action for assistance.

Part II of the Act relates to employment rights. Ss.23–5 amend maternity rights in order to comply with the EC Pregnant Workers' Directive. Ss.26–7 extend and enhance the right of employees to receive from their employer a written statement of main employment particulars. These provisions implement the EC Proof of Employment Directive.

S.28 protects employees against being victimised by their employer for taking certain specified types of action on health and safety grounds. It implements the employment protection requirements of the EC Health & Safety Framework Directive.

S.29 entitles all employees, irrespective of their length of service, hours of work or age, to complain to an industrial tribunal if they are dismissed or selected for redundancy because they have sought to assert one of their statutory employment rights.

S.33, most importantly, amends the Transfer of Undertakings (Protection of Employment) Regulations 1981 (TUPE) so as to ensure that the Regulations fully reflect the interpretation of the EC Acquired Rights Directive 1977 which they implement. The 1977 EC Directive requires member states to ensure that, whenever a business or part of a business is transferred, employees are transferred on the prevailing terms and conditions. It also prohibits dismissal arising from a transfer. However, UK law has always limited this to 'commercial ventures', with the implication that it did not apply to the public sector. As a result of a number of decisions of the European Court of Justice

(ECJ), followed by a number of British cases, it became clear that the UK's 1981 TUPE Regulations did not comply with the EC Directive and would have to be amended: hence s.33. The implications of this for the government's contracting-out and market-testing programme are likely to be very considerable indeed.

S.34 makes a number of changes to the redundancy handling procedures contained in ss.188–98 of the 1992 Act. These provisions implement the EC Collective Redundancies Directive, first adopted in 1975 but revised in 1992. The definition of redundancy for consultative purposes has been widened to include any dismissals for reasons not related to the individual. Consultation must be undertaken by the employer with 'a view to reaching agreement with the trade union representatives' about ways of avoiding dismissal, reducing the number of dismissals and mitigating the consequences of dismissals.

Part III of the Act is entitled 'Other Employment Matters', the most significant of which is s.35 which in effect abolishes Wage Councils by the repeal of Part II of the Wages Act 1986. Ss.36–42 relate to industrial tribunals and the Employment Appeal Tribunal (EAT) and provide for certain types of proceedings to be determined by an industrial tribunal chairman sitting alone, without lay members.

Finally, ss.43 and 44 refer to ACAS. S.43(i) removes ACAS's general duty to encourage the extension of collective bargaining. S.44 states that ACAS may charge a fee for any of its services, where it thinks appropriate, and further gives the Secretary of State power to direct ACAS to charge fees for any of its functions. ACAS has subsequently made clear that although it will be charging for conferences, seminars and 'self-help' clinics and some advisory publications, it 'has no plans to charge for any other ACAS activity as to do so would compromise ACAS's impartial and independent approach' (ACAS, 1993).

Other legislation

Since 1993 there was no further legislation by the Conservative Government on collective labour law. There was, however, the Employment Rights Act 1996 which consolidated individual employment law in the same way that the Trade Union and Labour Relations (Consolidation) Act 1992 consolidated collective employment law. The Industrial Tribunals Act 1996 was also a consolidation measure. There was in addition the Disability Discrimination Act 1995, whose employment provisions came into force in December 1996, providing protection from discrimination in employment for disabled employees and disabled job applicants where organisations employ 20 or more staff. In 1995 there was also a new Code of Practice: 'Industrial Action Ballots and Notice to Employers'. In 1996 the Health and Safety (Consultation with

Employees) Regulations came into force which require employers to consult with employees or their representatives who are not covered by representatives appointed by a recognised trade union.

The new Labour Government of 1997 has no proposals for legislation on industrial relations for the first session of Parliament. However in July 1997 a Private Member's Bill – the Employment Rights (Dispute Resolution) Bill – was introduced with Government support in the House of Lords which will provide for an arbitration alternative for unfair dismissal claims.

A Government White Paper in May 1998 is promised, presumably with a view to legislation along the lines of its electoral commitments in a subsequent Parliamentary session.

The Labour Government's election commitments were for:

(a) A National Minimum Wage (and a Low Pay Commission was established in 1997);
(b) the restoration of trade union rights at GCHQ (which was carried out in 1997);
(c) the ending of the UK's opt-out from the EU Social Chapter (which was carried out in 1997);
(d) statutory recognition rights where a majority of employees are in favour;
(e) the ending of the three-yearly renewal of the check-off;
(f) some protection for dismissed official and lawful strikers.

There is no commitment to a dismantling of the main Conservative legislation, for example on ballots, secondary action, the closed shop and so forth.

The use of law

The conventional wisdom, based to a large extent on the debacle of the 1971 Act (Weekes *et al.*, 1975), was that legal constraints imposed on trade unions would not succeed. This proved not to be the case in the 1980s. On the contrary, the use of law proved highly successful in restraining trade union power and in contributing to the defeat of unions in a number of major disputes. Evans (1987) recorded 77 cases of injunctions actually sought between May 1984 and April 1987, of which 11 related to picketing, 16 to secondary action and 47 to pre-strike ballots. In 65 of these cases the plaintiff was the direct employer (or ex-employer) of the defendants or their union. For the majority of employers their single aim in seeking the injunction was to lift the industrial action.

Injunctions were secured in 73 cases and refused in four. In only 13 cases were the defendants members, workplace representatives or local full-time officials compared with 67 in which the unions were defendants. In 31 cases the industrial action complained of was lifted immediately or otherwise quickly rendered ineffective (for instance, by the withdrawal of support by the union or other workers). In only three cases were damages sought against unions, so it remains clear that in the overwhelming majority of cases employers were only really interested in an immediate injunction to stop industrial action. The use of injunctions at that time seemed to be most marked in three sectors: printing, public services and shipping.

In a more recent study Gall and McKay (1996) report 169 applications by way of injunctions between 1983 and March 1996. Of the grounds for seeking injunctions over the period 1980–95, 36 related to picketing, 32 to secondary action, and 62 to balloting (there were 39 others). Injunctions sought by industry included 36 for print/publishing, 18 for public services, 32 for rail/sea, 16 for post/telecommunications and 29 for manufacturing. The unions or their members receiving the largest number of injunctions were the Graphical Paper and Media Union (GPMU: 33), TGWU (20), UNISON (18), the Communication Workers Union (CWU: 17), National Union of Rail, Maritime and Transport Workers (RMT: 15), and the Amalgamated Engineering and Electrical; Union (AEEU: 10). This pattern, however, as Gall and McKay point out, is somewhat misleading for there were considerable variations over time. Thus injunctions in print/publishing were overwhelmingly between 1983 and 1986, while in the public services they were overwhelmingly in the 1990s. Again, injunctions for picketing and secondary action were relatively high in the 1980s, while those for balloting were more evenly spread. Compared to the number of stoppages injunctions were used relatively infrequently, but this is not to say that their use or threatened use did not have a deterrent effect.

The effects of the law are shown through cases in the courts on three main areas – secondary action, picketing, and balloting before the taking of industrial action – as well as a number of other miscellaneous areas.

Secondary action

It will be recalled that secondary action was made unlawful by the 1980 Employment Act, with only certain very limited exceptions. Under the 1990 Employment Act even these exceptions were made unlawful.

Among the leading cases dealing with this aspect of the law was *Merkur Island Shipping Corporation* v. *Laughton* (1983), where the International Transport Workers' Federation (ITWF) had called on tugmen and lockmen to refuse to provide services for a Liberian registered ship with a Filipino crew which had docked at Tilbury. This call for action followed a complaint by a crew member of low wages, which the union had taken up and which the employer had refused to remedy. The shipowner applied for an injunction on the grounds of unlawful secondary action. The House of Lords held that it was indeed unlawful secondary action. The decision turned on whether or not there was an existing contract for services between the shipowner, who was the employer of the crew, and the port authorities. It was held that there was not, because the contract for services was with the charterers of the ship and not the owner.

Another leading case was *Dimbleby* v. *NUJ* (1984), where Dimbleby had transferred the printing of his newspapers, after a dispute with the NGA and the dismissal of his NGA workers, to the non-union firm of T. Bailey Forman (TBF). Dimbleby threatened to dismiss journalists who refused to cooperate with the transfer. The National Union of Journalists (NUJ) then called a strike of its journalists. The NUJ had been in dispute with TBF since the 1978 newspaper strike when TBF had dismissed its 25 NUJ journalists and gone non-union. On the application of Dimbleby, the High Court issued an injunction against the strike which was upheld by the Court of Appeal and the House of Lords The Court ruled that although the NUJ had a legitimate dispute with TBF, TBF did not print its own papers. This was done by a separate company – TBF Printers – and although the two companies had the same directors, the same address and the same telephone number, they were, in the eyes of the law, separate companies. The NUJ's action was therefore held to be unlawful secondary action because its dispute was with TBF and not with TBF Printers.

The *Messenger Newspapers Group* v. *NGA* (1984) was a *cause célèbre* in the early 1980s in that it was portrayed by most of the media as the 'small' man fighting for freedom against a powerful trade union; there were many scenes of violence on the picket lines, and it was the first case of sequestration of a union's assets under the Conservatives' overall legislative framework. From the late 1970s Eddie Shah's Messenger Group published a range of free newspapers in the Manchester area. The actual dispute revolved around three printing and type-setting companies set up by Shah. The first was Fineword Ltd, Stockport, established in 1979. Shah hired eight NGA members, agreed that there should be a closed shop and negotiated an agreement on pay and hours with the NGA. The second was a type-setting plant at Bury which was established in 1982. A closed shop was agreed, but there was a failure to reach agreement on pay and hours, whereupon Shah cancelled the closed shop agreement and engaged non-union labour. The third was a printing plant at Warrington which started to recruit labour while negotiations on the closed shop were still going on at Bury.

The NGA was concerned at the recruitment of non-union labour at Bury and Warrington, but employees at these two plants voted against NGA representation. The use of non-union labour was a breach of the industry's closed shop agreement and also counter to the union's rule which prohibited members handling work from non-unionists. The six NGA members at the Stockport plant consequently took strike action, and the company dismissed them. The NGA then obtained NUJ support, with the NUJ instructing its members at Stockport not to supply copy. The High Court ordered the NUJ to instruct its members to supply copy: the NUJ refused, but the journalists concerned supplied the copy anyway. The Court also issued injunctions to stop the NGA from exerting pressure on advertisers and to prevent NGA members from blacking origination work to the company on the grounds that these were both unlawful secondary actions. Another injunction was issued to stop secondary picketing at Bury and Warrington.

When the NGA intensified picketing at Warrington, the company sought sequestration of the NGA's assets for contempt of court. The Court at that stage turned down the request for sequestration but fined the NGA £50 000. The union refused to pay, but it then appeared that an agreement had been reached on union membership. However, the company refused to take back the six strikers and picketing was intensified. The Court then imposed a further fine of £100 000 and ordered the sequestration of the NGA's assets. In response to sequestration there was 'spontaneous' industrial action by NGA members on national newspapers, which stopped their publication for one day. Six of the national newspapers issued dismissal notices and all of them took out writs for damages, although none of these writs was ever followed up.

Meanwhile, mass picketing continued and the company took further action for contempt, but the case was adjourned when the NGA agreed to lift its picketing to enable talks to take place. The talks then broke down, picketing resumed, and there was a further fine on the NGA of £525 000. Thereupon, the NGA called on all its members to strike for 24 hours and also sought support from the TUC. A General Council sub-committee decided in favour of support for the NGA in the form of a 24-hour newspaper strike, but Len Murray, the then TUC General Secretary, cancelled the decision by ruling that the sub-committee had no power to take such a decision. At a full meeting of the General Council, the General Secretary's action was upheld and TUC support for the NGA in what was clearly unlawful action was refused. This was a dramatic moment and a key turning point in the TUC's attitude towards the new laws.

Eventually, the NGA called off its action and decided to purge its contempt. The dismissed 'Stockport Six' were found employment elsewhere in the industry. Eddie Shah had successfully challenged the NGA's power and the closed shop with the help of the law.

Another major case concerned Rupert Murdoch and his News International Company; he had built a printing plant at Wapping, equipped with the latest technology, in order, allegedly, to produce a new evening paper – *The Post* – for which a separate company had been established: The London Post (Printers) Ltd. Negotiations with the print unions did not result in an agreement, despite unprecedented concessions by the unions including unilateral binding arbitration and the acceptance of the direct input of editorial and classified material. With the failure of negotiations, the NGA and SOGAT called strikes after ballots of their membership at the *Sun*, *The Times*, *The Sunday Times* and *News of the World* had produced overwhelming majorities for such action. The strike issue was a claim for security of employment and indexed wages, and it commenced in January 1986. The claim had been made in an attempt to avoid a charge of secondary action which might have arisen if the strike had been about the London *Post*. The company then announced that it would print the papers at Wapping, where a new labour force had been engaged mainly from out of London. Journalists were ordered to report for work at Wapping or face instant dismissal: if they did report, they were to be given a bonus of £2000 and free private medical insurance. The NUJ National Executive Committee instructed its members at News International not to cooperate with any publications from Wapping, and to continue to work only at their normal place of work. The NUJ chapels disregarded these instructions and voted to work at Wapping, although in the case of the *Sunday Times* Chapel the margin was very small indeed. The company was thus able to produce its papers at Wapping. It had also arranged a new system of distribution – through a transport company, TNT, which it half-owned – so as to by-pass as far as possible the traditional distribution channels, which were organised by the Society of Graphical and Allied Trades '82 (SOGAT).

SOGAT and the NGA picketed Wapping and SOGAT called on its distribution workers not to handle News International titles. In February 1986 News International obtained an injunction which prohibited SOGAT from interfering with the distribution of its papers (*News Group Newspapers* v. *SOGAT*, 1986). The company also immediately dismissed all its striking print workers – over 5000 people – on the grounds that they were in breach of their contract of employment. SOGAT refused to obey the injunction and was first fined £25 000 for contempt of court and soon afterwards had all its assets sequestered. The injunction had been based on the grounds that SOGAT had not held a ballot of its members in wholesale distribution. It might equally have been on the grounds of unlawful secondary action. News International published its papers through two separate companies – Times Newspapers and News Group –while separate companies had been set up for distribution, for supplies and for advertising. Newspaper wholesalers' contracts were with the distribution company, but the primary dispute was with Times Newspapers and News Group, so that the union's action against the wholesalers could not be lawful secondary action under the 1980 Act.

Other legal actions at this time by Murdoch companies included a court order against the NGA to stop their members at Typematters and Northampton Mercury Company blacking material so as to prevent the publication of *The Times Literary Supplement* and *The Times Educational Supplement*; an injunction to stop SOGAT and the NGA from interfering with Northern editions of the *News of the World* which was printed under contract by Express Newspapers in Manchester; and an injunction against the Union of Communication Workers (UCW) on the grounds of unlawful secondary action by refusing to deliver *Sun* newspaper bingo cards. The law against secondary action had played a major part in Murdoch's defeat of the print unions, but also of great importance was the common law which enables employers to dismiss strikers for breach of their contract of employment.

Yet another much publicised dispute was that of *P&O* v. *National Union of Seamen* (NUS) (1988). Towards the end of 1987, P&O European Ferries had proposed drastic reductions in manpower and changes in working practices in order to cut costs to meet the forthcoming challenge of the Channel Tunnel. At this time there was an NUS strike at the Isle of Man Steam Packet Ferry Company (in which P&O had a 40 per cent stake) over proposed redundancies and changed working practices. Towards the end of January the Isle of Man Steam Packet Ferry Company dismissed the 160 striking NUS members. The NUS then called a national one-day strike over the sackings. P&O and Sealink immediately obtained an injunction on grounds of unlawful secondary action. The NUS defied the court order and the strike went ahead. P&O and Sealink then sought sequestration of NUS assets. The court refused sequestration but fined the NUS £7500. Meanwhile the Isle of Man dispute was settled with the help of ACAS conciliation, but the P&O seamen at Dover voted to continue their strike against P&O's cost-cutting proposals. Subsequent talks, with the help of ACAS, failed to end the dispute with P&O insisting that their proposals must be implemented within one year, whereas the NUS, now prepared to accept the changes, wanted them spread over three years. P&O then issued dismissal notices to the Dover seamen and the NUS countered that it would hold a national strike ballot. P&O then got from the court an unprecedented suspended order that the NUS should not hold a strike ballot because an affirmative vote would have led to unlawful secondary action. The NUS obeyed the Order, calling off the ballot; talks resumed only to break down again. The company then announced it would seek to resume services. It wrote individually to the striking seamen offering them jobs on the Company's new terms and conditions and advertised in the national press for workers. It also withdrew recognition from the NUS. At the beginning of May, two ships sailed and the NUS called for national industrial action throughout the ferry sector. A court hearing followed immediately and the NUS was fined £150 000 and had all its assets sequestered. Soon afterwards the NUS ordered the end of all secondary action and the strike eventually petered out.

Picketing

As a result of the 1980 Employment Act lawful picketing was limited to the workers' own place of work (s.16(i)). In addition, the Government produced a

Code of Practice on Picketing which came into effect in December 1980. The Code stated (among other things) that in general the number of pickets should not exceed six at any entrance to a workplace. It should be recalled that irrespective of the legal changes of the 1980s, the law has always required that picketing should be peaceful and that its purpose was peacefully to obtain or communicate information or to persuade a person not to work. Breaches of the law may give rise to civil liability, but there may also be breaches of criminal law: for example, by threatening violence, by being abusive, by obstructing the highway and by obstructing a police officer in the execution of his duty. The police indeed have very wide powers of discretion. Turning to some of the leading cases, in the *Stockport Messenger* dispute of 1984 (an account of which has already been given) the company obtained injunctions to prevent the NGA's secondary picketing at its Bury and Warrington plants: not only was there secondary picketing, but there was 'mass' picketing. The NGA continued its picketing despite the court order and after being fined for contempt of court, its funds were finally sequestered.

At the beginning of the miners' strike in March 1984, the then National Coal Board (NCB) was granted an injunction against the Yorkshire Area of the NUM to prevent secondary picketing of the still working Nottinghamshire pits, but the injunction was never enforced. According to Adeney and Lloyd (1986), the Minister, Peter Walker, with the support of his colleagues, decided to stop the NCB's action because it would generate sympathy for the miners. Also it might be noted that during the year-long dispute, like the NCB, neither British Rail nor British Steel (both of whom were subject to secondary picketing) took legal action. However, cases on secondary picketing did occur: for example, *Read Transport* v. *NUM South Wales Area* (1985), where Read, independent hauliers with contracts to transport coke from Port Talbot Steelworks to various destinations around the country, obtained an injunction to prevent the NUM picketing the works. Picketing continued and the NUM South Wales Area was fined £50 000 for contempt of court, and their funds were subsequently sequestered. In *Thomas* v. *NUM South Wales Area* (1985), the action was brought by working miners who claimed that they had been subjected to intimidation and abuse by pickets which interfered with their 'right to work'. The Court found that there had been regular abuse and intimidation and therefore that a tort had been committed, namely interference with the right to use the highway; it also pointed out that the pickets had been highly intimidating and that intimidation itself could amount to a tort. In granting the injunction the Court also ruled, in line with the Code of Practice, that the number of pickets should be limited to six. In effect the Court seemed to be saying that mass picketing, by its very nature, was intimidatory, as was the shouting of abuse. The actual circumstances in this case were that six official pickets had been agreed with the police and allowed to stand at the colliery gates, but there were also mass demonstrators who were kept by the police some distance from the gates. This case also raised the issue of 'vicarious liability'. Based on the ruling in *Heatons* v. *TGWU* (1972), the union was found liable for acts of its officials unless actively disowned.

In the miners' strike the main method used to counter picketing was the criminal law. It was calculated that nearly 10 000 were arrested in England and Wales and nearly 1500 in Scotland, of whom 81 per cent and 67 per cent respectively were charged. Over 4000 were charged with breaking the peace, nearly 1700 were charged with obstructing the police, 1000 for criminal damage and over 600 for obstructing the highway. In many of these cases, a common condition of bail was that the miners should not return to the picket line. Such a condition was upheld in *R.* v. *Mansfield Justices* ex parte *Sharkey* (1985). There was also the celebrated case *Moss* v. *McLachlan* (1985) where cars containing Kent miners were stopped at the Dartford Tunnel and turned back by the police, on the grounds that they were travelling north to picket and that they might cause a breach of the peace. The Court upheld the police action on the grounds that it was reasonable to suspect a future breach of the peace.

In the Wapping dispute, News Group Newspapers in July 1986 sought injunctions to restrain picketing and demonstrations at Wapping (*NGN and others* v. *SOGAT and others*, 1986(2)). The company alleged that the torts of nuisance, intimidation, harassment and interference with the performance of commercial contracts had been committed. The Court held that the events at Wapping had resulted in an unreasonable obstruction of the highway affecting the public at large. It went on to say that in order to bring a civil action for public nuisance, there was a need to show special damage, and this was the case with regard to some of the plaintiffs (for example, the cost of bussing workers). The Court also held there was private nuisance in that the owners of land adjoining the Wapping printworks had suffered damage. Further, the Court held that there had been intimidation: that is to say, violence or threats of violence. On the alleged tort of harassment, the plaintiffs relied on *Thomas* v. *NUM* where the High Court had ruled that working miners had a right to go to work without harassment and that they could bring an action against persons who interfered with that right. The unions argued that this was not a well-established tort but a 'new' one which did not come within any of the accepted torts. The judge said that he was inclined to agree but, as he had already ruled on nuisance and intimidation, it was unnecessary to take a final view on harassment.

On the allegation of interference with commercial contracts by unlawful means, the judge thought it likely that this had occurred in the case of the contract between News Group International and TNT Distributors, the unlawful means being intimidation and nuisance through the twice-weekly marches that were being carried out. The Court granted injunctions, first, to prevent the defendants from organising pickets and demonstrations in the vicinity of the Wapping premises, apart from six pickets whose purpose was peacefully to obtain and communicate information, and to require any marches or rallies to be organised so as not to interfere with the plaintiff's

compensation on the basis that they were in breach of their contracts of employment. This again was not on the basis of the 1980s' legislation, but on common law grounds. It nevertheless was highly significant and raised the question of whether such a thing as 'the right to strike' really existed at all. Clearly, it exists in the sense that 'lawful' strikes do take place. But strikers taking part in such actions can be legally dismissed by their employer without compensation. This threat was used effectively by the port employers in 1989 and was a not insignificant factor in the defeat of the TGWU, particularly as the threat was contrasted with the existence of a generous Government-backed voluntary redundancy scheme. There was, of course, nothing new in this. Strikers had almost always been breaking their contracts. It was still unusual for employers to dismiss them on these grounds. However, such employer action, or the threat of it, was arguably more effective in the economic and political climate of the 1980s and the 1990s than it had been in earlier post-war decades.

Another important legal issue was the nature and consequences of industrial action, other than strike action. This question had been raised a number of years ago in a case under the now defunct 1971 Industrial Relations Act: *The Secretary of State for Employment* v. *ASLEF* (1972). Here ASLEF's industrial action took the form of 'working to rule' and a ban on overtime. The Court held that to construe the rules 'unreasonably' and to put that unreasonable construction into practice, so that the railway system could grind to a halt, constituted a breach of the workers' contractual obligation to serve their employer in good faith. With regard to the ban on overtime, the Court held that this was a breach of contract of employment only if the overtime in question was obligatory under the contract; where the overtime was undertaken on a voluntary basis, a ban was not a breach of contract.

The issue of industrial action short of a strike has arisen in a number of other cases. One such case was *Wiluszñski* v. *Tower Hamlets Borough Council* (1989), where the plaintiff was employed as an estate officer in the housing department. The major part of his work consisted of dealing with the complaints and problems of council tenants, but he was also required to answer enquiries from councillors on estate matters and on average received one or two such enquiries a week. Due to an industrial dispute NALGO decided to boycott all councillors' enquiries and the plaintiff followed his union's instructions, while continuing to carry out his other duties. He was suspended and the Council refused to pay him any salary, whereupon he sued for the payment of salary. The Court of Appeal held that if, as part of an industrial dispute, an employee refused to perform certain parts of his contract of employment, he was in breach of his contract. The employer was then entitled to require the employee not to perform any of his duties until he was prepared to work normally and to refuse to pay him at all for the period during which he was in breach of contract. In *Miles* v. *Wakefield Metropolitan District Council* (1987), Mr Miles, who was the Superintendent of Births,

Deaths and Marriages, worked 37 hours a week. One of his functions was to conduct weddings on Saturday mornings from 9.00 in the morning to 12.00 noon. As part of a campaign of industrial action, Mr Miles, on instructions from his union, NALGO, though willing to work a 37-hour week and to work on Saturdays, refused to conduct weddings on Saturdays. The Council thereupon treated him as working only a 34-hour week and paid him accordingly. He sued for the rest of his salary. The House of Lords in their judgment held that the Council was correct in its action. In order to establish a right to wages, workers must prove that they were ready and willing to work in accordance with their duties. Mr Miles had not been willing to do so and his employers, as was their right, were not prepared to accept his incomplete performance.

An interesting case under the 1993 Act was *Blackpool & Fylde College* v. *National Association of Teachers in Further and Higher Education (NATFHE)* (1994). On 14 January 1994, NATFHE sent the College a notice of intention to 'hold a ballot of all our members in your institution'. A postal ballot was started on 24 January and completed on 7 February. The union informed the College that a majority of its members which had taken part in the ballot had voted in favour of industrial action. On 10 February, the union notified the College that it had instructed all its members at the College to take part in discontinuous action which would start with a strike on 1 March. The College sought an interlocutory injunction prohibiting the proposed action on the basis that neither the notice given before the ballot nor the notice of action following the ballot complied with ss.226A(2)(c) and 234A(3)(a) of the 1993 Act.

The 1993 Act laid down a number of new provisions requiring information to be given to employers both before and after any ballot. S.226A(2)(c) states that the notice of a ballot 'must describe (so that he can readily ascertain them) the employees of the employer who it is reasonable for the union to believe will be entitled to vote in the ballot'. S.234A makes the same requirement in respect of the notice of industrial action. The College argued that it was not sufficient for the union to have referred to its members employed at the College because the college did not know who these members were. It was claimed that only about one-third of the College's 900 or so employees were NATFHE members, and that only about one-third of the union's members used the check-off system. The High Court upheld the College's arguments and granted an injunction prohibiting the strike, and this decision was upheld by the Court of Appeal.

Finally, in November 1993, in an unusual case, an application by the Prison Service, an injunction against industrial action by the Prison Officers' Association (POA) was granted. The basis for the injunction was that prison officers had the status of 'constable' and therefore could not take industrial action. The Court ruling also called into question the POA's status as an independent trade union. The then Home Secretary subsequently included in the Criminal Justice and Public Order Bill clauses that would restore 'normal' trade union status to the POA, with the exception of the right to call industrial action. The provisions are retrospective and protect the POA from any liability from past actions it had taken when it was thought by all concerned to be a trade union. They also provide that the Certification Officer is to regard the POA as an independent union, despite the fact that by law it would be unable to take industrial action. This could be, of course, an exceedingly dangerous precedent.

There were no major leading collective law cases between 1995 and 1997. Significant cases and changes related more to individual rights, often through the decisions of ECJ, and some of these are dealt with in the next section.

The European Union

Introduction

The European Economic Community was created in 1958 by the Treaty of Rome. On 1 July 1968 the Customs Union came into being: all customs duties between the original six countries were abolished and a common tariff was adopted. In 1973 the Community was enlarged by the UK, Denmark and Ireland. In 1981 Greece joined, and in 1986 so did Spain and Portugal. Also in 1986 the twelve member countries signed the 'Single European Act' which amended the EEC Treaty and set the end of 1992 as the deadline for implementing the key legislative measures to create the Single European Market. In 1992 the Maastricht Treaty proposed a European citizenship and a European currency and a European central bank. These are sometimes referred to as European Political Union and EMU. In 1995 Austria, Sweden and Finland joined the EU, bringing the total of member countries to 15. Norway, following a referendum, rejected membership.

The two main means of achieving the EU's objectives are, first, by directives which are binding instruments on each member country, but leave to each country the choice of forms and methods; second, by regulations which are binding in their entirety and directly applicable in all member states.

Three of the main areas of impact of the European Community (EC) on employment relations have for some time been equal pay for equal work, collective redundancies and the transfer of undertakings. Health and safety measures have also been of great importance.

In December 1989 the Charter of Fundamental Rights of Workers (commonly known as the Social Charter), was adopted by 11 of the 12 member states (the UK being the exception), at the Strasbourg European Council meeting. The Charter was intended as a general statement of minimum social rights which would be applicable throughout the Community (see Appendix II). In January 1990, the Community unanimously adopted its 1990 Social

Action Programme (see Appendix III) which was designed as the first stage of the implementation of the Charter. During 1991 there was controversy among the 12 EU countries about the substantive issues involved and about the procedural issues; in particular, whether there should be a qualified majority or whether there should be unanimity.

The conclusion of this debate at the end of 1991 was the UK Conservative Government's refusal to sign the 'Social Chapter', (that is, the section of the Maastricht Treaty designed to accelerate the implementation of the Social Action Programme and the UK's opt-out from the Social Chapter which was approved by the other member countries as the Social Protocol to the Treaty (see Appendix IV)). The other member countries proceeded gradually to implement the Protocol, mostly by qualified majority. The UK was not able to take part in the discussions regarding the implementation of the Protocol.

However, the election of a Labour Government in 1997 led to the UK ending its opt-out from the Social Chapter. Indeed, as a consequence, the Treaty of Amsterdam 1997 provides for the Social Protocol to be included in the main text of the EU Treaty. Amsterdam also provided for the introduction into the Treaty of a specific chapter on employment. This commits the Community to contributing to a high level of employment by encouraging cooperation between member states and by supporting and (if necessary) complementing their action. However, it is clear that no power in this area will be transferred from the member states to the Commission, and no binding obligations are placed on individual member states in the area of employment policy.

Although Britain opted out of the Social Chapter, as a condition of signing the Maastricht Treaty, she has still been affected by many changes in European law and by decisions of the European Court, and will continue to be so in the future: for example, by the Working-Time Directive, the wider interpretation of Transfer of Undertakings Directive, the Collective Redundancies Directive, and the rights of part-time employees. First, the amended EU Treaty provides for qualified majority voting for matters related to the working environment as regards the health and safety of employees (Article 118A). Second, Article 118B provides for the Commission to endeavour to develop the dialogue between management and labour at European level which could, if the two sides consider it desirable, lead to relations based on agreement. Third, the UK remains affected by the Articles of the Treaty. Fourth, the UK is bound by directives which have already been passed and by any interpretation of these by the ECJ.

Equal pay and opportunities

With regard to sex discrimination, the principle of equal work was enshrined in the Community's founding treaty. Article 119 requires member states to 'ensure and subsequently maintain the application of the principle that men and women should receive equal pay for equal work' (Article 1). Progress was initially slow, but in 1975 the Council adopted the Equal Pay Directive. This directive expands on Article 119 by defining the principle of equal pay as meaning 'for the same work or for work to which equal value is attributed, the elimination of all discrimination on grounds of sex with regard to all aspects and conditions of remuneration'. Other Directives were subsequently passed including the Equal Treatment Directive 1976, whose purpose is 'to put into effect in the member states the principle of equal treatment for men and women as regards access to employment, including promotion, and to vocational training and as regards working conditions' (Article 1). The Directive goes on to explain that the principle of equal treatment 'shall mean that there will be no discrimination whatsoever on grounds of sex either directly or indirectly by reference in particular to marital or family status' (Article 2(i)).

As a consequence of these directives and subsequent cases the UK has had to amend its own sex discrimination legislation extensively. In 1983 the Equal Pay Act was amended in order to enable claims of equal pay for work of equal value to be brought. In 1986 after the ECJ's judgment in the Marshall case had established that discrimination in retirement ages was in breach of the principle of equal treatment, the 1986 Sex Discrimination Act was passed. Further measures which were required to implement the Equal Treatment Directive were contained in the 1989 Employment Act.

In the cases of Hertz and Dekker, the ECJ construed the Equal Treatment Directive in a way which gives substantial protection to pregnant women and those on maternity leave. In *Hertz* v. *Alidi Marked* (1991), the ECJ decided that it is a breach of the directive to dismiss a woman because she is pregnant: women are also protected against dismissal by reason of their absence on maternity leave. In *Dekker* v. *Strichting Vormingscentrum vor Jong Volurassenen* (1991), the ECJ decided that a decision not to hire a pregnant woman because of the financial consequences of her maternity absence was also a breach of the directive. These two judgments anticipated some of the provisions of the 1992 Directive on the protection of pregnant women at work (Cox, 1993) which has now been embodied in the Trade Union Reform and Employment Rights Act. In *Marshall* v. *Southampton and South-West Hampshire Area Health Authority* (1986), the ECJ ruled that compensation for discrimination should not be limited, and this now applies to both sex and race discrimination cases. In *Barber* v. *Guardian Royal Exchange* (1990) the ECJ ruled that payments made under a private occupational pension scheme, which is contracted-out of the state earnings-related pension scheme, were part of 'pay' and therefore there had to be no discrimination between men and women.

Yet another important case was *R* v. *Secretary of State for Employment* ex parte *Equal Opportunities Commission (EOC) and another* (1994). Under UK legislation (The Employment Protection (Consolidation) Act 1978), employees who work between 8 and 16 hours a week do not qualify for a statutory redundancy payment or the right to complain of unfair dismissal unless they have five years' service. Those who work 16 hours or more a week qualify after two years. Employees who work less than 8 hours a week never become entitled to these rights. The House of Lords in this case, brought by the EOC, declared that these different qualifying conditions were incompatible with EC equality law (namely Article 119 of the Treaty of Rome), and the Equal Pay Directive. Part-time employees are predominantly female, so the impact of the legislation was discriminatory on grounds of sex.

In *R* v. *Secretary of State for Employment* ex parte *Seymour Smith* (1997), (see IDS Brief 586), the House of Lords considered whether the two-year qualification period for unfair dismissal might be unlawful because of discrimination against women, who generally have shorter periods of service then men. The House of Lords referred a number of questions to the ECJ concerning the test for determining whether the qualifying period is contrary to Article 119 of the Treaty. The outcome is awaited.

Transfer of undertakings

Turning to the Directive on the Transfer of Undertakings (sometimes known as the Acquired Rights Directive), this concerns the rights of workers when a business is transferred. Broadly, it requires that employment should, as far as possible, be continuous before and after the transfer; it discourages dismissals on transfers; and requires employee representatives to be informed and consulted (Benson, 1993). The UK, in response to the directive, introduced TUPE in 1981. It eventually became clear, after a number of important judgments by British courts and the ECJ that TUPE did not properly reflect the EC's Directive. An amendment to British law was necessary and this was undertaken in the 1993 Trade Union Reform and Employment Rights Act. In particular, it was necessary to make clear that the directive applied to the public sector and not just to the private sector. This has had important consequences for the Conservative Government's policy of contracting-out of services.

Among leading cases were *Dines and Others* v. *Initial Health Care Services Ltd and Pall Mall Services*, where the Court of Appeal (1994) ruled that when a contract changed from one private contractor to another, TUPE still applied. In this case the Health Authority had not renewed its cleaning contract with Initial Health Care Services but awarded it to Pall Mall Services. Initial Health Care made about 100 of its staff redundant, most of whom were engaged by Pall Mall but on less favourable terms and conditions. In *Spar* v. *Schmidt* (1994) the European Court of Justice held that the contracting-out of the work of a single cleaning lady was a transfer because of the similarity of the work undertaken pre- and post-transfer. In *Rask and Christensen* v. *Kantineservice* (1993) the ECJ held that there was a transfer when a canteen was contracted-out even though the activity transferred was ancillary to the main business. In *Kenny* v. *South Manchester College* (1993) the High Court ruled that the contracting-out of prison education services was a transfer of undertaking. However, in *Suzen* v. *Zenacker* (1997) (Case C, 13/9) which again involved a cleaning lady, the ECJ ruled that the TUPE Directive did not automatically apply in the case of a contracted-out service transferring from one provider to another. It depended on the facts in each case, including the transfer of tangible or intangible assets and the taking-over by the new employer of a major part of the workforce. There would appear now to be some ambiguity in the interpretation of the law as a result of this new decision. In *Wilkins & Others* v. *St. Helens Borough Council* (1997) the Court of Appeal considered the position where the contracts of employees are terminated on a transfer, and they accept employment with the transferee on less favourable terms and conditions. The Court held that a termination in such circumstances is effective in law if it is for an economic, technical or organisational reason entailing changes in the workforce, in which case the employee is employed on the new terms and conditions agreed with the transferee. But where the reason or principal reason for the dismissal is the transfer itself, or a reason connected with it, and no economic, technical or organisational reason is shown, the termination is ineffective in law and the employee's original terms and conditions continue to apply.

In *The European Commission* v. *the UK* (1994), the ECJ ruled that the UK was in breach of EU law on transfers and on redundancies (see below).

Collective redundancies

Turning to the Directive on Collective Redundancies, this was first adopted in 1975 and revised in 1992. In the UK, the 1975 Directive was incorporated in the 1975 Employment Protection Act and the 1992 revisions were included in the 1993 Trade Union Reform and Employment Rights Act. The definition of redundancy for consultative purposes has been widened to include any dismissals for reasons not related to the individual. Consultation must be undertaken by the employer with a view to reaching agreement with employee representatives about ways of avoiding the dismissals, reducing the number of dismissals and mitigating the consequences of the dismissals. In *The European Commission* v. *the UK* (1994), the ECJ ruled that the UK was in breach of EU law on transfers of undertakings and on redundancies. British employers now have to consult employees, whether the organisation is union or non-union, when planning to make more than 10 redundancies or when transferring workers from one business to another. Furthermore, the obligation under the directive is to consult representatives 'with a view to reaching an agreement' and not merely to inform them.

The British Conservative Government gave effect to this judgment by passing new regulations as follows:

1. Employers may choose to consult either a recognised trade union or representatives of the employees affected. Elected representatives must be employees of the company.
2. Standing arrangements for such consultation are not required. Effective *ad hoc* arrangements are acceptable.
3. Elected representatives have the same rights as those from a trade union to:
    (a) time off with pay for this specific purpose;
    (b) not to be dismissed or to be treated
       detrimentally because of these activities;
    (c) complain to a tribunal that the employer
       has failed to consult in accordance with the law;
4. The need to consult arises only where an employer proposes to dismiss 20 or more employees at one establishment over a 90-day period;
5. Consultation should be done 'in good time' and not as previously required 'at the earliest opportunity';
6. only those who meet the normal qualifying conditions to bring a claim for unfair dismissal may do so in connection with a transfer.

It will be seen from the above that the opportunity was taken to weaken the position of unions. The TUC has sought a ruling from the Commission that parts of these regulations are not in accordance with the ECJ judgment and the Commission has agreed. The Labour Government has set up a committee to consider the matter.

Working-Time Directive

Next, there is the Working-Time Directive which was adopted in 1993 under the health and safety provisions of the Treaty. The British Conservative Government challenged the legal basis of the Directive in the ECJ claiming it was not a health and safety directive and therefore should not have been passed by a qualified majority vote. In 1996 the ECJ gave its judgment which upheld the directive as a health and safety measure, thus rejecting the British Government's case. The main provisions of the directive are:

(a) a maximum 48-hour week (including overtime) on average over 4 months;
(b) 11 consecutive hours' rest per day;

35 consecutive hours' rest per week, in principle including Sundays, although this would not be mandatory (these weekly rest periods can be averaged out over 2 weeks, and the 35 hours can be reduced to 24 for objective technical or work organisation reasons);

(d) rest breaks during the day for all workers working over 6 hours' duration and terms to be fixed by collective agreement or national legislation/practice;

(e) three weeks' paid annual holiday for the first 3 years after implementation (that is, until 1999) and thereafter 4 weeks paid holiday;

(f) certain protections for night workers.

However, there are many exceptions and derogations concerning different types of work pattern and occupation: for example many services (including transport) and most utilities, as well as seasonal work, and industries where work cannot be interrupted on technical grounds. In addition employers may get around the maximum 48-hour week if employees agree to changes and if those that do not so agree are not penalised. Most other areas are subject to flexibility provided compensationary arrangements are made. The only exceptions are for paid holiday leave, the additional provisions to protect night workers' health and safety, and the general requirement to organise work to take account of health and safety needs.

European Works Councils

Of major importance is the EU Directive on European Works Councils (EWC) which came into effect in September 1996. The Directive covers more than 1200 large and medium-sized multinational companies across Europe, the majority with operations in the UK. The companies covered are those which have at least 1000 employees within the member states (other than in the UK), and at least 150 employees in each of at least two member states.

The UK was not directly covered by the EWC Directive because of the Conservative Government's opt-out from the EU's Social Chapter, although it will be soon as a result of the Labour Government's ending the opt-out. However, many companies operating in the UK, including many which are UK-based, are covered by the Directive because of their operations elsewhere in Europe. Overwhelmingly these companies have included their UK employees in the EWCs they have set up, so undermining much of the opt-out.

According to the TUC (1977) by January 1997 around 400 EWCs had already been set up across Europe, including at least 57 in UK-based companies: for example, Barclays Bank, British Airways, British Steel, Courtaulds, Pilkington and Unilever. The Directive provided for voluntary agreement on the establishment of EWCs by September 1996. Since then management has been required to take part in negotiations to set up an

EWC, either on its own initiative, or if requested to do so by at least 100 employees in two member states or their representative body. If they fail to do so within six months of the request, or fail to reach agreement within three years, then 'the subsidiary requirements' of the Directive (or minimum terms) for an EWC will be imposed. Companies cannot therefore escape their obligations to set up an EWC by endlessly spinning out negotiations. Agreements which were reached before September 1996, or as a result of the negotiations referred to above, are not subject to the subsidiary requirements.

Medium-Term Social Action Programme

In 1995 the European Commission produced its new Medium-Term Social Action Programme 1995–97. This contained relatively few new initiatives but rather concentrated on dealing with a number of outstanding issues. However, it is a rolling programme and the European Trade Union Confederation (ETUC) and the European Parliament have pressed for additions. One new initiative which has emerged is the possibility of national company councils for consultation and information.

Passed in 1996 was the Posted-Worker Directive which aims to ensure that workers temporarily posted or sub-contracted to work in another member state enjoy the same employment rights concerning pay and working conditions as similar workers in the host country. Also, the Young Workers' Directive was due to be implemented in all member states by June 1996, but the UK has an opt-out clause for the first four years on some of its provisions.

Social dialogue

The 'Val Duchesse' process of social dialogue between the ETUC, the Union of Industrial and Employers' Confederations of Europe and the European Centre of Enterprises with Public Participation has existed since the mid-1980s. The Social Policy Agreement of the Maastricht Treaty gave the Social Partners not only a formal consultative role in the development of new social legislation, but the possibility of concluding European-level agreements either on their own initiative or as a substitute for proposed legislation, which could be given legal force by a Council decision. Indeed under the Treaty of Amsterdam, 1997, the majority of new social proposals will go straight to the Social Partners for possible negotiation as a framework agreement.

The first such agreement reached was on Parental Leave in 1995, which is backed by a European Directive. A second agreement – reached in 1997 – covered permanent part-time workers with the purpose of giving part-time workers the same employment rights as full-time workers. The Agreement will establish in the UK:

(a) the legal principle of equal rights for part-time workers without having to demonstrate sex discrimination;
(b) equal access to pay, bonus, shift and other additional payments for comparable workers;
(c) equal contractual terms – such as occupational sick leave and paid holiday leave – for comparable workers;
(d) equal access to all benefits such as share options, staff discounts and occupational pensions for comparable workers;
(e) equal rights for male part-timers who are effectively excluded from claiming parity with full-time workers because the only route available is to prove sex discrimination.

A Directive is expected later in 1997 and there will be two years to transpose the Directive into domestic legislation, with the possibility of a further year's extension.

The Social Dialogue process, if continued, has the potential in the longer term for developing a degree of multinational bargaining.

Conclusion

The leading cases in the courts are only the tip of the iceberg. Their existence indicates that there are large numbers of occasions when both employers and unions consult their lawyers about the relevance of the law to the options they are considering. There is no doubt that these occasions are far more numerous than they were before the 1980s. Moreover, in their day-to-day working, trade union officials in particular have to be aware of what the law says. Unions can be easily put at risk by the actions of members which 18 years ago were not unlawful, and which many would still regard as ordinary trade union behaviour. The risks involved can include the union's very existence through the sequestration of its funds and property. The law is now an important part of the daily practice of industrial relations.

Strikes and conduct connected with them, such as picketing and secondary action, are heavily represented among the cases in the 1980s and among the practical issues on which the law bears. In the 1990s, with the fall in strikes, issues such as picketing and secondary action hardly arose. The injunction has become a handy weapon for some employers, although the number of cases where an injunction restraining unions might successfully be applied for is legion compared with the number which are taken. Many employers regard them as more trouble than they are worth, but they are always potentially available. An injunction is a holding action rather than the full legal action; yet the cases show that the penalties for contempt which may follow disobedience of the injunction can be greater than the punishment exacted for guilt of the crime itself. This would seem to indicate that the procedure for securing an injunction should give the union every opportunity to be heard. Yet the procedure is dominated by the need for speed, and judges make decisions at unlikely times and in odd places. Since so much can hang on the decision the procedure should, at least, make certain that the union has the same opportunity to make its case as the employer who applies for the injunction.

This is a prime example of the limits of the legal system when it is called on to deal with a new crop of industrial relations cases. The subject matter has its own special characteristics and, while the legal system is general in its applications, its acceptance requires understanding of the environment in which people work. Now that the law on industrial relations is so extensive, the legal system should display a greater willingness to understand the context of cases.

Brown, Deakin and Ryan (1997), in the most recent and thorough review of the effects of the legal changes on industrial relations, have no doubt that, for trade unions, the legislation produced new financial burdens and obstacles to the recruitment and retention of members. It also provided employers with powerful new sanctions. However, the apparent success of the laws cannot be seen in isolation from the changes in the economic environment.

Elgar and Simpson (1993) reached the following conclusions, after a major study into the impact of the law on industrial disputes in the 1980s:

1. The law has in general become a more important factor across the spectrum of industrial relations.
2. To understand the impact of the law it is essential to locate it in the context in which it operates, and this varies considerably between different sectors.
3. One aspect of the law stands out, namely the need for trade unions to hold a ballot before calling on workers to take industrial action.
4. There is an increased awareness among employers of the vulnerability of the individual worker who takes industrial action to disciplinary sanctions, including stopping pay and, most important, summary dismissal.
5. The law contributed to a climate where there was a general awareness of a continuing shift in the balance of bargaining power.

We would not dissent from any of these conclusions, but two other conclusions emerge from our own review of changes in the law. First, there is the growing influence of EU law on British employment law, particularly in terms of individual rights, and in terms of consultation, participation and information: the whole concept, indeed, of social partnership.

Second, there is the election of the Labour Government in 1997. As stated earlier, the Labour Government is committed to:

(a) ending the opt-out from the Social Chapter;
(b) the introduction of a NMW;
(c) the restoration of trade union rights at GCHQ;

(steps have already been taken with regard to these first three)

(d) the introduction of a mechanism for statutory union recognition when a majority of employees so desire;
(e) the ending of the three-yearly renewal of the check-off;
(f) some protection for lawful strikers against unfair dismissal.

These are not insignificant measures, but there are no other firm commitments to amending the Conservative legislation, although some may be forthcoming. The unions would certainly like more change.

Indeed, as argued in Chapter 4, there seems to be a new broad consensus on much of the legislation: for example, on ballots before industrial action, the end of the closed shop, and on secondary action. In the future the law will continue to play an important part in industrial relations, both in terms of the collective constraints applied, but also in terms of the provision of individual rights and consultative and participative rights through Europe. This last item depends to some degree on whether the UK, under a Labour Government continues to follow the American path of individualism and deregulation, or whether it moves closer to the EU concept of social partnership, which itself is under some attack on the Continent as a result of economic pressures.

CHAPTER 6

Employer and management strategies in the private sector

Introduction

In this chapter we look at changing employer industrial relations attitudes and strategies in the 1980s and the 1990s. One of the major academic debates during the period was whether or not there had been a major shift by employers towards policies of macho-management, unitarism and anti-trade unionism. There has also been an extensive debate about Human Resource Management (HRM): what it means, how widely it has been adopted, and what are its implications for traditional industrial relations and personnel management? Along with this there has been a debate about individualism and collectivism in employee relations. These debates are in a sense part of the still wider question as to whether a 'new industrial relations' developed in this period. These issues are addressed in this chapter, although a final assessment is not made until Chapter 12.

The economic and political environment has already been discussed in Chapters 3 and 4, and only two points need to be emphasised here. The first is that the election in 1979 of a Conservative Government and its re-election in 1983, 1987 and 1992 meant above all that throughout the 18 years from 1979 to 1997, when a Labour Government was finally elected, there was a government which was pro-business and anti-trade union. It was a government pledged to reducing trade union power and removing burdens on industry. It was also a government pledged to reducing public expenditure, redistributing income and the tax burden in favour of the better-off: all objectives which most employers readily supported. The second is that employers faced a far more competitive environment than they had previously, and that both business organisations and competition were becoming more and more globalised. Alongside Conservative Government support for the small firm sector, multi-nationals were extending their market share and were playing an ever-increasing role in world trade.

In 1979/80 British industry almost immediately faced a major and unprecedented crisis. As outlined in Chapter 3, the country was plunged into the worst recession of the post-war period. The impact on profits was drastic, above all in manufacturing industry. Industry's immediate response was wholesale redundancies and the widespread closure of plants. It was this response which gave rise at the time to the term 'macho-management'. The extensive closures and redundancies indeed would certainly appear to justify the term. However, employers were preoccupied with survival. They were in business to make profits and not to create 'good' industrial relations. Industrial relations policy was subsidiary to wider changes in business organisation, strategy and policy, which were considered necessary to deal with recession and ever-growing world competition. Within this wider framework employers' industrial relations objectives were to control the work process and improve cost effectiveness; to assert managerial authority (although in some cases it was alleged that compliance was not enough for economic success: what was required was commitment); and to move towards a more unitary approach and away from pluralism which had developed in the earlier post-war decades (Poole and Mansfield, 1993). As part of this process there was also a move towards 'individualism' and away from 'collectivism'.

There is, of course, a great danger in generalising about employers' objectives. There are variations in objectives, as well as in managerial styles and perhaps above all in the circumstances of individual firms, which in turn affect objectives, policies and style. Thus the type of company, its stage of development, its products, the product markets, its labour markets, the degree of competition it faces, its technology, its traditions and philosophy all play a major part in determining its industrial relations objectives and the policies it adopts to attain these objectives (see Sisson and Marginson, 1995). Nevertheless, the above objectives will serve as a starting point for considering companies' industrial relations policies. These policies will be examined under the following headings:

(a) human resource management and management style;
(b) attitudes to unions;
(c) collective bargaining;
(d) involvement, consultation and participation;
(e) flexibility;
(f) levels and methods of remuneration.

Human resource management and management style

HRM became an 'in' phrase in the 1980s, although its meaning was by no means always clear. First, it can be used as just another term for personnel management with nothing else changed. Second, it can be used as another term for personnel management, but suggesting or providing much greater emphasis on certain aspects of personnel work, such as training, motivation and employee development, and a decreasing emphasis on some traditional areas, such as industrial relations. Third, it can be used to imply a completely new concept whereby labour is regarded not so much as a cost but as an asset or resource, which needs to be developed to its maximum, so that emphasis is on the individual employee and on his or her motivation, training and development. Often this approach is allied to the stated belief that HRM is primarily the responsibility of line managers and not personnel managers. HRM can thus simply be a form of public relations or a major change in corporate policy with a distinctive approach to labour management or another form of management style. Storey (1992) points out that HRM has its 'hard' and its 'soft' versions. 'Hard' HRM puts the stress on the idea of a 'resource' that is something to be used dispassionately and in a formally rational manner, as with any other economic factor. 'Soft' HRM lays stress on the term 'human', thus conjuring up echoes of the human relations school, and emphasises communication, motivation and leadership. What is striking is that the same term is thus capable of signalling dramatically opposite sets of assumptions.

Guest (1987, 1989) suggests that HRM consists of a combination of policies designed to produce strategic integration, high commitment, high quality and flexibility among employees. As he argues, in its full meaning, HRM should properly denote a package embracing a strategic and integrated approach to 'people management': the integration of employees on the basis of commitment and not mere compliance with instructions and an organic and devolved business structure as against a bureaucratic and centralised one. HRM thus involves the use of a coherent approach, matching HRM activities and policies to business strategy, and seeing employees as a strategic resource for achieving competitive advantage. Guest (1989) concludes that the evidence of such an integrated approach in Britain is so far limited, and this is confirmed by Millward (1994) based on Workplace Industrial Relations Survey (WIRS) 3 and Storey (1992). However, he argues that the underlying values, reflected in HRM policies and practices, would appear to be essentially unitarist and individualistic in contrast to the more pluralist and collective values of traditional industrial relations. The unitary approach views the organisation as a team, all owing allegiance to the organisation, and where all share the same objectives: the pluralist view sees the organisation as a coalition of groups whose interests in some respects may differ and need to be reconciled. HRM can pose a threat to trade unions in three ways. First, in companies in which unions are recognised, HRM objectives are likely to be pursued through policies that tend to by-pass the union. Second, by practising 'good' management, the employees' need for the union as a protective device against 'poor' management is likely to be reduced. Third, in companies where unions are not recognised, HRM policies might obviate any felt need for a union. Certainly in the USA HRM has been used by many companies as an anti-union device. In our interviews with managers, none spontaneously mentioned HRM as being a major new development in their employee relations. Mainly they regarded HRM as 'good' personnel policy and practice.

Storey (1992), from his research in mainstream British organisations, says that there was clear evidence of extensive and sustained activity directed at employment/management matters. Management had seized the initiative and were experimenting with a host of approaches. There was some degree of commonality in the initiatives. The touchstones were a retreat from proceduralism; an emphasis upon adaptability; direct communications with employees; managerial leadership; and the moulding of a more tractable labour force:

> The overall trend was incontrovertibly towards more individualised arrangements. Many of the particular devices had a rather patchy application but the pressure was found to be continuing in this direction. The basic tenets of HRM would seem to be enjoying some wide appeal among managers – if only in furnishing an aspiration and a sense of direction. (Storey, 1992)

Sisson (1994), in a review of developments in personnel management and HRM concludes that: 'The rhetoric may be the people-centred approach to the "soft" version: the reality is the cost reduction approach of the "hard" version' (p. 15). The use of the language of HRM has, however, spread rapidly in the 1990s and so have some of its component policies. However, there is evidence that the 'psychological contract' between employee and employer has suffered damage as a result, for example, of down-sizing, delayering and insecurity of employment (I. Kessler and Undy, 1995).

In the space available, it has not been possible to provide a full discussion of HRM, but of course there is no shortage of literature on the subject. Our concern has been the effect of HRM on industrial relations.

Turning to management style, Purcell and Sisson (1983) have, following Fox (1974), identified four 'ideal' types of industrial relations management. First there are *traditionalists*. These have unitary beliefs, and are anti-union with forceful management. An example of such a company was Grunwicks, which became a *cause célèbre* in the 1970s (see Chapter 11).

Next, they identified *sophisticated paternalists*. These are essentially unitary, but there is a crucial difference from the first type in that they do not take it for granted that their employees accept the company's objectives or automatically legitimise management decision-making; they spend considerable time and resources in ensuring that their employees have the right approach. Examples of such companies given by Purcell and Sisson (1983) are IBM and Marks & Spencer.

Third, there are *sophisticated moderns.* To quote Fox (1974):

> Management legitimises the union role in certain areas of joint decision-making because it sees this role as conducive to its own interests as measured by stability, promotion of consent, bureaucratic regulation, effective communication or the handling of change. It recognises that its discretion is being limited in certain areas of decision-making but it legitimises these limitations and therefore does not counter with low trust behaviour and attitudes. (p. 302)

Purcell and Sisson sub-divide this category into:

(a) *The constitutionalists.* These include, for example, Ford, where the limits on collective bargaining are clearly codified in the collective agreement. In those areas of decision-making where management is under challenge from the trade unions, or where it may be expedient to concede joint regulation (in return for concessions from the union elsewhere), the frontier of control may be moved back, but is then firmly entrenched in a specific codified agreement. Clegg (1979) has described this as 'the statute law' model of collective bargaining where 'the formal assumption . . . is that management is free to take their own decisions on matters which are not the subject of collective agreements' (p. 117).

(b) *The consultors.* These accept collective bargaining, but there is no desire to codify everything in a collective agreement. On the contrary, every effort is made to minimise the amount of joint regulation and great emphasis is placed on joint consultation with 'problems' having to be solved rather than 'disputes' settled. Examples of such companies given by Purcell and Sisson are ICI, BP and Esso, but in recent years the oil companies have been de-recognising unions.

Finally, there are the *standard moderns* (pragmatic or opportunist). These are considered to be by far the largest group. Trade unions are recognised, but industrial relations are seen as primarily fire-fighting and assumed to be non-problematic unless events prove otherwise. Consequently, the significance of industrial relations' considerations waxes and wanes in the light of changing circumstances. Unlike the earlier groups, there does not appear to be a set of values or assumptions which are held in common. Examples given by Purcell and Sisson are GEC, GKN and Tube Investments.

Taken together, the categories form a spectrum in which the adjacent ones shade into each other. Looked at in this way the categories are useful because a number of managers do see their firms as having shifted their position in the spectrum towards the earlier categories. The 1980s saw them, if they had been consultors, among the sophisticated moderns, reducing the scope of collective agreements compared with the 1970s, and getting managers' solutions to problems accepted.

Purcell (1987) argues that Fox, 'in distinguishing between pluralist and unitary frames of management provided a powerful impetus to the debate about management style, but the mutually exclusive nature of these categories had limited further development' (p. 546). Moreover, wide variations can be found within the unitary approach and within the pluralist approach. He therefore suggests an alternative distinction of 'individualism' (policies related to the individual employee) and 'collectivism' (the extent to which groups of workers have an independent voice and participate in decision-making with managers). Companies can and do operate on both these dimensions of style.

Purcell and Ahlstrand (1994) have taken the debate further and argued that aspects of individualism and collectivism can be found simultaneously and have developed a matrix with individualism along one axis and collectivism along the other. Along the individualistic axis they put cost minimisation, paternalism and employee development, while along the collective axis they put unitary action, adversarial conduct and cooperation. This is developed further by Kessler and Purcell (1995). Storey (1992) says that many individualistic measures have been introduced alongside the continuing recognition of unions and the continuation of collective bargaining. This he has called 'dualism'. In this connection it is interesting to note that WIRS 3 showed that unionised workplaces had adopted certain HRM measures to a greater extent than had non-unionised workplaces. Storey and Bacon (1993) argue that individualism and collectivism can be ambiguous concepts, and say that it was useful to use Gospel's (1992) division of a firm's employment policy into three sub-categories: work relations, employment relations and industrial relations –

> Work relations covers the way work is organised and the deployment of workers around technologies and production processes. Employment relations deals with the arrangements governing such aspects of employment as recruitment, training, job tenure and promotion, and the reward of workers. Industrial relations is concerned with the representational systems which may exist within an enterprise: in the British context this has often meant management–union relations and the process of collective bargaining'. (p. 3)

Gospel uses HRM as a generic term to cover the set of decisions which employers have long made in order to govern their enterprises. He takes it to cover the above three areas. The concepts of individualism and collectivism can then be applied to each of these sub-categories.

Policies are likely to vary according to the type of product and product markets, technology and skill level. Indeed, a firm may well have a number of different styles for different occupational groups. For example, the treatment and development of managers may well be very different from that of shop floor workers, as may the treatment of core-workers and peripheral workers. As Purcell (1987) concludes: 'Once we recognise that modern companies are capable of making strategic business choices we must allow for preferences to exist in the way employees are managed, albeit in constrained circumstances' (p. 547).

The debates about the unitary as against the pluralist approach, the individualistic as against the collectivist approach and the categorisation of organisations are valuable frameworks for analysis, but their main purpose is not to provide a practical typology. Rather, they help the analysis and understanding of developments in organisations. In the 1970s the trend in management was towards a greater acceptance of pluralism and collectivism, and there was some movement towards the 'sophisticated modern' model. In the 1980s and since, the movement has been towards the unitary and individualistic approach and towards the 'sophisticated paternalistic' model in some cases, as well as towards a cost minimisation policy (in other words 'soft' and 'hard' HRM). Indeed one leading personnel director stated that 'there had been an irreversible shift to the involvement of the individual in the workplace. There will be no return to the collective masses.' However, such a view was not that of all the managers we interviewed. A number of managers believed that they had significantly increased efficiency and in this achievement unions had played a full cooperative part. We return to this issue later in this chapter.

Attitudes to unions

The macho management policies of many manufacturing companies in the early 1980s were interpreted by some commentators as an employers' counter-offensive against alleged union excesses in the 1970s. The survey carried out by Mackay and Torrington (1986) showed a harder management attitude towards trade unions.

Further evidence was based on widely quoted specific examples, such as the (then) British Leyland Company, which at the end of the 1970s and early 1980s drastically cut manpower, confronted and defeated union power and imposed changed methods of work and changed procedures (Willman, 1984), and the P&O and Wapping disputes (see Chapter 5), and subsequently certain other national and provincial newspapers. However, early widely based surveys such as Millward and Stevens (1986), Batstone (1984), Edwards (1987), and Marginson *et al.* (1988) have suggested that there was not a major frontal assault on unions. Recognition has not been withdrawn in the over-whelming majority of cases, although of course, it has occurred in a number of well publicised instances and some not so well publicised. A study (Claydon, 1989) recorded 49 cases of de-recognition in 1986/7, but there is evidence of an increase in de-recognition in the second half of the 1980s and in the 1990s (Gregg and Yates, 1991; Marginson *et al.*, 1993; Smith and Morton, 1993; Gall and McKay, 1994; Claydon, 1996).

WIRS 3 (Millward *et al.*, 1992) demonstrated conclusively that, contrary to what some had claimed, there were major changes in employee relations during the 1980s. The most important of these was the decline in the representation of employees by trade unions and the decline in the coverage of collective bargaining, particularly in the private sector. Thus the percentage of establishments overall which recognised unions rose from 60 per cent in 1980 to 66 per cent in 1984, and then fell to 53 per cent in 1990. In private manufacturing the fall was from 65 per cent in 1980 to 44 per cent in 1990; in private services the fall was from 41 per cent to 36 per cent, and in the public sector from 94 per cent to 87 per cent. WIRS 3 concludes that 'the fall was stark, substantial and incontrovertible'.

However, Marginson *et al.* (1993) in their Second Company Level Industrial Relations Survey, which was conducted in mid-1992 among a representative sample of 176 multi-site companies with 1000 or more UK employees, reported that 69 per cent of companies recognised trade unions; in 25 per cent of these companies recognition covered all establishments, in 17 per cent unions were recognised in most establishments and in 27 per cent unions were recognised in some establishments only. In the previous 5 years, 19 per cent reported that recognition for negotiating purposes had been partially or wholly withdrawn, while 7 per cent of companies reported extending recog-nition. On acquired sites, 90 per cent had maintained the status quo, 5 per cent had withdrawn recognition and 3 per cent had granted recognition. On new sites 24 per cent had granted recognition at all sites, and 17 per cent had done so at most or some sites. But in 59 per cent of cases no recognition had been granted (pp. 55–7).

WIRS 3 shows that the decline in recognition was primarily a feature of small establishments, and that newer workplaces were considerably less likely to have recognised unions than older ones. Workplaces which were less than 10 years old recognised unions in only 23 per cent of cases, whereas in workplaces which were more than 20 years old, 52 per cent did so. In the private sector only 1 per cent of managers reported that they had de-recognised unions between 1984 and 1990, but cases of new recognition were also rare.

Had they wished, senior managers could have ended the recognition of trade unions in many more places. That they have not done so was largely because the majority of companies did not regard established recognition as an issue. Where unions were recognised, in the vast majority of cases managers accepted them. As one employer representative told us, de-recognition had not taken off because it had not been necessary. He added that what mattered for managers was putting their policies into action, and the presence of unions seldom stood in the way of that objective. Managers could take the initiative and succeed in taking the matters forward which were of concern to them. Some firms have taken a more sophisticated approach and, in cooperation with the unions, have endeavoured to ensure that the nature of the competitive threat is understood by their employees. That has meant putting across the details of the business, and it has sometimes led to seeking common solutions to problems. In those cases the unions have become positive partners rather than passive bystanders.

The maintenance of union recognition and of collective bargaining machinery where it has been maintained does not, however, tell us much about the relative power and relations of the parties. Indeed, there can be little doubt that bargaining power during most of the period had swung decisively in favour of management and the effect of this will be considered later, as will the argument that management, rather than launching a frontal assault on unions and joint machinery, had sought to by-pass them and to seek ways of doing things which reduced union involvement.

Unions have, however, found it harder than ever to gain recognition in greenfield sites (Beaumont, 1987; Marginson *et al.*, 1993; Millward, 1994),in new companies and in companies and sectors where recognition has always been difficult to obtain (for example, large parts of the private service sector where there has been considerable growth in employment). Indeed it was apparent from our interviews that managers often held a different attitude to unions in existing plants from that held towards the recognition of unions in a new or unorganised workplace. In the majority of cases if they can avoid recognition they will, and if they cannot they often have a strong preference for a single union. This indicates that managers have different strategies according to whether they have the choice. They may have a good working relationship with unions where unions are recognised but nevertheless keep them out, or only admit the one they select, on greenfield sites. They want whatever arrangement gives them the greatest freedom to take successful initiatives.

Employers have indeed had more choice than at any time in the post-war period as to whether they recognise a union or not, and also a choice of which union they want to recognise and the terms on which they would grant recognition: for example, a single union and a no-strike agreement. Unions no longer have a legal method for obtaining recognition (as they do in many other countries and as they did briefly in this country between 1975 and 1980), although there is likely to be one provided by the Labour Government. The nature of the unorganised trades and the growth in part-time employment were among the major reasons for the lack of success in gaining membership and hence the likelihood of recognition.

Collective bargaining

Three major developments in collective bargaining took place in the 1980s; the first concerned the reduced coverage of collective bargaining, the second concerned the level and the third its scope. With regard to coverage, WIRS 3 shows that overall the proportion of employees covered by collective bargaining was reduced from 71 per cent in 1984 to 54 per cent in 1990. In the public sector, the fall was from 95 per cent to 78 per cent, much of this being due to the substitution of Review Bodies for collective bargaining in the cases of teachers and nurses. In private manufacturing the reduction was from 64 per cent to 51 per cent, and in private services from 41 per cent to 33 per cent. In the private sector as a whole the fall was from 52 per cent to 41 per cent. When it is recalled that WIRS was limited to establishments with 25 or more employees, it will be appreciated that in the economy as a whole under half of all employees by 1990 must have been covered by collective bargaining.

With regard to the level of bargaining, there was a continuation in the reduced importance of industry-wide bargaining arrangements. This was shown first in the abandonment of industry-wide bargaining in a number of cases in recent years: for example, in the road passenger transport industry, national and provincial newspapers as far as journalists are concerned, the London clearing banks, multiple retailing, the water industry, independent television, the cement industry, and engineering. Brown and Walsh (1991, p. 49) state that at least 16 major national bargaining groups covering a total of over a million employees, have been terminated since 1986. The decline in multi-employer bargaining is confirmed in the 1990 WIRS, and is interestingly discussed in Brown (1993). Where industry-wide bargaining has been retained, as in construction and commercial printing, its substantive agreements are more and more safety nets and there is usually considerable freedom for companies to reach their own agreements on most matters, although in construction there are no company agreements.

It is above all in the public sector that industry-wide bargaining has until recently been maintained, although even here measures have been taken towards decentralisation and pay flexibility. This is discussed in Chapter 7. In the former public corporations, privatisation had as one purpose putting activities on the same basis as other commercial firms with the expectation that decentralisation would occur. What has happened so far in practice has varied. For example, in gas there was originally virtually no change but this has recently altered, and British Telecom still has central agreements. However, in iron and steel, electricity, the water industry and railways there has been major decentralisation from national level (Pendleton and Winterton, 1993).

In private industry, there has been a continuing move from industry-wide bargaining to enterprise bargaining. Within some enterprises there has been a further move towards decentralisation: that is to say, from corporate level down to divisional, subsidiary company or plant levels. This trend, however, is by no means universal, for example in manufacturing, Ford still maintains company-wide bargaining and this is perhaps more importantly true of much of the private service sector, including most of the large banks, the insurance companies and the large multiple retail chains. Although, in some banks and large insurance companies, there has been a degree of decentralisation on a business basis, the effect of this has not been very significant. It is, of course, also true that, for example, the retail stores may pay different rates in different geographical areas, and not just London versus the rest, but these variations are determined centrally. Indeed, even where bargaining is at plant level, there is conclusive evidence from Marginson *et al.*'s study (1993) that guidelines and controls are often set down centrally and that the freedom of plant bargainers may be only within very strict limits.

Managers were asked whether the picture had changed over the previous ten years and if so, in which direction. Around 30 per cent reported a change over this period, three-quarters of whom said the most recent change was in the direction of increased decentralisation:

Moves in a centralised direction were most common in UK domestics, where companies were undiversified, where operating sites were deemed cost rather than profit centres, and where unions were recognised at all rather than some sites. Moves in a decentralised direction were more common amongst multinationals, financially devolved and highly diversified companies. (Marginson *et al.*, 1993)

Turning to sectoral differences, establishment-level negotiations predominated in the manufacturing sector. In the services sector, centralised bargaining structures were more common, with company level bargaining covering all sites being as important as establishment-level bargaining. Conglomerate companies were least likely to bargain on a multi-employer basis, and most likely to bargain at the level of the individual establishment: territorially-based divisional organisation was strongly associated with company level bargaining, as was the presence of divisions covering one single business.

Of the 79 companies concerned, corporate managers claimed to be involved in lower level negotiations in 65 per cent of cases. In 30 per cent of cases involvement took the form of direct participation in negotiations. Elsewhere intervention was indirect, the most common means cited being the issuing of guidelines to management negotiators at lower levels.

Regarding non-union companies, centralised decisions on pay determination covering all sites were more prevalent than decisions at intermediate or establishment level. Even where decisions on pay were taken at these lower levels, head office managers were indirectly involved in three out of every four cases. For each type of company and in each broad sector, pay determination in non-union companies appears to be more centralised than in companies recognising unions.

The Marginson *et al.* study (1988) has already made the important point that generally the decision to decentralise pay bargaining was not taken on industrial relations grounds, but because broader business strategy had decreed decentralisation and the establishment of decentralised cost or profit centres; it then followed, if managers were to accept financial responsibility at plant level, that they had to be allowed some responsibility for wage determination. An earlier view regarding bargaining levels put forward by Purcell and Sisson (1983) and by Kinnie (1987) was that management sought the bargaining level which best kept union influence away from the level where major company decision-making took place. Thus, for example, an insistence on plant level bargaining kept shop stewards and union officials away from strategic decision-making at corporate level.

WIRS 3 in fact shows that for all sectors between 1984 and 1990 the proportion of workplaces where pay was set by collective bargaining declined from 62 per cent to 48 per cent for manual employees, and from 54 per cent to 43 per cent for non-manual employees. Of those where manual pay was determined by collective bargaining, multi-employer bargaining declined from 40 per cent to 26 per cent, single employer/multi-plant remained at 13 per cent, and plant/establishment declined from 7 per cent to 6 per cent. For non-manual employees the respective figures were from 36 per cent to 24 per cent, from 13 per cent to 15 per cent, and from 4 per cent to 3 per cent. Where pay was not the result of collective bargaining, determination at workplace level went up from 20 per cent to 31 per cent for manual employees and from 30 per cent to 37 per cent for non-manuals. Determination at a higher level for manual employees increased from 11 per cent to 15 per cent, and for non-manuals from 15 per cent to 17 per cent (p. 219).

While the theme of decentralisation is general and powerful, it does not lead to a single pattern; the relations between establishment managers and those at the centre of a company vary widely. Moreover, there is change and movement going on continually in the balance between centre and periphery. For example, one major company, providing a service nationally, moderated the high degree of local autonomy to which it had moved because it had subsequently realised that the devolved local units were not sufficiently self-contained to justify the change. The performance of the network and services to customers depended on all the local units working together. Devolved management had set them against each other, while interdependence in the production of the service required central control.

A second large company argued that it was essential for it to preserve centralised bargaining. Its personnel director stated that he was 'terrified of the power which local union barons would exercise if negotiations were decentralised'. Another major company had decentralised its bargaining because all control was now exercised through budgets down to the local plant. The drive to decentralisation followed from the decision to put the responsibility for meeting profit targets on to plant managers, and the main pressure for it came from the variations in profitability between plants: managers claimed that they did not have the requisite flexibility. It is interesting that the company did not take the decision to decentralise bargaining until very late in the 1980s because of fear of a domino effect: that is to say, what was settled in one plant would be the basis of claims and settlements in others. Managers were judged by the financial results they achieved which were set out in monthly, quarterly and annual targets. A dispute was bound to make it unlikely that they would achieve the expected results and so they would be judged to have fallen short. In the view of the personnel director, there would be a strong tendency to buy off a strike in the interests of maintaining short-term profits. The next manager up the line was likely to take the same attitude because he too was judged by monthly figures. So the result could be that decentralisation would greatly increase the potential bargaining power of the unions. The same personnel director in a subsequent interview admitted that his original fears had not materialised. In a fourth large firm with a varied pattern of decentralisation in its component companies, the possibility of some return to centralisation was being actively considered. In a fifth firm bargaining had long been decentralised with subsidiary companies free to operate within a corporate framework, for example, so that settlements should reflect markets and profitability. But proposed offers and settlements are reported to and discussed at corporate level, and it had been centrally laid down that there should be no cuts in working hours or increases in holidays.

So from management's point of view the decentralisation of collective bargaining is not a simple story: some firms have gone further than others, some have yet to decentralise, some have drawn back, some have found that the appropriate level for decentralisation is not the same in all parts of the firm, and some have found that the nature of the product and the technology of its production are a determining influence. Even so, the general trend in management has been, and continues to be, a preference for more decentralised bargaining, although usually within a firmly controlled, centrally determined financial budget and/or central guidelines.

Turning to the scope of collective bargaining, the 1984 WIRS showed that there had been a considerable reduction in the range of subjects which was covered by collective bargaining between 1980 and 1984, although the 1990 WIRS did not show much change. Over the period as a whole, there was a reduction in overt bargaining over operational issues, and these were the issues where management had sought to reassert its authority and unilaterally determine such matters. This may be illustrated by an examination of a number of new-style procedural agreements, many of which state, for example, 'that the Union recognises the right of the Company to plan, organise, manage and decide finally upon the operations of the Company'. The old *status quo* and mutuality agreements found throughout engineering, whereby certain changes could not be introduced without prior agreement or the exhaustion of procedure, have gone, or been turned on their head, so that if there is a status quo clause at all, it normally says that employees shall carry out changes in practices required by management, even if they object and put the matter into the disputes procedure.

This is not to say that bargaining over work practices has disappeared. Notable productivity bargains have taken place in some organisations where union power is still significant (for example, British Telecom and Ford) and an analysis of the CBI data bank (Ingram, 1991b) showed that a considerable proportion of agreements contain productivity elements. A number of these were, however, in the nature of the exercise of superior force by management with the alternative to acceptance by unions being the closure of the plant or a managerially imposed condition for a pay increase. As one employer representative put it, these days managers talk confidently about making changes with few references to trade unions. They can make changes to increase productivity in ways which were unthinkable in the 1970s when they had begun by wondering how they could overcome union resistance, or elicit union cooperation. One personnel director stated that 'something for something' bargaining had become the norm in his company. The increases in productivity which had been achieved had been on such a scale that, despite considerable pay increases, the company was still internationally competitive on labour costs. Two other personnel directors used the same expression – 'something for something' – to describe their bargaining in the 1980s and since. But generally management was firmly in command.

In contrast to the considerable reassertion of managerial authority over operational matters, bargaining has continued over pay and other terms and conditions of employment although, as we have seen, the coverage is markedly lower than it used to be. Even here, however, there have been examples on pay of 'take it or leave it offers', or the unilateral imposition by management of its pay offer even where it has not been acceptable to the unions. However arrived at, the settlements have usually been above the rate of inflation (although less so in the 1990s than in the 1980s), thus facilitating acceptance. Also, through the growth of performance-related pay (PRP) schemes, which is discussed below, some managements have sought to negotiate the minimum general increase possible and reserve the maximum discretion for itself through 'merit' awards. Indeed, many have ended general increases altogether.

Involvement, consultation and participation

There is a long history of attempts by unions to increase worker participation in industry, although unions' prime concern has always been with collective bargaining. During the Second World War, and in the years immediately afterwards, participation primarily took the form at workplace level of the widespread establishment of joint consultative committees. Later some degree of disillusionment set in with joint consultation (McCarthy, 1966) and, with the growth in the number and power of shop stewards, there was a considerable expansion, in particular in engineering, in the scope of workplace collective bargaining (albeit on a largely informal basis). The development of productivity bargaining in the 1960s added a degree of formality to this process. In the 1970s, spurred by Britain's membership of the EC and the need to take a view of the EC's draft 5th Directive with its proposals for worker members on boards of directors, as well as by trade union realisation that the extended scope of collective bargaining did not touch the major strategic decisions taken by companies, there was the demand for employee representatives on boards of directors, a process culminating in the Bullock Committee Report (1977) and the subsequent Government White Paper on Industrial Democracy (Cmnd. 7231) (1978), and with limited experiments in the iron and steel industry and the Post Office. The then Labour Government's White Paper proposed that under certain circumstances there should be employee directors on company boards. However, legislation was not enacted before the 1979 election and, after the advent of Conservative Governments, and with the changed balance of power between employers and unions, any move in this direction came to an abrupt halt. The Conservative Government's view has been that such matters should be left to industry and that it would be wrong to seek to impose any statutory requirements (a view it has pressed within the EU as well as at home). The only concession made was the inclusion in the 1980 Employment Act of a requirement for companies to say in their annual reports what they had done, if anything, in this area. The government view has been strongly supported by most employers and their organisations.

Employers have, however, not been against greater communication, involvement, consultation and participation. On the contrary, many employers have claimed to be pursuing these matters with great vigour. Their objectives, their methods and their interpretation of the terms have, however, been very different from those of the unions. After the managerial dominance of the early 1980s, it became fashionable for some companies to espouse the cause of better communications and greater involvement. According to Purcell and Sisson (1983), there was a growing realisation that management dominance was not enough to meet current and future competition, and what was required was a workforce committed to the company's objectives. To this end many companies have espoused a wide variety of measures to communicate with and involve their workforce on an individual basis. Such measures have included direct communication by letter to workers at their homes or in their pay packets, briefing groups, attitude surveys and quality circles. On one interpretation, these are all means of by-passing union channels and the position and standing of shop stewards. What distinguishes all these methods is, first, that they are based on individualisation and not on a collective approach and second, as a consequence, they are entirely unitary, as opposed to pluralistic, in their purpose. They are aimed at enlisting employee opinion and behaviour behind management's objectives and not at incorporating the influence of employees' organisations in negotiated decisions. This has sometimes been called the 'consensual' rather than the 'adversarial' approach. Its unitary and individualistic nature is very apparent from a CBI statement on employee involvement, published in 1988, which is reproduced in full below. The CBI believes that employee involvement:

- is a range of processes designed to engage the support, understanding and optimum contribution of all employees in an organisation and their commitment to its objectives;
- assists an organisation to give the best possible service to customers and clients in the most cost-effective way;
- entails providing employees with the opportunity to influence and where appropriate take part in decision-making on matters which affect them;
- is an intrinsic part of good management practice and is therefore not confined to relationships with employee representatives;
- can only be developed voluntarily in ways suited to the activities, structure and history of an organisation.

Employment involvement promotes business success by:

- fostering trust and a shared commitment to an organisation's objectives;
- demonstrating respect for individual employees and drawing on the full range of their abilities;
- enabling employees to derive the maximum possible job satisfaction.

It is the responsibility of management to generate effective employee involvement through the systems and techniques at their disposal. These may include:

- systematic two-way communication on all company matters (within the limits of commercial confidence);
- regular consultation;
- problem-solving groups;
- decision-making at the lowest practicable level of authority;
- training for key communicators;
- financial participation;
- harmonisation of terms and conditions of employment;
- seeking individual contributions aimed at achieving continuous improvement in the organisation.

As already stated, the approach is individualistic and unitary, and some employers would regard their involvement policies as having failed if employees still attached importance to collective action through trade unions.

However, a more balanced approach is the Code of the Institute of Personnel Management and the Involvement and Participation Association on *Employee Involvement and Participation in the UK* (1990). The issue of involvement, participation and consultation is considered further in Chapter 9.

Flexibility

The concept and model of the flexible firm, which was first put forward by John Atkinson (1984) of the Institute of Manpower Studies (IMS), aroused considerable interest, although its relevance was as a framework of tendencies rather than as a practical description to what was found frequently on the ground. The flexible firm was said to consist of three groups of workers: first, the core workers who conduct key activities; as the nature of operations of the firm changes, they have to accept changes in their jobs through functional flexibility; they have good pay and conditions and relative security, as long as they are flexible; the firm invests much in their training and development. Second, there are the peripheral workers who have less critical activities and more routine functions to perform; they are hired on contracts which permit easy adjustment to their numbers as demand changes. Third, there are the external workers who are not employees at all: they represent activities from which the firm has distanced itself through sub-contracting (the provision of contracts of service instead of contracts of employment). The model of the flexible firm thus envisages these three groups of workers: core, peripheral and external. Flexibility takes the form of numerical flexibility, functional flexibility and distancing. A fourth flexibility – that of remuneration – may be added to the list, and is discussed later in the chapter.

Numerical flexibility, according to the IMS, takes four major forms; the use of more temporary workers, the use of more part-timers, the greater use of overtime and more flexibility in working time (for example, annual hours contracts and a growth in shift-working).

Functional flexibility, which was said to apply mainly in manufacturing industry, has taken three major forms: first, maintenance jobs are being expanded horizontally into related trades and give rise to so-called multi-skilled maintenance craftsmen: second, process and operator jobs are being similarly expanded to provide greater mobility between jobs at similar skill levels: third, there is vertical flexibility across group boundaries, such as operators engaging in quality control and in minor maintenance work. Distancing, according to Atkinson and Meager (1986), is associated 'with a wish to concentrate corporate resources in areas of comparative advantage, to find cheaper ways of undertaking non-core activities, to shift the burden of risk and uncertainty elsewhere and to reduce (or contain) formal headcount and wage bill'.

The concept of 'the flexible firm' has been much discussed and would appear to have been widely accepted in many management circles as the way ahead in times of rapid economic and technological change. It has, however, been strongly attacked by Anna Pollert (1987), who argued that managerial concern for flexibility was not new: for example, it was a major element in productivity bargaining in the 1960s and it was extensively analysed in dual labour market theory. What was new was the model's transformation of segmentation as a process into a deliberate management strategy for large firms, and this was not supported by the evidence. Insofar as there has been an expansion of insecure and irregular work, this can be explained by sectoral shifts in the structure of employment – in particular the growth of the service sector – and by cost-cutting measures. There was also little evidence of widespread development towards functional flexibility (Cross, 1988) or of employment security for a core labour force. Indeed, definitions of core and periphery employees were shifting and unsatisfactory. Pollert further argued that the model was a mixture of description, prescription and prediction, a picture of a radical break from the past was created and projected into the future as an inevitable trend. The model concentrated on labour flexibility as a panacea. 'The probability that changes in labour arrangements are the result of far wider concerns with production organisation, marketing and industrial relations was not considered. The pre-occupation with decentralisation trivialises the problems of coordination and control.' Moreover, the model neglected possible counter-productive effects of flexibility, such as lack of commitment by the peripheral labour force, and diverted attention from the need for training. Studies by McGregor and Sproull (1991), and Hunter and MacInnes (1991) showed that only a small minority of employers used non-standard labour (for example, part-timers and temporary workers) as a result of strategic considerations based on the concept of the flexible firm with its core-periphery design. The main reasons cited by employers for recruiting part-timers and temporary workers were found to be the traditional ones: to cater for tasks requiring only limited time inputs; to match staffing levels to variations in the demand for the product or service; and to take advantage of the preference for part-time work among some groups in the labour force.

Indeed, the model of the flexible firm has been questioned in further work by the IMS itself. Thus Atkinson and Meager (1986), in a major study for the National Economic Development Office (NEDO) and the DE of 72 large firms chosen at random in engineering, food and drink manufacturing, retail distribution and financial services, showed that while there had been widespread changes in work practice and greater flexibility, management interest (particularly in the service sector) was more marked in deploying cheap peripheral labour, rather than changing the employment culture at the core. 'The outcome was more likely to be marginal, *ad hoc*, and tentative, rather than a purposeful and strategic thrust to achieve flexibility; short-term cost saving, rather than long-term development, dominated management thinking, save where substantial new investment was involved.' Rather than a universal adoption, changed working practices broadly reflected the different business strategies which were emerging in the four sectors. Thus part-time working was mainly of significance in the service sector, temporary working and functional flexibility were more important in manufacturing, and flexible working was more an aspiration than a reality save among part-time workers. The two main factors underlying the growth of service sector part-time working were to match manning levels to changing consumer patterns and the reduction of labour costs. While the concept of the flexible firm may be highly questionable, there is no doubt that employers' search for greater flexibility in the employment and use of labour has been one of the important features of the 1980s and 1990s. As Sisson (1994) says, 'the impression given is that flexibility is everything and the desired state is that management can do and should be able to do anything it likes' (p. 13).

Levels and methods of remuneration

The move in the level of pay determination from industry level to enterprise level, and in some cases within enterprises to lower levels such as divisions and establishments has already been discussed. It is a move which had Conservative Government support on the doctrinal grounds that the labour market needs to be more flexible in order to take advantage of different supply and demand situations in different parts of the country, of different financial situations in different firms and in order to reward individuals on grounds of performance (Clarke, 1987). As well as exhorting the private sector, Conservative Governments sought to introduce greater flexibility in public sector payment systems.

Of the main developments in levels and methods of remuneration, the first has been the greater linking of pay to performance or, if one prefers, the greater 'individualisation' of pay. There is, of course, nothing new in this as far as managers in the private sector are concerned. What is new is, first, its spread to the public sector: for example, to civil servants, university lecturers and NHS managers; second, in the private sector, its spread downwards from managerial levels to other white-collar workers, including clerical and in some cases to blue-collar workers. In addition, the size of the 'merit' element in pay has been growing: indeed, increasingly some companies have announced that there will be no general pay increases at all (regardless of the rise in retail prices), and that all increases would be based only on merit (for example, the clearing banks). On the other hand, there are signs that some companies which have a long record of paying for individual performance have moved on to rewarding groups and teams and even to company-wide bonuses. PRP is further discussed in Chapter 12.

Second, there has been a growth of profit-sharing and employee share ownership schemes, stimulated in part by favourable tax legislation, but above all by a belief that such measures would increase commitment and, in some cases, increase incentive. Companies with long experience of profit-sharing do not exaggerate the incentive effect, but play up the significance of profit-sharing for developing a sense of involvement. They also emphasise the importance of its being an appreciable size every year, and that means less profit for the shareholders.

Third, there have been widening pay differentials, as shown in Chapter 10. Numerous surveys also show that managerial pay has gone up much faster than that of other employees, while the pay of top executives (not to mention their share options) has gone up even faster.

Fourth, there have been changes in pay structures, apart from the widening of differentials. Thus there has been a continuing simplification of pay structures, in particular fewer grades in order to achieve greater flexibility and to reduce job demarcations and a growth in banding. Along with the simplification of pay structures, there have been increasing doubts in some of the more sophisticated companies about traditional job evaluation. For one thing, it has been felt that job descriptions could inhibit flexibility and for another, that there was a trend towards paying people for what they could do and how they did it, rather than for what they did in a specific job at a specific point of time. Finally, there were a number of examples of integrated pay structures: that is to say, of manual and white-collar jobs (for example, in Midland Bank, Pilkington and a number of American and Japanese companies). The main reasons for this appeared to be a desire to encourage team-working and a feeling that everyone should be treated on the same basis, and to acknowledge the increased blurring of boundaries between blue-collar and white-collar jobs with the development of new technology. An added advantage from management's viewpoint related to the avoidance of equal pay cases, and this was certainly the major factor in Midland Bank's adoption of an integrated structure.

Finally, there has been a growth of regional allowances and other pay settlements to reflect local needs and skill shortages. In the late 1980s the London clearing banks startled everyone – not least the unions – with a massive increase in their London allowances (for Inner London from £1750 p.a. to £3000 p.a.) and with the introduction of a 'Roseland Allowance' of £750 for the rest of South-East England. It was, of course, a reflection of the shortage of labour in London and the South East at that time. Needless to say, their action was soon followed by many other organisations, including insurance companies and building societies. During the early 1990s, with the second major post-war recession which led to high unemployment hitting London and the South-East, many London allowances were frozen. Indeed in the Civil Service they were abolished for new entrants and replaced by a more flexible local discretionary allowance.

Conclusion

During the 1980s and 1990s management, operating in an environment of increased competition in product markets and greatly reduced bargaining power on the part of the unions, has been able to take the initiative in industrial relations. It has sought greater control over the work process and has in many areas asserted managerial authority. It has also sought to be more cost effective (Brewster and Connock, 1985). Three major developments are apparent. First, there is the adoption by management of (in many cases) a more individualist approach to its workforce and less of a collective approach, as shown for example by the growth of PRP, new measures for increased direct communications with employees, and attempts to secure greater involvement. A number of personnel directors we interviewed put considerable stress on individualisation, and believed that they were moving with the spirit of the times: it is not just that unions are weaker. There have also been drives for greater flexibility, new forms of employment contract and moves towards HRM. Indeed, many of these measures could be considered as part of HRM.

The second major development, stressed by all the managers and management representatives we interviewed, is management's greater freedom to launch initiatives and to succeed in carrying them through. It seemed to be irrelevant whether the company concerned was unionised or not. Thus one employers' association told us that throughout the 1980s there had been much more emphasis on productivity, starting with an industry-wide enabling agreement which became more specific so that each year there had been further developments. As the unions absorbed changes, so more were easier to make. There are now, it was claimed, comprehensive clauses in agreements which bear comparison with any other industry. This association had adopted an evolutionary or step-by-step approach together with the unions, which was in contrast to that of another association in an allied industry which had successfully adopted a 'big-bang' approach through confrontation and by seeking to break the unions. The main point made by the first association was that, in the 1980s and 1990s, management got where it wanted to in the end, virtually irrespective of the method chosen. Generally management believes that its success is due in no small part to a better understanding by employees and unions of the need to be competitive. Others, including one eminent union general secretary and one senior personnel manager, attributed it, in part, to the fear of employees as a consequence of greater insecurity at all levels. Thus another senior personnel manager (in a company with a long history of paternalism) stressed that redundancies had been a cultural shock, particularly for managers. They thought they had a job for life. Morale had suffered, and loyalty and trust based on 20–30 years' service was replaced by a short-term view.

The third development in some of the companies we interviewed is that industrial relations have been marginalised, as have those who specialise in fire-fighting, and so have many trade union officials. Industrial relations have ceased to be, if they ever were, a preoccupation of top management. It is one part of the implementation of corporate strategy and policy on products, pricing, investment and technology.

These developments and their implementation have not been achieved by large-scale de-recognition of unions or by destroying existing collective bargaining machinery, although the extent of recognition and those covered by collective bargaining has been markedly reduced, recognition in greenfield sites has become difficult and collective bargaining has become more decentralised and its scope more limited. Whether the changes amount to a permanent new form of industrial relations is as yet uncertain, and is considered further in Chapter 12. While the initiative has been very much with management and managers have been able to get what they want in ways which would not have been possible in the 1970s, much of it has been done with the agreement (or, at least, the acquiescence) of the unions and employees. The fact that unions have been weaker is no reason for supposing they have been of no account at all. A number of major companies have told us that they could not have achieved what they have so smoothly and quickly without the agreement and cooperation of their unions. This view is supported by some employer evidence to the House of Commons Select Committee on Employment (Taylor, 1994).

Our evidence supports the positive contribution of the unions in a number of cases, who have sometimes secured considerable increases in pay or conditions in exchange for what they have agreed to. Interesting examples where job security has been agreed in exchange for increased flexibility have included Rover, Blue Circle and United Distillers. The balance of power has moved decisively towards management, but the unions are still a part of the scene even if much reduced in influence mainly in large organisations, privatised companies and the public sector.

CHAPTER 7

Government as employer and quasi-employer

Introduction

The government has a direct responsibility for the pay of over 500 000 civil servants, some 200 000 members of HM Forces and for over 1 million employees in the NHS. With the removal of negotiating rights of school teachers by the Remuneration of Teachers Act 1987, it is also directly responsible for the pay of nearly 500 000 teachers. In addition, the government has an indirect, but powerful, influence on the pay of some 2 million other local authority employees through its control over a large part of local authority finance. Finally, it has influence over the pay of employees in the public corporations, the largest of which is the Post Office, again because of the large degree of government control over their finances. The size of the public sector, as Table 7.1 shows, is still considerable despite the Conservative Governments' cutbacks in the civil service, the pressure on the NHS and local authorities to contract out services and the privatisation of most of the public corporations.

In considering the public sector it is important in the first instance to distinguish between the public service sector, in particular the civil service, the NHS and local authorities (LAs), where for the most part there is no competitive market for their services and hence no prices (although with contracting-out, market-testing and the internal NHS market, this is no longer quite true), and nationalised industries where there are commercial markets for their products and a price mechanism exists. Largely because of this, comparability has for long played a major part in determining public service sector pay (S. Kessler, 1983). In the case of the non-industrial civil service, as we shall see, the role of comparability was formalised and institutionalised, whereas in the NHS and LAs it was more informal but almost equally as important. In two cases the comparability link has been by means of indexation: the police,

TABLE 7.1   Public sector employment, 1979–96

	Mid-year (000s)		Change	
	1979	*1996*	*(000s)*	*%*
Central government				
HM Forces	314	221	−93	−29.6
NHS	1 152	90*	−1 062	NA
Other	921	676	−245	−26.6
Total	2387	987	−1400	−58.7
Local authorities				
Education	1 539	1 183 †	−356	−23.1
Health and social services	344	408	+64	+18.6
Construction	156	79	−77	−49.3
Police and civilians	176	207	+31	+17.6
Other	782	774	−- 8	−1.0
Total	2 997	2651	−346	−11.5
Public corporations				
Nationalised industries	1 849	335	−1 514	−81.9
NHS Trusts	–	1 102	–	–
Other	216	75	−141	−65.3
Total	2 065	1 512	−553	−26.8
Total public sector	7 449	5 150	−2299	−30.9
(of which civil servants)	738	534	−204	−27.6
Total workforce in employment	25 393	25 906		
Public sector as percentage of the workforce in Employment	29	20		

Source: Based on 'Employment in the Public and Private Sectors', *Economic Trends*, March 1997.

* Overwhelmingly NHS staff are now employed by NHS Trusts. Because of re-classification the changes above must be treated with caution.

† Polytechnics, higher education establishments, grant maintained schools, further education and sixth form colleges are excluded, now being classified as part of the private sector.

whose pay was linked to the average underlying increase in whole economy earnings as a result of the Edmund Davies Committee of Inquiry (1978); and the firefighters, whose pay was linked to the upper quartile of male manual earnings as part of the settlement of their strike in the winter of 1977/8. Such indexation has led the police and fire service to obtain pay increases which were well in excess of the public service sector generally (see Chapter 10), but in the case of the police the formula was revised in 1994 to the median increase in private sector non-manual earnings.

Another important exception is that certain groups have had their pay determined by Pay Review Bodies: for example, the armed forces, doctors and dentists, senior civil servants, the judiciary and, more recently, nurses and professions allied to medicine, and teachers. Well over 1 million staff are covered by the Review Bodies. Among factors playing a major part in the Review Bodies' deliberations has been comparability, and as a consequence these groups have tended to fare better during the 1980s and 1990s than have other public service sector employees.

One final difference within the public service that it is important to note is that whereas the civil service and the NHS depend virtually entirely on government finance, LAs depend only in part (although by far the major part) on central government, and therefore they have had for much of the period a slightly greater degree of flexibility in determining pay.

The civil service

In 1979 employment in the civil service was over 700 000, of whom some 560 000 were non-industrial civil servants. The traditional view of government as an employer was that it should be a 'good' employer. This did not mean high pay, but pay determined by the principle of 'fair comparability'. This was judged by a Royal Commission (Priestley, 1955) as fair to the taxpayer and fair to civil servants. The Priestley Commission's recommendations were accepted and the system for determining fair comparability was institutionalised and improved by the establishment in 1956 of then Civil Service Pay Research Unit. The first Thatcher Government speedily disclaimed the principle of fair comparability, arguing instead that pay should be determined by 'ability to pay', which it determined itself by setting its own cash limits.

For 1981 and for subsequent years up to 1986, the government announced a specific pay 'factor' or 'assumption' contained within the overall cash limits. In each of these years, pay increases exceeded the pay factor but not by very much, and in effect the difference had to be made good by staff economies or declines in the quality of services. From 1986/7, however, the central pay assumption was replaced by decentralised departmental running cost budgets.

Access to arbitration was requested by the civil service unions in 1984/5 and 1985/6, but was refused by the government. Apart from strict control over pay levels, the government sought greater flexibility in pay. Thus, during 1985 a merit pay system was introduced for senior officials and there was the introduction of Special Pay Additions which consisted of temporary cash additions for a specified period – usually two to three years – to meet acute recruitment and retention difficulties in respect of particular skills and/or localities.

The result was that the pay of civil servants experienced a prolonged relative decline through most of the 1980s. The government withstood lengthy and costly industrial action in 1981, which the civil service unions took in response to a low pay offer and to the abolition of 'fair comparability'. The eventual settlement included the setting-up of an independent committee to make recommendations on the principles of future pay determination (Megaw, 1982). The committee, although criticising comparability as it had operated in the past, argued that it could not be ignored and recommended a modified form of comparability, whereby bargaining would take place within the inter-quartile range of pay increases for comparable employees in the private sector. To ascertain this, an annual survey should be conducted into private sector increases, while every four years there should be a survey into the pay levels of comparable private sector employees. Within these limits civil service pay should be determined by the need 'to recruit, retain and motivate'. It was not, however, until 1987 that the first civil service agreement – with the then Institute of Professional Civil Servants (IPCS) – was concluded, embodying the Megaw principles. Apart from pay levels, the agreement included features which reflected the government's desire to increase pay flexibility, in particular the introduction of 'merit' increments (I. Kessler, 1990). This agreement with the IPCS was soon followed by similar agreements with the other civil service unions, namely the Inland Revenue Staff Federation (IRSF), the Civil and Public Services Association (CPSA) and the National Union of Civil and Public Servants (NUCPS). So the wheel had turned almost full circle, but in the meantime great damage had been done to the morale and to the relative pay of the civil service. It could be argued that the then government had come to recognise, mainly under the pressure of the Megaw Report and changes in the labour market, that comparability was inevitably the core of pay determination in the civil service, though in a form more suited to the 1980s and 1990s than that adopted after the Priestley Report 30 years earlier. The unions took some time to accept merit pay and local additions as part of the package until the IPCS broke the log jam. In negotiations with strong unions for its own employees the government changed its position to a marked degree by seemingly accepting the restoration of comparability, albeit topped up with individual and market payments. The agreements made in 1987 and 1988 seemed to indicate 'new realism' on the part of the government and the civil service unions. However, the rapid development in the early

1990s of semi-autonomous civil service agencies (discussed on the following pages), put an entirely different light on the determination of civil service pay.

In the non-pay area the government sought without success to eliminate index-linked pensions (Scott, 1981). It adopted a more robust managerial style. Thus in 1979, Sir Derek (now Lord) Rayner, from Marks & Spencer, was appointed to advise the Prime Minister on efficiency and he established a small Efficiency Unit which was continued under his successor, Sir Robin Ibbs from ICI. According to one study (Blackwell and Lloyd, 1989) 'attention was particularly focussed on the specification and achievement of clear objectives by managers and the need for managers to give much greater weight to value for money and cost considerations' (pp. 90–1). Further, 'this undoubtedly provided a major impetus to the development of the new managerialism, in particular by emphasising the role of line managers and demonstrating how responsibilities could be delegated and decentralised' (p. 91).

In addition, the government reduced the consultative role of the unions, reduced the time off allowed and other facilities for union lay representatives and terminated unilateral access to arbitration. Whereas the civil service Staff Handbook used to state that the government welcomed trade union membership, it ceased to do so: indeed, there is no longer a staff handbook. But the check-off has been maintained and it is the means by which most civil servants pay their union contributions. It survived the major strike in 1981, but the then government position became that the check-off was likely to be withdrawn where there was industrial action, and that was carried out in the case of the POA. However, the continuation of the check-off, and indeed recognition, is now a matter for agencies and departments.

The removal of the right to trade union membership at GCHQ Cheltenham in 1984, and the eventual dismissal of those who refused to renounce their membership, was a *cause célèbre* of the 1980s and was perhaps symbolic of the government's basic attitude to unions. The government's argument was that in the interests of national security it could not afford to have its communications network subject to possible industrial action. The civil service unions, in order to meet this argument and prevent de-recognition and the banning of union membership, offered a no-industrial action agreement which was accepted by Sir Robert Armstrong, the head of the civil service. He was, however, overruled by the Prime Minister. GCHQ civil servants were offered £1000 each if they relinquished union membership and the Conservative Government set up a staff association in lieu of unions. The staff association was given sole bargaining rights, although the Certification Officer subsequently ruled in 1992 that it was not an organisation independent of the employer, and this ruling was upheld by the Court of Appeal.

In protest at the government's action there was a well-supported one-day strike called throughout the civil service. The unions also took the government through the courts, but the House of Lords eventually ruled that the government's action was protected because it was allegedly taken on grounds of national security. The unions also took the issue to various international bodies, including the International Labour Organisation (ILO), which condemned the government's action as incompatible with the ILO's convention on freedom of association, of which the UK government was a signatory; all to no avail. However, one leading union participant in these events believed that in some ways they represented a major victory for the unions. 'It brought general opprobrium on the government, especially in international circles, and there was less possibility of the government's approach being extended to other civil servants.' One of the first acts of the new Labour Government in 1997 was to remove the ban on trade unionism at GCHQ.

Finally, over the years the number of civil servants was substantially reduced. In 1980, the Government announced that it would seek to reduce manpower by some 100000 by April 1984. This target was in fact exceeded, and a new target of a further reduction of 6 per cent by 1988 was announced. The reduction has mainly been in industrial civil servants and achieved by contracting out (for example, there used to be some 10000 cleaners and now there are only a few hundred); and by privatisation, (for example, the sale of the Royal Ordnance factories). Privatisation, market-testing and contracting-out have been growing markedly in the 1990s. Because pay increases are meant to be self-financing, this will also put further pressure on civil service numbers.

The Conservative Government following the Ibbs Committee Report (Ibbs, 1988), decided to devolve a large number of civil service functions, and the staff who provided them, to semi-autonomous agencies. It was envisaged that these agencies would behave in a more business-like manner. Each would have a chief executive, and would be given more freedom to manage from day to day in the style of the private sector, although still being responsible to ministers. Performance targets would be set and they would have a degree of freedom in determining their own establishments and in determining levels of pay and pay systems.

By the summer of 1990, 33 agencies employing 80000 people had been launched but by 1993, the Government's review of agencies (Next Steps Agencies in Government, 1993) reported that there were 92 agencies employing 60 per cent of the civil service. These included some very large organisations such as the Inland Revenue, Customs and Excise, the Employment Service, the Benefits Agency and HM Prison Service, as well as some very small ones. Indeed, agencies and announced candidates for agencies in the home civil service represented 78 per cent of the total. Most significantly, the Government announced the delegation of pay determination so that from April 1994 half of all civil servants were covered by delegated pay agreements and by April 1995 two-thirds were covered. By 1996 there was 100 per cent delegation of pay determination (with the exception of 3500 senior civil servants – Grade 5 and above – who have individual contracts of employment). National pay agreements ceased to exist. However, agencies in determining their pay and pay structures are operating within overall limits set by the Treasury and within the requirements of Treasury approval. For example, if an agency wanted to maintain incremental salary scales this would not be permitted as Conservative Government policy was for all staff to be on PRP. It was in a White Paper (1994) that further delegation to departments was announced. Departments will decide for themselves what efficiency measures they want to introduce, how many officials they need, and at what level. Each agency has a parent department and these departments are responsible for supervising the delegated arrangements using the rules set out for their guidance by the Treasury. The framework within which everyone operates is at a very high level, and there is considerable freedom within it. Delegation includes discretion for managers to use local rates of pay within their pay bill total, provided that they are within the permitted range.

The speed with which pay has been delegated is quite remarkable. The implications for staff and the civil service unions are very considerable indeed. The main change is to separate pay agreements for each department and agency. Most large agencies now have their own pay structures and their own procedural agreements.

Local government

Local government employs nearly 2.5 million workers. Apart from the police, firefighters and nearly half a million teachers, there are some 700 0000 manual workers and some 600 000 white collar workers in administrative, professional, technical and clerical (APT&C) grades. Up to the late 1960s industrial relations in local government, like the rest of the public service sector, were peaceful, and pay and conditions were determined nationally. A number of factors contributed to a changed climate of industrial relations, including the introduction of bonus schemes for manual workers following Report No. 29 of the NBPI (1967a); the effects of incomes policy; the growth of unionisation and the policy of some of the unions to encourage decentralisation and the increase in the number of shop stewards; and the increasing formalisation of industrial relations at local level.

LAs account for over one-third of total public expenditure. Given this level of expenditure, it was inevitable that a government committed to reducing public expenditure and to controlling inflation would seek to exert considerable pressure on, and control over, local government. This took three main forms (I. Kessler, 1989). First, there was an emphasis on reducing LA manpower. Second, there was an emphasis on the need for LA services to be 'efficient' and 'to provide value for money'. The pressure and eventually the statutory obligation to put out to tender many LA services were part of this process, as well as being ideologically in tune with the then government's philosophy. Third, and most fundamentally, there were major changes in the financial framework within which LAs had to operate. Central government exerted an increasingly tight control over LA expenditure by such means as cash limits, targets, penalties and charge-capping.

This culminated in the introduction of the poll tax or community charge in 1990 in England and Wales, it having been introduced a year earlier in Scotland. As a result of the poll tax and the introduction of the uniform business rate, some three-quarters of LA income was put under the direct control of central government. With the 1991 Budget and its large subsidy to reduce the poll tax, paid for by an increase in VAT, the proportion controlled by central government became even greater. Indeed, with the power to charge-cap, it could be argued that central government has virtually 100 per cent control over LA income and expenditure. The subsequent change from poll tax to council tax made no real change to this situation.

Such financial control obviously gave central government major influence over LA pay and terms and conditions of service, and indeed for most of the 1980s LA pay – both manual and white-collar – fell significantly behind that of the private sector (see Chapter 10). In 1978/9, LA manual workers' industrial action was a much publicised feature of the so-called Winter of Discontent. They were one of the first references to the Clegg Standing Commission on Pay Comparability, established in April 1979 to deal with the problem of public service sector pay. LA manual workers got a significant, but not exceptional, pay award – the award being nowhere near what the unions had claimed – but in subsequent pay rounds they slipped behind again. Approximately two-thirds of LA manual workers are part-time women, employed mainly in the two largest LA services – education and social services – as school meals workers and cleaners and as home helps and care assistants. The remainder are mainly full-time male workers employed in refuse collecting and disposal, roadworks, leisure, parks and housing. In 1986, the LAs and unions jointly undertook a major job evaluation exercise which resulted in 1987 in a new six-grade structure. Particular weight was given in this exercise to the question of equal pay for equal value, and it resulted in a substantial change in the rank order of jobs: in particular home helps and care assistants scored highly relative to, for example, the refuse collectors (Lodge, 1987).

White-collar APT&C workers had well under a quarter of their number employed part-time and the range of occupations covered was widespread, ranging from clerical and secretarial staff to social workers and other professional workers such as surveyors, architects, accountants and lawyers. Six unified APT&C scales plus senior officer and principal officer scales ranged across a 49 point 'spinal column'. While the national manual agreement allocated each occupational group to a grade, the white-collar agreement allowed LAs to adapt most job requirements to fit the salary scale they wished to pay. At the beginning of the 1980s, APT&C grades benefited from an 'in-house' comparability exercise which they preferred to conduct for themselves, rather than be referred to the Clegg Commission. In subsequent years, like their manual counterparts, their pay increases fell below those in the private sector.

Financial constraints by central government on local government in the 1980s and 1990s meant not only a fall in relative pay, but constant pressure for increased efficiency and reductions in the size of the labour force. Employers had in addition sought greater flexibility. While the employers achieved significant changes, on the whole peacefully, NALGO scored a major victory in 1989 when by selective industrial action it succeeded in raising the employers' pay offer from 6 per cent to 8.8 per cent and the complete removal of the conditions which had been attached to the pay offer, namely:

(a) provision for PRP, including the ability to withhold increments if performance was not satisfactory;
(b) the deletion of some grades from the pay scale, leaving them to individual authorities' discretion;
(c) grading decision appeals to terminate at local level (that is to say, there would be no appeal to regional or national level);
(d) authorities would be allowed to negotiate local variations from the national agreement on working time and weekend pay.

Nevertheless, despite NALGO's victory, there seemed little doubt that the employers would continue their search for greater flexibility. Thus at the end of the 1980s the growing uncompetitiveness of LA salaries at the top end led to greatly enhanced salaries and remuneration packages, often including the provision of a car and generous resettlement packages. In London and the South-East salaries were also proving uncompetitive at lower-levels and enhancement and up-grading were becoming common. The biggest step to cope with this problem and the consequent shortage of labour was taken by Kent County Council in 1989, when it withdrew from the national APT&C agreement in order to pay significantly higher salaries because of its recruitment and retention difficulties. However, so far its withdrawal has only been followed by Buckinghamshire and Surrey and a small number of mainly district councils. The recession in the early 1990s eased the labour market pressures on recruitment and retention.

The commitment of local government employers to a national framework for industrial relations, while seeking substantial reform was demonstrated by their policy document, *Single Status Employment* (Local Government Management Board, 1994). A number of basic considerations underpinned this review, including that most local authorities continue to support a nationally negotiated framework; that the national framework must be flexible enough to cope with the different needs of a wide range of authorities; that recent and forthcoming developments combine to present an opportunity for significant reform of national machinery, procedures and agreements; and that change should be negotiated with the unions and not imposed. Among the ideas pursued through negotiation were the promoting of single status; developing common core conditions of service; distinguishing mandatory core provisions in national agreements from voluntary non-core provisions enabling authorities to adopt nationally negotiated conditions to a greater or lesser degree, but still staying within the national agreement; merging APT&C, manual workers and craft-negotiating bodies (single table bargaining); adopting a common pay review date for all of the merged groups; and developing a common pay spine for all of the merged groups.

A new monumental Local Government Agreement was signed in July 1997 on the above matters, including single status, the merging of blue-collar and APT&C negotiations, a single pay spine and a standard 37-hour week from 1 April 1999. The three former employer associations have merged into one – the Local Government Association – and on the new negotiating body, UNISON has 31 seats, the General, Municipal and Boilermakers' Union (GMB) 16 and the TGWU 11. Interestingly, the new procedural agreement provides for unilateral arbitration (Industrial Relations Services, *Employment Trends*, 639, September 1997).

The unions supported the main objectives while the employers believed that their agenda was the right way forward to find a sustainable balance between maintaining a relevant nationally negotiated framework and sufficient local flexibility .

It was a constant feature of the period that a considerable proportion of local authorities was under Labour control. In addition, many Conservative authorities were unenthusiastic, if not openly hostile, to the then government's policy towards local government. As a consequence, Conservative Governments had not been able to further their objectives through the employers' side in negotiations. This was a major reason why they relied heavily on direct control of local government income and expenditure and on ever-increasing pressure for services to be put out to tender and to be contracted out.

Teachers

Teachers' pay in the 1980s had been subject to government constraints, as had most of the public sector, and dissatisfaction was evident for much of the period. Pay had fallen behind in the second half of the 1970s and teachers were one of the references to the Clegg Comparabilities Commission. The Clegg Report (1980) provided a substantial increase ranging from 17 per cent to 24 per cent, although the teachers' unions were disappointed that the award did not completely restore the Houghton Committee (1974) relativities. The 1980 pay negotiations ended in a failure to agree and in a substantial arbitration award of nearly 14 per cent. In 1982 there was again a failure to agree and the unions 'withdrew goodwill' in order to force a reference to arbitration. (The previous agreement, whereby reference to arbitration could be made unilaterally by either side, had been changed to a reference only by the agreement of both sides.) In 1984 there was again a failure to agree, with the unions asking for arbitration and the employers refusing. In order to obtain arbitration selective industrial action followed, including withdrawal from lunchtime supervision and selective one-day and then three-day strikes by the NUT. Finally, the employers conceded a reference to arbitration, although the eventual award of 5.1 per cent was a great disappointment to the unions.

It was 1985, however, that saw the most prolonged industrial action and the most bitter dispute. The unions' claim was for 12.5 per cent and a common pay scale: the original management offer was 4 per cent. There followed prolonged industrial action by the NUT, starting with the withdrawal of goodwill and accelerating to extensive selective three-day strikes. The NUT's action was followed by the NAS/UWT and eventually even by the Assistant Masters' and Mistresses' Association (AMMA). Action continued throughout 1985 and into 1986 (Seifert, 1989) when ACAS eventually got the agreement of the unions and employers to the establishment of an Independent Panel, headed by Sir John Wood, Chairman of the CAC. The terms of reference were:

> To guide, advise and assist as a matter of urgency, the management and teachers to provisional agreements on the pay, structure and career progression of the teaching profession and any other related matters, e.g. conditions of service and procedures for negotiation, which either party may wish to bring forward for discussion and negotiation.

It was agreed to set up four working parties, each chaired by a member of the Independent Panel, covering pay and structure; duties; appraisal; and future negotiating machinery. Discussions were complex and lengthy but, at a four-day residential negotiating session at Coventry at the end of July 1986, the Terms of Agreement was signed by the employers and five of the six teaching unions, the exception being the NAS/UWT who considered that the proposed top salary for the main professional grade was inadequate. Discussions continued through the working parties to try to resolve the many outstanding points of detail. A further residential negotiating session was planned for Nottingham early in November 1986 to resolve outstanding issues. Shortly before this took place – on 30 October 1986 – the Secretary of State announced government measures for ending the dispute: increased financial resources were to be made available, the Government having previously insisted that no more money would be forthcoming. However, the Government proposed a different salary structure from that agreed by the parties in outline at Coventry, and laid down other conditions. The Government also announced its intention to introduce legislation to repeal the Remuneration of Teachers Act 1965, thus abolishing the then existing negotiating machinery – the Burnham Committee – and give the Secretary of State power to impose settlements, with the help of an advisory committee.

The negotiations at Nottingham took place against the background of this bombshell. However, after very extended negotiations, agreement was reached covering in detail pay levels, salary structure, duties and coordination of service between the employers and unions representing a majority of teachers. Efforts were made to keep the overall cost of the agreement within the limits set by the Government, but the agreed pay structure was more expensive than that proposed by the Secretary of State. He therefore indicated that he would not be prepared to provide the additional funding, and early in 1987 Parliament passed the Teachers' Pay and Conditions Act under which collective bargaining for teachers was abolished, at least up to 1990, and the agreed settlement reached by the parties under the auspices of ACAS was set aside and replaced by terms and conditions imposed by the Minister.

Pay was increased by an average of 16.4 per cent, to be achieved in two stages: January and October 1987. A basic nine-point incremental scale was introduced from £7900 to £12700, and five additional above-scale allowances of £900, £1800, £2800, £3800 and £4800. On conditions of employment, teachers' contracts were unilaterally altered by an increase of working days in the year to 195, of which 190 were to be for teaching and other duties and the other five, so-called 'Baker Days', were to be for training. Teachers also had to be available for 1265 hours a year, excluding time required for preparation, marking and so forth. Standing in for absent colleagues was also required for up to three days. Teachers, however, were no longer required to undertake mid-day supervision, unless employed under a separate contract to do so. Many of these conditions had also been included in the defunct negotiated settlement but the unions had obtained certain assurances in return (for example on class size).

It needs to be recalled that the employers' side had had since 1965 an informal concordat with the Government that it would only make offers and reach settlements with the Secretary of State's agreement. However, at the end of 1986 the employers' side had renounced that concordat. As we have seen, in the face of industrial action, they proceeded to make an agreement without the Minister's approval. The Conservative Government's response was to abolish the teachers' negotiating machinery and to take over direct control of teachers' pay, aided by an Interim Advisory Committee under Lord Chilvers. Ministers were committed to the eventual restoration of negotiating machinery and in July 1990 the Secretary of State announced that a Bill would be introduced in the next parliamentary session to establish new negotiating machinery, which would not, however, become effective before the 1992/3 pay round. The Conservative Government then had second thoughts and in April 1991 announced that teachers' pay in future would be determined by a review body; they introduced legislation to put this into effect.

Teachers' pay and conditions had also been the subject of a prolonged dispute in Scotland, but with a different outcome. In December 1984 a campaign of selective industrial action began after a refusal by the Secretary of State for Scotland to agree to a request by the teachers' unions to the establishment of an independent salary review. The request for an independent review was supported by the Scottish local authority employers, but was not agreed to by the Conservative Government until over a year later – March 1986 – when a committee of enquiry was appointed, chaired by Sir Peter Main. The report of the Main Committee (1986), which proposed a restructuring of salary scales and changes in terms and conditions of employment, provided a basis for the eventual peaceful settlement of the dispute without the removal of the bargaining rights of the Scottish teachers.

Since 1990 there have been a number of disputes between teachers and government, in particular on national testing and on the introduction of PRP. A teachers' boycott largely prevented school testing being carried out in 1993. On pay, teachers have done somewhat better under the review body than have groups which negotiate. However, a new salary structure provides for extra pay increments to be made for performance as well as for extra responsibilities. The Conservative Government had also for some time been encouraging the opting-out of schools from local authority control. From an industrial relations viewpoint this could mean the possibility of pay being determined at individual school level, or at least performance-related elements.

The National Health Service

The NHS employs over 1 million people, the main categories being doctors and dentists, nurses, paramedics, technicians, clerical and administrative, ancillary workers, and ambulance workers. The NHS is primarily funded by the Government, although the staff are not now employed by the Government but overwhelmingly by the self-governing trusts.

NHS ancillary workers, along with LA manual workers, were in the forefront of the public's perception of the 1978/9 Winter of Discontent. Their immediate pay problem was solved through the establishment of the Clegg Comparability Commission, mentioned earlier. Not only were ancillary workers referred to the Clegg Commission but so also were ambulancemen, professions allied to medicine and nurses.

The Conservative Government's view was that public sector pay should be determined on the basis of ability to pay, not on comparability, and the NHS was no exception. This led to the pay dispute of 1982, when the Government offered a pay increase of 4 per cent to ancillary and clerical staff and 6.4 per cent to nurses. Limited industrial action ensued, the unions' actions being coordinated by the TUC Health Services Committee. The dispute was lengthy. However, concern for patients prevented the calling of an all-out strike and, with the Government standing firm, the unions were defeated, although they did succeed in getting a small increase in the original offer. Throughout the dispute the Royal College of Nursing (RCN) also campaigned for a higher pay offer, but they refused to engage in industrial action. Indeed, the RCN held a ballot on whether to change its rule prohibiting industrial action, which resulted in a large vote against such a change. In January 1983 following the dispute, the Government established a Review Body for nurses and midwives and for the professions allied to medicine. This was largely a reward for the RCN not engaging in industrial action and for having pledged not to do so in the future. (However, a minority of nurses are members of unions, in particular NUPE, and the Confederation of Health Service Employees (COHSE) – now part of UNISON – which have not renounced the strike weapon: neither has the British Medical Association (BMA). Indeed the RCN changed its rules in 1995 to permit industrial action.) As a consequence, from that date, more than half of the NHS staff – doctors, nurses and the professions allied to medicine – had their pay determined through the mechanisms of the Review Bodies. The result has been that those whose pay was determined by the Review Bodies have done better than those negotiated by the Whitley Committee machinery.

A second major development in the NHS was the appointment of general managers as the chief executives of health authorities, which followed from the Griffiths Report (1983). Moreover, a system of merit pay was introduced for these general managers dependent on their performance. Such PRP had by 1990 spread to other senior managers and to those in middle-management positions. It was due to be applied to doctors, starting with hospital consultants in 1995, but the BMA strongly opposed it.

A third major development was the pursuance by the government of a policy of encouraging 'efficiency savings'. These were to accrue from the increasing drive to contract-out ancillary services, from more efficient management, improved working methods and a reduction in staff costs. In addition, from 1980 onwards, the Government refused to fund pay awards above the percentage norm for the public sector. This underfunding provided strong pressure on Health Authorities to effect savings. Moreover, in 1983 manpower targets were set for all staff, and Regional Health Authorities were asked to monitor staff numbers closely and achieve a reduction in overall staff numbers of between 0.75 and 1.0 per cent. Each year Regional Health Authorities reminded Districts what was required of them and revised targets were set at the beginning of each financial year (Mailly Dimmock and Sethi, 1989a).

Of particular significance was the Conservative Government's policy of ordering Health Authorities to put out to tender cleaning, catering and laundry services. In 1981 the Minister of State for Health wrote to Regional Local Health Authorities suggesting that they consider contracting-out their 'hotel' services. There was little response, and in 1983 a further circular was sent requiring the Health Authorities to seek bids for their cleaning, catering and laundry work. As the FWR had been abolished in 1983, private contractors were no longer obliged to pay NHS terms and conditions, although many Authorities required that they should do so. However, in 1984 the Minister wrote again to the Health Authorities instructing them not to require private contractors to abide by Whitley pay rates and terms and conditions. The Government's policy had a significant effect, not primarily because private sector tenders were always the lowest, but because in order to win the contract in-house, substantial economies in staffing often had to be made. As in central and local government, contracting-out was often applied at the expense of the lowest paid workers. The services put out to tender were mostly performed by those on the lowest rates of NHS pay. The effect of the contracting-out was to lower the rates of pay and worsen the conditions offered for the same work by the private contractors. The same workers were often employed by the contractors, who in many cases expected them to do more work with less supervision. Those who were most in need of protection because of their weakness in the labour market had their position worsened. It was not the case that these changes challenged the position of strong unions with monopoly power protecting well-paid employees. They picked out the weak for penalties. With the acknowledgement by the Conservative Government in 1993/4 that TUPE applied to contracting-out in the public sector (see Chapter 5) the ability of private contractors to cut wages and conditions became more limited.

Finally, with effect from April 1991, certain NHS hospitals were encouraged to set themselves up as self-managing trusts, with freedom to determine the pay of their own staff, with the exception of junior doctors and existing staff who were entitled to stay on Whitley terms. In the following three years trusts became virtually universal: by April 1994 trusts were providing 95 per cent of all hospital and community care. The creation of trusts as the employers of NHS staff and with the responsibility for providing health care and for financial viability has profound implications for industrial relations. It is likely to spell the eventual end of national pay determination. However, to date progress by trusts towards their own pay structures and employee relations policies has been very slow. This is not surprising given all the problems they have had to face in the transitional period. There can be no doubt that trusts will be developing their own policies and structures eventually. They have to be financially viable, and labour costs are the major proportion of their total costs. Government is pushing hard: for example, in its evidence to the Review Bodies for a greater element of pay to be determined locally and for the introduction of PRP. Indeed in June 1994 the Chief Executive of the NHS Management Executive instructed NHS Trusts to present action plans by October 1994 and have local pay bargaining machinery in place by February 1995. As a consequence Trusts have had to determine their policy with regard to union recognition. This was in line with overall Conservative Government policy to seek to end or diminish public sector national agreements, as with civil service agencies. However, so far the policy of local negotiations has not been very successful, despite the Review Body for nurses allowing a certain amount to be settled locally. The amount was really too small to be conducive to local pay bargaining, but there has been negotiation on matters such as skill mix. Meanwhile, the new Labour Government has announced it will uphold national agreements. How these will react with Trust bargaining remains to be seen. It may be that the new local government agreement will provide some kind of model for the NHS.

The nationalised and former nationalised industries

As stated earlier in this chapter, Conservative Governments since 1979 have had an inherent dogmatic suspicion and distrust of public enterprise and public expenditure and an equally inherent and dogmatic belief in the superiority of private enterprise. However, the 1979 Government did not include wholesale privatisation in its election manifesto and such a policy only emerged after the 1983 general election. Nevertheless, the extent of privatisation in the 1980s was extensive. In the first instance a number of publicly owned companies or parts of companies were sold off: for example, Cable & Wireless, Rolls-Royce, British Aerospace, British Leyland and Inmos. These had been taken into the public fold in an earlier period, in most cases to save them from bankruptcy. Then, as Table 7.2 shows, in 1982 National Freight and Britoil were sold, and in 1983 Associated British Ports: in 1984 British Telecom (BT) was privatised and the process of selling off parts of British Shipbuilders commenced: in 1986 British Gas was privatised and the process of selling off the subsidiaries of the National Bus Company began. The year 1987 saw the sale of British Airways, the British Airports Authority, the Ministry of Defence Dockyards and the Royal Ordnance Factories, while in 1988 British Steel was sold and the privatisation of Passenger Transport Executives began. In 1989 the British water industry was privatised, and in 1990–91 the electricity industry.

Virtually all that was left in public ownership was the Post Office, British Coal, British Rail and London Transport, nuclear power and the BBC. In 1994

TABLE 7.2   Privatisation, 1982–97

Company	Year	Employees
National Freight Company	1982	28 000
Britoil	1982	14 000
Associated British Ports (formerly British Transport Docks Board)	1983	–
Enterprise Oil (separated from British Gas Corporation)	1984	–
British Telecom	1984	250 000
British Shipbuilders: various dates from	1984	–
British Gas Corporation	1986	89 000
National Bus Co. Subsidiaries	1986–88	30 000
British Airways	1987	36 000
Royal Ordnance Factories	1987	17 000
British Airports Authority	1987	7 000
British Steel	1988	53 000
Passenger Transport Execs: various dates from	1988	8 000
Regional Water Authorities & Water Authorities Association	1989	40 000
Girobank	1990	6 700
Area Electricity Boards and National Grid Company	1990	119 000
National Power and Powergen	1991	26 400
Scottish Power	1991	9 800
Northern Ireland Electricity Service	1993	5 000
British Coal Mines	1994	
British Rail	1995	
British Energy	1996	

Sources: Based on 'Employment in the Public and Private Sectors', *Economic Trends*, January 1994; *Economic Trends*, March 1997; press reports.

legislation to privatise British Rail and British Coal was passed, and the Government announced its intention to privatise parts of the Post Office. As a result of back-bench opposition the Government decided not to push ahead with privatisation of the Royal Mail. However, British Energy, which owned the eight modern nuclear power stations, was privatised in 1996. The number of employees in nationalised industries fell from 1.85 million in 1979 to 0.33 million in 1996.

The Government was, of course not the direct employer of workers in the nationalised industries; nevertheless it could and did exercise considerable influence over pay and employment matters, mainly through financial controls and targets, but also through the appointment of Chairmen and Board members who were in tune with Thatcherite beliefs and policies. In addition, the development of the policy of wholesale privatisation had a major effect on Nationalised Boards. In order to be saleable, the industries had first to be made profitable if they were loss makers, and this had implications for pay, manning levels and redundancies. It was, of course, not true that all nationalised industries were loss makers. For example, gas, electricity, the British Airports Authority and BT consistently made surpluses, as does the Post Office, under the Government's own rules: the only big and consistent loss makers were the coal industry, steel and the railways, although others like British Airways had spells in the red.

Coal

The coal industry in 1979/80 had 232 500 wage earners on the colliery books and produced 109 million tons. Throughout the last 15 years, the British coal industry faced competition from other sources of energy: oil, natural gas, nuclear energy and cheap imported coal. In the early 1980s the demand for coal fell steadily due not only to competition from other fuels, but as a result of the recession. Output and manpower were reduced, as was the number of working pits. The decrease was, however, gradual until 1984 when the NCB announced that over 30 pits would close in 1984/5. This led to the miners' strike.

With the NUM's complete defeat and subsequent powerlessness, management was free to pursue its own policies with impunity. Growing competition, including that which arose from the privatisation of electricity, and tight government financial constraints and targets, meant hard-line management in an effort to attain government targets and to bring down costs and prices. This meant restraint on national pay increases, changes in payment systems with great emphasis on piecework, local pay variations, large-scale closures, and major changes in working methods. As a consequence, by early 1994, in the years since the miners' strike, the number of pits had been reduced from 170 to 17 and the number of men employed from 150 000 to 15 000. The speed of the contraction has been staggering. It is questionable whether the 'macho-management' style, adopted by British Coal after the 1984/5 strike, was necessary. After all, very substantial reductions in the number of pits, in output and in manpower had been achieved in earlier decades without a major confrontation. However, a senior British Coal executive told us that, in his opinion, the progress which has been made and the changes in attitude could not have been achieved without the strike and the comprehensive defeat of the NUM.

Privatisation in 1995 resulted in most of the industry being owned by RJB Mining. The NUM and the Union of Democratic Workers (UDM) have been largely marginalised. There is no company bargaining, and issues are determined at pit level.

Railways

Like the coal industry, the railways had experienced secular decline during most of the post-war period, largely as a result of competition from other forms of transport (in particular, the growth of car ownership and the growth in the size and the use of lorries). It is true that the railways had an advantage in the movement of bulk commodities, such as coal, iron ore and steel, but these were also areas of long-term decline. The railways' predicament from such competition was accentuated in the 1980s by the Government's policy of alleged non-interference, free competition, drastic reductions in financial assistance, tough financial targets and a refusal to consider the social costs of competition. The result in industrial relations terms was a hard-line attitude on pay which meant that pay rates fell below those achieved elsewhere, and reasonable average earnings could only be obtained by the working of excessive overtime. It also meant determined drives to change working practices in order to increase efficiency. One such attempt resulted in a strike by ASLEF in 1982 which was unsuccessful from the union's point of view: however, in 1989 a series of one-day strikes by the NUR (and ASLEF) over pay and against changes in bargaining structure and other industrial relations procedures was successful, in that the pay offer which British Rail had sought to impose unilaterally was significantly increased and the proposed procedural changes were not imposed, but referred to a joint union-management working party for further consideration, with the assistance of ACAS. Agreement on new procedures was eventually reached.

However, with privatisation and the form it took of splitting the system into a large number of separate companies (the RMT now has agreements with 80 companies), the new procedures were thrown into the melting pot. The new companies inherited the terms and conditions and the procedures laid down in the agreement with British Rail, but all wanted to re-structure. Recognition and negotiating procedures had to be settled with each company. Recognition does not appear to have been a major problem, but there is no sign of an employers' association and no sign of single union agreements or single-table bargaining. Cuts in the labour force have continued, and improved pay and conditions have usually been conditional on changes in working practice.

Steel

The steel industry was nationalised in 1967 and was privatised in December 1988. Its story needs to go back to the mid-1970s when the Steel Corporation had 230 000 employees. It was suffering from gross overcapacity for it had been building capacity for an estimated UK demand in 1980 of around 39 million tons, whereas actual demand turned out to be 14 million tons. There was also overcapacity in the world steel industry. However, UK costs were high and productivity relatively low; there were also heavy financial losses. Management then decided that there had to be a strategy for change, the main elements of which included the closure of uneconomic steel-making plants and concentrating production on modern technology, the slimming of manpower, decentralisation to increase business identity, improving direct communications with the workforce, and having an active social policy contribution to alleviate the effects of change and to create a climate within which change became acceptable. The first closure took place at the end of the 1970s.

In 1979/80 there was a major national strike lasting some three months in an industry which had long been noted for its good industrial relations. The dispute was overtly over pay and it is difficult to avoid the suspicion that the Conservative Government had played a part in the original low offer. Be that as it may, the strike was also covertly about power. Management claimed that they had not been looking for a showdown: they had not thought it necessary. In retrospect, managers believed that they could not have moved as fast as they did if it had not been for union weakness and exhaustion as a result of the strike.

The reduction in manpower happened rapidly: by 1985 manpower was down to some 65 000 while in 1990 it was some 53 000. Closures were very extensive and included many major works, such as Shotton and Corby. Apart from closures there were substantial manpower reductions at surviving plants. For example, at Llanwern, between September 1979 and December 1980, manpower was reduced from over 9000 to under 5000, and man hours per ton reduced from 7.0 to 4.2. This was achieved, according to management, through reducing the number of management levels, increased flexibility between craft and process workers and manual and staff grades, increased mechanisation, greater use of contractors, higher work tempo and the cutting-out of inessentials. These achievements were attained against the background of a threat of complete closure of one of the major plants in South Wales. There was also very intensive local consultation and negotiation. Redundancy pay was relatively generous and was helped by European Coal and Steel Community (ECSC) funds.

Overall, labour costs as a proportion of total costs came down from 37 per cent in 1980 to 19 per cent in 1989. From heavy financial losses in the 1970s British Steel made a trading profit of £91 million in 1985/6 and £425 million in 1987/8 (the last year before privatisation). In terms of efficiency and profitability steel thus became a success story – a success achieved while the industry was still nationalised – but a success achieved by a reduction in the labour force of over three-quarters and hence at a great social cost. In the early 1990s British Steel's profitability came under pressure with the recession and with surplus capacity in Western Europe. There was further pressure in

1997 with the high exchange rate of sterling. There have been further cuts in manpower but not on the earlier scale.

British Steel has favoured a more devolved business structure in order to respond with greater flexibility to the varying commercial and economic pressures which faced the different businesses. Four main divisions were established, of which the two largest – General Steels and Strip Products – employed nearly 20 000 each. Since the beginning of 1990, bargaining has been decentralised to the separate businesses, and corporation-wide bargaining has ceased. The unions had been strongly opposed but eventually reluctantly accepted the new bargaining structure. The businesses varied in the decentralised negotiating arrangements they adopted. The two large businesses – General Steels and Strip Products – established joint bodies at business level, whereas the others have decentralised further down to their constituent companies. Bargaining took place at business unit level round a 'single table'. There has been no de-recognition, and the check-off still applies. There was no change in the established grievance and disciplinary procedures, except that matters cannot be referred beyond the business unit level. Arbitration arrangements were rationalised and are now in every case by mutual agreement only.

On pay systems, the steel industry has always put considerable weight on local bonuses linked to productivity, and in recent years more and more emphasis has been put on locally determined bonuses. Bonuses are now related both to departmental and plant performance.

Finally, management unquestionably considered that the cause of major initial change was the parlous economic state of the industry. It was not the law, or Thatcherism, or privatisation.

Electricity

The electricity industry in post-war Britain has had a long history of expansion. It also has had a long history of technological advance and rising productivity. Thus the Chairman of the Electricity Council in its last annual report (1988/9) stated that it was appropriate to record briefly what the industry had achieved over the past 30 years since the Electricity Act 1957 which set up the Electricity Council's twelve area boards and the Central Electricity Generating Board:

> In this time the number of customers has increased by about 50 per cent, sales have increased by more than 220 per cent, while the number of staff employed has fallen by more than 55 000. Output has trebled, productivity increased more than four-fold and technical efficiency has dramatically improved. Thirty years ago there were more than 250 power stations; today there are only 72 producing three times as

much electricity. Thermal efficiency at coal and oil-fired power stations increased from 26.77 per cent to 35.47 per cent, representing a saving of more than £1 billion per annum at present day prices.

He added that there had been an operating profit in 1988/9 of £777 million, that the industry was able to finance its capital investment programme entirely from internal resources and that it had reduced its net borrowings by £1779 million.

The industry has also been a model of industrial relations stability. The only significant industrial action taken in the post-war years was an overtime ban by the manual workers in 1972. The effects of this limited action were almost immediately apparent and potentially so serious that the Government set up a Court of Inquiry: the action was called off and the Inquiry recommended a significant pay increase. Indeed, so essential is electricity to the economy and to society generally that the unions had overwhelming bargaining power. However, it could be argued that they dared not use it to the full because of the dire consequences of industrial action for society. Nevertheless, it is difficult to argue that the unions abused their power. They cooperated in technological change, productivity increased steadily and earnings rose significantly, but not noticeably faster than the national average over the years. Moreover, manpower was gradually reduced as a result of technological change and increased efficiency, but without any traumas. The industry had long-established collective bargaining machinery at national level and elaborate consultative arrangements at all levels: it was a pioneer of productivity bargaining in the 1960s and one of the first to engage in moves towards harmonisation of the terms and conditions of blue-collar and white-collar workers. All this was achieved within the centralised bargaining arrangements; there was no move to decentralised negotiations. Certainly it can be argued that in the 1980s in contrast to, say, coal and the railways, industrial relations remained non-confrontational and cooperative, presumably a reflection of the fact that it was a successful and profitable industry, and hence less susceptible to government pressure. The continuation of central bargaining during a period of change and of manpower reductions had also helped to preserve stability.

With privatisation in 1991, after a transitional period, industry-wide central bargaining ceased and the generating companies and the regional distribution companies introduced their own procedural and substantive agreements. There have been very substantial reductions in the labour force in both the generating companies and the distribution companies. Another common feature has been the taking of senior members of staff out of collective bargaining and on to individual contracts.

The industry has been in a state of flux with many take-over bids, mainly by American companies. There have also been some cross take-over bids: for example, Scottish Power bought MANWEB and Southern Water; NORWEB bought N.W. Water and renamed itself United Utilities; and South Wales Electricity Board bought Welsh Water and renamed itself HYDER. However, National Power and PowerGen were stopped by the Conservative Government from taking over regional electricity companies. Some regional electricity companies are engaging in electricity generation, mainly through gas-fired powered stations. Indeed there were two revolutions in the industry: privatisation, and the use of gas-fired stations which now account for nearly half of the electricity generated. A gas-fired station needs 40 people compared with 400 at a coal-fired station.

The picture in the regional distribution companies varies greatly, but they are all moving in broadly the same direction. In one company, by way of example, there are now only two bargaining units: the first, professional and managerial down to and including foremen; the second, covering all manual workers and clerical workers. In effect, there are two 'single tables' and an integrated single pay structure for manual and clerical workers, a major driving force for which was equal pay. The only group not covered is senior management, numbering some 200 people. For these there has been de-recognition (although some still have representational rights) and personal contracts. For the professional and management group the agreement provides for bargaining over the minimum and maximum, but not over what each individual gets within that. For the staff group there is no PRP but there are appraisals and personal development plans. Incremental scales have been maintained for this group, but increments can be doubled or withheld. Single status has been achieved.

Gas

The story of the gas industry has been very similar to that of electricity. It had well-established industrial relations procedures and good industrial relations, with a virtually complete absence of industrial action over the years of nationalisation. At one point in the post-war period it looked as if the industry was due to stagnate, and indeed decline in the face of its dependence on coal as a raw material and competition from oil and electricity. Enterprising management, however, sought other ways of obtaining gas, including using oil as a feed stock, the extraction of methane from the NCB pits and the importation of frozen methane. The industry was subsequently transformed by the discovery of natural gas in the North Sea. Its history has been one of growth and high profitability.

The industry bargained at national level, both for manual and white-collar workers, although particularly for white-collar workers there was flexibility at local level in the pay scales. For manual workers, incentive schemes have long been in operation following the NPBI report (1967a). Earnings have been relatively high, but by no means the highest in industry, and again there is no evidence of the unions exploiting their strong bargaining position. Industrial relations in the nationalised gas industry were cooperative and not confrontational. Like the electricity industry, it did not suffer undue interference from government in the 1980s. Again like electricity, this was doubtless the result of its growth, steadily increasing productivity and profitability.

In the early years of privatisation, industrial relations did not change significantly. Management's intention was to preserve industry-wide bargaining and indeed to strengthen national pay structures with national standard job specifications. In a single-product business, they believed that there must be common terms because the work was identical wherever it was done. Sufficient flexibility was provided through regional bonus schemes related to performance, and there was local control of the amount of overtime and the schedules of stand-by and call-out.

However, the new measures announced in 1994 to introduce more competition into the gas industry greatly affected industrial relations arrangements. In a major restructuring, which was expected to result in the loss of about 25 000 jobs over five years, the company set up five business units: Public Gas Supply, Business Gas, TransCo, Service and Retail. With effect from January 1995, bargaining arrangements were devolved to business unit level. In April 1997, there was a further major restructuring with British Gas broken up into, first of all, Centrica, comprising gas sales to homes and business premises, servicing, retailing of appliances and Morecombe Bay Gasfield: second, into British Gas plc, comprising exploration and production businesses, TransCo pipeline and transmission company, gas supply to users abroad, research and technology, properties and leasing. Each company at the time employed some 20 000 staff. Redundancy was almost entirely voluntary, with some three-quarters due to contracting-out. Relationships with the unions are good and the unions were described by one senior manager as having 'mature and progressive attitudes'. There has been no de-recognition, even of managers who are in the Gas Managers' Association. In TransCo, employees moved in 1997 to PRP from top to bottom. There are no longer annual agreements for general increases. The unions now negotiate the size of the pot and the method for its distribution.

The Post Office

The Post Office and BT were separated in 1981. The universal expectation was that BT was the growth area and that the Post Office faced inevitable decline. This latter expectation proved to be false and the Post Office experienced a boom period which was greater than ever before in its history. Social mail had gone down, but business mail had increased enormously.

The Post Office had been run on civil service lines. In the 1970s, one senior manager originally from the private sector believed that 'Management didn't manage.' He considered that the traumatic postmen's strike of 1971, won by management, had the paradoxical effect of management almost bending over backwards to make concessions. They had found the conflict distasteful and wanted to reintroduce 'sound' relationships.

In contrast to the 1970s, the 1980s had been a good decade in the sense of successful achievement of business objectives. It had been a period of change. Management faced various restrictive practices: for example, a ban on the mechanisation of sorting and a virtual ban on the use of part-timers. Changes had to be achieved and management was determined to achieve them, using persuasion, inducement and, in the last resort, a determination to act uni-laterally, regardless of union opposition (for example, on part-time workers and on Sunday working).

Management, he believed, had been greatly helped by the new climate of industrial relations: weaker unions and stronger management. They had also been helped by the new industrial legislation and government policies. The Post Office had been a significant user of the legislation, in particular using injunctions to deal with walk-outs.

In the unions' view it was the government's financial targets and rates of return which had been the main influence, and not the legislation. During the 1980s there had been a series of national enabling agreements, and details of change were then determined locally. There had been three or four major disputes, and in the late 1980s a series of short-lived local disputes. There had therefore been industrial relations troubles but the Post Office had succeeded in bringing about substantial change, and there had also been business success.

In 1986 the Post Office had created three separate companies: Royal Mail, with 160 000 employees out of a total Post Office labour force of 210 000, Parcel Force and Post Office Counters. Counters was being restructured, with small offices closed so that there will eventually be only 500–600 main post offices.

Further decentralisation took place in 1992. In Royal Mail, nine independent business centres were created instead of 64 divisional districts. Each business centre is in charge of its own quality of service and its profit and loss account. The UCW in turn reduced its branches from 700–800 to 102, and a shop steward convener was introduced with 20/30 area representatives. There are now no central negotiations covering the whole of the PO. Each of the companies conducts its own negotiations. The unions did not like the separa-tion but accepted it. It means that there are now 16 main bargaining units. According to management, the main pay increases had been similar but the corporate agreement enabled different grading structures to be introduced, as well as different productivity schemes. According to the unions, each of the companies tries to put its individual stamp on its agreements. Following the changes in business structure, 1992 also saw the launch of a new industrial relations framework agreement between the Royal Mail and the UCW. The agreement encouraged trade union membership and participation and there was great emphasis on joint problem-solving, in which the help of ACAS was enlisted.

In the Post Office there had not been the removal of collective bargaining for managers to the same extent as there had been in BT and British Rail. However, personal contracts and PRP had been introduced for the top 30 managers a number of years ago, and then extended to a further 3000 managers. There is no intention of going radically further and there are some 14 000 junior managers and front-line supervisors for whom collective bargaining applies.

Finally, there had been a post-entry closed shop agreement with the UCW and the Communication Managers' Association which ceased. Union membership however remains high, at about 85 per cent. The check-off had not been affected. Management cooperated in securing the renewal of mandates, and is doing so again, although there was a 2.5 per cent service charge.

In 1994 there had been a number of unlawful walk-outs in Royal Mail, and in January 1995 there was one in London. The Post Office applied for an injunction which it obtained and there was then a fine on the union for contempt of court because it had not repudiated the action. Since then the union has repudiated all unlawful action, but this means that it cannot be active in getting the men back to work.

In 1996 there were eight one-day official stoppages after an agreement between Royal Mail and the union's negotiating team had been turned down by the union executive. The main disputed issue was team-working, which local union representatives thought would marginalise them. They had a strong local base which enabled them to allocate overtime, determine the allocation of jobs and ensure that seniority applied.

The strikes were ended by the setting-up of two working parties under ACAS chairmanship covering working practices and delivery structure. Difficulties in postal rounds could be contrasted with the acceptance of new technology for sorting.

British Telecom

BT, with a labour force of some 250 000, was privatised in 1984. It had been previously separated from the Post Office in 1981. Like the Post Office its management and industrial relations were steeped in civil service traditions. Indeed one senior executive described it at that time as 'more civil service than the civil service . . . at every level throughout the business there was joint management with the unions'.

The major change has been in management, in no small part (according to a union general secretary) through the importation of people from outside who had brought in a different culture. 'Change used to be gradual and joint. Now it is quick and, if necessary, unilaterally decided . . . In the past if the union's response to a proposal was "no" the management would drop it. But now they persist and impose it if necessary.'

Major changes had taken place in BT, partly as a result of management, partly as a result of technology and partly because of increased competition. The labour force has been markedly reduced although, because of turnover, and because of a generous early retirement and voluntary redundancy scheme, this so far has been achieved without compulsory redundancies. By 1997 the labour force was down to 123 000.

There were a number of significant disputes during the 1980s, in particular the 1981 Society of Civil and Public Servants (SCPS) strike over pay differentials; in 1983 over connecting Mercury and privatisation; and in 1987 over BT's linking of the annual pay increase with demarcation changes. In all three cases management had acted firmly: indeed, they had sought to escalate the action in order to put financial pressure on the unions. The 1981 strike, which was selective, went on for 21 weeks and achieved no gain for the union on management's last offer. In the 1983 industrial action, staff were not allowed to work their normal hours if they refused to do overtime. They had to sign a document saying that they would work as management directed or not work at all. Management won, but a senior executive admitted that 'industrial relations had been poisoned and scars were left on many managers'. The 1987 industrial action had begun with an overtime ban. Overtime was necessary to run the system without interruptions, and working overtime was part of the contract of employment. Management decided that it was best to exclude operational staff from the international exchanges, and they were run by managers. The main cost of the action to BT was a large backlog of faults which took a year or more to catch up.

Management had not resorted to the use of the law, not least because there had been no illegal action. The unions kept a tight control on their membership. If there was trouble at local level, management resorted to the union head office and not to the law. 'What matters are the working relationships and they have got to take the responsibility; importing legal decisions would worsen them.' However, it was accepted by both management and unions that the legal changes had altered the backcloth. 'They had made it respectable to stand up to union strength.'

Negotiations in BT are still largely centralised. While this is expected to continue, there is likely to be more flexibility and discussions are beginning on a single pay spine. The unions, according to one general secretary, made agreements which had helped management to reach its objectives. He believed that you 'had to do the best you could and that there was no percentage in just resisting management's pressure . . . So there was acceptance, though reluctant, of changes.' The CWU had never had a closed shop but its membership is over 90 per cent. Its clerical section (formerly part of the

CPSA) had a closed shop and lost membership on its termination in 1983. The check-off is still in full operation and management had fully cooperated in securing the renewal of members' mandates. There had been no problems, but the Society of Telecom Executives (STE) was now mainly on direct debit. Under the old system there had been collective bargaining for every level of staff up to the Board. Individual contracts were introduced for the top 100, then the next 250 and the next 600, and then the main group of 5000 managers. By 1997, some 10 000 managers had been de-recognised and were on individual contracts, and only the bottom two grades in the management structure – some 19 000 (the first two lines of supervision and junior professionals) – had union recognition and collective bargaining. In order to keep it the STE recognises that it will have to be flexible. In 1997 a form of PRP was introduced instead of a general increase, and the STE will probably only be able to bargain about the size of the pot and the ranges. The CWU lost substantial membership as a result of BT's large cuts in its labour force. However, it has cooperated in change and was able to do so on the basis that so far compulsory redundancy had been avoided. A senior manager said that agreeing with the union that there should be no compulsion was a price worth paying. They could have done it without the union, but not as well. The unions had been a positive help. The same manager also stated that 'while the collective relationship is significant, it is not a substitute for each manager developing an excellent individual relationship with each of our people'.

Conclusion

The public sector has been the main area of conflict in industrial relations since 1979. This was because the Conservative Government, either as employer or paymaster, started with the belief that the public sector was intrinsically inefficient: it was overmanned, bureaucratic, a drain on the public purse and the home of powerful trade unions which were unconstrained by market forces. Government policy was therefore to create a more commercial environment through stricter financial controls, increased competition, contracting-out or the threat of contracting-out, and eventually privatisation in order to achieve greater efficiency. Indeed as the Conservatives' belief in wholesale privatisation developed, this in itself became a major factor in the drive for greater profitability for unless there were a sufficient level of profitability, privatisation would not be possible.

As a consequence of government pressure – above all financial pressure – industrial relations moved from consensus to confrontation. As Ferner (1989) notes: 'This is not to say that the government has deliberately provoked public sector strikes in order to force a showdown with the unions . . . But the government's pressure on management has created conditions in which conflict became more likely if not inevitable.' Financial pressure has been applied, both to the public service sector and to the public corporations, in order to reproduce the conditions under which the private sector was believed to operate and to introduce what were believed to be private sector management practices. Consequently pay moved from being determined mainly by comparability to being determined allegedly by ability to pay and the need to recruit and retain labour. Moves were made to decentralise bargaining and to reduce the importance of national pay scales: merit pay was introduced, and so were allowances based on geographical shortages of labour and skill shortages. Staff numbers were reduced, and increased flexibility in the use of labour sought. Organisational change was introduced and also cultural change, often driven in the public corporations by the appointment of 'right-minded' chairmen and board members from the private sector.

As a consequence industrial relations in much of the public sector changed almost beyond recognition, although Pendleton and Winterton (1993), in their book which reviews the main public and former public corporations, conclude that 'there are elements of change and continuity in the industrial relations of public and privatized enterprises'.

Towards the end of the 1980s there were some signs of change, not in government hostility or basic objectives with regard to the public sector but in a recognition of certain realities. Thus tightening labour markets and rising inflation meant some relaxation in the policy of holding down public service sector pay: indeed, comparability in the form of the new civil service agreements briefly re-emerged in an institutionalised form, but by the early 1990s new pay limits were put on public sector pay increases. There was also perhaps a partial realisation that constant denigration and confrontation was not the way to obtain the best results from employees. However, these limited examples of improvement were dwarfed by numerous examples of continued disregard of 'good' industrial relations practice, such as constant refusal to compromise in order to avoid disputes and refusal in virtually any circumstances to permit the help of a third party, in particular arbitration; permitting pay increases to fall behind that of the private sector and indeed in some cases below the RPI: and reductions in time off and other facilities for union representatives.

In the first half of the 1990s, the pace of change in the public service sector accelerated, with changes in the civil service and the NHS (as indicated earlier in this chapter) being particularly marked. (See also Winchester and Bach, 1995; Bailey, 1996; I. Kessler and Purcell, 1996.) The main development has been the decentralisation of management to agencies, NHS Trusts and even to schools, which carries with it implications for industrial relations: mainly the end of central agreements and separate pay determination in the new management units. Whether pay review bodies will survive is an open question, although perhaps the return of a Labour Government in 1997 will make their survival more likely. However, it is too early to tell what difference, if any, the Labour Government will make in this area. The Labour Government has no commitment to re-nationalising any of the privatised industries, or to changing the new agencies in the civil service. It is, however, committed to ending compulsory contracting-out, particularly in local government, and to major change in the internal NHS market.

CHAPTER 8

Trade unions

Introduction

During the 1980s and 1990s the trade union movement under successive Conservative Governments experienced greatly reduced membership, reduced influence with Government and in society generally, and greatly reduced bargaining power *vis-à-vis* employers. The environment in which unions had to operate was the crucial cause of their problems, although this is not to say that there were not deficiencies in union organisation, policies and behaviour which contributed.

Metcalf (1991, p. 22) argued that the decline in union membership in the 1980s was 'the result of a complex interaction of five factors: the macroeconomic climate, the composition of the workforce, the policy of the state, the attitudes and conduct of employers and the stance taken by unions themselves'. With regard to the first factor, the record post-war level of unemployment in the first half of the 1980s was undoubtedly a major reason for the decline in membership, but the substantial reduction in unemployment and the increase in the labour force in the second half of the 1980s did not lead to an increase in membership, although the rate of decline fell significantly. The second major recession, at the beginning of the 1990s, saw further substantial falls in membership and the subsequent slow economic recovery again did not lead to an increase in membership. The second factor – changes in the composition of jobs and the workforce with major declines in manufacturing and manual male employment and major increases in the service sector, female part-time employment and in professional, managerial and highly skilled work – unquestionably contributed to the decline in union membership and density. So did the decline in large units. However, these labour market trends were also present in the 1970s when union membership and density grew to unprecedented levels. The third factor – Conservative Government policy and, in particular, anti-union legislation – was also of significance: for example, the outlawing of the closed shop, the ending of statutory recognition procedures and the need to renew the check-off every three years. The fourth and fifth factors – the behaviour of employers and of unions – are of key importance. Unions needed to both extend recognition and avoid de-recognition. While de-recognition has not happened on a major scale, there are some well-known examples, as well as a number of less widely known cases. Securing recognition in hitherto unorganised sectors has proved very difficult, with many employers taking a much harder line than they did in the 1970s.

Two studies on reasons for the fall in trade union density give somewhat contradictory results. Freeman and Pelletier (1990) calculate that changes in UK labour law reduced union density by 1 to 1.7 percentage points per year from 1980 to 1986, which cumulatively amounted to 9.4 percentage points: effectively the entire decline in UK density in that period. They therefore conclude that 'the vast bulk of the observed 1980s decline in union density in the UK is due to the changed legal environment for industrial relations' (p. 141). In contrast, Disney (1990) concludes that it is macro-economic factors that explain the upturn in union density in the 1970s and the downturn in the 1980s. Employment composition effects moved in a perverse direction (relative to membership) in the 1970s and played little part in the decline in the 1980s. He further concludes that industrial relations legislation of the period seemed to have had no direct effect. Neither of these studies is entirely satisfactory. In a subsequent study, using data from the WIRS Disney, Gosling and Machin (1994) argue that 'it seems that union recognition became significantly harder to achieve in new establishments in the 1980–90 time period and it is this rather than the derecognition of unions in existing establishments which has been driving the down-turn in unionisation'. Our own view is that the decline in membership is due to an amalgam of the five factors enumerated by Metcalf, and that it is impossible to put figures to each of them.

Most of the main environmental changes have been discussed in earlier chapters. In this chapter we consider the effects of these changes on trade union membership, on trade union finances and organisation, on union responses to changes in employers' policies and to changes in the law. We also consider changes in the organisation, role and policies of the TUC.

In many respects the major issue is whether the trend of union decline is a permanent trend which will continue and lead to the complete marginalisation of unions, or whether the events of the 1980s and 1990s did not basically change the institutions and procedures of workplace industrial relations, and the future will see a readjustment of union attitudes, objectives and methods to the changing environment and a revival of union fortunes. Connected to this issue is the so-called 'New Unionism' or 'New Realism' which some have argued is essential if unions are to survive in the future (Bassett, 1986; Roberts, 1987).

Trade union membership

The fall in trade union membership has been dramatic and was made even more so by the rapid increase in membership enjoyed by unions in the 1970s. Between 1969 and 1979 total trade union membership increased by nearly 3 million (from 10.5 million to 13.3 million) and union density increased from 45 per cent to 54 per cent. TUC membership over the same period increased from 9.4 million to 12.1 million. In contrast between 1979 and 1995, the total number of trade union members declined from 13.3 million to 8.2 million (a fall of over 5 million), and union density declined from 54 per cent to little more than 30 per cent. TUC membership over the period 1979–96 declined from 12.1 million to 6.8 million. So in terms of numbers of members, the gains of the 1970s were more than lost by the 1990s. Moreover, the loss of membership has continued every single year since 1979.

Union density is actual union membership as a percentage of potential membership. Potential membership can be defined in a number of ways. The traditional method, as used by Bain and Price (1983), is to take potential membership as being the number of employees in civil employment plus the unemployed, and this is the method used to produce the figures quoted above. A second method would be to take only those in civil employment and not include the unemployed in the denominator. For the early post-war decades, with very low unemployment, the result of using either method would not be very different. With the high unemployment of the last decade and a half, however, the result is significantly different and the decline in density if the unemployed are excluded would be from 57 per cent in 1979 to 36 per cent at the end of 1995, compared with 54 per cent to 33 per cent if the unemployed are included (see Table 8.1). Bain and Price mainly justified the inclusion of the unemployed on the grounds that many unemployed kept their union membership, at least to begin with. This may have been true particularly of craftsmen, and when periods of unemployment were of short duration, but is arguably less true with mass unemployment and the large increase in the number of the long-term unemployed. A third method of measuring union density would be to take as the denominator the total civil labour force, thus including the self-employed. There is no one 'right' method: it depends, as Kelly and Bailey (1989) have stated, on the purpose for which the figures are being used.

One further point needs to be made on union membership, which also affects calculations of union density. This is that union membership figures have traditionally been taken from the returns made by unions to the TUC, to the Certification Officer and to the then DE. It has long been realised that some of the union membership figures have been exaggerated for a number of reasons, one of the most common being that some unions include retired people in membership. Light has now been thrown on the extent of this

TABLE 8.1   Trade union membership, 1979–95

Year	Union membership (000s) (1)	No. of unions (2)	Potential union membership (000s)			Union density	
			Employees in employment (000s) (3)	Unemployed (000s) (4)	Total (000s) (5)	(1) ÷ (3) % (6)	(1) ÷ (5) % (7)
1979	13 289	453	23 206	1 301	24 507	56.9	54.2
1980	12 947	438	22 386	2 137	24 523	57.8	52.8
1981	12 106	414	21 580	2 782	24 362	56.1	49.7
1982	11 593	408	21 101	2 949	24 050	54.9	48.2
1983	11 236	394	21 169	2 956	24 125	53.1	46.6
1984	10 994	375	21 363	3 106	24 469	51.5	44.9
1985	10 821	370	21 418	3 133	24 551	50.5	44.1
1986	10 539	335	21 389	3 121	24 510	49.3	43.0
1987	10 475	330	21 956	2 569	24 525	47.7	42.7
1988	10 376	315	22 513	2 038	24 551	45.5	41.7
1989	10 158	309	23 004	1 635	24 639	44.2	41.2
1990	9 947	287	22 662	1 853	24 515	43.9	40.6
1991	9 585	275	21 865	2 551	24 416	43.8	39.3
1992	9 048	268	21 521	2 973	24 494	42.0	36.9
1993	8 700	254	21 658	2 780	24 438	40.2	35.6
1994	8 278	243	21 871	2 418	24 289	37.9	34.1
1995	8 031	238	22 142	2 235	24 377	36.3	32.9

Sources: *Labour Market Trends*, February 1997, for number of unions and union membership; *Employment Gazette* and *Labour Market Trends*, various, for employees in employment and the unemployed.
Employees and unemployed figures are for UK, seasonally adjusted, for December each year.

exaggeration by the inclusion for the first time in the Labour Force Survey (LFS) for 1989 of a question on union membership. The results for Great Britain give an estimated figure of 9.1 million for membership and a union density of 39 per cent in the spring of 1989 (Stevens and Wareing, 1990). The membership figure compares with 10.2 million for December 1988 as compiled by the DE. Among reasons given for the difference were that the LFS question was only asked of those in employment and therefore excluded those who were unemployed or economically inactive during the 'reference week' in question; the LFS estimate counted individuals in membership rather than individual memberships (those belonging to two unions would appear twice in the DE figure but once in the LFS figure); and the fact that retired people who were currently union members were excluded from the LFS survey.

The LFS figure receives a considerable degree of support from some research work (Bailey and Kelly, 1990, p. 9) which sought to adjust the DE membership figures to less inflated ones. They produced revised figures for trade union membership and density, with figures adjusted to account for the inclusion of non-UK citizens, retired members, unemployed members and self-employed members. Their deflators, based largely on a survey of TUC unions conducted in 1988, depend 'on one very important assumption: namely that the proportion of non-Great Britain retired and unemployed workers in trade unions has not varied significantly over the years'. Their estimate for 1987 gave union membership of 9.427 million for Great Britain compared with the DE's 10.475 million for the UK, and put union density at 44.1 per cent. The main reasons for the difference were that union returns in 1986 included an estimated 500 000 retired people, 190 000 unemployed and some membership in Northern Ireland as well as some in the Irish Republic. As a result of the recent process of the centralisation of union membership details and their computerisation, a number of major unions accept that there was a degree of inflation in their earlier figures. They are now convinced that their present lists are accurate.

For our purpose the measure of trade union density which best indicates the decline of union bargaining power is one which excludes the unemployed from the denominator and retired and unemployed members from the numerator. That measure according to Stevens and Wareing (1990), was 39 per cent in the spring of 1989. According to Bailey and Kelly (1990), it was 44 per cent in 1987 compared with 53 per cent in 1979: a fall of 17 per cent. The series, which is continuous from 1979 in Table 8.1, shows quite clearly that a decline in density has taken place in every year since 1979.

Table 8.1 also shows that between 1979 and 1995 (December), the number of unions declined from 453 to 238, thus continuing a long decline which goes back to before the turn of the last century. It should be recalled that there are still many very small unions in existence. Thus 141 unions (59 per cent of the total) had a membership in 1995 of less than 2500 each, accounting in total for only 1 per cent of total union membership. At the other extreme, there were eight unions with a membership of 250 000 or more each, accounting for over 60 per cent of total union membership.

The impact of the overall fall in union membership on individual unions is shown in Table 8.2, which lists the 14 largest TUC affiliated unions (those with a membership of over 100 000 at the end of 1996). It will be seen that the fall in membership is not evenly distributed. Some white-collar unions – for example, the National Communications Union (NCU) and the Banking, Insurance and Finance Union (BIFU) – stand out against the trend, although BIFU has in recent years had a considerable fall in membership as a result of staff cut-backs in banking. Other white-collar unions, such as the Association of Scientific, Technical and Managerial Staff (ASTMS) before its merger with TASS to form the MSF in 1988, experienced a decline of some 20 per cent; and the

**TABLE 8.2 TUC membership, 1970–96, January (000s)
(affiliated unions with a membership of over 100 000)**

	1970	1979	1996	change 1979–96	% change 1979–96
1. UNISON[1]	–	–	1355	–	–
2. TGWU	1639	2073	897	−1176	−57
3. GMB	853	965	740	−225	−23
4. AEEU[2]	-	–	726	–	–
5. MSF[3]	–	–	446	–	–
6. USDAW	330	462	282	−180	−39
7. CWU[4]	–	–	275	–	–
8. GPMU[5]	–	–	217	–	–
9. NUT	311	291	175	−116	−40
10. NAS/UWT	57	112	157	+45	+40
11. PTC[6]	–	–	150	–	–
12. BIFU	89	126	123	−3	−2
13. CPSA	185	225	122	−103	−46
14. UCATT	–	321	107	−214	−67
Total number of TUC affiliated unions	142	112	73	–	–
Total TUC membership	10 000	12 100	6790	−5 310	−44

Source: TUC statistical statements.

[1] UNISON: merger in 1992 of NALGO (744 000), NUPE (579 000), and COHSE (203 000).
[2] Merger in 1992 of AEU (622 000) and the Electrical, Electronic, Telecommunication and Plumbing Union (357 000).
[3] Merger in 1986 of ASTMS (390 000) and TASS (241 000).
[4] CWU formed in January 1995 by merger of UCW (167 000) and NCU (122 000).
[5] Merger in 1990 of SOGAT (166 000) and NGA (123 000).
[6] PTC formed by merger of NUCPS (105 000) and IRSF (55 000) in 1996. NUCPS itself had been formed by the merger in 1986 of the SCPS (89 000) and the Civil Service Union (30 000).

Association of Professional, Exexcutive, Clerical and Computer Staff (APEX), which is not shown in the table, experienced a decline of some 50 per cent before its merger with the GMB, also in 1988. Another union not shown in the table, the NUM, had its membership reduced from 253 000 in 1979 to 10 000 in 1995 as a result of the cutbacks in the coal-mining industry following its defeat in the 1984/85 strike, and the breakaway movement which resulted in the formation of the UDM. Some other smaller unions – for example, the NUS and the Agricultural Workers' Union (the latter eventually merging with the TGWU and the former with the NUR) – were also greatly reduced in size.

Outside the TUC, the RCN grew from 162 000 in 1979 to 300 000 in 1995, and the Association of Teachers and Lecturers (ATL; formerly AMMA) reached over 170 000 in 1995.

The change in membership of individual unions needs to be treated with some caution. Thus in some cases the loss is understated because of mergers with other unions. This is true, for example, of the GMB. Sometimes a heavy fall is the result of special factors separate from the general trend (for example, the NUT, part of whose loss was due to teachers switching to other teachers' unions).

The variation in the fortunes of different unions reflected to a large extent the varying fortunes of different sectors of the economy. Union membership and density, even in its heyday, had varied in different sectors, with the highest density in the public services and the rest of the public sector, high density in much of the manufacturing sector, particularly in large establishments, and very low density in much of the private service sector. With the severe contraction of manufacturing in the 1980s and early 1990s, and the decline in the number of large establishments, unions with membership concentrated in that sector suffered the most, as also did parts of the then public sector such as coal-mining and iron and steel where there were drastic cut-backs in employment, whereas those in the public services, taken together, suffered the least.

The LFS gave an estimated union membership of 7.2 million in 1996. Based as it is on individuals, the LFS gives a wealth of detail on the characteristics of union membership. Table 8.3 shows a union density in Great Britain in 1996 for males of 33 per cent and females 29 per cent: manual density is 31 per cent

TABLE 8.3   Union density of employees, autumn 1996 (Great Britain) (LFS)

	Density %
All employees, of which:	31
Men	33
Women	29
Full-time	35
Part-time	20
Non-manual	31
Manual	31
Public sector	61
Private sector	21

Source: Adapted from *Labour Market Trends*, June 1997.

and non-manual also 31 per cent; for manufacturing it is 31 per cent; density of full-time employees is 35 per cent and for part-timers 20 per cent. As the WIRSs have shown, there is a strong association of density with size of workplace. Thus density is 16 per cent in workplaces employing under 25, and 39 per cent for workplaces employing 25 or more.

Table 8.4 shows union density of employees by occupation. The outstanding point is the highest density for professional occupations and for associate professional and technical occupations. Table 8.5 shows union density

TABLE 8.4   Union density by occupation, autumn 1996 (Great Britain) (LFS)

	Density (%)
Managers and administrators	20
Professional occupations	52
Associate professional and technical occupations	47
Clerical and secretarial	27
Craft and related occupations	36
Personal and protective service	28
Sales	11
Plant and machine operatives	41
Other	26

Source: Derived from *Labour Market Trends*, June 1997.

TABLE 8.5   Union density by industry, autumn 1996 (Great Britain) (LFS)

	All	*Men*	*Women*	*Non-Manual*	*Manual*
Agriculture, forestry, fishing	8	10	5	10	8
Electricity, gas and water	61	67	42	54	75
All Manufacturing	31	34	22	16	41
Construction	25	28	12	19	31
Wholesale and retail	11	10	12	10	14
Hotels and catering	7	5	8	8	6
Railways	75	78	–		84
Postal services	64	71	44	42	75
Telecommunications	50	54	42	41	70
Banking and building societies	49	41	56	50	–
Public administration	61	65	56	63	44
Education	55	65	51	65	29
Hospitals	54	58	53	41	33

Source: Adapted from *Labour Market Trends*, June 1997.

by industry. Density is much higher in the public sector than the private sector. Within the service sector, public services (and the former public services) still have a high density, although falling in recent years, but in most of the private service sector union density is very low.

Between 1989 and 1996 (as recorded by the LFS) union density fell from 39 per cent to 31 per cent. The decline was particularly marked among male employees, manual employees and those in production industries. In 1996, an estimated 37 per cent, or 8.1 million, of all employees were covered by collective bargaining.

Union mergers

Over the years many smaller unions have simply disappeared, while others have merged with larger unions. However, mergers have not simply been between small unions and large ones, but between medium-sized unions and between large unions. Thus some of the notable mergers have included that of ASTMS (with a membership of 390 000) and TASS (with a membership of 241 000) to form the MSF; the GMB (membership 800 000) and APEX (membership 80 000); and the Civil Service Union (30 000) and the SCPS (89 000) to form the NUCPS, all three mergers taking place in 1988. In 1990 there was the merger of NGA (123 000) and SOGAT (166 000) to form the GPMU, and the merger of the NUR (110 000) and the NUS (22 000) to form the RMT. Of great significance was the formation in 1992 of UNISON – now Britain's largest union – as a result of the merger of NALGO (744 000), NUPE (579 000) and COHSE (203 000), and the formation of the AEEU in 1992 through the merger of the AEU (622 000) and the Electrical, Electronic, Telecommunications and Plumbing Union (EETPU) (357 000). In 1995 there was the merger of the UCW (167 000) and the NCU (122 000) to form the CWU. In 1996, the IRSF (55 000) and the NUCPS (110 000) merged to form the Public Services Tax and Commerce Union (PSTCU).

Earlier, in the 1980s, the Boilermakers (120 000) merged with the General and Municipal Workers to form the GMB in 1982; the POEU and the CPSA (Posts and Telecommunications Group) merged to form the NCU in 1985; the National Association of Theatrical, TV and Kine Employees (20 000) and the Association of Broadcasting Staffs (16 000) merged to form the Entertainment Trade Alliance in 1984 (subsequently there was a further merger in 1991 to form the Broadcasting Entertainment Cinematograph and Theatre Union); the Metal Mechanics (33 000) and the Tobacco Workers (16 000) transferred their engagements to TASS; and the Amalgamated Textile Workers (19 500) transferred their engagements to the GMB in 1986. The trend in mergers has been such that more than one general secretary has talked about there being only a few super unions at the end of the century.

McCarthy (who, together with Undy, had been conducting a review for the TUC on union mergers: TUC, 1991c) makes a number of interesting points, among which is

> that the underlying motives of most contemporary mergers are defensive, or consolidatory, rather than expansionist. The merger partners wish to recover lost membership, or improve their bargaining position in established areas; many are experiencing financial problems and need the support of larger and more stable organisations. Some wish to bring to an end long-standing and wasteful rivalries in the face of a more effective employer challenge. (p. 20)

Further he believes that

> the merger process will continue and grow over the next ten years. It should at least halve the number of TUC unions before the turn of the century. Yet it will not lead to any discernible ideal 'model' or optimum union size. From the outside, according to traditional classifications, British unions will look as illogical and unplanned as before. From the inside, I think, they will be much leaner and fitter; with more effective and improved services, and a greater ability to fight their corner if required. (p. 20)

McCarthy concludes that care must be taken to ensure that the merger trend does not lead to counter-productive rivalry and dissension between unions, and that it was here that the TUC had a vital role to play.

Willman (1989) contrasts 'market share' unionism, by which he means unions competing for their proportion of a declining membership base in high density sectors, with 'expansionary unionism', by which he means attempts to extend union membership into low density sectors. He argues that competition by unions in the membership market is financially unrewarding and difficult, as is individual recruitment in unorganised areas:

> To the extent that competitive 'market share' unionism dominates over 'expansionary' attempts to extend union membership into low-density sectors, we may expect a long-term stagnation or decline of union membership. Under such circumstances, the limits to membership will be roughly set in the aggregate by employment in the manufacturing and public sectors – assuming no wide-spread de-recognition – while the expanding private services sector characterised by female employment, part-time work, small establishments, self-employment and employer hostility will remain un-unionised. (p. 261)

All the union general secretaries we interviewed stressed that the problems arising from mergers were much greater and more time-consuming than they had anticipated. However, none had doubts that their endeavours would be well worthwhile in the longer term. Future mergers are highly likely (for example, among banking unions, MSF and the Institute of Professionals, Managers and Specialists, or IPMS, and probably in the longer run the TGWU and the GMB).

Trade union finances and organisation

The loss of membership has been accompanied by straitened financial circumstances. The British trade union movement has never been well endowed financially, particularly compared with many West European countries and the USA. This is largely the result of low subscriptions, both absolutely and as a proportion of average earnings. Falling union membership in the 1980s has worsened the position. Willman and Morris (1988), after looking at the period 1975–88, stated that given the loss of members 'the data convey a picture of remarkable financial health' (p. 96). This conclusion, as shown in Table 8.6, does not appear justified. Indeed, in two later papers, Willman himself seems to have had second thoughts (Willman, 1989, 1990). In the latter work, he used a number of ratios to measure the financial position of unions and concluded that overall they indicated 'financial health and stability from 1950 to 1966; a period of financial decline during membership growth from 1967 to 1981, and some financial recovery during membership decline in the 1980s' (p. 318). His data further showed that

> per capita income, expenditure and net worth moved broadly in line up to 1968. Thereafter, to 1979, real income and expenditure per capita continued to rise as membership rose, but real net worth per capita fell very steeply. The financial and membership conditions of the 1980s differed again. This was a period of rapidly rising per capita income, expenditure and net worth, but of sharply contracting membership. (p. 319)

He concluded that in 1988 'the financial position remains relatively weak. Reserves are historically low as a multiple of expenditure. There remains, in addition, the structural problem of the shortfall of membership income' (p. 324).

It will be seen from Table 8.6 that total income between 1979 and 1995 rose by 176 per cent, although income per head rose by 353 per cent. Total income from members rose by 169 per cent and income per head by 335 per cent. These figures are in money terms, and have to be discounted by inflation which increased over the same period by 139 per cent. They also have to be compared with a rise in total expenditure of 200 per cent, and a rise in

TABLE 8.6 Trade union finance, 1979–95

	Total			Per head		
	1979 (£m)	1995 (£m)	% increase	1979 (£)	1995 (£)	% increase
Total income	230.9	636.7	176	17.5	79.3	353
of which income from members	194.7	524.7	169	15.0	65.3	335
Total expenditure of which	208.8	623.4	199	15.8	77.6	391
admin. expenditure	154.6	545.6	253	11.7	67.9	480
expenditure on benefits	45.9	77.8	69	3.5	9.7	177
Total assets of which	318.5	792.1	149	24.1	98.6	309
fixed assets	76.5	242.0	216	5.8	30.1	419
Membership (millions)	13.2	8.0				

Source: Based on *Annual Reports of the Certification Officer*, 1980 and 1996, all listed unions.

expenditure per head of 391 per cent. Most of the increase in expenditure was not on benefits, but on pay and administrative costs, which rose from 74 per cent of total expenditure in 1979 to 88 per cent in 1995.

The increase in union total assets looked healthier: from £318.5 million in 1979 to £792.1 million in 1995 and £24.1 per head in 1979 to £98.6 per head in 1995. In real terms, the increase in total assets was only 7 per cent, while in assets per head it was 122 per cent; the reason for this increase was the decline in membership. While it is perfectly true that assets per head had increased considerably, they were still far too small to finance strike action for any length of time, as they always have been.

Among the consequences of strained finances were, first, that even the largest unions, such as the TGWU, the AEU and GMB were forced during the 1980s and 1990s to reduce their staff numbers very substantially and make other economies as their membership fell. British unions have traditionally relied for most of their activity on unpaid (by them) lay officials. With the need to provide new services and to recruit new members, as well as having to cope with more local and decentralised bargaining, there is a requirement to provide for more officials, not fewer. Moreover, overreliance on shop stewards who in turn depend on employers providing time off and other facilities can be dangerous given some employers changing attitudes and policies. Similarly, unions rely overwhelmingly for the collection of their income on managements' deductions of subscriptions from pay through check-off agreements. It is for such reasons that Willman (1989) refers to unions as 'employer dependent'.

The practice of the check-off grew markedly in the early 1980s. It is, perhaps, surprising that this should have happened during a period of union weakness and a growth among some employers of anti-unionism. In 1990, according to WIRS, check-off existed in 83 per cent of workplaces where unions were recognised (manual or non-manual): in private services, the figure was 85 per cent, while in manufacturing and the public sector it was 75 per cent (Millward *et al.*, 1992).

The issue of the check-off became of vital importance in 1993/4 as a result of s.15 of the 1993 Act, which provides that if an employer is lawfully to make check-off deductions from a worker's pay there must be prior written consent from the worker by August 1994, and renewed consent at least every three years. Additionally, if there is an increase in the amount to be deducted, the employer may only deduct the increased amount if the worker has been given at least one month's advanced notice of that increase, with a reminder that the worker may withdraw his consent to the arrangement at any time.

There can be no doubt that the Conservative Government's intention in enacting such a measure was to secure a reduction in union membership. The effect has been for the TUC and individual unions to set up mechanisms and to give top priority to securing the required individual authorisations. Originally there were estimates of a possible loss of membership of between 10 and 20 per cent.

In the event the unions' campaign succeeded in keeping losses to a minimum, although it has been impossible to obtain any precise figures. Some even suggested that in the process of renewal they had actually recruited new members, while some estimated there had been overall a 5 per cent loss. Most of the large companies we interviewed at the time had been cooperating with their unions in the process of obtaining the written consent of employees. In 1996/7 the process of renewal was, by law, repeated, although generally in a much lower key, and with most employers fully cooperating. The Labour Government is committed to ending the renewal process every three years.

While the check-off is a much more effective way for unions to receive subscriptions than their old methods, it works best when the labour force is relatively stable. There is clearly an argument for direct debit which carries on irrespective of a change in employer. Indeed a number of unions, particularly white-collar unions such as the RCN, BIFU and the teachers' unions, already have a considerable proportion on direct debit. They and certain other unions are actively encouraging members to use direct debit. The argument by employers in favour of threatening to end the check-off if there were industrial action was that it made no sense for the employer to collect subscriptions which the union then used to support strike action. Such a threat had been made in the civil service, but it had not had any practical effect on the unions' position in bargaining. In the prison service, the check-off agreement was ended by management because prison officers had taken industrial action in 1988. The POA, however, has been successful in getting their members to pay by direct debit and is not interested in having the check-off restored. British Coal in 1993 ended their check-off arrangement with the NUM after a one-day strike. Also in 1993 British Rail ended their check-off arrangement with the RMT in retaliation for the union calling a one-day strike. This involved the union in a great deal of effort, but it claimed that some 80 per cent of members were on direct debit or cash collection.

For most unions, particularly predominantly manual unions, there is no doubt that check-off is vitally important. One may well ask why then did the check-off not only continue during the 1980s, but actually grow? The answer would appear to be that generally employers have not attacked unions head-on, and the ending of the check-off would surely be such an attack. Furthermore, some employers value the role of unions for the part they play in securing orderly industrial relations, and as a partner in obtaining change. In such circumstances, an unrepresentative union would be a disadvantage and no real help. Also, as we were told by a leading employers' organisation, if the alternative is stewards wandering around the establishment to collect subscriptions, employers would prefer the check-off. Moreover, the check-off does give the employer information, not only about total union membership in the enterprise, but its distribution (for example, whether it is high or not in certain key areas, such as computer centres).

A second consequence of strained finances has been that a considerable number of unions have been forced to merge. Examples of such mergers were given earlier in this chapter. Third, financial constraint has often been one of the most important factors in forcing unions to become more efficient. One general secretary of a major union argued that although he would rather not have experienced it, 'Thatcherism had been good for the unions because it had made them face up to the issues.' As a result of financial pressures his union had undertaken drastic changes which included a reduction in the number of branches by 20 per cent in two years; the merging of districts and closure of offices; income and expenditure had been centralised and channelled through head office; the number of officials and staff had been considerably reduced; sophisticated computerisation had taken place; 'ghost' membership had been eliminated; and they had a revised strategy of moving from a geographical basis for organisation to an industrial one. Fourth, financial constraints have been an important factor for unions in considering their tactics on industrial action. All-out comprehensive strikes are very costly, whereas selective strikes or other forms of action are much less so.

One major organisational change for some unions has been the development and strengthening of their regional organisation. This is particularly so for unions in the public and former public sector where bargaining has been increasingly decentralised. However, more generally there has been a strengthening of the centre in terms of administrative and financial control and in the need for central approval for industrial action (Undy *et al.*, 1996).

Trade unions and their members

The pressures of the 1980s and 1990s have caused unions to react in a number of ways in their attitudes to their membership and to their potential membership. First, with regard to their membership, legislation, as we have seen, has ensured that general secretaries, presidents and national executive members have to be subject to election and to re-election at least every five years. While it is true that many unions prescribed such elections in their rule books (Undy and Martin, 1984) long before the legislation, the new required method of secret postal ballots was important. Undy *et al.* (1996) have produced a major and fundamental study of the effects of the legal and other environmental charges on unions.

The legislation also required that lawful industrial action could not be undertaken without a secret individual ballot. These changes were intended by the Government to increase the power of the individual rank and file members, who were deemed to be sensible and moderate, against that of the leadership who were deemed to be militant and autocratic. Whether these adjectives were justified or not is another question, but the effect has been to increase the power of the rank and file. Interestingly, it has not necessarily done so at the expense of the power of general secretaries. This point was put to us by a civil service union leader who argued that the power of at least civil service union general secretaries had been enhanced by the legislation for two reasons. First, they had previously been appointed and now that they were elected they could claim a greater legitimacy: this, he argued, was not so much with regard to the membership, but *vis-à-vis* union activists. Second, the obligatory use of the ballot over industrial action has been extended to other matters, such as determining pay claims and pay settlements, which again enhanced the position of the general secretary *vis-à-vis* activists by appealing over their heads to the wider membership. Thus, for example, he continued, the power of annual conferences, usually dominated by activists, has been greatly reduced, although conferences are still important as policy-making bodies. Confirmation of this view came in a report that Inland Revenue staff had, at a special delegate conference in 1990, voted to withdraw from a PRP scheme introduced two years earlier. In response the general secretary said that the union's executive would press for improvements to the current scheme rather than seek its abolition. The executive, he added, took its mandate from the membership, which had balloted in favour of a comprehensive settlement, including performance pay. A similar view was put by another general secretary from a large public sector white-collar union, who believed that the move from an appointed general secretary to an elected one had transformed his position.

The general secretary of a large industrial union believed that the legal obligation on unions to keep a central list of members had led to computerisation, more accurate membership figures, greater administrative efficiency and increased power at the centre *vis-à-vis* branches and districts. An additional change in his union, which had also shifted the balance of power, had been the decision to channel all income and expenditure through head office. The check-off had removed the need for branch collections of subscriptions for the majority of members. Their friendly society benefits, which used to be paid out by the branch, were now paid direct from head office to the member.

Another factor which has affected the relationship between unions and their members was the series of cases by 'working miners' (see Chapter 5) taken during the coal-mining strike. The interpretation of the courts (that in effect there was a contract between the individual member and his union) was of great significance in establishing that at common law members had substantial rights *vis-à-vis* their unions. Additional to the common law position was the legislation of the late 1980s which gave a number of specific rights to individual members (see Chapter 5), and which also established the office of a Commissioner for the Rights of Trade Union Members. Perhaps more important than the legal position was the eventual acceptance by many union leaders that they were out of touch with their members, that the views of members had often been neglected or taken for granted, and that this needed to be rectified. Thus one leading union official stated that the members had become disillusioned with their leaders in 1977–9, believing that they were getting 'too big for their boots'. The Winter of Discontent had strengthened this belief and was connected with the support by many trade unionists for a Conservative Government's legislation. Another leading official said that the votes of trade unionists, especially in the south, were a key factor in the return of a Conservative Government in 1979.

Consequently, many unions in recent years have taken steps to improve two-way communications: for example, through attitude surveys, internal restructuring, the use of 'consultants' (often, but not exclusively, academics) to advise on changes and the more frequent use of ballots, even when not required by law. The successful campaign carried out by unions in 1984/5 to secure favourable votes for the continuation of their political funds was an educational process which helped greatly in improving communications. This balloting on political funds took place again in 1994/5 alongside the renewal of mandates for the check-off.

With regard to potential membership, a number of unions have made some effort to recruit in areas where they have previously been weak: for example, in retail distribution, hotels and catering and finance. There have also been efforts particularly directed at women, at youth, at part-time employees and at ethnic minorities. As part of making themselves more attractive to members and potential members, unions have developed individual services: for example, financial services such as advantageous insurance policies, mortgages, loans, holidays, discounts on purchases and legal advice, usually in association with other organisations (for example, Unity Bank).

Unions have also sought to improve their image and to make more effort in the field of public relations. Too rosy a picture should not, however, be drawn, (see Kelly and Heery, 1989). Union resources are limited, and there are great difficulties in breaking into unorganised sectors. As one leading general secretary put it, in the early 1980s the unions were too occupied in coping with redundancies: there had also been a major collapse in union morale. Moreover, unions had not done any real recruiting for 20 years so they did not know how to do it. Officials had not regarded themselves as recruiters; they had become the providers of services to existing members. In the 1970s members came into unions without much effort. Unionisation was often regarded as inevitable by many employers and as a natural state of affairs. In the 1980s and 1990s the attitudes of many employers changed and anti-unionism became more prevalent: a feeling was encouraged by the Conservative Governments and by some employers that there was a better way to deal with employee relations than through unions. Thus far unions have not shown that they can recruit new members and hold them in the private services sector on a greater scale than they have in the past. However, a major new effort on organisation and recruitment was highlighted by the TUC in 1996, based on the USA where the American Federation of Labor/ Congress of Industrial Organizations had set up an organising Institute to train 500 young organisers. Experiences in Australia and Holland were also drawn upon.

One problem for a number of unions is the high turnover of members: for example, in USDAW about one-third leave every year and in the TGWU about one-fifth leave every year: they had failed to recruit enough to replace those who had left. While it is not usually difficult to get a new employee to join a union in a well-organised workplace, when employees leave and move to another less well organised one their membership often lapses because the check-off stops. So it is still the case that the continuity of union membership depends on workplace recruitment. The situation had led one general secretary to argue that there needed to be a new basis for joining a trade union which meant that individuals would remain members wherever they worked. Subscriptions would be paid to head office by direct debit, making the membership long-term, if not permanent. For that, the member would get a wide range of services and membership would be valuable, even if in a particular workplace the union was not recognised for collective bargaining. This 'insurance'-based union membership is a long way from current practice and attitudes. However, many unions are putting much greater emphasis on the provision of services to members and on representative recognition rights.

enterprise, but this does not mean that their objectives and the means of achieving these objectives are always identical. Divergences arise and these have to be accommodated and reconciled: how they are accommodated is the very heart of industrial relations. However, there is a New Unionism in the sense that unions are seeking a partnership with employers and stressing cooperation rather than antagonism.

In Chapter 6 we argued that management's attitude to unions in the 1980s and 1990s was not one of frontal assault, except in a number of extreme cases, but often of diminishing the power of unions by restricting the scope of collective bargaining and by by-passing unions and stewards through more direct approaches to individual employees. De-recognition was limited (Claydon, 1989), although growing later in the period (Claydon, 1996), but union attempts to secure recognition at greenfield sites and at non-union enterprises have been mainly successfully resisted. Where recognition has been granted it has usually been on management terms: that is to say, it has often been exclusive to a single union. Management has chosen the union (the so-called 'beauty contests') and management has largely determined the procedural agreements: for example, in some cases no-strike agreements with binding arbitration (conventional or pendulum). There has been an absence of the traditional 'status quo' clause, and often a clause stating that management had complete freedom in operational matters, including the use of labour. The unions' efforts on recruitment have been mentioned earlier and it is only necessary to repeat that increased efforts have been made to recruit new members, although success has been limited, particularly in the growing services sector. They have also developed new services to attract members and have sought to target specific groups such as women, part-timers, the young and ethnic minorities. One consequence has been increased inter-union competition, which the TUC has sought to keep within reasonable bounds.

On collective bargaining procedures, as we saw in Chapter 6, management, as a broad generalisation, sought first to reduce the importance of industry-wide bargaining or eliminate it altogether and decentralise to company, divisional or establishment level, and second, to restrict the scope of bargaining by reasserting managerial authority, particularly on operational matters. On the level of collective bargaining, the union response has been mixed. In some instances, unions have sought to defend industry-wide agreements, although rarely to the extent of taking industrial action. Two notable exceptions were in British Rail and in local government (white-collar APT&C grades), both in 1989 when industrial action (admittedly related to pay as well as to procedural change) was successful in resisting management proposals. In the docks industry, the ending by the government of the National Dock Labour Scheme in 1989 was followed by strike action to try to obtain a national agreement with the port employers in place of the scheme. The port employers refused to negotiate a national agreement, preferring local agreements, and the strike collapsed after a relatively short period. In most other cases union opposition was not taken to such lengths. For example, there was reluctant acquiescence to the ending of industry-wide bargaining in the London clearing banks (1987), in the water industry (1989) and in commercial television (1989).

On the scope of collective bargaining it has long been union policy – formally and informally – to seek to extend the scope of bargaining. In response to employer attempts to restrict the scope, either through changing agreements or unilaterally changing work practices, there were a number of well-publicised pitched battles: for example, at British Leyland at the end of the 1970s and early 1980s; in the newspaper industry, particularly at Wapping, but also in parts of the provincial press; at P & O, and in coal-mining; all of which resulted in major union defeats. Elsewhere (for example, in the television industry) unions on the whole have had to retreat and accept the assertion of managerial authority. Sometimes this has been expressed in agreements, and at greenfield sites it has often been one of management's conditions for recognition: for example, the Nissan agreement provides for 'complete flexibility and mobility of employees'. More often it has been less a question of changes in formal agreements, and more of changes in the way the establishment was managed.

On involvement, consultation and participation, unions have long argued for the maximum consultation with employers, although consultation was seen by many as an inferior process to collective bargaining since the former, however genuine and thorough, meant that in the last resort management had the right to take the final decision. In the 1980s and 1990s, as outlined in Chapter 6, many employers sought to improve direct communications with their workforce, to involve individuals to a greater degree in the work process, and to some extent by-pass established joint consultative and joint negotiating committees. Such practices (of a varying kind) were on the whole not resisted by unions; indeed, unions were often in no position to do so, even if they had wanted to. There were a few examples of resistance (for example, to the introduction of quality circles at Fords), but these were exceptional. At national level, however, the TUC continued to advocate greater union participation in management decision-making, including the greater disclosure of information, further arguing that without statutory obligations many employers would not pursue such policies. Given Conservative Government and employer opposition to such a step, TUC hopes for progress switched to the EU and to the European Social Charter.

The move by employers to more direct communications with individual employees and attempts at greater involvement in job-related tasks may be seen as part of a change in management style and, in its most developed form, as part of a move towards HRM. In the early 1980s, the style and actions of many managements was considered as 'macho-management', as typified by British Leyland and British Steel, albeit that such action was usually the result of recession, falling demand and increasing competitive pressures. This term was used in relation to the mass redundancies and closures which were widespread in British industry at that time. It also related to managements riding rough-shod over established procedures and agreements and to major unilateral changes in working practices. What was perhaps surprising was the absence of strong union resistance, in particular to the drastic cut-backs in the labour force. In part it would appear in some cases to have been due to a feeling of inevitability, and in other cases to relatively generous severance payments which at the time were attractive to many of the workforce. Thus even if union leaders had wanted to fight, and thought they could do so successfully, they were unable to carry their members with them. With the growth of HRM and the apparent change in style and approach, unions, as previously stated, have not generally shown any major resistance, although they have often been suspicious of management's motives and policies (which have been a move towards individualisation and away from a more collective approach). A more participative style on the part of management is in any case difficult for unions to resist. Moreover, the second major recession in the early 1990s meant that unions' bargaining power remained weak and it did not significantly increase with the subsequent recovery. Many large companies continued to reduce their labour forces drastically, although now the prime factor often appeared to be enhanced profits rather than competitive necessity.

Another aspect of management policy in the 1980s and 1990s has been the drive for greater flexibility on the part of the labour force. It is impossible to generalise about unions' reactions to this, for it varies over thousands of different workplaces. Greater flexibility, leading to the more efficient use of resources and higher productivity, is difficult to argue against, even if there was a desire to do so. Moreover, if unions and workforce are convinced that greater flexibility is necessary for a given enterprise, to survive in a world of ever-increasing competition, then it is unlikely to be resisted. Open communications and consultation, and a willingness to negotiate rather than impose change, are crucial for the peaceful and willing acceptance of change. Moreover, where management has been willing to compensate for the acceptance of change, there is likely to be more willing acceptance. Having said all this, there are limits to which unions and employees can be expected to accept greater flexibility, and suspicions have been voiced. Some practices and agreements developed over the years which might be viewed by employers and government as 'restrictive', are viewed by many employees as 'protective' and may be deemed essential for social reasons, for reasons of health and safety and for economic reasons. For example, temporary and casual employment are not likely to be welcomed by their recipients, and neither is the absence of any limits on daily hours of work. Unions have therefore been cautious, and a more realistic approach is to examine existing working practices on a systematic basis rather than condemn them all out of hand and proclaim that 'flexibility' is the answer to all problems and needs. The achievement of greater flexibility can mean a worsening of working conditions for employees.

On pay increases, these have not in general been a major bone of contention in much of the private sector in the 1980s and 1990s. Average earnings have kept ahead of the cost of living throughout the period. On the whole private employers sought to reduce costs by cutting numbers rather than reducing the real pay of their surviving employees. In the public sector it has been a different story. While some of the nationalised (or former nationalised) industries (for example, electricity and gas) provided pay increases in line with the private sector, others (such as British Rail and coal-mining) did not. The main sufferers, as a result of government cash limits, were employees in the public service sector who received pay increases below that of the private sector, except for the favoured few (primarily the police and firefighters and those covered by the Review Bodies). In this sector, there was union resistance and several notable strikes took place during the 1980s – for example, civil servants, NHS staff and school teachers – but with only very limited success, if any.

Apart from the level of pay increases, there have been attempts by management in both the private and public sectors to achieve the greater individualisation of pay, in particular through PRP schemes. Among unions there were major differences of approach. Many unions have traditionally been suspicious of such schemes on the grounds of possible subjectivity, favouritism and divisiveness, and because of their belief in 'the rate for the job'. Some (for example, NALGO) opposed it and would have nothing to do with its operation. Others (for example, BIFU) sought to control it and sought safeguards against abuse, through negotiating the size of the kitty and the criteria for the operation, and through advising members on how to argue about it with managers.

Overall, whether there was union opposition or not, PRP has spread widely throughout the private and public sector. Similarly unions have traditionally had reservations about profit-sharing and employee-share ownership schemes, but this has not prevented their growth, and unions have in recent years been more prepared to consider them favourably. The other major pay development has been the very substantial widening of pay differentials and, despite the efforts of many unions to improve the lot of the lower-paid, differentials have continued to widen.

The Trades Union Congress

The TUC has two major roles, the first being that of spokesman and representative of the trade union movement. During the Second World War and in the early post-war decades this role developed into acting as the representative of unions with regard to:

(a) government;
(b) employers;
(c) the public;
(d) international institutions.

The second major role has been that of maintaining order and keeping the peace between unions, as typified by the Bridlington Agreement of 1939 and the work of the TUC's inter-Union Disputes Committee; the provision of certain services (for example, trade union education and training and research facilities); the provision of guidelines on important issues (for example, picketing and disputes procedures); and finally having a regard for the wider interests of the trade union movement.

Before considering the TUC's role and the changes which occurred in the 1980s and 1990s, one preliminary remark is necessary: namely, that it must be appreciated that the TUC is the servant of its affiliated unions and not their master. It was the unions which created the TUC and not the other way around. The TUC's powers over affiliated unions are very limited, and in the last resort consist essentially of suspension and then expulsion. Such power has to be used sparingly or it becomes self-defeating. The TUC was often in the early post-war decades portrayed by the media as all-powerful, but this was a far cry from reality. However, all trade unions recognise that when they agree to get together through the TUC they may have influence. It has been the role of the leaders of the TUC to secure that unity in order that the unions' influence should be maximised. The 1980s saw rather more occasions when they disagreed than when they agreed by comparison with, say, the 1960s, but this is much less true of the 1990s.

The role of the trade union movement with regard to its affiliated unions, government and employers is considered in the next three sections. Here we briefly consider internal changes in the TUC, the TUC's role *vis-à-vis* society in general and internationally.

The TUC conducted important reviews in 1980 and 1984: *The Organisation, Structure and Services of the TUC* (TUC, 1980) and *TUC Strategy* (TUC, 1984). The former was adopted by Congress in 1981 and led to the TUC Development Programme which, among other things, sought to extend the number of TUC industry committees and strengthen its regional organisation. The latter review discussed the changing environment and its effects on trade union aims and objectives, functions and methods. As a consultative document it did not make recommendations, but posed a series of questions for unions to consider. A further review was conducted between 1987 and 1989 through the establishment of a Special Review Body, whose two reports are discussed in the next section of this chapter. Finally, 1993, which was the 125th anniversary of the formation of the TUC, saw the election of a new general secretary, John Monks, and another review which resulted in a 'relaunch programme' for the TUC in March 1994 entitled *Campaigning for Change: A New Era for the TUC*

(TUC, 1994a). This programme saw the TUC as a campaigning body. It also introduced far-reaching internal changes, in particular the permanent suspension of the TUC's 17 policy and industry committees and their replacement by a single executive committee answerable to the General Council. Use is being made of task groups: the Executive Committee meets monthly and the General Council only meets four times a year instead of monthly. Regional activities have been strengthened.

Also in 1994 there was a major reorganisation of staff structure. In departmental terms, the Organisation and Industrial Relations Department merged with the Trade Union Education Department to form a new Organisation and Services Department. Some changes in departmental boundaries and titles were introduced so that the Equal Rights Department concentrated solely on equality issues and the Economic Department was enlarged to cover economic and social affairs. A new unit was created, responsible to the Assistant General Secretary, to cover Europe, and the Press and Information Department was replaced by a new Campaigns and Communications Department with a wider remit for campaigning and lobbying at Westminster.

An earlier major internal change was in the composition of the General Council in 1983. Until then, members had been nominated by some 20 trade groups, but with all affiliated unions entitled to vote in their election. However, Congress approved changes, which came into effect in 1983, whereby all unions with a membership of 100 000 or more were automatically entitled to at least one seat (section A). Smaller unions (section B) – those with under 100 000 members – were allocated 11 seats for which elections were held, but in which only the smaller unions were entitled to vote. In addition, six seats were reserved for women (section C), in the election of whom all unions were entitled to vote. The change was particularly significant in that it had an effect on the political balance of the General Council in favour of moderation. It also reduced the power of the very large unions in that they no longer dominated the votes in the election of the members from the smaller unions. To a considerable extent the change in the composition of the General Council reflected the changing composition of union membership: relatively more white-collar members, more public sector members, and more women members. A further change in the composition of the General Council, although a less fundamental one, took place in 1989, creating four sections as set out below.

Section A: consisting of members from those unions with a membership of 200 000 or more:

200 000–399 999	–	2 seats
400 000–649 999	–	3 seats
650 000–899 999	–	4 seats
900 000–1 199 999	–	5 seats
1 200 000–1 499 999	–	6 seats

Where the total number of women members of any union in Section A was 100 000 or more, that union had to nominate at least one woman.

Section B: members from those unions with a membership of 100 000 up to 199,999. Each such union was entitled to one seat.

Section C: between 6 and 11 members elected from those unions with a membership of less than 100 000. The total number of seats available depends on Section C membership in any given year.

Section D: four women members, all of whom were members of unions with less than 200 000 members.

The main reasons for this change were first to secure a more even balance of members per seat between the smaller and the larger unions and second to ensure a larger number of women on the General Council.

Subsequently, the following was agreed:

Section E: consisting of one black member from a union with membership of 200 000 or over;

Section F: consisting of one black member from a union with less that 200 000;

Section G: consisting of one black woman member.

The General Council, on the above basis, consisted in 1997 of almost 50 members.

In recent years the TUC has suffered from financial problems and has been forced to make economies, basically for the same reason as most of its affiliates: namely, the fall in union membership. In 1995 the TUC's expenditure was £13.9 million and its total income £12.6 million. The financial difficulties of many individual unions make it hard for the TUC to increase its affiliation fee continually. The 1994 internal changes in its operation, and a sharper definition of its objectives and functions, should result in greater cost effectiveness.

The TUC is the acknowledged spokesman of the trade union movement in relation to society or the public at large. Unlike a number of other countries, where there are separate trade union centres based on religious, political or occupational (for example, white-collar and manual) differences, the British trade union movement has only one central organisation. It is true that there are a considerable number of unions outside the TUC, but most of these are extremely small and the total non-affiliated membership is of the order of only

1 million. The non-affiliated unions of any size are the RCN (303 000 members in 1995) and the ATL (171 000 members in 1995). Recently a number of smaller organisations have joined the TUC: for example, UNIFI (Barclays Bank Staff Union), the Halifax Staff Union, the Managerial and Professional Officers, and the British Orthoptic Society.

In its role of spokesman, the TUC seeks to inform the public of union objectives and policies, not only on trade union matters but on matters relating to society more generally (for example, education, social security, the economy and international affairs). In the later 1980s and the 1990s, more emphasis has been given to expounding the virtues of trade union membership, and indeed of the necessity for the existence of trade unions in a democratic, pluralistic society. The TUC through its Special Review Body (TUC, 1988b, 1989), started to re-think its role and purpose in the changing environment in which it has to operate, and among other matters has sought to help unions in publicity and public relations, in the development of services and in coordinated recruitment drives.

Under the 1994 Campaign for Change programme, the TUC is focused on promoting a renewal of confidence in the concept of full employment, on developing trade union responses to the HRM agenda, and on campaigning for a right of representation for workers in relation to their employers, and rights for trade unions in relation to trade union organisation and recognition (TUC, 1995). The TUC has also campaigned for social partnership in industry, stressing common interest in efficiency, and in general arguing for cooperation and not confrontation (TUC, 1996a).

In addition, the TUC is taking a pro-active approach to European integration. Thus a new TUC European Unit has been set up to service unions and lead the TUC's campaigning and lobbying work in Europe. The Unit has embarked on a new project on information and consultation in multinational companies, and is compiling a comprehensive database for unions on multinational companies operating in Britain. In 1993 the TUC also established an office in Brussels which works closely with the European trade union bodies and the European Commission.

Internationally, the TUC is a prominent member of the International Confederation of Free Trade Unions (ICFTU) which was formed in the early post-war years and has its headquarters in Brussels. The ICFTU consists of 196 affiliated organisations in 136 countries, with a combined membership of approximately 124 million. It is the spokesman for much of the international trade union movement and presents trade union views on world economic, social and political issues to the public at large and to relevant international institutions, such as United Nations agencies. Second, the TUC represents the British trade union movement at the ILO, an agency of the UN with headquarters in Geneva. The ILO is a tripartite organisation, with each country's delegation consisting of representatives from government, employers and unions. It is concerned with setting international labour standards and guidelines, mainly through conventions and recommendations, on a wide range of matters, such as freedom of association, safety and training, minimum pay, minimum terms and conditions of employment. Third, the TUC is a leading member of the ETUC, which is based in Brussels and which has 56 affiliated organisations from 28 countries with a combined membership of about 53 million. A major concern of the ETUC is the EU. The ETUC makes representations to the EU on matters of trade union interest, and is consulted on such matters. Indeed, at European level, if not in the UK, the trade union movement is acknowledged as, and treated as, one of the social partners. In addition, the TUC is represented on the EU's Economic and Social Council and on a range of Advisory Committees: for example, on the Advisory Committee for the Free Movement of Workers, on the Committee for Vocational Training, and the European Social Fund Committee.

Individual unions have also been playing a significant role in EU deliberations, either through the ETUC or through their international organisations (for example, BIFU through its membership of the International Federation of Commercial, Clerical, Professional, and Technical Employees (FIET)). Other international activities include membership of the Trade Union Advisory Committee to the Organisation for Economic Cooperation and Development (OECD) and the Commonwealth Trade Union Council.

The TUC, on a number of occasions in the 1980s and 1990s, complained to the ILO about Conservative Government policy. For example, there were complaints about GCHQ and the ILO Committee of Experts determined that the British Government had been in breach of Convention 87 on freedom of association, and subsequently the ILO Conference deplored the dismissal of trade unionists from GCHQ. A second complaint concerned the 1987 Teachers' Pay and Conditions Act, which had abolished negotiating machinery and which the TUC argued was in violation of ILO Convention 98 on the right to organise and to collective bargaining. This complaint was also upheld by the Committee of Experts and by the ILO Governing Body. A third complaint concerned the 1988 Employment Act. The ILO Committee of Experts, who had conducted a review of British industrial relations legislation since 1980, found that large areas of the legislation were not compatible with Conventions 87 and 98 on freedom of association and protection of the right to organise, and collective bargaining. They asked the Conservative Government to have the 1988 Employment Act amended to restore to trade unions the possibility of disciplining members who refused to participate in a lawful strike or other industrial action, and to enable unions to indemnify members or officials in respect of fines imposed by the courts. The Committee of Experts also noted that the narrowing, since 1980, of protections in civil law for strikes had virtually excluded the possibility of taking boycott, protest, or sympathetic action, and that the definition of trade disputes imposed excessive restrictions on the right to strike. Employers could also take refuge behind subsidiary companies to deprive working people of the possibility of taking lawful industrial action. The experts asked the then Government to amend the legislation, and to introduce legislation preventing strikers from being dismissed or having other discriminatory treatment taken against them. They also asked the Government to stop the blacklisting of people on grounds of their trade union membership or activities. The experts commented that a positive statement of trade union rights by the Government would be of advantage. A more recent complaint which has been upheld by the ILO concerned s.13 of the 1993 Trade Union Reform and Employment Rights Act (see Chapter 5), which encourages employers to discriminate against employees who refuse to accept personal contracts by paying them less than those who do.

The Trades Union Congress and affiliated unions

In 1987 the TUC established a Special Review Body with the task of considering the future role of the TUC. Its first Report (TUC, 1988b) identified a number of key areas for investigation, namely:

(a) the need to review the problems of securing recognition, the terms on which recognition is gained, the pressures arising from inter-union competition, and the role of the TUC Disputes Principles and Procedures, linked to an assessment of employer attitudes;
(b) public perceptions of unions and the promotion of trade unionism generally, as well as among specific groups;
(c) the need to give further emphasis to consolidating membership and building the organisation in the light of the labour market trends in order to protect and to expand the 'frontier of trade unionism';
(d) the role of union and TUC services and the scope for their coordination, expansion and development.

It then identified three broad roles for the TUC:

(a) helping to improve and regulate inter-union relationships;
(b) helping unions to develop their organisation;
(c) helping unions to provide improved services to members.

With regard to inter-union relationships, the Report pointed out that on a number of occasions in the past the TUC had reviewed the complex structure of the trade union movement, but that Congress had not been able to agree on a particular form of trade union structure as being most desirable, and the TUC had no authority to impose general solutions. However, important initiatives had been taken to promote mergers on a broadly sectoral basis, to establish spheres of influence agreements between unions, and other joint arrangements, and, since 1970, to set up TUC industrial committees. Indeed, throughout its history, the TUC has sought to promote cooperation between unions and avoid (but, if necessary, resolve) inter-union rivalry and differences by discussion, conciliation and arbitration.

To this end, the Special Review Body recommended first that there should be a code of practice designed to set standards for unions seeking recognition, and second that there should be a modification to Principle 5 of the TUC Disputes Principles and Procedures. These recommendations were accepted by the 1988 Congress. The background to the review was that there had been rows between the big unions about single union agreements and the Bridlington Procedure was inadequate to deal with them. In particular, the EETPU had been in the forefront of signing single union agreements (often no-strike agreements). The purpose of the review was to prevent inter-union difficulties when unions sought to enter into single union agreements. To this end, a union in the process of making a single union agreement should notify the TUC and provide relevant details (including whether and to what extent any other union had membership, whether other unions were involved in making presentations claiming recognition to the company, and whether contact had been made with other unions). On receipt of the details, the TUC would aim to tender advice within two weeks. The Code also provided that:

> Unions, when making recognition agreements, must not make arrangements which specifically remove, or are designed to remove, the basic democratic lawful rights of a trade union to take industrial action. This is not meant to deter unions using arbitration, pendulum or otherwise, at the request of one or both parties. Unions must not make any agreements which remove or are designed to remove, the basic democratic lawful rights of a trade union to take industrial action in advance of the recruitment of members and without consulting them. If faced by circumstances where procedures are insisted on which remove the basic democratic right to take industrial action, the union should consult the TUC at the earliest opportunity.

It further provided that: 'Unions are expected to cooperate with any procedures, which have been approved by the General Council of the TUC, which are operated by the TUC, STUC, Wales TUC or TUC Regional Councils in relation to inward investment authorities', and also that:

> When negotiating recognition agreements which have implications for substantive factors, unions should have regard to the general level of terms and conditions of employment which are already the subject of agreement with the company concerned, or which have been set through recognised arrangements, and take all possible steps to avoid undermining them.

The Special Review Body pointed out that competition between unions concerning recruitment and recognition could result in the duplication of effort and the wasteful use of scarce trade union resources. It could also adversely affect the standing of unions with members, potential members and employers. To help overcome these problems the Special Review Body considered the possibility of 'designated organising' areas and 'protected' areas which would be considered further in its Second Report. There was also a discussion on the problems of multi-unionism, which would also be considered further in its Second Report.

With regard to helping unions to develop their organisation and to provide improved services, the Special Review Body's first report proposed enhanced contacts with national employers' organisations, in particular the CBI and the Institute of Personnel Management, to discuss practical industrial relations questions. Other proposals included pilot regional and local labour market surveys which would draw up an economic and employment profile and its implications for trade unions; a development programme on union services; improved public relations in order to promote trade unionism, using modern techniques including advertising, videos and opinion research; and the targeting of special groups such as women workers and young people. All these proposals were to be considered further in the Second Report.

The Second Report (TUC, 1989) reported on a number of matters, including the work carried out on labour market information, local labour market pilots and joint recruitment drives under the auspices of the TUC at Old Trafford Park, Milton Keynes and Dockland. On trade union services a major initial package of services had been established, available to all TUC unions. It covered pension services (arranged with Unity Trust), insurance and certain other financial services, and legal services on non-employment matters (arranged with the Law Society). On problems associated with multi-unionism, the Report promoted the concept of 'single table' bargaining and proposed to develop the concept further, while acknowledging that it was neither practicable nor desirable in all situations.

In 1993 the TUC produced a new edition of 'TUC Disputes Principles and Procedures'. This was made necessary above all by the 1993 Act, which broadly had the effect of:

> denying the right of a union to refuse admission to an applicant for membership unless the person does not satisfy union rules;
> removing the right of a union to exclude an individual from membership other than in very restricted circumstances; and
> making it unlawful for a union to exclude members as a result of a TUC Disputes Committee Award. (TUC, 1993)

It was thus an attack on a vital traditional role of the TUC.

The new provisions provide that all affiliates accept, as a binding commitment to their continued affiliation of the TUC, that they will not knowingly and actively seek to take into membership the present or recent members of another union by making recruitment approaches (whether directly or indirectly) without the agreement of that organisation. A new element is a moral responsibility on the part of the respondent union to offer compensation to the complainant union for any loss of income suffered as a consequence of any knowing active recruitment of its members. If the matter goes to a Disputes Committee then the Committee may adjudicate on a compensatory settlement.

During the 1980s, there were two other issues concerning inter-union relations which were of major concern to Congress. The first was part of the TUC's reaction to trade union legislation (which is discussed in a subsequent section): namely, the question of unions applying for government money to meet the cost of ballots. As part of its opposition to government legislation, Congress had decided that unions should not apply for such funds. However, the AEU and the EETPU both decided that they would do so. This raised the likelihood of a major clash which, if the two unions did not back down, could only lead to their eventual expulsion. Rather than face this possibility, Congress altered its policy and no longer sought to prevent unions applying for government funds. Virtually all unions then took public funds to pay for their ballots, the cost in 1992 being £3.4 million. However, in February 1993 the Secretary of State made regulations to phase out over three years the provision of public funds for balloting, and indeed for trade union education as well.

The second issue related to the Bridlington Agreement and perhaps its inadequacies, namely the policies and practices of the EETPU. The EETPU had for many years been pursuing its own policies (which it was, of course, fully entitled to do). But in doing so it was highly vocal in its criticism of many other unions and of mainstream Congress policy. This, needless to say, did not endear the EETPU to many other unions, particularly those on the left of the political spectrum. Conflict reached its height over the Wapping dispute (see Chapter 5) when the EETPU was accused of supplying labour to the Wapping plant and enabling News International to produce its newspapers despite the dismissal of the entire labour force (with the exception of the journalists) of the *Sun, The Times, The Sunday Times* and the *News of the World*. The print unions – SOGAT and the NGA – pressed hard for the disciplining of the EETPU and it was censured (TUC Annual Report, 1988, pp. 13 and 14), although its expulsion was avoided by a very narrow margin.

Having avoided expulsion over Wapping, the EETPU was expelled by the 1988 Congress for refusing to conform with two decisions of the TUC's Disputes Committee, and the subsequent General Council directives, regarding single union agreements into which it had entered, namely Christian Salvenson (Food Services) Ltd, Salstream and Orion Electric (UK) Ltd, Port Talbot (TUC Annual Report, 1988, p. 16). This was the first time that a major union has been expelled from the TUC in recent times (with the exception of the expulsion of a number of unions for registering under the 1971 Act), with the expectation on its part, and that of other unions, that it might not be returning. However, in 1992, the EETPU merged with the AEU and in its new form it returned to the TUC in 1993.

The Trades Union Congress and government

The role of the trade union movement as a 'fourth estate' or 'social partner' which existed for most of the post-war period, was arguably its most important one. In the TUC's own words:

> For over a century the prime role of the TUC has been to influence the actions of governments over a wide range of economic, industrial and social issues of major concern to trade union members. Since 1940 governments too have increasingly sought a working relationship with the trade union movement. The present (Conservative) government has moved in the opposite direction. (TUC, 1984, p. 13)

Since 1979, under Conservative Governments the role had been reduced to virtually nothing. Indeed it could be argued that it has diminished even further still in that trade unions are regarded as not even a neutral element but, in Mrs Thatcher's phrase, as 'the enemy within'. The reasons for Conservative Governments' attitude to trade unions were discussed in Chapter 4, and it is not necessary to repeat them here. What is necessary is to give a brief account of how the reduction in the influence and participation of trade unions has taken place.

In the post-war decades up to 1980, trade unions had a recognised and accepted involvement in a number of areas of national life, the main areas being:

(a) economic affairs and particularly incomes policy;
(b) social policy;
(c) training;
(d) health and safety;
(e) ACAS;
(f) representation on a range of bodies, from the Boards of Nationalised Industries to Royal Commissions.

First, trade union involvement in economic policy was typified by the existence of the NEDC in which the TUC had, at least in theory, an equal voice with employer representatives and Government, and (again in theory at least) equal control over the NEDO. The TUC boycotted meetings of the NEDC for a time as a protest against the Conservative Government's ban on trade union membership at GCHQ in 1984. NEDC's role in a supposedly 'free market' economy was always a questionable one, and it was perhaps no surprise that the government in July 1987 should have decided unilaterally to curtail its activities drastically, to reduce the 38 Economic Development committees to 18 new Sector Groups, and to cut its staff by half. It was to meet less frequently; the Prime Minister would not again take the chair, and the Chancellor of the Exchequer would do so only infrequently.

As a further pinprick the Government declared that the convention whereby TUC nominees were accepted as the trade union representatives on the NEDC was ended and it proceeded in 1988 to appoint as a Council member the general secretary of the EETPU, which had recently been expelled from the TUC. In 1992, the Government abolished the NEDC completely.

However, in the 1960s and 1970s, the major involvement of the unions in economic affairs was through incomes policy which existed directly or indirectly through most of that period. Although the TUC frequently passed resolutions in favour of 'free collective bargaining', involvement in incomes policies, paradoxically, meant not only influence over pay determination, but some influence over matters relating to pay determination, such as prices, profits, dividends, taxation, and macro-economic policy generally. Conservative Governments of the 1980s condemned incomes policies of the past and declared that they would not be part of their economic policy; pay was to be a matter for free labour markets. Given a declared absence of incomes policy there need be no TUC involvement. But the declared absence of incomes policy did not mean that there was no policy on incomes. For most of the 1980s and the first half of the 1990s there was a policy to keep pay down in the public service sector, primarily through cash limits; and in the public corporations, primarily by strict financial targets. In the private sector, pay was to be restrained by high unemployment and greater competition in labour and product markets.

Second, the trade union movement, as a prime progenitor of the welfare state, had in the post-war decades a major interest in social welfare (for example, regarding pensions, sickness benefit, industrial injuries and unemployment pay), and its view and policies in this area were not without influence on successive governments. But Conservative Governments, from the beginning, were concerned to reduce public expenditure as far as possible in this area and a trade union input which sought to protect (and indeed improve) social welfare was therefore unacceptable. By the third Thatcher government it might be argued that Conservative Party policy was not one of merely restricting social welfare expenditure, but one of dismantling the welfare state, which was being characterised as 'the Nanny State', and as incompatible with the 'enterprise culture'.

Examples included the linking of state pensions to the cost of living and not to earnings, the reduction in benefits from the state earnings-related pension scheme, the encouragement of personal pension plans and private health insurance through tax concessions, the much harsher conditions required in order to obtain and retain unemployment benefit (now the job seekers' allowance) and the refusal to index the value of child allowances.

Third, there had been a long involvement of trade unions in the development of state support for training to remedy the deficiencies of British industry in this respect. From its inception, the MSC was a tripartite body with full union representation, and this was equally true of the ITBs and the

Area Manpower Boards. The Thatcher Governments progressively abolished these bodies, starting in 1980 with the abolition of most of the ITBs. This increased the importance of the MSC whose then chairman – Sir Richard O'Brien – was succeeded by David Young. In 1985 the MSC was abolished and replaced by the Training Commission, which was still tripartite; but this was reduced in scope when the Employment Service returned to the DE. In 1990 the Training Commission was abolished, along with the few remaining ITBs and the Area Manpower Boards, and replaced by 82 newly created locally based Training and Enterprise Councils (TECs) and the Training Agency. The Training Agency had hardly got off the ground when it too was abolished, and national training policy was back in the DE's Training, Employment and Enterprise Division, to be assisted only by a purely advisory body called the National Training Task Force. The Government laid down that TECs were to consist of two-thirds senior managers from private industry and one-third from the public sector, education, local authorities, voluntary organisations and trade unions. At the end of 1990 a Parliamentary Answer, quoted in *Personnel Plus* (1991), recorded TEC Boards as consisting of 378 employers, 29 trade unionists, 50 local authority representatives, 59 people from the educational field and the remainder from voluntary organisations and employers' federations. The decision to create TECs and the Training Agency was the key to the ending of tripartism in the training field. Nevertheless, what is remarkable is the long and successful record of tripartism in the 1980s in which the TUC exercised considerable influence. Moreover, recently the TUC, which has always put great emphasis on training, has been successfully seeking to work more closely with TECs and with union representatives on TECs, the number of whom has increased considerably. In 1996, the TUC signed a national training accord with 81 TECs in England and Wales. The TUC–TEC 'Bargaining for Skills' project is primarily aimed at raising awareness among shop stewards and other union representatives of training and development initiatives such as national vocational qualifications (NVQs) and the modern apprenticeship scheme.

Fourth, since the passing of the Health and Safety Act in 1974, and related regulations, recognised independent trade unions have had certain statutory rights at the place of work, and the whole field of health and safety has been administered at national level by a tripartite body called the Health and Safety Commission. Trade union involvement in this area has not been changed.

Fifth, another area where trade union involvement has not been basically changed is ACAS, whose Council remains tripartite, consisting of union and employer representatives and independents. Although appointments are made by the Secretary of State, the TUC in effect used to nominate the three union representatives, but in 1989 the Government asserted itself and appointed an additional representative from a non-TUC union as well as an additional businessman. However, it could be argued that although ACAS undoubtedly performs invaluable industrial relations functions in the field of conciliation, arbitration and advisory services, its Council is hardly a major policy-making body. Thus the ideological disadvantage to the Conservative Government of union involvement was not so great as the practical advantages.

Finally, there was a widely diverse field of institutions where it was accepted practice for trade union nominees, or at least people with a trade union background, to participate. Such bodies ranged from the Boards of nationalised industries and Regional and District Health Authorities to Royal Commissions and numerous quangos. Trade union membership in such bodies was progressively reduced. However, importantly, it is still present on Industrial Tribunals.

While the Conservative Governments had a general objection to the presence of trade union nominees and their influence on official bodies, it saw the force of the argument in favour of representation in the cases mentioned above. The three most important were the Health and Safety Executive, ACAS and the Industrial Tribunals. In all three the function to be performed is hardly conceivable except on a tripartite basis. If parties are to be conciliated or to take some responsibility for safety at work, their representative bodies have to be involved. The TUC, in its policy document *Campaigning for Change* (1994a), acknowledged that its influence in Whitehall and Westminster had diminished:

> Government departments no longer consider it necessary to consult the TUC on all matters of importance to the economy and employment . . . The TUC is thereby having to refocus its links with Whitehall and Parliament in order to maximise its influence on public policy. It needs to build understanding of trade union work and objectives across the political spectrum.

With the election of a Labour Government in May 1997 there has been a major change in atmosphere. This does not mean a return to the corporatism of the past. The Labour Party promised the unions 'fairness, not favouritism', and this has been accepted by the unions. The Labour Government immediately rescinded the ban on unions at GCHQ and announced that it will be signing the Social Chapter of the Maastricht Treaty. The Labour Government has also established the Low Pay Commission, including three trade union nominees, with a view to introducing an NMW Possible legislation on employee rights was not in the Queen's speech, but a consultative paper is expected in May 1998.

Reaction to legislation

In the early part of the 1980s, the unions and the TUC reacted strongly to government trade union legislation. The TUC wanted a re-run of the opposition to the 1971 Industrial Relations Act. Thus it proclaimed its complete opposition to the 1980 Employment Act and organised public demonstrations on 9 March 1980, and a Day of Action on 14 May 1980. The support, however, was poor compared with the protests against the 1970 Industrial Relations Bill, and it was clear that the TUC had misjudged the mood of the members. There was not the same hostility to the Government's proposals. Further TUC opposition was announced to the Government's Codes on Picketing and the Closed Shop and subsequently to the 1982 Employment Bill. At a Special Conference of union executives at Wembley in April 1982, it was decided:

(a) to campaign widely against the legislation;
(b) not to take part in membership agreement ballots;
(c) not to accept government funds for balloting;
(d) that the General Council would help unions in difficulties, if requested, including financial assistance;
(e) that a Special Defence Fund would be established.

A major economic recession was in progress with massive redundancies, and public opinion, including the opinions of many union members, seemed strongly of the view that unions had become too powerful and that some change in the balance of power was required.

However, a number of unions seemed prepared to ignore the new legislation. A crisis point was reached in the 1983 *Stockport Messenger* dispute (see Chapter 5). The point came when the TUC's then general secretary, Len Murray, immediately denounced the decision of a committee of the General Council to support the NGA's request for a newspaper strike, and his view was subsequently supported by the full General Council. Len Murray's opposition was based partly on the grounds that this would most likely have exposed the TUC to contempt of court, and partly because it would have meant TUC support for unlawful action. This arguably was the major turning point for the trade union movement. However much the TUC might oppose the new trade union laws, it would not engage in unlawful action. Murray, at this stage, also thought in terms of trying to arrive at an understanding with the government, remembering that it had just been returned for another five years. But this was not to be, for there almost immediately followed the de-recognition of the civil service unions by the government at GCHQ. Not only was there de-recognition, but staff at GCHQ were required to give up their union membership or face possible dismissal. The 'stick' of the threatened dismissal was accompanied by 'the carrot' of a £1000 bonus if staff relinquished their union membership. The government persisted in this policy despite the offer by the civil service unions of a no-strike agreement, and proceeded to establish a staff association, pronouncing that this would be the only body with whom it would deal. A well-supported one-day protest strike throughout the civil service failed to move the government. The unions then resorted to legal action, which failed on the grounds that the government – because it had claimed to be acting for 'national security' reasons – could not be challenged in the courts. The GCHQ episode convinced Murray that no deal was possible with the government and, indeed, it was followed not long afterwards by his decision to take early retirement.

The next major clash between unions and government was the coal-miners' strike of 1984/5. The TUC was not directly involved in the early months of the strike, not least because the NUM preferred it that way (Adeney and Lloyd, 1986). The NUM did not seek TUC help but sought support by direct approaches to certain individual unions: for example, the NUR, ASLEF, the NUS and the TGWU. At the 1984 Congress the NUM did seek help from the TUC, and a resolution to that effect was overwhelmingly carried. However, during the debate a number of union leaders, while backing the resolution, made clear that any support in the shape of industrial action would have to be conditional on the approval of their members who would be actually involved (for example, at power stations). The request for TUC help came very late in the day and what was given – other than moral support – was very limited and virtually confined to a hardship fund. The only active role played by the TUC was towards the end of the dispute, by which time the NUM was clearly facing defeat. At the request of the NUM, the TUC tried to retrieve something from the debacle in the form of an agreed settlement, but its efforts were rebuffed eventually by both Arthur Scargill and the government.

The complete defeat of the NUM was regarded by many as the low point for the trade union movement. If the NUM – allegedly the most powerful of unions – could not win, then who could? But other battles did take place. In the public sector, the long-drawn-out action of the teachers' unions resulted in the government removing the bargaining rights of some 400 000 teachers in 1987, imposing a unilaterally determined settlement and taking the power to impose further terms and conditions for at least the following three years. In the private sector, the strike of the print unions against News International in 1986 demonstrated that the law, particularly with regard to secondary action and picketing, could be effective, and the same was true of the seamen's dispute with P&O in 1988. In both cases, the unions were fined and had their funds sequestered. Following these events, it can be argued that the unions had learnt the hard way the inadvisability of openly defying the law and that they had to operate within the law, as the TUC had determined in 1983. Thus (for example, in the 1989 strikes in British Rail and the docks) the unions were meticulous in conforming to legal requirements. It can also be argued that the unions learned to use strike ballots as a bargaining tool, and that an affirmative vote gave unions a powerful weapon with which to seek an improved offer from management (see Chapters 5 and 11).

Unions and the Labour Party

First it needs to be recalled that the TUC is not affiliated to the Labour Party: it is individual unions which are affiliated, if they so decide. Although most unions of any size have a political fund, not all are affiliated to the Labour Party. Indeed, a declining proportion of TUC membership is in affiliated unions. Trade union/Labour Party links at national level have been strong, through union presence at the Labour Party Annual Conference and the existence of the block vote; strong union representation on the Labour Party's National Executive Committee; the unions' participation in elections for the leadership; and the high dependency of the Labour Party on union affiliation fees and special contributions at election times. All this is not to say that the Labour Party is dominated by the trade unions which are affiliated to it. 'The proof of the pudding is in the eating', and Labour Governments in the post-war decades have often differed fundamentally on certain policy issues with the trade unions (for example, on incomes policies). Moreover, recently important changes have taken place in the Labour Party: for example, the 'One member one vote', the ending of direct sponsorship of MPs and reduction of the unions' vote at Conference to under 50 per cent. In addition, more significant changes are likely in the near future, reducing the influence of the unions in the Labour Party still further.

Since 1979 a number of important issues have arisen with regard to the trade union/Labour Party relationship, the first of which related to trade union legislation. In the early 1980s, both the TUC and the Labour Party completely opposed the government's trade union legislation, and in the 1983 election, the Labour Party pledged its repeal. Towards the end of the 1980s both the TUC and the Labour Party started to reassess their position with regard to the legislation and accepted that much of it was here to stay (for example, ballots before industrial action, the election of National Executive Committee members and national leaders, restrictions on certain kinds of secondary action and secondary picketing, and the ending of the closed shop). It was clear that such measures had public support and that a complete return to the pre-1980 legal position would greatly harm the Labour Party's electoral prospects. From the union viewpoint, it was for some an acceptance of the inevitable: for others, there was an appreciation of the advantages to unions of some of the legislation: for example, strike ballots and obligatory and secret ballots to elect top officials and executives. Further, in supporting the EU and, in particular, the Social Charter, complete opposition to a legal framework became impossible. Indeed, the TUC came to appreciate that, given the relative weakness of unions, some of their objectives could only be realised through legislation. The 1990 Congress and the 1990 Labour Party Annual Conference provided a victory for those in the Labour movement who accepted this view.

A second issue was that after the 1987 election the Labour Party had come to appreciate that too close an identity with the unions was harmful to its electoral prospects. The unions, for their part, had begun to appreciate that a considerable proportion of their members did not vote Labour; indeed, there is some evidence that in the general election of 1983 more trade unionists than non-trade unionists voted Conservative (Himmelweit *et al.*, 1985, p. 208), and that the composition of union membership had been changing markedly, in particular the growing proportion of white-collar workers.

A third issue was that of ballots for trade union political funds, in which arguably the unions gained a very rare victory over Conservative Government legislation. The 1984 Trade Union Act required that unions which wished to retain their political funds (or establish such a fund) had to achieve a majority by secret ballot. The expectation at that time was that a number of unions would not be able to obtain a majority. In the event, every trade union which balloted secured a majority to continue their fund, and some unions, such as NALGO and the NCU, which previously had not had a political fund, voted in favour of such a fund. Such ballots have to be held at least once every 10 years, so that in 1994/5 ballots were held again to approve political funds, with complete success from a union viewpoint.

A fourth issue which arose during preparations for the 1984 Trade Union Act was the question of 'contracting-in' or 'contracting-out' of the political fund. The government was considering substituting 'contracting-in' for 'contracting-out' but, after discussions with the TUC, the Employment Secretary, Tom King, decided not to proceed with a clause to the Bill providing for 'contracting-in' if the TUC would issue appropriate guidelines to affiliated unions concerning their political fund arrangements. This the TUC subsequently did, in particular drawing the attention of unions to ensure that no obstacles were placed in the way of members who wished to 'contract-out'.

Unions and the European Union

Towards the end of the 1980s, there was a marked change in the TUC's attitude towards the EC, from a degree of caution to one of positive enthusiasm. At the 1988 Congress a General Council Report on *Europe 1992: Maximising the Benefits; Minimising the Costs* (TUC, 1988a) was approved. This preliminary report stated that the UK Conservative Government had been able to veto many progressive EC measures because of the need for unanimity in the Council of Ministers.

However, the Single European Act now permits new directives for 'improvements, especially in the working environment, as regards the health and safety of workers' to be adopted by a qualified majority, thus by-passing the

UK veto. The report continued by pointing out that this promising develop-ment was qualified by the lack of a clear definition of 'working environment' and by the continuing requirements for unanimity for directives relating to the 'rights and interests of employed persons'.

The Single European Act had also asked the Commission to endeavour to develop the dialogue between management and labour at a European level which could, 'if the two sides consider it desirable, lead to relations based on agreements'. A number of meetings have taken place, in what has become known as the Val Duchesse process, between ETUC and representatives of the European employers' organisations.

The Report concluded with a final chapter on 'TUC Strategy – Next Steps', which listed a number of issues for immediate action which the General Council intended to pursue. Also of great significance in 1988 was the invitation to the President of the Commission, Jacques Delors, to address Congress, which he did, arousing much enthusiasm as a result of his emphasis on the need for a social dimension to the Single European Market. He proposed a platform of social rights based on the European Social Charter, and the introduction of legislation on European companies which would provide for the extension to working people of information, consultation and negotiating rights, and for a permanent right to training.

The TUC Report (1993) to Congress sets out a trade union programme to take forward key demands to the European Parliament elections in 1994, and beyond to the next round of intergovernmental negotiations in 1996. For the TUC and ETUC, full employment and a solid basis of workers' rights are the priorities and go hand in hand. The TUC was convinced that the UK's opt-out would prove untenable in the longer term, for industrial no less than for political reason.

Indeed, with the election of a Labour Government in 1997 the new Government has declared that it will sign the Social Chapter. In *Britain and Europe – Next Steps* (1997a), the TUC outlined its views and policies for the future, arguing that 'the European social model of high productivity com-bined with strong welfare states, effective public services and trade union worker rights had proved fairer than the US and Asian Tiger models – although unemployment remains a major problem'. The TUC puts consider-able weight on 'The Employment Title' in the Treaty of Amsterdam (1997) on the integration of the Social Protocol and Social Agreement into the Treaty creating a single legal basis for social policy, and on the majority of new proposals going straight to the social partners for possible negotiation as framework agreements. If the negotiation track is not adopted then they will go back through the legislation route.

The TUC and many of the larger unions are paying increased attention to European developments and to strengthening links with their counterparts in Europe. For example, one union we interviewed has regular six-monthly meetings with its German equivalent, and has set up similar arrangements with Holland and Scandinavia. There have been officer exchange programmes and seminars for representatives from all European plants of multinationals concentrating on the setting up of EWCs. Most interestingly, in 1997 the GMB signed a joint membership agreement with the German Chemicals Union. For its part, the TUC has created a Europe Unit at Congress House and a Multinational Information project, which has established a data bank giving details of UK companies with subsidiaries in Europe. Many UK based multinationals have established EWCs, and the number will increase with the UK signing of the Social Chapter. The TUC has continued with its Network Europe Contact Points which is open to all affiliated unions (TUC, 1994a). In 1993 the TUC opened an office in Brussels, and it has continued to be active in the work of the ETUC and in the advisory committees of the EU. In 1996/7 the TUC has been active in helping unions in the establishment of EWCs (TUC, 1997b).

Conclusion

In the 1980s some observers stressed the importance of New Unionism. What was meant by that term was not always clear, but it was a form of 'business unionism'. It was exemplified in some of the 'new style' agreements with a number of Japanese and other companies, mainly at greenfield sites. The ingredients were typically recognition of a single union: a no-strike clause, usually with compulsory pendulum arbitration as the final means of settling disputes; the complete flexibility of labour; single status; and a high degree of consultation (for example, through a company council). Although such agreements were well publicised, their number was very limited – about 50 – and the number of employees covered was perhaps no more than 20 000. As Millward (1994) said, 'Quantitatively the new style agreements did not form the starting point for a "new industrial relations" in Britain' (pp. 126–7).

One might also query what is new about New Unionism (see Heery, 1996). Many unions have sought, and often achieved, single union agreements; it has long been the policy of manual unions to seek harmonisation of blue-collar and white-collar terms and conditions of employment; unions have always sought consultative processes with employers: and strikes have nearly always been a weapon of last resort, with many unions, particularly in the public sector, preferring arbitration. It was after all the Conservative Government and not the unions in the early 1980s which ended unilateral arbitration in the public sector, as did most private sector employers where it existed (for example, the clearing banks), and it has been employers who have resisted the harmonisation of terms and conditions.

However, as the 1990s progressed, if we have not seen New Unionism on a widespread scale, we have seen a degree of New Realism in the unions if by that is meant a growing acceptance of the realities of the changing environment in which unions had to operate. Thus unions have accepted many of the legal constraints imposed upon them and, unlike the reckless disregard of the legal consequences shown on occasion (for example, by the NGA in the *Stockport Messenger* dispute and the NUS in the P&O dispute), great care has been taken to abide by the law, especially in the docks dispute and the British Rail dispute, both in 1989. Certainly, balloting before the taking of official industrial action has become the norm. Unions have become more aware of the more competitive environment in which firms have to operate, and have been receptive to the introduction of new technology.

They have also recognised that they need actively to recruit new members and that in order to do so, they need to market themselves and to make themselves more attractive; hence the new services being offered. Insofar as these are offered to individuals, they also pinpoint a change in direction in seeking to meet the needs of individual employees, as well as the more traditional role of collective representation. Most of these services can be provided to members even where employers do not grant recognition.

Unions seem to have acknowledged that there are certain objectives which can be better achieved through legislation than through collective bargaining, as illustrated, for example, by the adoption by the TUC for the first time in 1986 of a resolution in favour of a national minimum wage and a statutory recognition mechanism, the 'FLARE' (Fair Laws and Rights in Employment) campaign of the GMB and support for the extension of individual legal rights at work.

For the future, the trade unions seem to be placing considerable hope on developments in Europe, including the extension of individual rights, protection at work and the growth of participative processes. It may be that in practice such participative processes will become more extensive and important than collective bargaining.

Not only have many individual unions sought to adjust to the changing environment and look to the future, but so has the TUC. The work of the TUC's Special Review Body is evidence of this, as is a series of TUC consultative documents on, for example, *Unions in Europe in the 1990s* (TUC, 1991c), *Collective Bargaining Strategy for the 1990s* (TUC, 1991b), and *Towards 2000* (1991b), and *Campaigning for Change* (TUC, 1994a). Taylor (1994) discusses in some detail the ways in which the TUC and individual unions are adjusting to change.

How far the New Realism is an adjustment to the adverse balance of power in a changed economic, political and social environment (which might be reversed if and when the pendulum swings), or how much it is the result of a fundamental change in attitude, is considered in Chapter 12. We would argue that there is a New Unionism, in that unions and the TUC have accepted the new environment and are seeking a cooperative approach to management and not an adversarial one. As the general secretary of one major union put it,

'What we used to regard as given no longer holds . . . purity of ideology is a consolation for the soul but you have to respond to the world as you find it.' This view was indeed typical of virtually all the general secretaries interviewed. They are in fact seeking social partnership (TUC, 1996a).

The effects of the Labour Government, elected in 1997, remain to be seen. Certainly there will not be the persistent overt hostility shown by the Conservatives to trade unionism *per se,* and there has already been the restoration of trade union rights at GCHQ, the commitment to sign the Social Chapter and the establishment of the Low Pay Commission, and an important commitment on statutory union recognition. Significantly, the TUC (1995), in a major policy document, seeks not only recognition for collective bargaining, but consultation and representation for individual members. However, major changes in the Conservative legislation seem unlikely. The biggest problem for the unions remains how to stem the continuing fall in union membership.

CHAPTER 9

The institutions of industrial relations

Introduction

Some aspects of the institutions and processes of industrial relations have already been discussed – in particular collective bargaining and consultation, involvement and participation – in the context of employer strategy (Chapter 6) and in terms of trade union reaction (Chapter 8). In this chapter we concentrate more on the implications of the changes that have, and are still, unfolding. In the early post-war decades there had been, particularly in much of manufacturing industry, a great growth in informal and fragmented workplace bargaining, in the importance of custom and practice, in the power of workgroups and shop stewards, and in wage drift (see Chapters 1 and 2).

Among the consequences were the undermining of industry-wide agreements, of national union officials and of employers' associations. The Donovan Commission described and analysed these developments and, by way of remedy, recommended management initiatives to obtain formal agreements at company and/or plant level. The NBPI in the 1960s in its reforming role had adopted a similar approach, and on the substantive side encouraged, for example, the introduction of job evaluation systems and the reform of payment systems and pay structures. In the early 1970s, the CIR encouraged the development and formalisation of company and plant procedures, including the role of shop stewards and their facilities. Progress indeed was made in the 1970s in the formalisation of both substantive and procedural agreements, although this progress was overshadowed in the public perception by rapidly escalating inflation, the re-emergence of major national strikes and the felt need by government, both Labour and Conservative, for a national incomes policy.

At that time, looking forward to the 1980s and 1990s, most industrial relations experts and practitioners would have expected a continuation of the trends of greater unionisation, a widening of the extent and scope of collective bargaining and more formalised procedural and substantive agreements. One example of academic thought (McCarthy and Ellis, 1973) was that there would be a very large extension of joint decision-making. The fact that most of these trends did not continue, and indeed were drastically reversed, must be explained in terms of the changed economic and political climate and the parties' reactions to the changed environment.

What happened, generally speaking at first, was increased formalisation in many procedures: for example, disciplinary and grievance procedures and increased formalisation of pay structures and systems through the extension of job evaluation and PRP. But on operational matters, there was a complete reversal of the trend with much greater freedom for managers to take unilateral action.

As stated earlier, what has happened to the institutions of industrial relations had been the subject of debate, with one school of thought originally arguing that fundamentally there had been little change in that the institutions were still in place despite the traumas of the 1980s and early 1990s, mass redundancies, high unemployment, a decline in union membership and fiercely anti-union legislation (Batstone, 1984, MacInnes, 1987). The second school of thought argued that there had been fundamental changes which had marginalised, and will continue to marginalise, unions and the joint institutions of industrial relations (Bassett, 1986; Phelps Brown, 1990).

WIRS 3 has shown conclusively (see Chapter 6) that there were major changes in the 1980s. The most important of these was the decline in the proportion of workplaces which recognised unions, and the decline in the coverage of collective bargaining, particularly in the private sector. Where unions are recognised the joint institutions are still in place, although in many industries and companies they have undergone marked change. But what has changed above all has been the balance of power. Management has been dominant and, as a result, it is the use to which the institutions have been put (rather than their retention, abolition or change) which is perhaps the crucial factor. Management has been pursuing its own objectives, often under the banner of HRM, and some observers have talked about the collapse of institutional industrial relations. It is also arguable that the changing use of the institutions has been affected by the changing attitudes and behaviour of employees and unions towards more cooperation and less confrontation. This has also been the subject of much debate and is returned to in Chapter 12.

In Chapter 6 it was argued that the main developments in collective bargaining which had taken place since 1979 had been, first, the reduced coverage; second, the changed level – away from industry level to company level and within companies to some extent to plant/divisional level – and third, the reduction in its scope. Before pursuing these developments, it is necessary to look briefly at what has happened to employers' associations.

Employers' associations

Historically employers' associations were major actors in British industrial relations, but they have been consigned in the last two decades or so to virtual oblivion by most academics and commentators. Attention has rightly been focused on individual companies and their industrial relations objectives and policies, particularly in view of changing developments. But, like trade unions, whatever the knocks they have suffered, employers' associations still exist. A limited number continue to engage in collective bargaining and all are seeking a new role for themselves in a changing world. The CBI was largely ignored by Thatcher Governments in favour of the more politically and ideologically acceptable Institute of Directors, and the CBI distanced itself from the TUC in a reaction against the corporatism of the 1970s. But it has a membership of some 250 000 companies and most employers' and trade associations are members. It has no rival as the national representative body of employers. In the early 1990s this seemed to be more appreciated by the Conservative Government and there was also some movement towards a better relationship with the TUC.

The major trend towards the decentralisation of collective bargaining continued in the 1980s. Brown and Walsh (1991) state, 'the decline in multi-employer bargaining has almost certainly accelerated in the second half of the 1980s. At least sixteen major national bargaining groups, covering a total of over a million employees, have been terminated since 1986' (p. 49), the most important of which was that of the engineering industry. Brown, Deakin and Ryan (1997) suggest that the importance of industry-wide bargaining has fallen even further in the 1990s, and so has the coverage of collective bargaining.

However, industry-wide bargaining still exists: for example, in electrical contracting, construction (particularly the building sub-contracting industries), printing, engineering construction and the garage trade, and also in a number of other industries which are mainly characterised by a large number of small establishments and with relatively low capital requirements.

In these industries employers clearly still see advantages in having industry-wide agreements. Usually there is two-tier bargaining although, in electrical contracting and engineering construction, standard rates are successfully applied. In commercial printing, for example, where industry bargaining sets a floor, the industry is dominated by small firms spread all over the country with a wide diversity of products. These are characteristics which, according to the British Printing Industries Federation (BPIF), indicate that a national agreement on pay is required by member firms. There is two-tier bargaining in both large and small companies, although its importance varies between sectors, being particularly marked in periodicals, graphics and reproduction. At domestic level it is mainly associated with measures to increase productivity, and the Association's staff spend a considerable amount of time in advising member firms on productivity improvements. In 1993 there was a failure to reach a national agreement and the GPMU pursued its claim at individual firm level with some degree of success. But in 1994 the two sides got together again in national negotiations.

In building, again an industry with numerous small firms throughout the country, although with a few very large ones as well, a survey of members of the Building Employers Confederation (BEC) showed 100 per cent support for continuing with the national agreement, despite the rise in self-employment. The individual companies tend not to have formal pay bargaining with the unions, but are largely dependent on the national agreement. They believe that the industry agreement supports the unions nationally and enables them to exert some control on sites when needed.

The Engineering Employers Federation (EEF) which still has 5000 member firms, abandoned industry-wide bargaining in 1990 in the midst of its dispute with the unions over a shorter working week. However, the EEF is not resigning itself to a minor role. It sees its role increasingly as an advisory one for member companies and as a spokesman and pressure group for the industry. This latter role is becoming more important, it believes, particularly with regard to developments in Europe. It has in recent years designed new categories of membership and is seeking to attract more members, including some very large firms. It believes that what firms want is a representative voice in Brussels which it is seeking to provide.

While there is no doubt that industry-wide agreements negotiated by employers' associations have been in decline as they have been abolished or their content has been narrowed, they still continue to be of importance in a few sectors. It is not the case that employers' associations have completely ceased to have a role in industrial relations. WIRS 3 (Millward *et al.*, 1992, p. 45) does show, however, that in 1980 as many as a quarter of establishments had been members of employers' associations; by 1990 the figure had fallen by half to just 13 per cent, or one in eight. Membership remained highest in engineering (32 per cent), textiles (32 per cent) and construction (75 per cent). WIRS 3 also shows that employers' associations are far less the main source of advice for many firms than they used to be. In 1980 they were the most commonly used by workplaces for advice: in 1990 they were one of the least commonly used. One cannot quarrel with the WIRS 3 conclusion (p. 351) that 'employers' associations were a far less important part of the institutional structure of industrial relations in 1990 than they were a decade or more earlier'.

Collective bargaining

For present purposes, collective bargaining can be analysed first in terms of recognition and bargaining agents, and second in terms of bargaining level and scope (Bain, 1971; McCarthy, 1971).

Recognition and bargaining agents

It is widely accepted that the degree of de-recognition has been relatively low (Claydon, 1989) although there are some indications that it is more wide-spread than originally thought (Gregg and Yates, 1991) and that it has been increasing in recent years (Geroski, Gregg and Desjonqueres, 1994; Gall and McKay, 1994; Claydon, 1996). There have been some widely publicised cases, such as the de-recognition of the print unions at Wapping; the NUJ in most of the national newspapers, in parts of the provincial press and in parts of publishing; the then NUS at P & O, the TGWU in the horse racing industry, and at Tilbury following the 1989 abolition of the National Dock Labour Scheme and in parts of the oil industry; some parts of the hotel and catering industry; senior managers at British Rail, BT and in the electricity and water industries, and groups of white-collar workers elsewhere. Examples of de-recognition have increasingly spread beyond the confines of a few industries.

De-recognition has been increasing, however: although not extensive, the impetus has been growing. As one employer representative put it, 'De-recognition has not taken off because it has not been necessary since the unions do not stand in the way of change.' He added that some employers who are hostile to trade unions have been content to stand aside and watch trade union membership fall and wither on the vine. Another stated that 'they had got all the cooperation they needed from their unions to make changes which were necessary to achieve great increases in productivity', while a third company (which had made major strides in efficiency) said that 'the unions could not have been avoided in making changes on such a scale; they had to be integrated into the process'. A fourth company – an important privatised company – moved to single status and a common 37-hour week. White-collar workers had been on 35 hours and blue-collar on 39. 'The 37 hour week could not have been achieved without the unions. Their value was that they represented the workforce and could make an agreement – it was the agreement which brought in 37 hours and management alone could never have done it' (HRM director).

If most managers have not been actively pursuing de-recognition, their attitude towards recognition at greenfield sites in unorganised parts of the economy has been very different. They have, on the whole, been unwelcoming with regard to recognition and often positively hostile. There are, of course, exceptions. Thus we were told by the personnel director of a large company with both retail and manufacturing interests, which recognised unions on the manufacturing side, that on the retail side the union had been given access to employees in company time. The company had offered recognition for any group which achieved 50 per cent plus one membership and union representation in any shop if they achieved 50 per cent plus one. Despite such a favourable attitude by the employer, the Union has only attained between 3 and 4 per cent membership.

One senior union official said that US companies have always been anti-union but that they have been relaxed about it and have an open-door policy. He added that Japanese companies tend to follow whatever is the local attitude: thus they follow the US companies in Scotland and are anti-union, but in the North-East and in South Wales they recognise unions because other employers do so.

What is clear is that employers for the first time in many decades have a choice as to whether they recognise a union or not. They are free to consider the advantages and disadvantages of recognition and to make their own decisions. In the 1970s, apart from a number of exceptions, employers felt that union recognition was not an issue because they fell in with it. By contrast in the 1980s and 1990s it became the norm among managers not to recognise unions where they were not already recognised. Just as employers have the power to recognise or not, in most instances they also have the power, if they decide to recognise, to determine which union should be the bargaining agent for its employees. In most cases they have gone for single-union recognition, while unions have often been subjected to a 'beauty competition' so that employers can satisfy themselves as to the most appropriate – or perhaps the least troublesome – union to choose.

Over a period of 18 years unions have found it difficult to secure recognition for the first time, and most union membership is in establishments where the union was recognised in an earlier period. As new places of employment are a growing part of the economy this failure to secure recognition has been eroding union membership and the coverage of collective bargaining. Managers may not have de-recognised unions on a wide scale but by, for the most part, not extending recognition, they have secured a withering away of the extent of collective bargaining.

Bargaining unit level and scope

The movement of bargaining level from industry to company, and within some companies from corporate to divisional and/or plant level, has already been discussed in Chapter 6. It should be noted that alongside the major trend in decentralising collective bargaining, there has been a move to widen the bargaining units at any given level. This reaches its extreme in 'new style' single union agreements where the bargaining unit is usually the whole of the labour force, excluding only management. In brownfield sites, where several unions may already have recognition and where historically there may be a number of separate bargaining units (for example, for process workers, for craftsmen, for clerical workers and for technicians and supervisors), there are moves in some companies towards the TUC's idea of a 'single table'. This at best means one joint negotiating body and one set of negotiations covering manual and non-manual workers, and an integrated pay structure. It may be too large a step in some companies and a half-way house has been one joint body covering all manual workers, and another joint body covering non-manual workers.

Turning to the consequences of these trends, the first is that, with an emphasis on domestic bargaining, the importance of shop stewards should be enhanced and the importance of the full time officials reduced. The one important caveat is that with the major swing of bargaining power to employers, shop stewards may feel exposed, with few volunteering to put their heads above the parapet. They may be less likely to put their future at risk by opposing management plans, and indeed WIRS 3 reported that the role of full-time officials had increased. But discrimination against stewards has not been a major issue and there have been no complaints of a campaign against stewards, although there have been a number of unfair dismissal cases.

Second, as Brown (1986, p. 165) has argued:

> shop steward organisations are proving relatively easy to isolate from the wider union movement . . . they identify their interests more with the success of the enterprise . . . It is hard to avoid the conclusion that the structure of trade unionism, originally developed for the strategies of employee solidarity, is increasingly being shaped to the needs of employers.

The needs of employers have increasingly been towards 'enterprise orientated rather than occupationally orientated trade unionism'. It is clear from our interviews with senior managers that they now frequently communicate more directly with employees rather than through shop stewards and that is indicative of the reduced significance of stewards in many workplaces.

Third, domestic bargaining has made it possible and meaningful to include productivity elements in negotiations. Thus the CBI (1989) reported that 'every year during the 1980s, more than one in every five pay settlements in manufacturing has featured changes in working practices as part of the deal' (p. 9). But WIRS 3 reported that recent productivity increases were an important factor in pay increases in only 5 per cent of workplaces in the private sector (p. 239). The cost of living was by far the most frequently mentioned, followed by economic performance, ability to pay and labour market conditions. It is interesting that this was equally true of union and non-union workplaces. However, some of the personnel directors interviewed reported that 'something for something' bargaining had become the norm in their companies. In some ways this is a paradox for, as is argued in an earlier chapter, the scope of collective bargaining in many cases has diminished as a result of growing managerial power and assertiveness. As Terry (1995) states, managers have been increasingly prepared to introduce change and to take decisions without prior negotiation, although they may consult and inform.

In some cases, management has obtained new procedure agreements which expressly state that it has complete control over operational matters, such as the movement and flexibility of labour. In other cases, it has been less a question of changing procedures, and more of changes in the style and method of management and management's ability to make unopposed changes in working practices. As one union general secretary put it, managers can certainly achieve more than they used to be able to; they drive things through forcefully. He was not critical of this, but he argued there are two types of manager. There are those who say that certain things have to be done and they go to some lengths to carry the unions with them, even if it means dragging them along, but there are others who adopt a take it or leave it attitude and therefore impose their will. The vital difference between the two types is that the former sort pay attention to longer term considerations while the latter do not.

The paradox mentioned above is also partly explained by differences in the balance of power. In some cases (although a reducing number) unions still retain considerable power or influence, which means that management either has to negotiate over changes in working practices or believes it expedient or worthwhile to do so in the interest of future good industrial relations. In other industries and companies, management may never have conceded influence over operational matters to the unions (for example, in retail distribution and banking), while in others, union power may have been destroyed or greatly diminished (for example, in coal-mining, the docks, iron and steel and newspaper publishing).

In the public service sector, management has also largely been in control, and the Conservative Governments were determined to push through change. Where the government was the employer, as in the civil service, or was ultimately responsible for management, as in the NHS, it sought to institute change directly through weakening or abolishing centralised bargaining and national agreements, as well as through a financial squeeze. The establishment of NHS Trusts and civil service agencies greatly enhanced this process. In other parts of the public service sector – for example, local authorities – it has again sought to ensure change mainly through financial pressure, but also more directly through legislation: for instance, with regard to teachers' pay and terms and conditions of employment, through allowing and indeed encouraging the opting-out of schools and local authorities from the national agreements, and through the local management initiative for schools and the enforcing of compulsory tendering. In the public corporations, pressure for change has been created largely through the setting of financial targets, the removal or reduction of subsidies, deregulation and ultimately through privatisation. Indeed, it is arguable that in recent years the degree of change has been more marked in the public sector and former nationalised industries than in the traditional private sector, for in the latter case it has been mainly a continuation of previous trends that had been taking place for many years.

The conclusion is that the major changes in the institutions of collective bargaining are in decentralisation, reduced coverage and in the use to which they are being put. Management has been taking the initiative and tabling its own requirements, such as de-manning, changes in working practices, in payment systems and in pay structures. It is no longer simply a matter of unions putting forward their annual claims for pay increases and improvements in the terms and conditions of employment. The subject matter has become much more focused on what workers do rather than on what they are paid. In a programme of negotiations for change, pay is considered in parallel, or pay claims are met, with a set of required associated changes in workplace practices.

In the private sector, as corporate objectives have required more decentralised operations, so the determination of pay and the management of labour have been decentralised to where management has thought it most suitable. This has made the local agenda more comprehensive and less subject to oversight by, and dependence on, corporate or industry bargaining: this process was underway before the 1980s. In addition, manpower matters are increasingly in the hands of line managers because the more efficient use of labour has become a major line management responsibility. Moreover, with more quiescent labour, the case for industrial relations specialists to negotiate has arguably become weaker. Manpower use and labour costs are part of a bigger set of managerial questions. Industrial relations decisions follow behind those made about products and investment. As a starting point, managers ask what changes must be made if these are to be the products, rather than what changes will the unions agree to. Managers, where they negotiate at all, believe that the negotiations are the means for facilitating the achievement of their objectives. They do not approach them in the spirit that the unions can determine whether or not the changes are to be made.

Indeed, it is clear that the significance of industrial relations in many firms has diminished. It is part of a management-controlled operation, and a small part of HRM. It is no longer a high profile problem-ridden part of personnel management as it so often was in the 1970s. The role of the unions has become more centred on achieving the best bargain for the changes which plant management wants. Increases in average earnings above inflation have made that enforced strategy one which has often paid off for some individual members (or at least those who have retained their jobs).

Productivity bargaining

It is interesting to compare the 'something for something' bargaining of the 1980s and 1990s (where it exists) with productivity bargaining, which had its heyday in the 1960s. There is a strong common thread in that in both cases bargaining is about what is done for pay as much as about what pay shall be; bargaining in both cases is usually at domestic level and carried out by plant managers and shop stewards; settlements are not normally one-off but are linked together on both pay and work in a stage by stage approach; and implementation of the changes is part of the follow-up to a settlement.

However, the strongest common feature is that management is responsible for taking the initiative because it can translate the plant's economic objectives – products, costs, investment – into labour requirements. Thus, one personnel director of a large manufacturing company told us that the productivity bargaining of the 1960s and 1970s had 'set the juices running' so that in the 1980s productivity bargaining had become the norm. Another personnel director, also of a large manufacturing company, accepted that what they had been doing in the 1980s could be called 'productivity bargaining' and that it had been remarkably successful. Productivity had increased substantially and the labour force had been reduced by well over one-third without a single stoppage and without a single compulsory redundancy. The tribute to productivity bargaining in this case is particularly noteworthy for this was a company which, in the 1960s, had stood aloof from productivity bargaining on the grounds that the organisation of work and other operational matters were solely the concern of management.

What is missing in the 1980s and the 1990s is an element of joint control, by which is meant the shared, cooperative exercise of control over the uses to which labour is put. For Allan Flanders (1964), the leading advocate of productivity bargaining in the 1960s, its essence included the introduction of an element of joint control as shown by his famous dictum that 'In order to regain control management must be prepared to share it.' But this of course was at a time when unions were strong. Flanders also argued that it was management which had to be the key actor in the process: for too long managers had been passive and had taken little interest in industrial relations. It was an essential part of Flanders' message, from his study of Esso's Fawley oil refinery, that management had to take the initiative if labour was to be used more effectively. This message he repeated in his evidence to the Donovan Royal Commission and it was indeed adopted by the Commission (1968) in its final report, which emphasised time and time again the responsibility of management to initiate reform. The Commission also stressed the need for companies to engage in plant/company formal bargaining for 'in most industries such matters cannot be dealt with effectively by means of industry-wide agreements' (1968, p. 262).

Ahlstrand (1990) shows how Esso at their Fawley refinery continued to engage in productivity bargaining through the 1960s and 1970s and into the 1980s. However, he also shows that the gains were limited, that there was a significant creep back to old working practices, and that Esso was never really interested in joint control, but solely in the restoration of management authority. It would appear that Flanders was overoptimistic about the effects of the Fawley agreements, but this does not negate his message regarding the importance of management initiative and of domestic bargaining.

Thus, managers have come to be where they are now not only because of what happened in the 1980s. Many of them have been endeavouring since the 1960s to promote the efficient use of manpower to as prominent a place in bargaining as pay. The present bargaining norms owe a great deal to what used to be called productivity bargaining. In the 1980s and early 1990s, productivity bargaining was facilitated by the decentralisation of management authority. However, it has been given a different drive by management's dominance and the unions' acquiescence. But an important point is that in some cases the unions are involved, not excluded.

However, the extent of productivity bargaining must not be exaggerated. Where it has existed, unions have retained an element of power. Far more common is management introducing change unilaterally.

One way forward for the unions is to challenge management and seek to establish a rival centre of power. Another is to engage in setting the agenda for negotiation and to have a strategy for manpower which complements that of management, based on an assessment of the interests and aspirations of their members at work. The latter is more in line with the way in which industrial relations has been developing in recent years in response to the swing of power to management, and has been espoused by many unions. This approach rejects the idea of a backlash of union power and argues for a measured strategy of seeking partnership and improving the quality of union participation in bargaining and consultation: for example, through the TUC (1995) concept of minimum standards agreements including access to training and education.

Third party intervention

Traditional third party intervention in industrial relations continues to be primarily provided ACAS. ACAS was established in 1974 and put on a statutory basis by the EPA. Its duties are as laid down in that Act which basically transferred to ACAS the functions of conciliation, arbitration and advice, which were previously discharged by the DE, and the enquiry functions, which up till then had been provided by the CIR.

ACAS is one of the few tripartite organisations which survived the Thatcher years. Its survival might at first sight seem surprising, particularly its objectives of promoting the improvement of industrial relations and of encouraging the extension of collective bargaining as well as its provision of free advice and services, which would appear to run across 'the bottom line' philosophy of Conservative Governments since 1979. Indeed, the objective to encourage the extension of collective bargaining was finally eliminated in the 1993 Act. But every industrialised country has a need for a conciliation, mediation and arbitration service. The mere existence of ACAS has the enormous advantage of enabling government to appear to distance itself from industrial disputes and their settlement.

Since 1979 the use of ACAS's collective conciliation and arbitration services has declined significantly. The number of completed collective conciliation cases fell from 2284 in 1979 to 1197 in 1996, and the number of cases referred to arbitration and mediation from 363 to 117 (ACAS, 1980a, 1997), although there has been greater stabilisation in recent years. The individual conciliation case load has been very heavy and increasing with over 100 000 cases received in 1996, of which nearly 47 000 were on unfair dismissal.

The decline of arbitration is explicable in the same terms as the decline of strikes. The parties have usually been able to reach a settlement themselves. In cases where breakdown would mean arbitration, as well as ones where it would mean a strike, the parties have found an answer for themselves. Management dominance has been the main explanation. In the private sector arbitration has always been a last resort and has normally been voluntary: that is to say, it could only be invoked by the agreement of both sides. Similarly ACAS has no power to impose arbitration on the parties without their joint agreement. Since 1979 management has normally been unwilling to go to arbitration, and because of their dominance have been confident that their final offer would be accepted. In the prevailing climate unions, if dissatisfied and denied arbitration, would in most cases be unwilling to take industrial action.

In the public sector, the position was historically different in that arbitration was usually the normal means of solving differences between the parties which could not be settled by negotiation. Sometimes reference to arbitration was the norm as a result of custom and practice. In many other cases there was a right, laid down in procedures, for either party to invoke arbitration unilaterally. In the early 1980s the Conservative Government sought (and largely succeeded) in terminating public sector unilateral arbitration agreements. Where resort to arbitration depended on both sides' agreement, the Conservative Government almost invariably withheld agreement and pressurised other public sector employers to act likewise.

The Conservative Government's hostility to arbitration was partly because it believed that arbitrators split the difference, partly because it alleged that arbitration awards were inflationary, partly because it believed it wrong to give a third party control over pay and cost decisions which should rest with the employer, and above all because it wished its own view to prevail. The big public sector strikes of the 1980s would in other times probably have been settled by arbitration. The then government thus preferred to settle disagreements by force rather than by peaceful means and, having engaged in a dispute, was determined to win, regardless of cost. In some ways such an attitude was paradoxical for the government had supported 'new style' agreements, such as those entered into by many Japanese companies, which provided for obligatory arbitration in the event of the parties failing to agree. Many of these agreements provided for 'pendulum arbitration', which means that the arbitrator had to make a choice between the final offer of the employer and the final claim of the union. There was no scope for an award in between. The main stated advantage over conventional arbitration was that it encouraged realism on the part of both parties as an unrealistic offer or claim was likely to lead the arbitrator to award in favour of the other party. The main stated disadvantage was the lack of scope and flexibility given to the arbitrator (S. Kessler, 1987). To date there have been far too few cases for any kind of judgement to be made although Milner (1993) made a brave attempt to do so.

One further point needs to be made with regard to third party intervention in the 1980s and since, and that is that it has been of the traditional kind; in other words, it is essentially concerned with helping to keep the peace. It has not had a reforming purpose (although arguably some of ACAS's advisory work could fall into this category), unlike certain earlier third party institutions such as the NBPI and the CIR (see Chapters 1 and 2). The main reason for this was the Conservative Government's stated policy of non-intervention in industrial matters; it should all be left to the parties. In reality, they sought reform through changes in the law and in the public sector also through financial squeeze, privatisation and so forth: private employers have sought reform through their own policies and through the widespread use of private consultants. However, it is true that ACAS advisory work has flourished during the 1980s and 1990s, subject only to imposed financial constraints. In 1996 ACAS completed 540 'advisory mediation' projects. These are aimed at encouraging non-adversarial approaches to preventing and resolving problems at work by facilitating joint working groups of employers, employees and their representatives. A study assessing this work was very favourable (I. Kessler and Purcell, 1994).

Joint consultation

Theoretically there is a clear distinction between collective bargaining and joint consultation: bargaining is a process which normally results in a joint or agreed decision by the parties, whereas in joint consultation decisions are unilaterally determined by management, albeit after consultation. This theoretical distinction is usually mirrored in practice by the existence of separate machinery for bargaining and for consultation, although WIRS 3 reported some 30 per cent of consultative committees were also concerned with negotiation (p. 157). There are also normally separate agendas. Collective bargaining machinery is concerned with the determination of pay and other terms and conditions of employment, whereas joint consultation is concerned with what are considered non-negotiable matters, such as welfare, health and safety, production and efficiency (matters supposedly of common interest). In practice, there is often an overlap and blurring on certain issues.

It was Flanders (1964) who fiercely attacked the separation of the two processes, arguing that it was not only artificial, but positively harmful. If efficiency was left to the consultative machinery and pay was left to the negotiating machinery, management (seeking to improve productivity through the cooperation of workers and their unions) could only resort to exhortation. However, exhortation alone was unlikely to be successful. Attempts to improve efficiency needed to be linked to increased rewards, and hence Flanders' advocacy of productivity bargaining: a process which required the enlarging of the content of collective bargaining and including matters which had hitherto been dealt with by joint consultation.

With the growth in productivity bargaining in the second half of the 1960s, this widening of collective bargaining took place and joint consultation declined somewhat. Indeed, McCarthy (1966) has argued that, with the growth of shop steward power and workplace bargaining, joint consultation would inevitably decline, for it was regarded by stewards as an inferior process to bargaining on the grounds that it left decisions to be unilaterally determined by management. WIRS 3 showed that in private manufacturing 23 per cent of workplaces had joint consultative committees in 1990, compared with 36 per cent in 1980. In the public sector almost 50 per cent of workplaces had committees in 1990 compared with a fifth of those in the private sector. Overall, the proportion of workplaces with committees fell between 1984 and 1990 from 34 per cent to 29 per cent. WIRS 3 concluded that the fall in workplace consultative committees was primarily due to the changing composition of workplaces: that is to say, it was not due to a tendency for workplaces to abandon committees, but to a fall in the number of larger, more unionised workplaces who were much more likely to have committees. Marginson *et al.* (1993), in their survey of large companies, report that 57 per cent had regular consultative meetings at company level. Such arrangements were more likely to be present when unions were recognised. Other methods of communication and involvement were common but 'overall there appears to be little evidence that non-union companies are pursuing approaches characterised by extensive use of forms of employee communication and involvement' (p. 65).

Marchington (1989) has argued that there are four different models of consultation which can be seen in action in Britain. First, consultation may be used as an alternative to collective bargaining and to prevent its establishment. Here management is essentially unitarist, but much more sophisticated than the traditional anti-union owner-manager. Thus it seeks to promote harmony and the willing acceptance of management decisions. The process is mainly one-way and basically educative in its nature. One large retail chain, whose personnel director we interviewed, does not recognise unions, but has an elaborate consultative system. There are 'communication groups'; in all stores and distribution centres, meetings take place every six weeks or so, but representatives recognise that decisions are left to management.

Second, consultation may be seen as marginal within the enterprise by employer and employees and achieve little or nothing for either party. This is likely to be the case where there is little trust, where the parties use opportunistic tactics to undermine each other and where there is little management commitment to joint arrangements.

Third, it may be seen as being in direct competition with collective bargaining, with management seeking to upgrade consultation so that negotiations become less meaningful or necessary. In order to succeed management must make consultation appear more significant. The agenda will therefore cover important topics, such as new products, investment plans, efficiency and marketing. In such companies, there are often developments in other forms of involvement, designed to convince employees of the reasons for management actions (for example, briefing groups, employee presentations and reports, and quality circles).

Fourth, especially where trade unionism is strong and well developed, consultation may be seen as a valuable adjunct to collective bargaining. Here the two processes are kept separate, although the representatives of each committee will be largely the same people. Thus the personnel director of a large manufacturing company, which was highly unionised, told us that their present position is the opposite of macho management. Competition is severe and they need effective communications to ensure that the competitive threat is understood. That requires a coming together on the details of the business. In the 1970s it was a war described in battle terms. Now they seek common solutions and are constantly asking, 'How do we improve relationships?' There has been much more growing together and recognition of the others' interests. Accommodation has been achieved which, fifteen years ago, he would not have believed possible. The unions, he said, could not have been left out in making necessary changes. They had to be integrated into the process. To achieve this, management really did open the books.

In Chapter 6, it was argued that in the 1980s and since, management in many cases had sought better communications and greater involvement because they realised that they required a workforce committed to company objectives. It was also argued that this approach was based on unitary beliefs and on seeking greater individualisation. Thus, much of management's efforts are now focused directly on their employees and not only or mainly through representative channels. Such efforts – aimed as they are at enlisting employee opinion and behaviour behind management's objectives – must inevitably threaten to weaken the union's traditional position.

Joint consultative machinery is therefore (like negotiating machinery) still in place, although its coverage has declined. But the use to which it is now put is often different from what it used to be. Moreover, it is now supplemented by a range of management methods to communicate and influence employees directly and individually. The Conservative Governments since 1979, together with employers, had strongly resisted any suggestion of a statutory obligation on companies to engage in consultation. They had also strongly resisted any such development through EU action.

However, consultation is being given a boost through the EU. First, as detailed in Chapter 5, the EU passed a Directive on EWC which came into effect in September 1996. Many British multinationals have already established EWCs because they met the Directive's criteria, and they have not excluded British representation despite the UK's opt-out of the Social Chapter. Moreover, the Labour Government is pledged to end the opt-out so that many more British companies will be affected. Moreover, the EU is considering a directive on works councils in each member country, probably at company level. Second, again as detailed in Chapter 5, as a result of an ECJ judgment, the UK's practice with regard to consultation on transfers of undertakings and on redundancies has had to change. Consultation now has to take place in union or non-union companies, and has to be 'with a view to reaching an agreement' and not merely to inform.

Furthermore, the TUC (1995) in *Your Voice at Work* put considerable emphasis on consultation, along with statutory rights for recognition for collective bargaining and for individual representation. How the Labour Government reacts to these proposals remains to be seen.

Conclusion

In the 1980s and 1990s there were significant changes in the institutions of industrial relations, in particular the reduced coverage of collective bargaining, its decentralisation and the development by employers of more direct means of communication with their employees, often by-passing traditional union channels. Some observers have written about the end of institutionalised industrial relations and of employers no longer seeing collective bargaining as the focus of their thinking on employee relations.

As important as the changes in the institutions has been the use to which they have or have not been put.

The roles of the parties were substantially different. Management seized the initiative as a result of the change in the balance of power and the changing economic and political environment. The assertion of managerial authority meant in many cases a reduction in the coverage and scope of collective bargaining and an increase in the ability to act unilaterally: for example, in reductions in the labour force, in introducing organisational and technological change and 'something for something' bargaining.

There are three main features which have a bearing on the future and are further discussed in Chapter 12. First, in the late 1980s during the period of economic expansion, as well as in the recessions before and after that period and in the economic recovery of the mid-1990s, the new power relationship between managers and trade unions in the private sector continued with a continuing fall in union membership and with a reduction in the coverage of collective bargaining. How far and to what extent the traditional institutional framework will survive in the future is an open question.

Second, it was in the public sector, and particularly in the public services, where the changed relationship was more difficult. The institutions had, of course, been put under stress by extreme financial pressures and by conflict in some parts. But there have been drastic changes (for example, in the NHS and the civil service, as outlined in Chapter 7). Overt conflict and pay failing to keep up with that of others provided a less congenial background for changes which, in the private sector, could sometimes be justified by both sides by improvement in both pay and productivity.

Third, there are the effects of the EU and the likely policies of the Labour Government to be considered. A new framework, with more emphasis on consultation and partnership and less on collective bargaining, is a distinct possibility.

CHAPTER 10

Pay and productivity

In this chapter we look first at government's objectives and policy with regard to pay determination since 1979; second, at the outcomes of policies on pay; and finally, at how and why outcomes differed from intentions.

Government objectives and policy

The Conservative Government's objectives with regard to pay were clear and were derived from their fundamental belief in the free market. Britain's post-war record on pay was thought to be poor and was the result of government interference through incomes policy and other regulatory means, such as Wage Councils and the Fair Wages Resolution (FWR); overfull employment; too powerful trade unions; industry-wide bargaining and consequently in-dustry-wide pay rates; protected product markets; too large a public sector, where the price mechanism did not work and comparability reigned supreme; and too generous unemployment pay and too easy conditions to qualify for benefit, as well as a taxation system which discouraged the will to work. The consequences were said to be high wage inflation, inflexibility, inadequate differentials, and pay increases unrelated to performance and profitability, to the supply of (and demand for) labour, which in turn resulted in uncompe-titive British goods and services and indeed unemployment itself as the unemployed had 'priced themselves out of jobs'.

Perhaps the best statement of government views was contained in a lecture given by Kenneth Clarke, the then Minister of State at the DE, at the City University Business School in February 1987. The Minister stated that:

> the inflexibility of our labour market produced the gradually increased employ-ment we have experienced postwar ... greater flexibility in the labour market is essential to tackle unemployment ... At the heart of our economic problems since

the Second World War has been the problem of paying ourselves more as a nation than we can afford in higher productivity and output growth.

In pursuit of greater flexibility he argued that we must change the way we bargained about wage levels and wage increases. 'We must move towards a system more clearly based on market forces, on demand and supply, on competition and on ability to pay', and we must move away from the annual pay round, the going rate, comparability, job evaluation and national pay bargaining. Two particular changes he identified as crucial were, first, a move from national to local bargaining; second, employers introducing payment systems which rewarded merit and performance:

> If we can move to a system where pay increases are primarily based on performance, merit, company profitability and demand and supply in the local labour market, we will dethrone once and for all the annual pay round and the belief that pay increases do not have to be earned.

The defects of the post-war British system were clear in the eyes of the then Government; so were the remedies, which followed directly from this analysis of defects. As far as the economy as a whole was concerned, and the private sector in particular, it was not for government to interfere directly. What government needed to do was to provide employers with the appropriate environment to conduct their own affairs. This involved the following elements:

1. Increased unemployment.
2. Laws reducing the power of trade unions.
3. Reducing the burden on industry: for example, through reducing regulations on hours of work; reducing regulations on the employment of women and young people; changing the burden of proof in unfair dismissal cases; increasing the period of employment to two years before a degree of protection applied to employees, such as unfair dismissal; and increasing the number of hours that part-time employees had to work before they became entitled to a degree of protection.
4. Abolishing or reducing legal minimum wages, and terms and conditions entitlements where they existed by the abolition of Schedule 11 of the 1975 EPA, the FWR and the Wage Councils.
5. Encouraging the break-up of national wage agreements.
6. Encouraging a reduction in the pay of young people so that they could be priced into jobs.
7. Encouraging PRP, profit-related pay and share ownership.
8. The ending of 'the wage round' and the concept of 'the going rate'.

In the public sector the government sought to reproduce the conditions and policies which existed (or rather which the government thought ought to exist) in the private sector. Thus, to produce financial pressure in lieu of product market pressure, strict financial limits and targets were imposed; PRP was introduced; local allowances were permitted to provide pay flexibility to meet geographical and skill shortages; industrial action was resolutely resisted as the unions had to be defeated; the right to unilateral arbitration was removed wherever it existed, and recourse to jointly agreed arbitration almost invariably denied; comparability was considered irrelevant (until towards the end of the 1980s when it partially re-emerged for a short period in the IPCS Agreement and other subsequent civil service agreements); the need 'to recruit and retain' was paramount as a useful doctrine in the years of high unemployment; finally, there was privatisation either of complete public corporations or of designated services through contracting-out and market testing. By the early 1990s a policy of hiving off central government functions to agencies, which would have a degree of freedom to determine pay, was underway. By the mid-1990s this programme was almost complete and central pay bargaining in the civil service was at an end. In the NHS government pursued a similar policy of down-grading national negotiations and ensuring 'local bargaining' by NHS Trusts (except for doctors). Success in this objective was less complete than in the civil service, as the continued retention of the Pay Review Bodies provide problems. Local authority employers and unions have succeeded in retaining national bargaining in their 1997 agreement, although with a more flexible framework providing considerable local discretion. Finally, for the year 1992/3 the Government introduced a pay limit in the public sector of 1.5 per cent. This was followed for the year 1993/4 by a complete freeze on public sector wage and salary bills, which has continued every year since then. Any increase in pay has had to be paid for by efficiency gains which, given the high labour content in the public services, meant job losses. The Labour Government has so far indicated no change in this policy.

In the following sections, we consider the results of nearly two decades of such policies.

The growth of earnings

Average earnings for all men increased by 286 per cent between April 1979 and April 1996, and average earnings for all women increased by 349 per cent (Table 10.1). The increase in RPI was 180 per cent, so there was an increase in average real earnings of 38 per cent for men and 60 per cent for women. In terms of reducing the increase in earnings, government policy got off to a disastrous start. Between April 1979 and April 1980 average earnings increased by over 20 per cent compared with an annual rate of increase of 10 per cent when Mrs Thatcher took office. The Government sought to lay the blame on the awards of the Clegg Comparability Commission, but the real reasons

TABLE 10.1 Average gross weekly earnings, 1979-96 (UK)

	Male						Female						
Year	Manual	%	Non-manual	%	All	%	Manual	%	Non-manual	%	All	%	RPI
April													
1979	93.0	100	113.0	100	101.4	100	55.2	100	66.0	100	63.0	100	100
1980	111.7	120	141.3	125	125.4	124	68.0	123	82.7	125	78.9	125	121.8
1981	121.9	131	163.1	130	140.5	139	74.5	135	96.7	147	91.4	145	136.4
1982	133.8	144	178.9	158	154.5	152	80.1	145	104.9	159	99.0	157	149.3
1983	143.6	154	194.9	172	167.5	165	87.9	174	115.1	174	108.8	173	155.2
1984	152.7	164	209.0	185	178.8	176	93.5	169	124.3	188	117.2	186	163.3
1985	163.6	176	225.0	199	192.4	190	101.3	184	133.8	203	126.4	201	174.6
1986	174.4	188	244.9	217	207.5	205	107.5	195	145.7	221	137.2	218	179.9
1987	185.5	199	265.9	235	224.0	221	115.3	209	157.2	238	148.1	235	187.5
1988	200.6	216	294.1	260	245.8	242	123.6	224	175.5	266	164.2	261	194.9
1989	217.8	234	323.6	286	269.5	266	134.9	244	195.0	295	182.3	289	210.5
1990	237.2	255	354.9	314	295.6	292	148.0	268	215.5	327	201.5	320	230.0
1991	253.1	272	375.7	333	318.9	314	159.2	288	236.8	359	222.4	353	244.5
1992	268.3	288	400.4	354	340.1	335	170.1	308	265.5	402	241.1	383	255.0
1993	274.3	295	418.2	370	353.5	349	177.1	321	268.7	407	252.6	401	258.3
1994	280.7	302	428.2	379	362.1	357	181.9	330	278.4	422	261.5	415	265.0
1995	291.3	313	443.3	392	374.6	369	188.1	341	288.1	437	269.8	428	273.7
1996	301.3	324	464.5	411	391.6	386	195.2	354	302.4	458	283.0	449	280.3
% increase in real earnings 1979/96		16		47		38		26		63		60	

Source: Based on *New Earnings Surveys* (adult full-time employees whose pay was not affected by absence).

that pay increases had been escalating as a consequence of the Discontent, and partly (and most importantly) there was a very ase in the cost of living as a result of the government's own fiscal and monetary policy, namely a hefty rise in interest rates and a major increase in indirect taxation in its first budget (in particular the doubling of VAT at a stroke). The rapid escalation in the RPI which ensued was followed by an equally rapid escalation in pay settlements.

In the following two years, however, during the depth of the first post-war recession, there was a major de-escalation in pay increases, followed by several years of stability with annual increases in earnings of between 7 and 8 per cent, compared with RPI increases of about 5 per cent. In 1987/8, however, the rate of increase started to move up again and this continued in 1989 and 1990. With the second major post-war recession between 1990 and 1992, and the high and rapid increase in unemployment and the fall in the RPI, the rate of increase in earnings declined markedly and did not increase in the mid-1990s when recovery slowly took place. Between 1993 and 1996 earnings increased by some 4 per cent per annum and the cost of living by about 3 per cent per annum.

Throughout the 1980s pay increases had been above those of our main industrial competitors (Table 3.6), and throughout the decade earnings increased more than the cost of living, so that real earnings continued to increase. What was remarkable was that earnings should have increased to the extent that they did despite very high unemployment for most of the decade and despite the reduction in union power. Whatever the reasons (returned to later) it was clear that at the end of the decade, with earnings rising at an annual rate of some 10 per cent (which was far higher than that of our main competitors), ten years of Thatcherism had not solved the problem of excess increases in money earnings which had been a major feature of post-war Britain. It is true that the 1990s saw a substantial fall in the rate of increase in earnings. However, it was higher than that of our competitors (although much less so). Unemployment was still high and, in view of past experience, it must be questioned how long this trend will continue. It must also be questioned whether more reasonable trends in earnings and RPI can only be achieved at the cost of large-scale unemployment.

The distribution of earnings

If the Conservative Governments had been unsuccessful for the best part of 20 years in reducing earnings increases to satisfactory levels, it could be argued that they had certainly succeeded in changing the distribution of earnings. The distribution changed in two major aspects. First, non-manual earnings increased far more than manual earnings (see Table 10.1): for manual males, between 1979 and 1996 the increase in money earnings was 224 per cent (or 16 per cent in real terms), compared with a money increase of 311 per cent, and a real increase of 47 per cent for non-manual males. For manual women, money earnings increased by 254 per cent and real earnings by 26 per cent, compared with 358 per cent and 63 per cent respectively for non-manual women.

Second, the higher paid did very much better than the lower paid (Table 10.2). Between 1979 and 1996, the lower quartile for all men as a percentage of the median went down from 80 per cent to 73 per cent while the upper quartile as a percentage of the median increased from 125 per cent to 138 per cent. For all women the lower quartile as a percentage of the median fell from 82 per cent to 75 per cent, and the upper quartile as a percentage of the median increased from 125 per cent to 140 per cent. Between 1979 and 1996, for all men the lowest decile as a percentage of the median fell from 66 to 56, while for all women it fell from 69 to 59. In contrast, the upper decile for all men as a percentage of the median rose from 157 to 189, and for all women from 159 to 181. Management, and above all directors' salaries, as evidenced by various salary surveys, increased at a far faster rate than pay generally, to a point at the end of the 1980s where such increases actually drew a rebuke from Mrs Thatcher and an appeal for restraint. This was apparently in vain for it was repeated by the Chancellor of the Exchequer in 1994 (again without any success).

Supporters (or apologists) for the markedly changed distribution of income in favour of the better-paid (even without taking into account the income tax cuts for the higher paid) argue that it is all the result of market forces, and that wider differentials are necessary for the success of 'the enterprise culture'. How directors' pay, normally determined by non-executive directors who primarily owe their appointment to the full-time directors, can be said to be determined by market forces is not always easy to understand. Certainly, the climate created by the doubling and trebling of managing directors' annual salaries (to reach, in some cases, £1 million or more) was not conducive to restraint and responsibility in pay claims at lower levels. Some of the implications of the explosion of pay at the top are discussed in McCarthy (1993).

Earnings by occupation

The distribution of earnings has thus changed markedly, with the lower paid getting relatively less and the better paid getting relatively more while non-manual employees as a whole gained substantially compared to manual workers. These, however, are very broad categories and we need to look

TABLE 10.2 Distribution of earnings, 1979–96 (UK)

	Males						Females					
	Manual		Non-manual		All		Manual		Non-manual		All	
	1979	1996	1979	1996	1979	1996	1979	1996	1979	1996	1979	1996
Median Weekly earnings (£)	88.2	280.0	103.6	399.5	93.9	334.9	53.3	178.7	60.8	268.7	58.4	248.1
Lowest decile as % of median	68	62	63	53	66	56	70	67	70	60	69	59
Lower quartile as % of median	82	78	79	72	80	73	83	80	82	76	82	75
Upper quartile as % of median	122	128	127	137	125	138	118	129	126	139	125	140
Highest decile as % of median	149	162	163	189	157	189	141	163	161	175	159	181

Source: Adapted from *New Earnings Surveys*, 1979 and 1996 (adult full-time employees whose pay was not affected by absence).

more closely at changes in occupational earnings. A comparison of changes in occupational earnings between 1979 and 1990 based on the New Earnings Survey (a comprehensive comparison between 1979 and 1996 is much more difficult because of subsequent changes in occupational classifications), shows that among non-manual groups which did particularly well were those in 'the professional and related [areas], supporting management and administration', where the overall average increase in earnings was 244 per cent for males and 253 per cent for females, and where, for males, accountants' earnings increased by 237 per cent; finance, insurance and tax experts by 280 per cent; personnel officers and managers by 255 per cent; and marketing and sales managers and executives by 234 per cent. Other groups which did particularly well were nurses, with male earnings up by 229 per cent and female earnings up by 271 per cent; general practitioners, with male earnings up by 247 per cent; and journalists, with male earnings up by 232 per cent. Non-manual groups which did worse than average included clerical workers, with male earnings up by 177 per cent and female earnings by 204 per cent; sales people and shop assistants, with male earnings up by 177 per cent and female earnings up by 185 per cent; and professions relating to science, engineering and technology, where males' earnings increased by 198 per cent.

As far as manual occupational groups were concerned, it needs to be repeated that their overall increase in earnings was 155 per cent for males and 168 per cent for females, in contrast with the non-manuals' increase of 215 per cent for males and 226 per cent for females. Indeed, very few of the manual categories exceeded the non-manual average. Among those significantly below the manual average increase were female hospital orderlies with 119 per cent, male hospital porters with 131 per cent, bus and coach drivers with 134 per cent, male railway workers with 142 per cent, and face-trained coal-miners with 145 per cent.

Earnings by industry

The average increase between 1979 and 1996 for manual males was 224 per cent for all industries and services, and 231 per cent for manufacturing. For non-manual males the increase was 311 per cent for all industries and services and 307 per cent for manufacturing. For manual females the increases were 254 per cent for all industries and services and 254 per cent for manufacturing: for non-manual females the increases were 358 per cent and 360 per cent respectively. There was thus remarkably little difference over the period between manufacturing and all industries and services.

Comparisons by industry are complicated by changes in the Standard Industrial Classification, but if earnings by industry are arranged in descending order of earnings in 1979 and 1996, they show basically how little change there has been in the 'pecking order' over the period. For manual males, of the top 10 industries in 1979, seven were still in the top 10 in 1996. Within the top 10, there was some change in order between 1979 and 1996, but the changes were not very significant. Of the bottom 10 industries in 1979, nine were still at the bottom in 1996.

The picture for non-manual males was similar. Seven of the top 10 industries were the same in 1996 as in 1979, while of the bottom 10 industries nine were the same.

Looking at average gross weekly earnings for women by industry in 1979 and 1996, there was again a high degree of stability. For manual women, five out of the top six industries were the same in both years, while five out of the six bottom industries were the same. For non-manual women five out of the top six industries were the same in 1979 and 1996, while five out of six of the bottom industries stayed the same. Thus, despite the economic and political upheavals of the 1980s and 1990s, taking men and women together, pay relativities between industries have on the whole shown remarkable stability.

Public sector pay

Public sector pay deserves to be looked at separately for a number of reasons. First, the public sector still remains a significant part of the economy despite cuts and privatisation. Second, it was the centre of most of the major industrial disputes of the 1980s and 1990s. Third, it has been the subject of special government treatment, whereas the private sector has been free to make its own settlements, subject to the market and to government-induced environmental changes. In one sense there was nothing new about the public sector receiving special treatment. In effect, this was true of the 1960s and 1970s as well, because incomes policies always bore more heavily on the public sector than the private sector. The difference was that under incomes policies there was no overt discrimination against the public sector. It was just that it was easier for the government as a direct or indirect employer to enforce incomes policy norms than for it to enforce those norms on the private sector: in the 1980s and 1990s, however, the discrimination was overt. Fourth, despite all the evidence (Bailey and Trinder, 1989), there are myths, misconceptions and indeed prejudices about public sector pay.

During the 1960s and 1970s public sector pay fell behind private sector pay in periods of incomes policy and was then restored to its approximate former relationship. In the earlier decades this was often done by special *ad hoc* Committees of Inquiry, such as Houghton (1974) on teachers, Halsbury on nurses (1975), and the Clegg Comparability Commission (1980) which dealt with much of the public service sector. For most of the 1980s and 1990s, the public service sector again fell behind, but this time there has not been a policy or body established to restore former relationships.

Table 10.3 shows the changes in average weekly earnings in the public and private sectors between 1981 and 1996. We have chosen 1981 as the base year rather than 1979 because if we took the latter it would mean including the Clegg awards and the special settlements for many of the public sector groups. This would clearly be wrong for these awards were a catching-up exercise on the relative loss sustained by the public sector in the second half of the 1970s.

Average weekly earnings for all men increased by 168 per cent between 1981 and 1996 in the public sector as a whole compared with 190 per cent in the private sector, while for all women the respective increases were 201 per cent and 228 per cent (see Table 10.3). There can therefore be no doubt that pay increases for employees in the public sector were markedly less than those in the private sector and that this is true of all broad categories: national government, local government and the public corporations.

However, there were considerable variations in the treatment of different parts of the public sector. Among the then nationalised industries, some fared better than others, with employees in the more profitable corporations doing the best and suffering the least government interference (for example, gas and electricity), while British Rail fared badly.

In the public service sector, between 1981 and 1996, those who did worst were lecturers in higher and further education, university academic staff, local authority manual workers and NHS ancillary workers. Those that fared best were police, firefighters, teachers and nurses.

These results are not, of course, surprising. Broadly, of those that did relatively well, police and firefighters were privileged by having pay agreements, dating back to the late 1970s, which linked their pay to general movements in earnings in the economy as a whole, and others (such as nurses and doctors) had the advantage of pay review bodies. Of those doing exceptionally badly, further education and university lecturers, as well as being subject to severe government financial constraints, had little bargaining power. Others, such as local authority manual workers and NHS ancillary staff (among the lowest paid groups in the economy), suffered through their services being made open to private tendering by the government.

Towards the end of the 1980s, there had been small relative improvements for some public service sector groups. This was partly because of the restoration of some limited degree of comparability in the civil service (see Chapter 7). For certain other groups, with the economy booming for a period, the relative fall in earnings led to severe labour turnover and shortage problems, particularly in London and the South-East, so that extra pay was forthcoming, although not so much through national agreements as through local allowances. However, in the 1990s further constraints were put on public

TABLE 10.3 Average gross weekly earnings, public and private sectors, 1981–96

	Manual			Non-manual			All		
	1981 £	1996 £	% Increase	1981 £	1996 £	% Increase	1981 £	1996 £	% Increase
Men									
Public services	110.1	271.5	146.6	166.7	429.0	157.3	146.8	392.7	167.5
Central government	112.7	265.5	135.6	165.0	402.8	144.1	146.9	380.8	159.2
Local government	108.9	273.2	150.9	167.7	442.5	163.9	146.8	398.2	171.3
Public corporations	137.0	308.5	125.2	171.2	503.3	194.0	147.5	397.3	169.4
Public sector	127.2	289.0	127.2	168.0	442.6	163.5	147.1	394.0	167.8
Private sector	119.2	306.4	157.0	158.1	474.2	200.0	135.8	393.1	189.5
Women									
Public services	75.1	205.2	173.2	111.3	326.8	193.6	105.8	317.9	200.5
Central government	77.0	201.2	161.3	97.4	290.7	198.5	94.5	286.9	203.6
Local government	73.5	206.0	180.3	125.7	342.5	172.5	117.3	330.7	181.9
Public corporations	97.2	226.4	132.9	101.0	325.1	221.9	100.3	314.1	213.2
Public sector	78.7	213.2	170.9	109.9	326.3	196.9	105.1	316.8	201.4
Private sector	72.9	193.0	164.7	83.6	284.6	240.4	80.3	263.1	227.6

Source: Based on *New Earnings Surveys*, 1981 and 1996 (full-time employees whose pay was not affected by absence).

sector pay. For 1992/3 the maximum permitted increase was 1.5 per cent. For 1993/4 there was a freeze on public sector pay bills, although permitted pay increases were around 2.5 per cent. In the following three years the Conservative Government continued the freeze on public sector pay bills. This policy has not been changed by the new Labour Government. However, it is questionable whether this policy can be continued indefinitely. Whatever else Conservative Government policy on pay may have achieved, it has certainly not solved the problem of pay determination in the public sector.

Regional pay

The significance of local labour markets has been much discussed since 1980, partly because of large geographical differences in the incidence of unemployment for much of the period, partly because of the decentralisation of pay bargaining in private industry, but above all because of the Conservative Government's policy of seeking to break up national pay bargaining in the public sector and its rhetoric with regard to the virtues of local pay determination in the economy as a whole. Government policy was based on a belief in free labour markets, so that if pay determination was locally based, employers would be able to take advantage of labour surpluses in areas of high unemployment and pay lower wages there than in areas of low unemployment. This would, it was claimed, lower labour costs as well as increasing employment in areas of high unemployment. It would also encourage the unemployed in low-paying areas to move to areas of high employment and higher pay unless differences in housing costs prevented it.

Table 10.4 shows gross regional average weekly earnings expressed as a proportion of national average weekly earnings. The outstanding conclusions from the table are, first, that the issue of regional pay is overwhelmingly a London problem. It is London, and London alone, where pay is markedly above the national average. Even the rest of the South-East is only slightly above the national average. The second conclusion is that London pay compared with the national average has increased markedly since 1979 for men from 14 per cent in 1979 to 32 per cent in 1996, and for women from 16 per cent to 29 per cent. For the rest of the South-East the increase for men went from being virtually the same as the national average in 1979 to 5 per cent above it, and for women from again being virtually the same as the national average in 1979 to 3 per cent above it. An additional measure of the relative increase in London pay is to take London earnings as a percentage of pay in the lowest region. This shows that for men the difference increased from 25 per cent to 49 per cent between 1979 and 1996, and for women from 23 per cent to 47 per cent. These figures do not therefore support a policy of

TABLE 10.4   Regional average gross weekly earnings as proportion of national average, 1979–96

	All men		*All women*	
	1979	*1996*	*1979*	*1996*
Greater London	113.9	131.8	116.3	129.0
Rest of South-East	100.5	104.6	100.5	103.2
East Anglia	94.3	91.3	95.6	93.9
South West	91.1	93.2	95.2	92.3
West Midlands	96.7	92.0	97.5	90.8
East Midlands	95.8	90.1	94.8	87.9
Yorks and Humberside	97.7	89.6	94.3	89.2
North-West	97.8	93.9	96.0	93.7
North	98.3	89.6	96.2	89.0
Wales	96.2	88.4	97.5	88.4
Scotland	99.8	92.8	95.9	92.6
% difference between Greater London and the lowest region	25.0	49.1	23.4	46.8

Source: Based on *New Earnings Survey*, 1979 and 1996 (full-time employees whose pay was not affected by absence).

decentralisation of pay determination in the public sector. The regional problem is specifically a London problem. This conclusion was also reached by Brown and Rowthorn (1990), who argued that the Government policy of decentralisation was flawed since it was based on a fallacious view of labour market mechanisms and a misunderstanding of private sector practice. Where pay bargaining has been decentralised within private sector companies, it was usually on a product, and not a geographical, basis.

Productivity

Figures on productivity were given in Chapter 3 (see Table 3.1). Basically they showed that productivity – both for the whole economy and for manufacturing industry – declined at the beginning of the 1980s, during the depths of the recession, but thereafter in manufacturing there were substantial increases in most years until near the end of the decade when there was a marked slow-down, which continued into the early 1990s with the second major post-war recession but then started to improve. Output per person for the whole economy moved in a similar fashion, but increases were at a much lower level than they were for manufacturing. Thus between 1980 and 1996 output per person for the whole economy increased by 38.8 per cent, while for manufacturing it increased by 95 per cent.

The increase of productivity in manufacturing was hailed as a 'miracle' by Conservative politicians and seen as part of the so-called 'Thatcher Economic Miracle'. Claims from such a source that an economic miracle had taken place may be treated with scepticism, especially with the severe recession of the early 1990s. However, the claim of a productivity 'miracle' has been made in a number of academic articles. In one such article, Metcalf (1990a) argued that of the four explanations usually advanced for the turnaround, three were not valid. First there was no 'batting-average effect'. The plants that closed in the recession of the early 1980s did not have low labour productivity, so composition effects did not account for the increase in productivity. Second, the capital:labour ratio did not grow more rapidly in the 1980s than the 1970s. Third, the quality of inputs did not improve, comparatively in the 1980s: for example, spending on research and development and on human capital remained low. Consequently, he concluded that the explanation must be that labour was being used more efficiently. Elaborating on this conclusion, he argued that three major factors and the interaction between them were the major reasons for higher productivity: namely, the shock effects of the recession in the early 1980s, more competitive product markets, and the reduction in union power. The shock effects, which elsewhere Metcalf (1990b) called the fear factor, arose on the workers' part from mass redundancies and high unemployment and on management's part from fear of bankruptcy.

TABLE 10.5   Labour productivity in the business sector, 1960–95
(average annual per cent changes)

	1960–73	1973–9	1979–95
UK	3.9	1.5	2.0
USA	2.6	0.4	0.8
Japan	8.4	2.8	2.2
Germany	4.5	3.1	0.9
France	5.3	2.9	2.2
Italy	6.4	2.8	2.0
OECD	4.6	1.7	1.9

Source: Derived from *OECD Economic Outlook*, No. 60 (December 1996).

This conclusion has not been without its academic critics, in particular Nolan and Marginson (1990). However, both Metcalf and his critics agreed that whatever the causes of higher productivity in the 1980s, there were grounds for scepticism about its continuation in the 1990s. Sustained improved productivity requires increased capital investment, increased expenditure on research and development, and increased investment in human resources through education, training and development. These were certainly not forthcoming in the 1980s or in the first half of the 1990s (see Table 10.5, previous page).

Labour costs per unit of output

Table 10.6 shows the movement of labour costs per unit of output during the 1980s and first half of the 1990s. It will be seen that, after a horrendous increase of over 20 per cent in 1980, there was a rapid decrease during the

TABLE 10.6   UK unit wage costs, 1980–96
(per cent increase on the previous year)

Year	Manufacturing	Whole economy
1980	22.9	21.9
1981	9.2	9.6
1982	4.5	5.2
1983	1.1	3.8
1984	3.6	6.5
1985	5.0	5.4
1986	4.0	4.6
1987	2.3	5.1
1988	2.7	7.2
1989	4.4	9.9
1990	6.7	9.9
1991	5.7	7.0
1992	0.8	3.6
1993	−0.4	0.1
1994	0.0	−0.3
1995	3.1	1.4
1996	4.3	1.7
1996 (1980=100)	176.7	213.2

Sources: Based on various *Employment Gazettes* and *Labour Market Trends*.

early 1980s in the rate of increase in unit wage costs for both manufacturing and for the economy as a whole. Thereafter, the rate of increase moved upwards, with the exception of 1986 and 1987, with the increase accelerating very markedly towards the end of the decade. However, the recession of the early 1990s, and the subsequent years of slow recovery, did show a marked fall in the rate of increase. For the complete period 1980–96, unit labour costs rose markedly less in manufacturing (76.7 per cent) than they did for the economy as a whole (113.2 per cent). Thus, the persistence of increases in money earnings in excess of productivity caused increases in unit labour costs throughout most of the period, even in manufacturing in those years when productivity was rising especially fast.

Conclusion

A number of features are readily apparent from this discussion of pay. First, there was a significant increase in both money and real earnings during the 1980s and early 1990s, although there was a marked slow-down in both in the mid-1990s. Second, this increase was not evenly spread; rather there was a very marked widening in the dispersion of earnings, the lower paid doing far worse than the higher paid. Thus, manual workers did worse while non-manual workers did much better, and within the white-collar group, the higher paid – managers and professionals – did best. Third, the public service sector as a whole did far worse than the private sector, although there were exceptions, such as doctors, nurses, police and firemen.

What is clear is that the Conservative Governments which were in office until May 1997 had not solved the problem of wage inflation although there was greater stability in the mid-1990s. Whether this will last is an open question, as is what level of unemployment would be required to maintain it. One of the enigmas of the 1980s is the extent of the rise in money and real earnings, despite very high unemployment, record interest rates and mone-tary squeeze, and a great weakening in trade union power. This is further discussed in Chapter 12.

What is also clear is that the problem of public sector pay was not solved in the 1980s and 1990s. The Conservative Government early on abolished comparability as the main criterion and replaced it by 'recruitment, retention and motivation'. For most public sector employees this has meant a sub-stantial decline in their pay relative to that of the private sector. Motivation was forgotten, and certainly not enhanced by the Conservative Government's berating of public sector employees, of whom teachers were a prime example. Towards the end of the 1980s, the Conservative Government sought to increase motivation through the introduction of PRP and in the 1990s determined that public sector pay bills should be frozen so that any pay increases had to be financed by so-called 'efficiency savings'. The Labour Government has taken no measures as yet to change this position. The problem of public service sector pay is again one to which we return in Chapter 12.

CHAPTER 11

Strikes

The litmus test of the Conservative Government's objective of curbing the power of trade unions was strikes. Overpowerful unions were, in the eyes of the Conservative Party, too ready to use strikes to get their way: 'strikes are too often a weapon of first rather than last resort' (Conservative Party Manifesto, 1979). In the Party's demonology stood the miners' strike of 1974 which had challenged, and some would say brought down, a Conservative Government. Moreover, the general election of 1979, which the Party had won with a majority of 43 seats over all other parties in the House of Commons, had taken place in the shadow of the Winter of Discontent and extensive strikes among public service workers. Strikes had become for the Conservative Party, the symbol of the abuse of their power by trade unions. This dedication to using the law to curb strikes persisted after the strikes had withered away. The Trade Union Reform and Employment Rights Act 1993 was the sixth piece of legislation since 1980 to make provisions on strike action, and its passage coincided with the smallest annual number of strikes ever recorded. The Labour Government elected in May 1997 was not committed to any change in the legislation about strikes apart from some protection against the dismissal of strikers.

This chapter looks first at the place of strikes in industrial relations and then at the strike record since 1980, comparing it with earlier periods and with other countries. It then summarises the changes in the law affecting strikes and the impact on ballots, picketing and secondary action is examined.

Strikes and industrial relations

Before embarking on a detailed examination of strike activity since 1980, it is as well to keep a sense of proportion about the significance of strikes. In the

239

1970s an annual average number of 2.6 million workers were involved in strike action, or about 1 in 8, so it was somewhat more than a once-in-a-decade event on average for employees. In the 1980s the annual average number involved was about 1.1 million and by the end of the decade it was down to less than 0.8 million; going on strike had become less than a once-in-two-decades event on average. In the first half of the 1990s it fell to 0.24 million, which was about once in eight decades. The proportion of all days which could be worked but which were lost through strikes was minute in the 1970s (0.2 per cent); in the 1980s it became even more minute (less than 0.1 per cent); and by the 1990s it had virtually disappeared (at about 0.01 per cent). The decline in strikes since 1980 has been dramatic and strikes have been transformed from major to a minor feature of the industrial relations scene. But an understanding of strikes is essential to an understanding of changes in industrial relations since 1980.

Of course, there are some ways in which the statistics underestimate the effect of strikes: the method of counting stoppages ignores other forms of industrial action, such as bans on overtime and working to rule; strikes lasting for one day or less causing the loss of less than 100 days' work are not counted in the official statistics; many stoppages, especially short ones, have repercussive effects for which the number of days' work lost is an inadequate proxy for the cost.

Going beyond the statistics, strikes have a symbolic significance because they are the open use of power to inflict damage in order to extract concessions or to defend existing positions. The use of terms such as 'militant minority' indicates a belief that strikes are war-like conflict. On that view, if a strike is in breach of agreed procedures and is unofficial, the conclusion to be drawn is that control has passed to the 'militant minority'. For those who see management as the unitary government of workplaces, strikes, especially those in breach of procedure agreements, are challenges to the established order. The Government's claim in its 1979 manifesto, that 'a minority of extremists in the trade unions had the power to abuse individual liberties' and that 'Labour had enacted a "militants' charter"', gave strikes a heightened importance and made the reduction of stoppages a test of the Government's reforming zeal.

The practitioners of industrial relations tend to see strikes in less political terms although they are well aware that strikes are the most politically charged part of industrial relations. They emphasise that strikes have always to be seen in the context in which they occur. If there are agreements laying down a procedure for resolving disputes then a strike indicates that they – the negotiators – have failed. Most procedures recognise that when they end the unions may call a strike and the threat of it is taken on board in the negotiations. The right to strike is acknowledged in democratic countries because it is a legitimate last resort, the existence of which is part of the balance of the relative power of the two sides. This is well understood by negotiators, but for most of them it is a background point remote from day to day negotiations. The lock-out and the dismissal of employees are in theory the employers' equivalents of the strike although, as became clear in the early 1980s, it is the closing of a place of work, or the threat of it, and the making of workers redundant which is the equivalent in practice.

For most managers and trade unionists there is a continuing long-term relationship in which the same individuals have to live together, and that shapes the use which both make of the measures available for bringing their maximum bargaining power to bear. In most places of work a strike is a sign of failure because for most of the time the two sides are well enough attuned to each other's potential power to take account of it in bargaining. But if it comes to a strike, though it may be a failure on the negotiators' part, it is not a failure of industrial relations; rights of last resort are there to be used when people feel justified in employing them. Sometimes managers prefer to accept a strike because they believe that the eventual settlement will be better for them than the agreement which would have avoided the strike. In the end, virtually all strikes conclude with a negotiated settlement, although the parties may need the help of a third party to reach it. In that sense, strikes are extensions of negotiations beyond the agreed procedure.

There are cases where strikes occur in breach of procedure agreements. Exceptional impatience on the part of employees and undue frustrations on the part of managers can cause understandable explosions. So long as they are rare the procedure can usually survive. But frequent and deliberate breaches of procedure involving strikes indicate some deep-seated problem.

Strikes are bound to occur from time to time even with the best procedure agreements and the most sophisticated negotiators, because there will always be cases where one side or the other miscalculates the determination or bargaining power of the other. This is quite compatible with a general policy of seeking to reduce the use of strike action. It is also compatible with a belief that people on both sides can bring matters to a point where a strike occurs in order to meet objectives which lie outside the current negotiations if they are determined to do so. 'Militant' shop stewards may precipitate strike action and 'militant' managers may provoke it.

In some industries strikes always have a high political profile because of the nature of the product or service they provide. This is particularly so in the public services where the citizen is a captive non-commercial customer and there is no feasible alternative supply. Strikes in some parts of the private sector, like the sale of petrol and bread, have something of the same significance, and the privatisation of utilities like gas, water, electricity and telephones has added to them. An element of cost to the customer is inherent in all strikes. The public look to government in a parliamentary democracy to reconcile the pursuit of sectional interests with regard for the public interest. It follows that, even on the negotiators' view of strikes, governments will from time to time have grounds for interfering in the way in which industrial relations are conducted, and that often means adding to or subtracting from the bargaining power of one side or the other and thus affecting the use of strike action. The argument is then about whether the public interest will be served more by whatever restriction is under consideration than by allowing legitimate sectional interests to run unimpeded. Between 1980 and 1993 the Conservative Government took legislative action directly affecting strikes with the objective of changing the balance of power between the negotiating parties, causing that of the unions to decline and that of the employers to increase.

The strike record

Table 11.1 shows Britain's strike record since 1950. The number of recorded strikes was larger decade by decade in the 1950s, 1960s and 1970s. The upward trend peaked in 1970 at 3906 strikes and by 1979 the number had fallen to 2080. But both the other two measures of strikes activity – the number of workers involved and working days lost – were historically high in the 1970s; indeed, taking a long perspective, 'it was the 1970s that were the peculiar decade, whereas the 1980s simply saw a return to the underlying trend of strike activity apparent since 1930' (Milner and Metcalf, 1993, p. 238). A comparison of working days lost in relation to the working population shows that in the 1970s there were only two years when less than 300 working days were lost per 1000 workers, whereas in the 1980s there were eight such years.

In the 1980s the decline in the number of strikes speeded up and there were major reductions in the other two measures of strike activity. WIRS 3 showed that in manufacturing in 1979/80 one-third of establishments experienced industrial action, and ten years later the proportion was only one-tenth; in the public sector, however, the proportion hardly changed, falling from 35 to 30 per cent (Millward *et al.*, 1992, pp. 280–1).

Large strikes have always had a disproportionate effect on the number of working days lost, and that was particularly true in the 1980s. Out of the 72 million days' work lost in the decade, 26 million (36 per cent) were accounted for by the miners' strike in 1984/5 alone. The biggest strike of the 1970s, the miners' strike of 1971, lost 6.25 million days, which was a mere 5 per cent of the days lost in that decade. If to the miners' strike of 1984–5 are added the four other strikes in the 1980s which exceeded 1 million working days lost – steel (1980: 8.8 million), local government non-manual workers (1989: 2 million), telecommunications (1987: 1.5 million) and postal workers (1988: 1 million) – the concentration is even greater, being 55 per cent of the total for the decade in just five strikes.

TABLE 11.1   Strikes, 1950–96: UK annual averages

Years	Strikes	Workers involved (000s)	Working days lost (000s)
1950–59	2 119	663	3 252
1960–69	2 446	1 357	3 554
1970–79	2 601	1 615	12 870
1980–89	1 129	1 040	7 213
1990–96	307	236	370

Sources: *Employment Gazette* and *Labour Market Trends*, various.

The miners' strike was so unusually large that it dominates any comparison with earlier periods. If it is excluded, the number of annual average working days lost in the 1980s comes down to 4.6 million, which is only about one-third of the average for the 1970s although it is still greater than the averages for the 1950s and 1960s.

Strikes of over half a million working days lost formed a bigger part of the total in the 1980s than in the 1970s, but it is their concentration in the public sector which stands out. Of the 13 such strikes in the 1980s, 11 were in the public sector: local government, the civil service, the NHS, railways, education, the Post Office, steel and coal-mining. By contrast, in the 1970s only six out of 16 such strikes were in the public sector.

This was a radical change. The 1980s were a decade when big set piece battles took place in the public sector. There had been major strikes in the 1970s in coal-mining, the Post Office, the civil service, the fire service and the NHS, but in the 1980s strikes in the public sector were more widespread and more bitterly fought, with the government and public employers coming out on top.

The private sector had virtually no big strikes in the 1980s, in stark contrast to the 1970s when British Leyland, Vauxhall, Ford and *The Times* each had strikes costing more than half a million working days lost, as also did the engineering, construction, docks, and road transport industries. The public sector became the cockpit of industrial conflict in the 1980s as major strike activity in the private sector almost ceased.

In the first half of the 1990s strikes were at their lowest level in living memory and in 1994 were the smallest number since records began over one hundred years ago. Strikes in which 50 000 working days were lost numbered five or less a year between 1993 and 1996. But even at this extremely low level, in the same period 52 per cent of days lost were concentrated in the transport and communications sector, covering mainly public sector organisations.

By contrast very short strikes, though declining too, became a much bigger proportion of all strikes. As Table 11.2 shows, strikes lasting no more than a day had grown to over half of the much smaller total number of strikes.

TABLE 11.2   Strikes lasting not more than one day, 1970–96: UK annual average

Years	Number	Percentage of all strikes
1970–5	601	20.6
1976–80	423	18.0
1980–4	432	31.7
1985–9	393	43.9
1990–2	201	48.2
1993–6	116	50.2

Sources: *Employment Gazette* and *Labour Market Trends*, various.

As already stated, the incidence of strike action – working days lost per 1000 workers – was markedly lower in the 1980s than in the 1970s, and in the 1990s very much lower still. In the motor vehicle industry it fell spectacularly. In the second half of the 1970s it had averaged annually 4626 working days lost per 1000 workers, but in the 1980s it was 1398; in the second half of the 1980s it was only 760; in the first half of the 1990s about 100. The decline in the incidence of strikes marked a major change in its industrial relations.

The coal-mining industry experienced average strike incidence in the 1970s in years when there was not a major dispute. But in the 1980s the incidence was much higher than elsewhere, quite apart from the 1984–5 strike. Between 1986 and 1989 an annual average of 1130 working days were lost per 1000 workers, nearly eight times the national average, but by 1994–6 the figure for a much smaller industry was seven.

Some of the causes of strikes are set out in Table 11.3. The major change since the 1970s has been the decline in pay as a cause of working days lost, although it bounced back a little in 1993–6.

Redundancy became a more important cause rising over the 20 years from 1975 from almost nothing to one-fifth of the working days lost in 1993–6, and reflecting the increasing uncertainty of continued employment in both blue- and white-collar jobs.

Strikes over manning and work allocation moved with the economic cycle, rising in recovery and falling when unemployment grew. By the mid-1990s both trade union matters, and dismissal and discipline, had almost disappeared as causes of strikes.

TABLE 11.3 Working days lost by principal cause of strikes, 1970–96 (UK: % of all days lost)

Years	Pay	Redundancy	Trade Union matters	Dismissal and discipline	Manning and work allocation
1970–4	87.2	n.a.*	n.a.	n.a.	n.a.
1975–9	84.2	1.5	6.5	3.4	5.4
1980–3*	68.5	9.6	2.9	4.0	4.0
1986–9†	69.4	6.6	2.5	2.7	13.5
1990–2	50.2	14.9	1.4	4.1	8.1
1993–6	58.2	19.5	0.5	2.0	10.1

Sources: *Employment Gazette* and *Labour Market Trends*, various.
* The definitions changed in 1973.
† The miners' strike was classified under 'redundancy' and since its size outweighs all other factors in the breakdown by cause for 1984 and 1985, those two years are omitted from the comparison in the table.

The annual series in Table 11.4 shows that there was a downward trend in the three measures of strike activity during the 1980s and into the 1990s, reaching an extremely low level in 1994 when the number of strikes was one-sixth of what it had been ten years before. Working days lost annually per 1000 workers were 330 between 1980 and 1983, but only 25 between 1991 and 1994. The somewhat higher figures for 1995 and 1996 were still at historically very low levels.

The main features of the declining level of strike activity since 1980 were that large strikes were virtually confined to the public sector, pay was a declining cause of strikes, and one-day strikes were a rising proportion of the total; by the mid-1990s strike activity was at an extremely low level.

Comparisons with the strike record in other countries

Comparisons of the UK's strike record with that of other countries is important for two reasons. The UK's historically poorer economic performance has often been put down in part to its greater strike incidence, so a reduction in strike activity might indicate better relative economic performance. The second reason is that the Conservative Government has taken the credit for reducing strike activity, mainly through its industrial relations legislation.

TABLE 11.4   Strikes 1980–96 (UK)

Year	Strikes	Working days lost (000s)	Working days lost per 1000 employees
1980	1 348	11 964	521
1981	1 344	4 266	195
1982	1 538	5 313	248
1983	1 364	3 754	178
1984	1 221	27 135*	1 278
1985	903	6 402†	299
1986	1 074	1 920	90
1987	1 016	3 546	164
1988	781	3 702	166
1989	701	4 128	182
1990	630	1 903	83
1991	369	761	34
1992	253	528	24
1993	211	649	30
1994	205	278	13
1995	235	415	19
1996	244	1 303	59

Sources: *Employment Gazette* and *Labour Market Trends*, various.
* Includes 22 400 for the miners' strike.
† Includes 4 000 for the miners' strike.

TABLE 11.5   Working days lost through strikes per 1000 workers, 1970–95: International comparisons, all industries (annual averages)

Country	1970–9	1980–4	1985–9	1990–2	1993–5
UK	570	480	180	43	21
France	210	90	60	37	129
Germany	40	50	less than 5	27	11
Italy	1310	950	300	272	178
Netherlands	40	20	10	23	45
USA	n.a.	160	90	43	44
Canada	n.a.	660	280	293	132
Sweden	n.a.	240	120	70	83

Sources: *Employment Gazette*, December 1990 and 1993; and *Labour Market Trends*, April 1997.

Reductions in strike incidence since 1980 have been experienced in other countries, as is shown in Table 11.5, and is 'in line with a world-wide decline in strikes' (Brown and Wadhwani, 1990, p. 69). During the 1980s the reductions in the UK's incidence were not larger than those of its major competitors. In the first half of the 1990s the incidence continued to fall in the UK, whereas it fell more slowly or turned up again in most other countries. The average for the EU in 1990–5 was 92 working days lost per 1000 employees compared with 32 in the UK.

So the improvement in the strike position in the UK was not unique; the incidence of strikes fell considerably in almost all industrial countries, and by the mid-1990s was lower in the UK than in any other EU country apart from Germany and Austria.

Causes of the decline in strike activity

The reasons why strike activity declined were the same as the reasons why employers were for the most part stronger and unions weaker in the 1980s and 1990s than in earlier periods. Strikes are not detachable from the rest of industrial relations; factors affecting the whole affect them as part of the whole. But because of the high political significance attached to strikes, their causes have to be examined separately.

The similarity in the decline of strike activity in most industrialised countries since 1980 is the appropriate starting point. The large reduction in strike activity in Britain seems remarkable until it is set beside the decline in other countries. So the causes are likely to have included ones which were at work generally rather than ones which were peculiarly British.

The world-wide recessions of the early 1980s and 1990s were the common cause, tipping the balance of bargaining power towards the employers and away from the unions. Redundancies in British manufacturing were greater than in most other countries, but unions in all countries were confronted with the threat of contractions and closures. Unions tend to be at their strongest in manufacturing even in countries where they are generally weak, and so it was the recession in manufacturing which brought unions face to face with employers who said that only if the labour force was drastically reduced and managers' proposals for improved productivity accepted could firms survive. In the US, reductions in real pay were often part of the package. The unions had to choose between resistance, including strikes, probably leading to closure, or survival on employers' terms with fewer jobs. In the UK acceptable redundancy terms helped the unions to choose the lesser evil. That general explanation of the way in which the unions adjusted to their weaker position is widely accepted among practitioners on both sides of industry.

However, there was a period of stability and expansion in the middle of the late 1980s, yet the decline in strike activity continued in most countries, as in Britain. So the explanation for the second half of the decade cannot be the continued threat of closures and the need to survive as output fell. The unions' bargaining power was tending to wax. There were perhaps three factors at work. First, the earlier period of widespread redundancies and closures of plants had been a traumatic experience for employees and their unions as well as managers. Those who had survived were chary of risking what had been bought at a high price.

Second, the expansion of output in manufacturing did not need more employees. Employment in manufacturing in Britain continued to fall until 1987 and in the next two years increased by less than 1 per cent; yet between 1981 and 1989 manufacturing output increased by over 32 per cent. So jobs were still on the line. Firms recruited on only a limited scale and, in the absence of sufficient natural wastage, regular programmes of redundancies remained a common feature.

Third, the rising output, with little or no increase in employees, was achieved by higher productivity. Unions had cooperated in implementing managers' proposals for improved use of labour to secure survival. The process continued as investment came on stream and output began to grow. Many managers involved union representatives in delivering the changes needed to improve productivity, and they offered pay increases accordingly. The unions in manufacturing found that their members who remained in jobs did well out of local productivity bargaining, and threatening strike action was not necessary.

Indeed, looking at the whole of the private sector, it is notable that pay has not been a source of major conflict in the 1980s. While higher productivity enabled employers in manufacturing to offer pay increases in excess of inflation, the rest of the private sector was able to offer pay increases as big as those in manufacturing because of the expansion of the whole economy which the government's economic policy facilitated in the second half of the decade, and because the rest of the economy was not exposed to overseas competition to the extent that manufacturing was. Even when expansion slowed down in 1989, pay continued to increase at least as fast as prices. The pay pressure underlying stagflation came not from the unions' threatening to strike over pay demands but from employers making acceptable pay offers. In the 1970s attempts to restrain pay increases had caused some of the biggest private sector strikes, such as Ford in 1978. But in the 1980s, when unions were weak by comparison, real wages forged ahead. No wonder there were fewer strikes.

However, as shown earlier, declines in strike activity were not universal, for there were sectors where strikes were at a high level. First, there were the large set-piece battles in steel in 1980 and in coal-mining in 1984–5 over the terms on which the Government intended to contract those industries, although in steel the ostensible cause of the dispute was pay. Second, there were strikes over pay in the public services as the Government imposed cuts in real pay which its policy required in the private sector too, but which the employers there would not adopt. Most of the public sector unions were not weakened by falling numbers of employees; the numbers employed in public administration and education increased in every year of the 1980s, and in medical and other health services in every year but one. Trade union density held up well. In the early part of the decade, the strikes over pay were defeated by the Government. In the latter part of the decade, the outcomes were more mixed. The local government officers' strike in 1989 secured sizeable increases in the pay offer and the teachers' protracted selective and partial strikes held the position on pay but lost the negotiating machinery. As the number of strikes declined in the 1970s and 1980s – in total and in all sectors – the proportion of the total which were in the public sector rose steadily: in 1974 it was only 19 per cent, but by the second half of the 1980s it was between 50 and 60 per cent (Dickerson and Stewart, 1993, p. 274).

The recession from 1989 to 1993 hit some private services and some public services particularly hard. They experienced then what manufacturing had been through in the early 1980s with extensive redundancies in, for example, banking, insurance, telecommunications and energy. Middle managers and professional workers were widely affected. Neither were manufacturing and construction exempt. The decline in strike activity in the early 1990s, as in the early 1980s, was mainly a reflection of the threat of unemployment.

The recovery in the mid-1990s saw some increase in strike activity but it was from a very low level in 1994 and was not general; a single strike in 1996 accounted for more than half of the working days lost in that year. There is therefore no reason to expect the level of strike activity to turn up to a marked degree as unemployment falls. Practitioners believe that the general state of job insecurity is the prime factor continuing to deter strikes, affecting employees in financial services and the public sector as well as manufacturing.

Was the legislation, particularly in its specific provisions on strikes, a cause of the decline in strike activity? Certainly it was not a major cause. In the first place it was only from the mid-1980s that the main legal provisions were in force and could exercise an influence. Although secondary action and picketing were curtailed in the 1980 Act and the unions' special legal immunity was abolished by the 1982 Act, it was not until the 1984 Act that a majority in a secret ballot was required before a strike could be called with immunity from the law.

Most negotiators believe that the legislation has had little effect on the conduct of industrial relations. But in the case of strikes the provision for a secret ballot lays down actual procedures to be followed which are new, and so the practice to that extent is different. Later in this chapter the impact of the changes in the law affecting secret ballots, picketing and secondary action is examined. The conclusion drawn is that while they have tended to discourage strikes, and to that extent have contributed to the decline of strike activity, they have not had a clear and unmistakeable effect of their own. There are hardly any cases where unions wanted to call strikes, or where outsiders have considered a strike the next logical step in the union's strategy, but where the legal provisions (especially the need for a majority vote) have stopped the strike weapon being used. The law's existence deters the calling of strikes without careful consideration of where the line of legal immunity is now drawn and of the likely result of a secret ballot. But where a strike is the appropriate next step, the law can make it more likely, not less, because the secret ballot offers a way of legitimising it.

The law requires ballots to be held and they take time. So it would be expected that short, lightning strikes would be deterred. But, as Table 11.2 shows, strikes lasting not more than one day, though declining in number, have been a growing proportion of the total. With such strikes the law is often, even in its more rigorous form, irrelevant. They happen suddenly and are quickly over. Union officials probably only hear of them when they occur and their main concern is usually to bring them to an end. Most employers want work resumed as quickly as possible so that there can be negotiations, and resort to the courts to penalise the unions will seldom help to achieve that objective. It is, therefore, not to be expected that the law would have a powerful restraining effect on the number of short strikes.

Changes in the law affecting strikes

Chapter 5 reviewed the legislation affecting industrial relations. Here the provisions affecting strikes are briefly repeated. Also in Chapter 5 the consequences of the legislation were analysed under the headings of secondary action, picketing and ballots on the basis of actions in the courts. In this chapter the significance of the legislation is examined under the same headings in terms of its impact on the conduct of employers, unions and government. Inevitably there is some overlap and repetition, although references to the content of the legislation and to court actions are kept to the minimum, the material in Chapter 5 being available.

The stream of Acts of Parliament since 1980 dealing with trade unions altered the legal position of strikers and their unions. Each new piece of legislation reflected responses to the previous ones, the political pressures which built up between the steps, and the preferences of successive Secretaries of State since each of the Acts was carried through by a different Minister.

The provisions of the 1980 Employment Act on strikes were limited to the connected issues of picketing and secondary action. James Prior, who was Secretary of State from 1979 to 1981, was particularly concerned that the law should prevent the extension of disputes beyond the primary employer and the aggressive picketing which often accompanied it. Both had been prominent features of the Winter of Discontent. He had the failure of the Heath Government's legislation – the Industrial Relations Act of 1971 – in the forefront of his mind. His 'purpose was to bring about a lasting change in attitudes by changing the law gradually and with as little resistance, and therefore as much by stealth, as was possible'. He was particularly concerned with 'the dangers of having tougher legislation which employers might in practice be afraid to use . . . and which the courts could not enforce, as had been the case with the 1971 Act' (Prior, 1986, p. 158). This cumulative, one bit at a time, way of dealing with the problem was applied not only to industrial relations as a whole, but to parts of it (such as strikes).

Broadly, the 1980 Act preserved unions' immunity from legal action where the industrial action and picketing to support it was confined to the employer with whom the union was in dispute. Secondary action was lawful only against employers buying from or selling to the primary employers. Strikers could only picket at their own place of work. The limit on the number of pickets to six was not in the Act but in the Code of Practice, and subsequent case law supported it.

The 1982 Act passed through its main stages when Norman Tebbit was Secretary of State for Employment (1981–3), and he regarded it as his greatest achievement in government and 'one of the principal pillars on which the Thatcher government reforms have been built' (Tebbit, 1988, p. 185). On strikes it made key alterations in the law which severely reduced trade union immunity from legal action. If the unions were to avoid losing immunity, they would have to give up certain types of strike action.

Although the Trade Union Act 1984 fell in Tom King's period of office as Secretary of State (1983–5), it was the product of Norman Tebbit's policy of handing the unions back to their members and had been heralded in his Green Paper in January 1983. Secret ballots had to be held before lawful industrial action could take place. The ballot had to be confined to those likely to be called out, and the question on the ballot paper had to allow a simple 'yes' or 'no' answer to strike action, or to whatever other action was proposed.

The Employment Act 1988 gave trade union members, as well as employers, the right to ask the courts to stop a strike where there had not been a ballot carried out according to law with a majority in favour. Moreover, even where there was a majority in favour of strike action, a union could not punish a member who went to work or who encouraged others to do so.

The Employment Act 1990 made two major extensions of legal penalties for strike action. It made unions responsible for strike action called by lay officials – unofficial strikes – unless repudiated. The other extension was also to do with unofficial strikes. WIRS reported that one-third of manual workers' strikes and one-tenth of non-manual workers' strikes were unofficial in 1990 (Millward *et al.*, 1992, p. 296). The Act made it possible for employers to dismiss selectively employees involved in unofficial strikes repudiated by unions. Furthermore, action by the unions to protect shop stewards who lead unofficial strikes and are dismissed is outside the law. So leaders of local strikes which flare up and quickly die down run the risk of dismissal. The Act also went back on the government's definition of legal secondary action in the 1980 Act and made all such action illegal.

The Trade Union Reform and Employment Rights Act 1993 tightened up the provisions on strikes in three specific ways: all strike ballots had to be postal, ending workplace ballots which had been secret since 1984; seven days' notice of the action had to be given to employers, thus allowing them to make preparation to render the strike ineffective; and the employers had to be given a list of all employees being called on by the union to vote and subsequently to take action, thereby revealing to the employer the union's members. These terms, prepared by Michael Howard when he was Secretary of State, seem to have had no other motive than hampering unions' ability to call effective strikes and are in a different category from the basic provisions for a secret ballot of the employees involved in earlier Acts. The unions believe that these provisions interfere with the right to strike, as defined by the ILO in its Convention on Collective Bargaining (No. 98) to which the Government is a signatory.

So the law on strikes is different in major ways now from what it was in 1980. The definition of strikes which unions can call without penalty has been narrowed, and secret postal ballots are needed in all cases. Strikes and limited picketing must be confined to the employer with whom the union is in dispute. Not only can employers go to the courts and get injunctions if these conditions seem not to be met, but so can trade union members. If union members choose not to strike, despite a majority vote in favour, they cannot be punished by the union, and the Commissioner for the Rights of Trade Union Members is there to protect their rights and pay their costs. Leaders of unofficial local strikes repudiated by unions for fear of loss of legal immunity risk dismissal. No secondary action is legal. The employer is entitled to seven days' notice of strike action, and a list of all employees who are taking part in a ballot and who may strike. Those changes can be summed up as meaning that 'while the British workers' "freedom to strike" has not been extinguished or fatally damaged, it can be deployed only in a more structured way and at greater risk' (McCarthy, 1992, p. 71).

There was one proposed legal restriction on strikes which was not pro-ceeded with, however. Strikes in essential services were part of the old order which the Conservative Government was intent on banishing. Of course, the definition of essential services was elastic; at its narrowest it was electricity, gas and water, and at its widest it included the health service, the fire service and certain parts of transport. The 1979 Manifesto said that the Government would 'seek to conclude no-strike agreements in a few essential services'. The 1983 Manifesto beefed up the 1979 commitment, about which nothing had been done, by undertaking to carry out 'further consultation about the need for industrial relations in certain specified essential services to be governed by adequate procedure agreements, breach of which would deprive industrial action of immunity'.

The national strike in water supply in 1983 brought the Conservative Government close to legal action on strikes in essential services. It was the first national strike there had ever been in water supply, and all previous governments had regarded such a strike as unthinkable. In the event its effects were not as drastic as had always been forecast. Despite its lasting for a month, the feared health hazards did not materialise. Had it lasted much longer they might have been serious, and the size of the settlement reflected that possibility, being larger than the government liked.

Even so, Norman Tebbit, the Secretary of State for Employment, was put under 'heavy pressure' to 'make strikes in essential services a criminal offence' (Tebbit, 1988, p. 198). He successfully resisted on the grounds that the same legal rules should apply to essential services as elsewhere, otherwise there was a danger that any special restrictions would be kicked over. His 1982 Act had narrowed the area of union immunity and the 1984 Act based on his 1983 Green Paper introduced ballots for strikes. So he stood the issue on its head. No special measures were needed to prevent strikes in essential services because the legal restrictions on all strikes would be so ferocious that they would be sufficient in the essential services.

The issue lay dormant until 1996 when the government issued a Green Paper on *Industrial Action and Trade Unions* (Cmnd 3470). The immediate cause of the renewal of interest was a group of strikes in 1995 and 1996 in the Post Office, the fire services, higher education and, most importantly, London Underground; between 1990 and 1995 nearly two-thirds (of a very small number) of working days lost through strikes had been in essential services (Sweeney and Davies, 1996). With a general election looming, the Conservative Government no doubt saw that more proposals for legislation to curb union power could be to their electoral advantage, as they had been in all elections since 1979.

The proposal was to render unlawful any strike that had 'disproportionate and excessive effects'. The problem of definition of essential services was avoided by handing it to the courts. An employer would apply for an injunction to stop a strike, all the legal requirements for ballots and notification having been met, on the grounds that it was in an 'essential service' and that the strike would have 'disproportionate and excessive effects'. While the judicial decision might be fairly straightforward for a widespread strike in the electricity supply industry, it would be less clear in the case of, for example, a ban on overtime in a Royal Mail sorting office.

The employers as well as the unions were opposed to such an extension of the legal control of strikes. The Labour Party proposed binding arbitration in essential services until the implications for government expenditure were realised (see Dunn and Metcalf, 1996). The issue is bound to reappear whenever a strike is in prospect in an essential service which could inconvenience the public. The attitude of those who are responsible for industrial relations in the essential services is that the legal restrictions on all strikes are as considerable a deterrent in essential services as elsewhere (Norman Tebbit's point), and where strikes do occur the existing arrangements contain many possibilities for finding solutions. That view is made more convincing by the absence of any commitment by the Labour Government when it came to power in May 1997 to change the law on strikes.

Strike ballots

As the law now stands, unless there has been a majority vote of those involved in favour of industrial action, unions lose their legal immunity when calling members out on strike in breach of their individual contracts. This was a major change in British industrial relations. It was legal intervention at the heart of unions' ability to damage employers' interests, or threaten to do so, in pursuit of claims or to protect themselves. Yet it did not figure in the Conservative Government's early plans, and the 1980 and 1982 Acts had nothing about strike ballots. But they were a main feature of the 1984 Act and came into force at the end of September 1984. That was too late to affect the miners' strike which began in March 1984, although the absence of a national ballot before that strike was used as justification for compulsory strike ballots during the passage of the Bill. The unions strongly opposed the change, seeing it as a deliberate attempt to weaken them. Not all employers supported the change, fearing that it would introduce rigidities which would make bargaining more, not less, difficult. So secret strike ballots were a political initiative taken by the government.

From 1985 to 1987 ACAS published statistics about strike ballots in its annual reports. Of course, its information was not complete for there was no notification system even of an informal kind; but through its regional offices and its monthly collection of strike statistics ACAS was better placed than any other organisation to collect data on strike ballots.

In the first fifteen months to the end of 1985 ACAS was aware of only 94 ballots; in 1986 the number was 246 and in 1987 it was 280. The numbers of unions involved were 37, 30 and 53 respectively. In the first year the proportion of ballots with a majority in favour of industrial action was 72 per cent, rising to 77 and 90 per cent in the two subsquent years. The turnouts were commonly above 75 per cent. In 1985, 23 (34 per cent) out of 68 ballots with a majority led to no action, and in 1986 the figure rose to 169 (89 per cent) out of 189. The proportion of ballots of which ACAS was aware with a majority in favour of industrial action continued to be above 90 per cent; in 1995, 219 out of 234 ballots supported action (ACAS, 1996).

From this meagre information, supplemented by the interviews, some general features do emerge. Although unions were punctilious about observing the need to hold a ballot before strike action was officially taken, there were large numbers of strikes on which no ballots had been held; in 1987 there were 1074 strikes, and ACAS knew of only 280 preceded by a ballot. However, 601 (56 per cent) lasted for no more than two days. Short strikes continued to flare up and end without time for balloting. Employers did not go to the courts because they had little or no notice of these strikes, and legal action after the event was likely to worsen their relationships with the unions.

The provisions of the 1990 Act allowing employers to dismiss strikers selectively, free of any claim for unfair dismissal if the strike were repudiated by the union, were intended to deter short strikes. (If the union fails to repudiate the strike it loses legal immunity.) There is no clear evidence that employers have used this power to dismiss unofficial strikers other than occasionally. Even so, the unions regard it as one of the legal provisions which they would most like to see repealed.

The level of participation in voting is high, but there are no doubt cases where it falls short of the 75 per cent which is common. Most ballots produce a majority for action but in only a small proportion of cases is a strike actually called. Indeed, strike ballots have been remarkably well integrated into union bargaining strategies, and ACAS reported this as early as 1985. Unions have learned to use the results of ballots as bargaining counters. Often the employer's offer is put to the members and, as the union negotiators recommend, is rejected. The union then holds a ballot strictly according to the rules of the Code of Practice in which a high proportion vote and there is a large majority for strike action. The union officials return to the negotiating table with authority to call a strike if there is no improvement in the offer. As ACAS reported, 'some employers have found (this) difficult to counter' (ACAS, 1987, p. 14). Some employers believe that a strike ballot should not be held until the negotiating procedure has been fully exhausted, but unions tend to hold it when it will help their bargaining position most. The ballot requirement has strengthened the union's hand in many cases and, faced with the choice of a strike or a better offer, the employer usually chooses the latter. The Conservative Government's Green Paper in 1996 sought to make it more difficult for unions to hold successful strike ballots by proposing that a majority, not of those voting, but of those eligible to vote, would be required, and adding the proposal of an increase from 7 to 14 days' notice of strike action by the union to the employer.

Everyone understands what is going on. The union members know that rejecting the offer will be followed by a strike ballot. The union officials will only recommend rejection of the offer if they believe there is a majority for strike action. A majority of union members vote for strike action knowing that it will probably not need to be called. The employer knows that they should keep back enough to be able to improve their offer in response to the likely majority in the strike ballot.

Of course, such neat ploys can go awry. The strike ballot may produce a minority for action, or only a small majority, in which case the union will rapidly settle for the employer's last offer. Even though there is a majority, it may not materialise if action is called for; voting for strike action to put pressure on the employer is one thing, but actually striking is another. The employer may have meant it when he said his pre-ballot offer was his final offer, so that the expectation that he would give in to the strike threat may be false and the union's bluff may be called.

All negotiations in a company or plant where there is a settled relationship contain a number of unspoken assumptions about each side's behaviour based on past experience. Strike ballots have been incorporated into these patterns. The word 'final' applied to an employer's offer has to be interpreted, and successful negotiations depend on both sides' interpretations being the same. No employer can deny that the offer being put to the employees is 'final', but it may well be that it is not his final 'final' offer. Strike ballots have clarified the role of the strike threat in negotiations. They have brought the possibility of a strike into the negotiations in more cases than formerly but, on the other hand, despite ballots, the number of strikes has been going down. Strike ballots have become tactics which are well understood by both sides (see Elgar and Simpson, 1993, pp. 102–5).

These responses to the legal provisions have been different from what the Conservative Government expected. Penalties for unions where strikes took place without secret ballots were intended to weaken the use of the strike threat and to give the members the opportunity to stop the 'militant minority' calling irresponsible strikes. The Government assumed that employers would seek injunctions against unions if strikes were called without a majority in a ballot, or if the technicalities of the ballot were not observed. Some employers have challenged ballots successfully, as did the port employers after the dockers' strike ballot in 1989. But in general employers have held back from the courts even when they knew they would win because, for example, those voting were not confined to those who would be called on to strike. Many managers say that they would only resort to the courts in very exceptional circumstances. This reluctance, as on other elements of industrial relations law, can be explained in terms of having to live with the other side afterwards and of believing that legal penalties would damage future relations.

The Conservative Government tried to stimulate individuals into taking legal action against unions to compensate for the employers' relative unwillingness to use the courts. It did this by setting up a Commissioner who could pay the legal and other costs of individual litigants. In the 1988 Employment Act the Government extended to union members the right to seek an injunction if a strike were called without a ballot, or if the ballot were not properly conducted. In the same Act the Commissioner for the Rights of Trade Union Members was created to facilitate these and other actions by individual union members. The Government's belief that individuals would be more willing than employers to bring in the law was not borne out in practice. The Commissioner reported that between 1990 and 1997, 68 complaints about strike ballots had been received but only six led to formal applications for assistance, of which two resulted in court actions.

The second provision was contained in the 1993 Trade Union Reform and Employment Rights Act. It set up a Commissioner for Protection Against Unlawful Industrial Action who could assist individuals to take proceedings against unions where strikes were unlawful. (The same person acted as Commissioner in both cases, operating from a single office, since there were so few applications.) Between 1993 and 1997, six formal applications for assistance were made and the Commissioner supported two, neither of which got beyond the advisory stage. In the report for 1995–96, the Commissioner said that the lack of applications reflected the fact that 'there have been few, if any, instances of unions being involved in unlawfully organised industrial action' (p. 22). Both attempts to use state funds to encourage individuals to institute proceedings, causing unions to step back from unlawful action or suffering punishment if the action is persisted in, seem to have been irrelevant in practice, either because there is so little unlawful action or because individuals do not wish to take up the offer of assistance.

A ballot gives legitimacy to strike action. If a union calls a strike it expects its members, including those who have voted against it, to observe the call, and there are usually sanctions in union rules which can be applied to those who work when called on to strike. The government decided to separate the issue of the vote in a ballot from that of the union's power to punish those who do not strike. The 1988 Act prevents unions punishing their members for refusing to strike after a majority vote in favour of action, or for encouraging other members not to strike. The provision has sharp teeth. After the strike action taken by NALGO in the summer of 1989 over a pay claim, a number of its members were fined for refusing to strike despite the majority in favour of strike action in the ballot. They took action against the union. The first case – *Bradley* v. *NALGO* – was determined by the EAT in February 1991, when it awarded £2520 compensation to each of the nine former members of the South Tyneside branch who had crossed picket lines. This was the minimum award possible, the EAT deciding *inter alia* that they could not be compensated for loss of union membership because they had attempted to resign.

The practical effect of this provision on unions is that they are even more reluctant to call strikes where the majority is small or where there is a large minority, some of whom may be inclined to work in defiance of the majority. But many managers doubt the efficacy of this provision because they antici-pate that the other, more informal, pressures on those who work during a strike may be more widely used, and they could carry over into day-to-day relations between unions and management in an unhelpful way.

The requirement that strikes should be sanctioned by a majority in a secret ballot is based on the clear principle that the decision should be made by the individuals concerned in private. It is a major improvement in the conduct of industrial relations that this is now almost universally accepted. The unions opposed it (as did many managers) when it was introduced, and only a Conservative Government could have brought it to pass.

However, some provisions of the 1988, 1990 and 1993 Acts which were designed to close loopholes were widely seen as unprincipled and vindictive. The main provisions open to that criticism are the submission of lists to employers of those entitled to vote in the ballot and of those to whom a strike call applies; postal ballots instead of secret workplace ballots; the complicated duties of scrutineers; and 7 days' notice of strike action to employers. These provisions, in the view of the unions, contain numerous possibilities for employers to mount legal challenges on matters of marginal detail. As a result the principle of a secret strike ballot, for which there is now universal approval, has got so many fuzzy edges that unions say they have difficulty in meeting every legal requirement, and employers acknowledge that in many cases they could quite easily find grounds for applying for an injunction to prevent the strike.

Picketing

Action to make strikes effective has always been contentious. If a strike has solid support from a disciplined labour force no picketing may be needed. But in most cases a picket on the entrance to the workplace is necessary to exercise persuasive pressure on those who do not favour strike action and may be willing to go against the majority decision and continue working. Pickets have been required to limit themselves to peaceful persuasion since the Conspiracy and Protection of Property Act of 1875.

Where a strike divides a body of employees and where the success of the strike seems to depend on stopping all those directly involved from working and, even more certainly, where the strikers believe that picketing is necessary to stop others (such as lorry drivers) entering and leaving the workplace, there is a recipe for damaging conflict which may turn into a challenge to the police. If people in no way directly or indirectly involved decide to join the pickets out of sympathy for the strike, that may sharpen the challenge.

Picketing only infrequently raises major issues of public order but in the 1970s there were two events, among others, which had a formative influence on the intentions of the incoming Conservative Government in 1979. The first was the victory of pickets over the police at the Saltley coke depot in February 1972. A strike in the coal-mining industry was in progress and the NUM wanted to stop the use of stocks in order to bring pressure on firms dependent on the supply of coal, or of coke in the case of the steel industry and some other consumers. On the morning of 10 February the NUM assembled a large number of 'flying' pickets, sufficient to prevent the police keeping the Saltley coke depot open. The police were greatly outnumbered. The depot had only one gate in a closely built up area and the Chief Constable, no less, decided to close the depot.

Several features contributed to this event's symbolic status and to the Conservative Party's conviction that it should never be repeated. The NUM had organised the transport of large numbers of pickets from far away. Arthur Scargill first achieved national fame as the organiser of these 'flying' pickets. The miners were strongly supported by numerous local trade unionists in the West Midlands, many from the engineering industry. The closing of the Saltley depot by picketing happened the day after a state of emergency had been declared by the Conservative Government and seemed to cock a snook at the power of the state. Deliberate planning of large-scale picketing had been shown to have the power to prevent the police keeping open places at some distance from the primary dispute and where the picketing was not designed to deter people from working.

The second event was the Grunwick dispute in 1976. There was a strike over recognition at a north London photographic film processing factory. The employer had refused to recognise the union when (in August 1976) 137 employees walked out over his treatment of them and then joined APEX. The employer held that they had dismissed themselves. The union authorised a strike, the factory was picketed and it escalated into a *cause célèbre*.

By March 1977 ACAS had reported under the statutory procedure then available recommending recognition. The employer refused to accept the ACAS recommendation and the TUC called for a boycott of the company, to which Post Office workers who delivered a significant part of the factory's work responded. The picketing built up in the summer. The entrance to the factory was in a confined street and the mass pickets tried to stop the police ensuring entry for those of the firm's employees who had continued to work. There were regular scenes of violence and on 13 June 84 people were arrested. Most of the pickets had not worked at Grunwick but were supporters of the claim for trade union recognition. Leading trade unionists and ministers in the Labour Government appeared on the picket line. Grunwick challenged the ACAS report in the courts, winning in the High Court but losing in the Court of Appeal. In August the report of the Court of Inquiry, which had been set up with Lord Scarman as chairman, recommended reinstatement and recognition of APEX while criticising the picketing. APEX then withdrew its support for mass picketing. The company still refused recognition and the dispute petered out; Grunwick had won. Picketing had not been successful but it had brought a running battle to a north London street and it seemed impervious to all the apparatus of the law, ACAS and a Court of Inquiry.

These two events entered the hall of fame of militant trade unionists and became models for extensive picketing during the Winter of Discontent in 1978–9. But no other events achieved the significance of Saltley and Grunwick for both militant trade unionists and the Conservative Party.

Picketing which challenged the police and was violent was a high priority for attention when the Conservative Government came into office in 1979, and so legal limitations on picketing were a major feature of the 1980 Employment Act. People involved in a dispute were confined to picketing peacefully their own place of work. Unions which authorised picketing beyond that faced legal action. This limitation meant that people could not picket the premises of other employers involved in the same dispute; pickets had to be drawn from those who worked in the workplace picketed. Limits were also placed on the picketing of other employers who, if their employees went on strike or took other action, might put pressure on the employer in the primary dispute. So from the beginning of the 1980s the law severely reduced the scope of legal picketing, and it seemed that the ghosts of Saltley and Grunwick had been laid.

Picketing is ancillary to strike action. In the early 1980s strikes declined in number and picketing was not an active issue, the new law being in general observed. But in the autumn of 1983 there was a dispute between the *Stockport Messenger* and the NGA which is described in Chapter 5. Picketing was only one feature of the dispute, but it was the scenes of picketing designed to stop the newspapers leaving the plant and the resulting conflicts with the police which claimed public attention. The union chose to defy the law and brought down crippling penalties on itself. The dispute showed that a union could be prevented from operating effectively if it persisted in picketing in the face of injunctions. Newspaper printing does not dominate the mainstream of British industrial relations but, even so, the lesson was plain for all to see. If injunctions against picketing were not observed, the unions' existence was at stake. The new legislation, when applied, could cripple unions.

Picketing was an essential part of the strategy used in 1984 by the NUM and its Areas to make the miners' strike effective. At the very beginning the ballots of South Wales lodges were 18 to 13 against strike action. But by the morning after these results were known there were pickets at every pit in South Wales and no one crossed the lines (Adeney and Lloyd, 1986, p. 96). That showed the superior power of picketing over the ballot. But in Nottinghamshire pickets from Yorkshire unsuccessfully tried to stop miners going to work and that picketing may well have been the crucial influence causing the Nottinghamshire Area of the NUM to vote against strike action by a three to one majority.

As is explained in Chapter 5, the NCB (in accordance with the wishes of Ministers) took no legal action against picketing because they feared it would cause sympathy with the miners, and it was the initiating of injunctions by a transport company and NUM members against picketing which led to the sequestration of the assets of the South Wales Area of the NUM.

However, it was the picketing at the Orgreave depot which brought to a head the consequences of the NCB taking no legal action against picketing. On 18 June 1984 10 000 pickets attempted to repeat Saltley and make the police concede the closure of Orgreave. Like Saltley, Orgreave was a source of coke for steel-making and the intervention was intended to prevent lorries leaving. It was not a picket to prevent people working. A month's picket had not prevented lorries going in and out, yet the Yorkshire miners made it the test of picketing. But unlike Saltley it was surrounded by fields and had more than one entrance. As the pictures on television showed, it became a pitched battle. The large numbers of pickets were insufficient to achieve their objective. Determined police, especially those who were mounted, broke the strikers' lines and the strikers left the field defeated. For some, it was seen as the turning point of the strike. In violent exchanges the police were a different proposition from those at Saltley; they used the force necessary to defeat the pickets. Mass picketing was not used again after Orgreave and attempts to bring the Nottinghamshire miners out by picketing their pits withered away.

The 1980 Act had been designed for such events as the picketing used in the miners' strike. Had injunctions been applied for they would undoubtedly have been granted. If ignored, they would have led to fines and the sequestration of the NUM and its Areas' assets in the first few weeks of the strike. That might well have caused the Areas to try to restrain the picketing. As it was, they were under no such restraint. Whether attempts to impose injunctions against picketing would have caused the Nottinghamshire miners to vote for strike action is questionable since it was the picketing itself to which they objected. But the decision not to use the law against picketing ensured that violence between pickets and the police became the norm, and victory was seen to belong to the side which had the superior force. By forswearing their own legal remedies, the government failed to do all they could to deter violent picketing.

Since the miners' pickets were defeated by the police, others who used picketing to exert pressure on employers and working employees could expect the same strenuous treatment. The Wapping dispute, in which News International used the law on picketing against the unions, is described in Chapter 5. The print unions staked their future on the success of the picketing at Wapping. They had to prevent the newspapers being sold for a time if they were to make the company negotiate. The pickets only had to close off the exit from the Wapping plant for a few hours each night to secure their end. The stakes were as high for the company as for the unions. Having moved to Wapping and dismissed all the previous staff, successful picketing might well have brought the company down. In such a case injunctions and penalties for not observing them could not stop the mass picketing on which the union depended and which the company had to overcome. The police were the key, and they gave News International its victory. The picketing failed because the police ensured that the newspapers could leave the plant. As one trade union official said to another on the first night that newspapers were printed at Wapping, seeing the lorries come down the ramp and the police successfully making way for them through the pickets, 'We have lost.' As at Orgreave, the police used the force necessary to overcome the pickets, night after night. A report by Northamptonshire police into police conduct at Wapping in January 1987 found that some officers were violent and out of control. Where the law itself was not enough to prevent mass picketing succeeding, the police secured its defeat.

This historical account shows how the practice of picketing influenced the content of the legislation and showed the limits of the law, together with the ultimate power of the police. In the past ten years the low level of strike activity has meant that the issue of legal restrictions on picketing has claimed little attention. So long as the climate of industrial relations continues to be non-confrontational for the most part, picketing will cease to be a topic of interest to practitioners.

Secondary action

Secondary action is that which is taken by a union against employers other than the one with which it is in dispute, to cause them to put pressure on the primary employer to make concessions to the union. It can take various forms, such as a refusal to touch material or components bought from, or being supplied to, the primary employer ('blacking'), or action against any employer who might do business of any sort with the primary employer. It may go much wider. Action may be taken against employers at some distance from the dispute to generate pressure on the employer to settle (sympathetic action). Where unions are in a weak position, as is often the case in recognition disputes like Grunwick, or where unions feel that the action of others may tip the balance their way, as with the NUM call for support from lorry drivers and railway workers to which there was a partial response in 1984–5, they appeal to the sense of trade union solidarity and to the feeling that others may need their support another day.

The Employment Act 1980 limited secondary action to that taken by the employees of a supplier or a customer who had a contract with the primary employer. That this was a significant narrowing of industrial action was shown in the Wapping dispute referred to above, and in the NUS's dispute with P&O Ferries in February 1988 when the union was made virtually bankrupt by the fines and sequestrations of its assets which followed its refusal to obey injunctions against illegal secondary action.

In the Employment Act 1990, however, the Government changed its position and all secondary action, including wider sympathetic action as well as action against customers and suppliers, was made illegal. This was a major restriction on the right to strike which could penetrate the scope of primary action if employers deliberately divided their activities between legally separate companies, as some did after the 1980 Act in order to reduce the scope of legal secondary action. It is the threat of industrial action which is most often used, not its actual occurrence, and if no supplier or customer of a firm in dispute can be touched, no convincing threats of action can be made and the right to take industrial action is severely curbed. It was for this reason that in 1980 James Prior had opposed making secondary action against customers and suppliers illegal: as a consequence of the 1990 Act 'the legitimacy of different workgroups supporting each other is now completely denied' (Elgar and Simpson, 1993, p. 78).

As with picketing so with secondary action; the restrictions in the 1980 Act had widespread support and the unions no longer oppose them. By virtually outlawing all secondary action the 1990 Act is seen by many as going too far. But the subject is no longer on the unions' active agenda because there has been a sustained period of low strike activity.

Conclusion

The decline in strike activity since 1980 has been continuous. It has two main features. First, during the 1980s strike activity about halved in terms of numbers of strikes, but at the end of the decade several million working days were still being lost each year through strikes. Second, the decline continued into the 1990s until in 1994 it bottomed out at an extremely low level: in that year there were 205 strikes and 278 000 working days were lost; in the last three years of the 1980s those figures on an annual basis had been 833 and 3 125 000. The slight rises in 1995 and 1996 do not alter the picture of strike activity having almost disappeared.

The fact that strike activity continued on a downward trend until it reached an almost irreducible level marks a major development in industrial relations, being a change of quality as well as of degree. Not only did set-piece national strikes disappear but so did almost all strikes in the private sector except for a small number of very short ones. The explanation is that industrial relations as a whole has changed, and that a number of factors have contributed to it.

The contraction of major basic industries with high densities of trade union members, like coal, steel and ship-building, has obviously reduced the area where strikes could occur, and the increase in the proportion of employees in service trades where unions are weak or not recognised has made the part of the economy in which strikes might happen much smaller. The ending of many national agreements, and the decentralisation of bargaining to companies and plants where managers and union representatives often have a cooperative relationship, have reduced the relevance of strike action. Apart from these structural factors, probably the most important influence working against strike action has been widespread feelings of job insecurity. High levels of unemployment and redundancies connected with 'delayering' and 'down-sizing' in a wide range of service trades like banking, as well as in manufacturing industries, have created a general uneasiness about continuity of employment. Many employees have felt that strikes, or threats of strikes, could only increase that insecurity. This is the view of both senior managers as well as trade union leaders.

So although the government's legislation affecting strikes seems not to have been a main reason for the decline in strike action, that legislation has changed the legal framework affecting strikes in major ways. The paradox that the practitioners claim the legislation has not been of major importance, although the legislative changes have been very considerable, is explained by the absorption of the new legal rules into the negotiators' practices and the unwillingness of most employers to use the law against the unions. The practitioners mostly believe that the reduction in strike action flows from general factors affecting the labour market and the ability of managers to take and keep the initiative in negotiations, with unions being less able to get priority for their claims. Yet government Ministers saw the six Acts, all of which affected strikes, as leading directly to a modification of conduct. It is a fair conclusion that the legal changes have been one influence, but by no means the dominant one, making for the reduction in strike activity.

Strike ballots are a good illustration. That the ballots amount to a major change in practices is unquestionable. Secret ballots are now held as a matter of course before strike action is taken, except for local strikes which suddenly flare up. In the vast majority of cases, of course, a majority in favour of strike action does not lead to one occurring. There is a general acceptance that secret ballots before strikes are a permanent feature of the practice of industrial relations. This can be put to the credit of the Conservative Government since Ministers had little support initially for the proposal from employers, and they faced opposition from trade unions. Now it is accepted all round. But its practical significance is limited. When ballots are called trade union members seldom reject strike action. Over 90 per cent of ballots are in favour of it, with high participation rates in the votes. Ballots have become part of the bargaining tactics of both sides. The union uses the ballot as a means of showing it has rank and file support, while the employer expects the union to prove the strength of its members' feelings through a ballot. The requirement for secret ballots on industrial action has improved the quality of negotiations without changing them in a fundamental way.

The ballot makes known to both sides what the majority of the individuals concerned prefer. It gives legitimacy to the union's position which could previously be said to be that of the active minority, and marks the end of the vote by show of hands at a hastily assembled meeting, often out of doors. Many more majority votes in favour of strike action are followed by negotiated settlements on an improved offer from the employer than are followed by strikes. Just as skilled union negotiators will only go to ballot when they have good reason to believe they will win, so a skilled manager will not make a final offer (or a final, 'final' offer) which risks being rejected in a ballot. It is proof of the value of the strike ballot provisions in the law that the negotiators have integrated them into their procedures so successfully.

The significance of the narrowing of the unions' legal immunity in calling strikes is more difficult to assess, as is that of the legal changes on picketing and secondary action. During the 1980s these changes seemed to be of little consequence, except in certain major disputes. Moreover, the miners' strike showed that it does not follow that because the law exists it will be applied. But the major reason why a firm conclusion cannot be reached is that industrial action has been running at such a low level, and one that has continued to fall, so that there have not been enough occasions on which the law might be tested for its practical significance to have emerged. It can be argued that the low level has itself been caused in large part by the legal changes, but international comparisons work against that view. If there were an upsurge of strike activity in the future, the significance of the changed legal framework might turn out to be greater than at present appears. However, so long as strike action continues to be insignificant, or even if it rose to somewhat higher levels, the changes in the law may well continue to be of little apparent importance.

After a sustained period of few strikes, especially in the private sector, it may be that the prospect of any upsurge in strike activity is slight. If it is the case that in many places of work changes are brought about through negotiations and by skilled management preparation and consultation, strike action could continue to be far less on the cards than it used to be. Experience in the car industry points in that direction. Perhaps the changes in the law on strikes came at the time when strikes were ceasing anyway to be significant.

The large strikes in the public sector in the 1980s were major events in the development of contemporary industrial relations, although they seem hardly relevant to the mid-1990s. There was a marked contrast between the private sector in which hardly any strikes of significance occurred, and the public sector where there was a long roll of set-piece battles, often in industries and services where strikes had previously been regarded as likely to damage essential services in politically unacceptable ways. In that sense, the 1980s were the years when the Government took on strikes far more readily than any previous post-war government had dared to do. The handling of strikes in steel, the civil service, water, the NHS, and above all coal, showed the Government's resolve. Strike action was extensively threatened and taken in the public sector because the changes proposed for running down and reorganising the industries and services were such strong challenges by government to union positions. The unions which called strikes all had to accept defeat, some more extensively than others. The Government's policy appeared to be that any challenge to it by strike action would meet with as crushing a defeat as could be mounted. Having defeated the miners, the Government was not going to lose to the nurses, teachers or ambulancemen. That determination to defeat unions which challenged the Government, which was particularly associated with Mrs Thatcher, was a major determinant of the quiescent state of industrial relations which has persisted since the 1980s.

As the Conservative Government proceeded with legislation affecting strikes from 1980, every move was opposed by the trade unions and some were resisted by employers too. At first the unions talked of the repeal of all the legislation but, by the 1992 general election, they had come to accept that the public were in favour of secret strike ballots and the other main provisions. But they had expectations at that time that a Labour Government would repeal what they regarded as the vindictive measures allowing the selective dismissal of unofficial strikers, the total ban on secondary action, and the requirement to give employers the names of union members before ballots were held and strikes called. But by the time of the general election of 1997, the Labour Party was committed to making no changes in the legislation as it affected strikes, apart from some protection against the dismisssal of strikers. It took account of TUC views in other directions, and undertook to provide a statutory recognition procedure and to end the legal requirement of a renewal of the check-off every three years. The adoption of the Social Chapter was also to the unions' advantage. The Labour Party's unwillingness to commit itself to any changes to the law on industrial action was a major blow to union hopes. It was motivated by a belief that such changes would be regarded by the electorate as being soft on the unions and so politically damaging.

The unions had no alternative but to acquiesce, although it is to be expected that if an opportunity occurs they will return to the subject at some time in the future. But for the time being, the election of a Labour Government uncommitted to changes in the law on strikes means that the existing legislation is likely to be the framework regulating strike action for the foreseeable future.

CHAPTER 12

Assessment and implications for the future

Introduction

In this chapter answers are attempted to the questions posed in the introduction to this book, and changes which have taken place since 1979 and their implications for the future are assessed. The first section surveys the changes in the environment of industrial relations, be they political, economic or social. Next the changes in the objectives, policies and structure of the two parties – unions and employers – are considered. Then the changes in institutions and procedures, in private and public sector pay, in productivity, and changes in the law, including such issues as strikes, recognition, the closed shop and the check-off are assessed. Finally, the future agenda for industrial relations, the effects of greater EU integration and the Social Chapter of the Maastricht Treaty are looked at, as is the election of a Labour Government in May 1997 after 18 years of Conservative rule.

The environment

The period since 1979 was one of profound economic, political and social change. Consequently, the environment within which industrial relations was conducted was radically different from that of the 1970s, and indeed from that of the earlier post-war decades. First, there was the political environment. The UK from 1979 to May 1997 was ruled by Conservative Governments. These governments pursued a brand of conservatism which was in marked contrast to that of earlier post-war Conservative Governments. Above all, they signalled the end of the post-war consensus, which had included commitment to full employment, the welfare state, Keynesian economics, a significant public sector and a degree of corporatism. In its place was a whole-hearted belief in a free market economy, private enterprise, monetarism, individualism, the creation of an 'enterprise culture' and the ending of any form of corporatism. In pursuit of these beliefs, the Conservative Government passed legislation which sought to restrict union power severely, and to limit union ability to take industrial action. The legislation also sought to enhance the rights of individual union members against those of the union leadership.

Conservative Government hostility towards unions did not however show itself only in legislation. The Government no longer treated the TUC and individual unions as social partners and as important participants in society. In its role as an employer and quasi-employer, the Government throughout the period sought to resist union demands and, in a series of public sector disputes, showed its determination to defeat the unions, virtually regardless of cost. This policy culminated in the year-long miners' strike of 1984/5. Once the miners had been defeated no one else was going to be allowed to win, neither teachers nor ambulance staff. The Government's conduct against the miners was a sign to others of what would happen to them if they chose to strike. While the removal of the right to union membership at GCHQ in 1984 was perhaps the most spectacular and extreme anti-union measure taken by the Government, the resistance to it perhaps prevented it being extended elsewhere in the civil service.

There can be no doubt that the Conservative Government's early industrial relations legislation had popular public support, there being a widespread belief (not least among some trade unionists) that the unions had become too powerful in the 1970s. However, the Government's antipathy to unions went much further than this. Given its ideological commitment to free markets, to managerial authority and to individualism, the existence of unions was considered a hindrance to the proper working of the labour market. Thus in its White Paper, *People, Jobs and Opportunity*, (DE, 1992) the Government stated: 'There is new recognition of the role and importance of the individual employee. Traditional patterns of industrial relations, based on collective bargaining and collective agreements, seem increasingly inappropriate.'

Logically, therefore, the Conservative Government's ultimate objective had to be the elimination of unions or, at the very least, their marginalisation. Except in these terms, or in terms of pure vindictiveness or political opportunism, it is difficult to see the rationale for much of the Government's later industrial relations legislation. Thus for trade unions the political environment was an exceedingly hostile one from 1979 to 1997.

The return of a Labour Government in 1997 marked a turning point. There is no longer an inherent enmity to trade unions. There will be interchange and the unions' voice will be heard. But there will be no return to corporatism, there will be no major change in the balance of power, and there will be no major change in Conservative legislation. Some legislation has been promised and this is discussed later. A Government White Paper is due in May 1998.

If the political environment was bleak for trade unions, so was the economic one for much of the period. As far as the labour market was concerned, unemployment doubled in the first two years of Conservative rule, and continued to increase to a peak of well over 3 million in 1987. Thereafter unemployment fell steadily (to around 1.5 million by the middle of 1990). However, the country then entered a new recession and unemployment again rose to nearly 3 million by the end of 1993. There was subsequently a slow developing economic recovery with unemployment falling towards 1.5 million by the summer of 1997.

As far as product markets were concerned, there was a great growth in competition, partly as a result of deregulation at home but mainly as a result of growing international competition: the consequence of the EU and the Single Market, developments in world trade and the growth of multinationals. This growth in competition – particularly in the manufacturing sector – led employers to seek greater flexibility, efficiency and cost effectiveness, with significant consequences for industrial relations. Multinationals compared the production costs of their various plants, and those plants at the bottom of the league faced threats of closure unless significant improvements were attained. There was thus internal as well as external competition.

For employers, the political and economic environment was mixed, although basically very favourable. On the one hand, there was a Government from 1979 to 1997 which was favourable to business. Direct taxation for individuals (especially the higher paid) and companies was greatly reduced. The Government favoured increased incentives for enterprise, and the pay of senior managers and top executives rose at an unprecedented rate (not to mention generous tax concessions on share options). Profits, dividends and share prices also increased very substantially for most of the period. At the same time, unions were put in their place and management authority was restored.

On the other hand, business faced more competitive product markets. It was manufacturing industry in particular which at times felt most beleaguered.

New Labour has gone out of its way both before and after the 1997 election to seek to work with business to secure a flexible, competitive and prosperous economy, although it has also promised unions and employees 'fairness at work'.

The third major environmental change was new technology, the development and application of which continued apace in the 1980s and 1990s. Again the consequences for industrial relations were highly significant, affecting the demand for different kinds of labour and skills, blurring distinctions between manual and non-manual workers, and greatly affecting the location and size of establishments, job descriptions and pay structures.

Finally, there were changes in the social environment. Phelps Brown (1990) has traced these changes, arguing that after the Second World War there was a growth in collectivism 'centred upon a sense of neighbourly obligation and the intervention of government to guide the economy and modify its workings in the cause of material advancement and social justice'. In the 1980s a new view has prevailed:

> people are no longer seen as dependent on society and bound by reciprocal obligation to it: indeed the very notion of society is rejected. Individuals are expected to shift for themselves and those who get into difficulties are thought to have only themselves to blame. Self-reliance, acquisitive individualism, the curtailment of public expenditure, the play of market forces [developed] instead of the restraints and directives of public policy, the prerogatives of management instead of the power of trade unions, centralisation of power instead of pluralism. (p. 1)

Phelps Brown argues that this change was partly the result of the perceived defects of collectivism, but also (and more importantly) the result of a new generation for whom 'a quarter of a century of full employment removed awareness that an unplanned economy was capable of inflicting great hardship . . . the very success of the welfare state made it seem unnecessary'. There was also the growth of consumerism; the effect of widespread car ownership and of home ownership; and the widening of income distribution and changes in the tax system, with a consequent undermining of egalitarianism. At the same time, there were (as a result of economic change) drastic changes in the structure of the labour force with the decline of the traditional trade union strongholds in manufacturing, the rise of the service sector and the increase in self-employment, with a consequent change in social outlook.

The whole process is described by Phelps Brown as 'one of downward extension of the middle class and its values'. The Labour movement had been based on a sense of common interest and purpose: the purpose was not only defensive but there was the belief that betterment could come through changes in society. This called for action at national level: hence the formation of the TUC and the Labour Party. It also meant unity and loyalty, which sprang from the individual worker's sense of common interest. Phelps Brown believed that loyalty had ebbed away and that there has been a 'dissolution of the labour movement'. This was the result of the social changes mentioned above and, in effect, of the 'localisation' of interests: of interests in the home and in the workplace as against solidarity with fellow workers and policy at national level. While some might think that this conclusion is too pessimistic, particularly in view of the election success of Labour in 1997, there can be little doubt that the social changes he describes have had a significant effect on industrial relations.

Looking to the future, most environmental pressures on industrial relations are unlikely to be greatly changed. The political environment for trade unions has become more supportive with the election of a Labour Government. However, as stated earlier, there will be no major reversal of the Conservative legislation. There will still be restrictions on secondary action, picketing and the closed shop, and there is no doubt that lawful industrial action will continue to require a prior individual ballot.

There will be some changes in legislation. There are commitments, for example, to the introduction of a statutory mechanism for unions to attempt to gain recognition, a strengthening of the rights of individual employees, a NMW, and the end of the UK's opt-out from the Social Chapter of the Maastricht Treaty. Above all, there would not be a consistent anti-union campaign led by a hostile government, as occurred between 1979 and 1997, and which was clearly meant to have an effect on employer attitudes and behaviour. The return of a Conservative Government for a fifth term would have meant no let-up in the efforts to marginalise trade unions further.

With regard to the economic environment, product markets are certain to remain highly competitive, and indeed with '1992' and the removal of the remaining barriers to the movement of trade, are likely to become even more so. There will also be the effects of the introduction of the Euro. The position in the labour market improved in the mid-1990s but there is still substantial long-term and youth unemployment, and job insecurity is substantial. Technological change will continue unabated, and there is evidence that its effects on parts of the service sector may equal that on manufacturing in the 1980s. Finally, with regard to social change, the election of the Labour Government shows a reaction to the extreme individualism of the Conservative years. However, the main social trends are unlikely to be reversed and all political parties now place 'the market', and hence the consumer, high on their list of priorities.

For employers, the future environment will continue to mean competition and technological advance which will make manpower reductions, especially in manufacturing, a continuing feature.

Trade unions

For unions, there have been two major developments since 1979. First, there has been the dramatic and continuous fall in overall union membership (from 13.3 million in 1979 to 8.0 million in 1995) and in the membership of TUC affiliated unions (from 12.1 million in 1979 to 6.8 million in 1996). Second, there has been the drastic decline in union power and influence in relation to government and employers.

There can be little argument about the change in the relationship between Conservative Governments and unions. At best, unions have been viewed as an irrelevance and at worst, as 'the enemy within'. Thus the TUC was seen as having no public role; tripartism was virtually eliminated (for example, in the field of training after 1985); the NEDC was first emasculated and then abolished; TUC advice and policy statements were ignored; and the practice of having TUC nominees on a range of public bodies was ended. Complete elimination of a public role for unions was, however, not achieved. ACAS was still in the hands of a tripartite council, union presence still existed both in the health and safety field and in the composition of industrial tribunals. There will be a better balance under the Labour Government, although no return to the corporatism of the 1960s and 1970s.

The changed relationship between unions and employers was a more debatable question in the 1980s (certainly among academics). One school of thought argued that the structure and process of collective bargaining had been maintained in the 1980s: there had been no widespread de-recognition of unions; the check-off had been maintained; and shop stewards not only still existed but, with the further decentralisation of bargaining, their role had to some extent been enhanced. Another school of thought argued that although the machinery of collective bargaining had been kept in place, the power relationship between the parties had changed to such an extent that management authority had been almost complete, and it was management which set the agenda. The unions were thought to be in a state of almost terminal decline: management had taken control and 'individualism' was becoming dominant.

By the 1990s there could be no doubt about management's supremacy. The second school of thought believes that management is now supreme, that unions have largely been marginalised and that their power and effectiveness have been minimalised. Management, it is argued, has been transformed. HRM is being widely adopted; unions are being by-passed with management communicating directly with individual employees; and employees are being directly motivated, not least through the growth of individual PRP. Cost effectiveness rules and management has been free to innovate, to adopt technological and organisational change, to reduce the labour force when required, and to achieve virtually complete flexibility. Moreover, it is claimed that the attitudes and behaviour of both unions and employees have significantly changed. There is a greater realisation of economic imperatives and, consequently, a willingness to cooperate with management initiatives.

The first school of thought, although accepting that many of the changes mentioned above have occurred, emphasises that they are neither universal nor immutable. The fact that unions are less powerful does not mean that they are powerless or that they are bound always to be as acquiescent as many now are. That there is so little overt conflict does not mean that they do not exert any pressure.

The real situation varies between companies and in different sectors of the economy. For example, union density is still high (although there has been some decline) in the public sector, the privatised sector and some large companies. Thus, overall, generalisations are to be treated with caution. There can be no doubt that unions have lost power and influence and that management authority has been asserted. There has been some de-recognition but its extent has been limited, although perhaps somewhat greater than was originally thought (Gregg and Yates, 1991; Gall and McKay, 1994; Claydon, 1996) and increasing in recent years. Unions have had great difficulty in gaining recognition in new plants (Millward *et al.*, 1992; Marginson *et al.*, 1993) and breaking into service industries, where they have traditionally been weak. On the other hand, there has been an extension of the now widespread practice of the check-off. Employers bent on weakening unions might well have ended their check-off arrangements, but they have not done so. Nevertheless, there is as yet no sign of a halt in the decline in union membership which has continued unabated for well over a decade and a half. Whereas towards the end of the 1980s there were signs of a slowing down in the rate of decline, the severe recession of the early 1990s, with its sharp increase in redundancies and unemployment, meant further substantial falls in membership and there has been no recovery in membership with economic growth in the mid-90s.

Turning to the unions themselves, by the end of the 1980s and into the 1990s, there was a very significant change in attitude and behaviour in most unions. The basic objective of unions has always been, and still is, the protection of their members' interests. This is an entirely legitimate objective in a democratic and pluralist society. Moreover, a strong and healthy trade union movement is an essential component of such a society.

Unions throughout their history have not generally sought confrontation, but have sought to achieve their objectives through securing recognition from employers and then establishing procedures for negotiation, consultation and grievance handling, so that issues and disputes could be handled peacefully. Industrial action has never been other than a last resort in most cases.

While the unions' basic purpose has not changed, they have certainly sought to adapt, rather belatedly perhaps, to the realities of the changing environment in which they have had to operate. As stated in Chapter 8, there has been a growing acceptance of some of the legal constraints imposed upon them. There has been a greater awareness of the more competitive environment in which firms have had to operate, and they have been more receptive to the introduction of new technology. There is a less confrontational approach and an attempt to seek a partnership with employers.

Unions have also recognised that they need actively to recruit new members, and that in order to do so they need to make themselves more attractive and to provide new services. They have also (under the pressure of falling membership and financial difficulties) sought to make themselves more efficient. Computerisation among the large unions is now universal: and in many unions there have been changes in internal structure to meet changing circumstances: for example, a strengthening of local and regional organisation to meet the needs of decentralised bargaining and the problems of individual members. At the same time, there has been more centralisation in other respects, such as financial control and over industrial action.

As part of the process of adaption to changed circumstances, there has been a spate of union mergers since 1979 which was discussed in Chapter 8. The trend towards mergers will probably increase. This should lead to stronger unions, the more efficient use of resources and the better provision of services. However, a note of warning should be struck: such gains are not automatically achieved. A merger between incompatible unions could be disastrous; competition between large general unions could be self-destructive; and giant unions could become bureaucratic and remote from the membership. Nearly all the union general secretaries we interviewed who had been engaged in mergers stressed that the problems they encountered were far greater and much more time-consuming than they had envisaged.

Since 1979 the decline in union membership and bargaining power has been unremitting. The longer it continues the more likely it is to be permanent. A generation of trade union leaders, national and local, has known little but threats of redundancy and managerial dominance as they have sought to defend their position against the continuous erosion of their significance as representatives of working people.

Will further new attitudes and behaviour develop in the years ahead? As already stated, unions (including the TUC) have sought a less adversarial approach and have sought a partnership role: New Unionism. This does not mean that there will never be strikes, or that unions will not seek to reach hard bargains.

Will trade union membership continue to fall in the years ahead? Many of the adverse factors which have contributed to the fall in union membership in the 1980s and 1990s will still be present: for example, continuing changes in the structure of the labour force away from manufacturing to services, the decline in manual employment and the growth of white-collar employment, the decline in the employment of men, and the growth in the employment of women and of part-time women in particular. However, these trends were also present in the 1970s and did not prevent union growth. More important will be the policies, attitudes and behaviour of government, employers and the unions themselves. Employers vary in their attitude to unions from complete hostility to active cooperation. Their attitude is influenced in no small part by the attitude and behaviour of unions themselves, but there has undoubtedly been a trend among employers of non-unionism. In this respect unions have to a large extent shown that they have absorbed some of the lessons of the recent past (Metcalf, 1991). In the workplace they are seeking to play a more constructive role while, in an effort to attract membership, they have sought to provide new services and have increasingly appreciated the importance of providing individual services as well as collective ones. A major advantage for the unions is the election of a Labour Government in 1997 which is not overtly hostile to unions in the way the Conservatives were and which is committed to some helpful measures, although nowhere near as much as the unions would like. Also helpful should be Britain's greater integration in the EU and the implementation of the Social Chapter. Whether the favourable factors will be enough to overcome the unfavourable ones is uncertain.

Employers

How have employers used their increased power? Many large organisations have drastically reduced their labour force, without any significant union resistance. This is particularly true of manufacturing, but is also true, for example, of the docks, BT, coal-mining, the railways, the clearing banks, the large insurance companies and the civil service. In a number of cases this has been achieved partly by generous early retirement schemes and voluntary redundancy packages (for example, BT), and partly by the threat of the loss of such benefits if voluntary redundancy is not accepted (for example, coal-mining and the docks).

Employers have regained control over operational matters where it had been lost. Most agreements in those greenfield sites, where unions have managed to gain recognition, have included a clause providing for flexibility of labour. Many employers have strengthened direct communications with their workforce and ceased to rely upon the union channel and shop stewards. There have also been attempts to secure greater employee involvement, not in the old sense of increased worker participation, but in the sense of moulding workers to employer objectives and policies. There has been a very marked widening of pay differentials and a growth in the application of PRP. All these changes can be typified as a growth in the 'individualisation' of industrial relations and a move away from 'collectivism'. What most employers did not do, despite their greater power, increased competition in product markets and the need for cost effectiveness, was to cut real pay (except at the lower end of the labour market).

Among a number of employers, the period saw an increase in hostility to unions, fostered in part by the Conservative Government's anti-trade union-ism. An overtly anti-union stance became seemingly respectable during the second half of the 1980s and 1990s in a way that had not been true in Britain for the last half a century, and in a way which more resembled the American scene than the West European one. It took the form, as we have shown earlier, not of widespread union de-recognition, but of the frequent refusal to recognise unions in greenfield sites, some de-recognition of managerial unionism, a greater reluctance with regard to white-collar unionism in general and in some cases to manual trade unionism. Above all, however, there were attempts to marginalise unions or by-pass them through direct communications with individual employees, through PRP and through other measures of 'individualisation'.

Such attitudes have not been universal. Many of the personnel directors interviewed paid tribute to the cooperation of unions in increasing efficiency and productivity, some going so far as to say that without union cooperation, such improvements would not have been achieved as smoothly as they had been. Others saw the unions as a declining force and believed that the future rested entirely with management. Some such companies laid great stress on the development of HRM, although what they meant by this was not always made explicit. As we pointed out in Chapter 6, the evidence which exists suggests that very few firms have espoused HRM in the full meaning of the term. Nevertheless, in looking into the future, this is the direction in which many major British firms claim to be moving. Others are putting the emphasis on cost minimisation.

There is some difficulty in reconciling HRM claims with the practice of large-scale cut-backs in the labour force of many such companies, the growing casualisation of employees, and the inadequacy of their investment in training and development. In answer it may be argued that HRM practices are meant to be applied to the 'core' workforce and not to the periphery. This begs many questions, not least how the core and the periphery are to be defined. Even if this is done satisfactorily, and different policies applied to each, does this mean that we are institutionalising a two-tier labour force? If so, what are the implications for 'team working', 'a common purpose', and loyalty to the organisation? Presumably such attitudes would only be expected of the selected 'core' workforce and nothing expected from those on the periphery. It is a cliché to say that management gets the unions and employees it deserves, but if responsibility and cooperation are expected from unions and employees, then management for its part must exercise an equal degree of responsibility and cooperation. The record of British management in this respect, with a few notable exceptions, has not been outstanding.

WIRS 3 showed that in 1990, establishments with no union recognition dismissed some two-and-a-half times as many workers employed per thousand as did those where trade unions were recognised. Compulsory redundancies were reported in 46 per cent of workplaces without recognised unions that had made workforce reductions, compared with 17 per cent where unions were recognised. Private sector workplaces were less than half as likely to have any form of health and safety representation if they were not unionised than if they were. A similar picture is painted by the National Association of Citizens Advice Bureau report (CAB, 1993) which stated that in 1991/92 the CAB dealt with nearly 1 million employment problems (an increase of over 10 per cent on the previous year). There was 'Increasing concern over the frequency with which employers are changing their employees' terms and conditions of employment. The most common changes are cuts in pay and/or increases in the hours employees are required to work' (p. 1). A more recent CAB report (1997) stated that flexible working was bringing insecurity to thousands of workers who had no paid holidays, sick pay or protection against unfair dismissal.

The WIRS 3 conclusion is highly relevant here in saying that:

> Employee relations in non-union industrial and commercial workplaces had relatively few formal mechanisms through which employees could contribute to the operation of their workplace in a broader context than that of their specific job. Nor were they as likely to have opportunities to air grievances or to resolve problems in ways that were systematic and designed to ensure fairness of treatment. Broadly speaking, no alternative models of employee representation – let alone a simple alternative model – had emerged as a substitute for trade union representation. (p. 365)

Marginson *et al.* (1993) also conclude that overall there appears to be little evidence of the emergence of a non-union model. In relation to communication and involvement, non-union companies were no more likely than those recognising unions to communicate information about business performance or to have profit-sharing or employee share ownership schemes. In fact, the unionised firms used a greater range of methods of employee communication and were more likely to use two-way forms of communication and forms of task participation.

Changes in institutions and procedures

As described in Chapter 9, the three major changes in collective bargaining have been its reduced coverage, the further erosion of industry-wide bargaining and decentralisation to company level (and, within some companies, to divisional/plant level); and there has been a reduction in the scope of collective bargaining. In addition, as already stated, there has been no widespread move towards active de-recognition. New procedures – where introduced – have tended to be more favourable to management: for example, the inclusion of managerial prerogative clauses and the ending of obligatory arbitration clauses where they existed, particularly in the public sector. Interestingly, the 1997 Local Government Agreement provides for unilateral arbitration, as does the 1997 Agreement at GCHQ. Paradoxically, most of the so-called 'new style' agreements have compulsory arbitration clauses, usually pendulum arbitration, but they are very few in number.

There have been moves to single union agreements, above all on greenfield sites, although there have been cases in established organisations: for example, Midland Bank's de-recognition of the MSF, leaving BIFU as the sole bargaining agent. Where, in established organisations, single-union agreements have not been deemed advisable or possible, there have been some moves towards 'single table' bargaining (that is to say, management bargaining with a single joint union side, consisting of all recognised unions). There has been the ending of many national agreements – for example, engineering, banking, shipping and commercial television – and the decentralisation of bargaining and other procedures to company, divisional or plant level. Decentralisation within companies has largely been the result of organisational changes made for purposes of business strategy and financial accountability, rather than for purely industrial relations purposes.

As Brown (1989) and Brown and Rowthorn (1990) have shown, such decentralisation has usually been on a product basis and not on a geographical basis to take advantage of different local labour markets. To the extent that the Conservative Government has ended national agreements and fragmented bargaining in the public sector, it appears to have misunderstood what has been happening in the private sector. Those companies interviewed who produced a single product, or who had integrated production spread over a number of plants, insisted that the maintenance of company-wide bargaining was essential.

There has been an end, where it had existed, to the 'single union channel': that is to say, employers no longer accept that communications and consultation should be solely or even mainly through elected union representatives. They proclaim that it is their right – indeed, duty – to communicate directly with their own employees, and this they have increasingly proceeded to do. In a number of cases, joint consultative committees now consist not only of elected union representatives, but of directly elected individual employees.

These trends are unlikely to be substantially reversed in the future. However, it may be, particularly if union strength recovers somewhat, that the dangers of leap-frogging in too decentralised a system of bargaining may lead to some reconsideration of a role for more centralised bargaining.

One final point on changes in institutions and procedures which needs to be made is the decline in the use of arbitration and other forms of third-party intervention (see Chapter 9). There are two main reasons for this. The first relates to the public sector where arbitration pre-1979 was the accepted peaceful method of resolving disputes. Its virtual disappearance is the direct decision of Conservative Government as employer and quasi-employer. The government regarded arbitration as inflationary and 'weak-kneed'. It was for government and other public employers to take the necessary decisions and not subject these decisions to arbitration which might result in a compromise award. There was no room for compromise in the policy and philosophy of the Conservatives from 1979 to 1997. If the price was industrial action, inconvenience to the public and severe financial cost, so be it.

The second reason relates to the private sector where arbitration was not institutionalised, as it was in the public sector, but was used mainly on an *ad hoc* basis. Here it was the mammoth shift in bargaining power to employers. Employers, on the whole, saw no need to go to arbitration, as in most cases they could in effect impose their final offer in the knowledge that employees, given economic insecurity, would be unlikely to take industrial action.

It is open to argument whether such attitudes will continue indefinitely into the future. It is the antithesis of 'good' industrial relations. Also, if a strong economic recovery takes place and unemployment is significantly reduced, then the balance in bargaining power may change. Employers may then be only too pleased for disputes to go to arbitration rather than have them settled by force.

Substantive changes

On the substantive side, the first and perhaps the most important change was the significant increase in average real earnings which took place, particularly in the 1980s, although the increase by no means applied universally and was largely absent in much of the public service sector. Given the weakness of unions throughout most of the period, it is difficult to blame (or praise) the unions for the rise in average real earnings. Pay went up as fast as it did more because employers offered it than because unions pressed for it. The key question must therefore be why employers acted in this way during a period when there was high unemployment, a surplus of labour, cuts in the size of many companies' labour forces, weak unions, strong competition (certainly in manufacturing), constraints on public sector pay, and the need to be cost effective? The answer can only be that employers, individually, considered that it was in their best interests to do so. Once the worst of the recession of the early 1980s was over, company profits increased dramatically; labour forces were drastically cut, and productivity – at least in manufacturing – increased significantly. Employers seemed to believe that their remaining employees should share in their company's prosperity. Employees had earned higher pay by accepting cuts and by accepting organisational and technological change, while flexibility had increased and had been generally accepted, so that increases in labour costs per unit were small for much of the period (again, at least in manufacturing). In much of the private service sector, international competition was absent, thus making higher pay less of a problem. In addition, some employers believed that higher pay was necessary to achieve involvement and agreement with management objectives. Towards the end of the 1980s, additional reasons for higher pay were labour and skill shortages in some parts of the country and a resumption of the upward movement in the cost of living. In the public sector, after many years of enforced restraint, there had to be some 'give'; if not on grounds of social justice, then on grounds of high labour turnover and growing labour shortages in at least some areas and in some occupations. With the recession in the early 1990s, increases in the cost of living, money earnings and real earnings were markedly reduced, and with the up-turn increases so far have been moderate.

Second, although there were substantial increases in average real pay, there was also a marked widening of differentials, as shown in Chapter 10. Non-manuals workers did better than manual workers, the higher paid did better than the lower paid, skilled and professional workers did better than the unskilled and semi-skilled. Moreover, in the 1990s there was increasing evidence of falls in real pay at the bottom end of the labour market. Above all, management pay, particularly top management pay, soared. Such increases were justified at the time on a number of grounds, including that it was performance-related and that as profits grew significantly, top management deserved significantly higher pay. This did not prevent at least one chief executive justifying a large pay increase, despite falling profits, by arguing that in difficult times the strain on top management was greater. Gregg, Machin and Szymanski (1993) show that between 1983 and 1991 directors' pay increased by about 20 per cent per annum on average, and appeared to be unrelated to company performance. Conyon and Gregg (1994) conclude from their research into 170 companies that there is no relationship between directors' pay and company profits. The Greenbury Committee did not appear to have had any moderating effect on directors' pay.

The third significant change has been the growth in the popularity of PRP and, to a lesser extent, in profit-sharing and employee share-ownership. While PRP had always been common for management in the private sector, during the 1980s and after it spread to lower level white-collar employees and (in a growing number of cases) to manual workers. In the public sector PRP had been rare, even among management grades, the most common system being incremental point scales with incentive provided by promotion prospects. However, the 1980s saw the introduction of PRP for management grades in the public corporations, such as British Rail, and in the public service sector, including the civil service, the NHS and universities. In addition to its spread, the size of the 'merit' element in pay has been increasing, and indeed some companies have declared that there would be no general pay increases at all and that all increases would be based on 'merit'. Such a policy might be easier to achieve in times of low inflation than in times of high inflation. While there is an arguable case for pay to be related more to performance, before management adopts such a policy there are some questions which it should consider. There is as yet little evidence of the effects of PRP on performance. Is management satisfied that performance can be accurately measured in every job so as to base pay increases on it? How much of the judgement is objective and how much is subjective? Is it possible that PRP can be divisive, and is not the need in many cases to encourage group performance rather than only individual performance? It also needs to be remembered that PRP can be demotivating for those who are judged not to have done well. If performance assessment for pay purposes is linked to the appraisal interview, as increasingly it seems to be, what has happened to the previously strongly held belief that the two should be separate in order that the appraisal interview can be conducted honestly and frankly, so that deficiencies could be admitted and hence the first step taken to secure improved performance? With regard to profit sharing and employee share ownership, while they may have great potential value, unless they are to be merely a trimming on the cake or a façade, management needs to be clear as to their purpose and their effects on employees. Objective evidence is so far limited, and what there is is far from favourable (Thompson, 1992, 1993).

I. Kessler (1994), however, makes the important point that individual performance pay has been used not only as an incentive to help bring about organisational change:

> More specifically this type of pay system has been used to facilitate changes in organisational culture; to weaken the influence of trade unions and undermine collective bargaining as the primary means of pay determination; to revitalize and strengthen the role of the line manager; to enhance employee commitment to the organisation; and to strengthen financial control over payroll costs. (p. 478)

Kessler (1994) suggests that

> the value of individual performance pay in enhancing employee motivation is always likely to be limited. The establishment of clear and consistent performance goals is highly problematic as a general managerial exercise and particularly so when applied to certain occupational groups . . . If, however, the distinctiveness of individual performance pay is seen to lie in its use as a lever for promoting organisational change, perhaps as part of a broader HRM strategy with the emphasis on its symbolic and rhetorical value in generating a new performance-driven company culture and supporting the principles of managerialism and individualism, the issue of impact assumes an entirely different form. (p. 490)

Other changes in pay systems have included simplification in pay structures (for example, fewer grades through banding, usually in the cause of greater flexibility) and the reduction of job demarcations. Along with the simplification of pay structures there have been doubts in some quarters about traditional job evaluation. For one thing, job descriptions can inhibit flexibility and there is a trend towards paying people for what they can do and how they do it, rather than what they do in a specific job at a specific point of time. There have also been a number of examples of integrated pay structures (that is to say, manual and white-collar), in Midland Bank, Pilkington and a number of Japanese and American companies. The main reason appears to have been harmonisation in order to encourage team-work and to acknowledge the blurring of boundaries between blue-collar and white-collar work. An added advantage relates to avoiding equal pay actions, and this was certainly the major factor in the case of Midland Bank. It is also a major factor cited in the 1997 Local Government Agreement.

There have been developments in other terms and conditions of employment. In 1979, the engineering unions had just won a reduction in weekly working hours from 40 to 39 per week, and the staggered introduction of a fifth week's holiday. During the early years of the 1980s, these concessions spread to many other industries. Coincidentally, in 1989, the engineering unions conducted a campaign, including selective industrial action, for a further reduction in the working week, originally for a 35-hour week and then in practice for a 37-hour week. They had a considerable degree of success, which led eventually to similar reductions in a number of other cases.

It is clear from the experience of the 1980s that the Conservative Government's 'free market' and monetarist policies failed to solve Britain's wage/price spiral, although there are new claims for a virtuous circle in the 1990s. If there were a sustained period of much lower unemployment the labour market would be tighter for employers, and trade unions and employees would be in a stronger position. In those circumstances, there would be a serious possibility of pay-induced inflation. However, the Labour Government, like its predecessors, is committed to a low inflation target, and no doubt financial and fiscal measures would be taken to restrain excessive growth. There certainly seems little possibility of attempts at constraint through any form of incomes policy.

Public sector pay

Increases in public sector pay, with only a few exceptions, fell markedly behind those of the private sector after 1979. The absence of agreed guidelines for the determination of pay in the civil service, local government and the NHS leaves open the possibility of the sort of pitched battles which occurred in the 1980s. However, Conservative Government measures for decentralisation (such as the widespread establishment of agencies in the civil service, self-governing trusts in the NHS, and the power of local authorities to opt out of national agreements) may make this less likely.

In all three services, changes in the 1980s and 1990s reduced the scope for future conflict. In the NHS, the inclusion of the nurses and some professions ancillary to medicine in the Review Body procedure means that more than half of the staff now have Review Bodies and do not have their pay determined by collective bargaining. The decision in 1991 to have school-teachers' pay determined by a review body was also of major importance.

In local government and the NHS, the obligation to put various services out to tender means that there is acute pressure to adjust pay and staffing to meet competition. With agencies and departments in the civil service determining pay separately, and the likelihood of NHS hospital trusts doing so too, there will be many public service employers who will each have to take account of comparability, with the attendant responsibilities for collecting the relevant information.

The central questions are the same throughout the public services: how should pay relate to that of comparable work outside? In a national or regional service what should be the relationship between pay in decentralised units of that service? How should the contributions of individuals and groups be rewarded? The public services include some professional groups for whom they are almost the only employer, as well as a wide variety of occupations similar to that found in the private sector. It is the financing of them from public funds which makes them different. Since 1979 the Conservative Government took advantage of that characteristic to hold back their pay, as had its predecessors from time to time.

It may be that what is needed in the longer run is a comprehensive approach to all public service pay: those covered by Review Bodies (doctors, nurses, teachers, armed forces, and others), those with formulae (police and firemen), those with an as yet untested degree of comparability (civil servants), all local government employees (manual and non-manual), the NHS outside the Review Bodies, and university and further and higher education staff. They total about 5 million employees.

All those listed need settled, regular and permanent access to independent pay comparisons. During the 1980s and 1990s only the groups covered by the Review Bodies had such comparisons fully taken into account. A single pay review body solely devoted to providing such information would have to be set up by the government with terms of reference which ensured that it delivered its findings impartially to both sides or to the Review Bodies. The viability of such an approach would depend on governments acknowledging that reviews of comparable pay were necessary because the settlement of public service pay had to take the results into account. Until that is accepted by governments as the employer or chief paymaster, there is always the likelihood that, in the absence of such data and an agreed intention to take it into account, parts of the public services will fall so badly out of line that strikes will occur or a special catching-up exercise has to be mounted. Any government intent on improving the quality of public services could not escape facing the need for some commitment to ensuring that public service pay kept up with the pay for comparable work outside (see Brown and Rowthorn, 1990).

The actual outcome depends essentially on whether governments put improving the services above the holding back of levels of expenditure. So long as public service pay is left to be settled piecemeal and without a framework of agreed guidelines, there is a danger that disputes will occur. Even if battles are avoided, the public services will continue to deteriorate as a consequence of low morale, high turnover and a failure to attract an adequate share of the best people.

Productivity and labour costs

Movements in productivity and labour costs per unit of output were discussed in Chapters 3 and 10. Reasons for the marked increase in productivity in manufacturing industry during much of the 1980s, and the fall in the rate of increase in labour costs per unit in manufacturing, were considered. By 1990, with the recession, as a result of the government's high interest policy, there was also a slow-down in the improvement of productivity and labour costs per unit.

The 'productivity miracle' of the 1980s appeared less of a miracle in the early 1990s. Mayhew (1991, p. 14) states that: 'it is generally agreed that the improved productivity performance in manufacturing was the result of a more effective use of resources rather than of a significantly greater investment in physical or human capital. The improved efficiency stems from better working practices and a more flexible use of labour.' As the recession gave way to recovery during the 1990s, productivity improved again. While changes in organisation and working practices have been important, sustained improvement in the British economy can only come from increased investment in physical and human capital.

Changes in the law

Between 1979 and 1993, Conservative Governments acted through legislation to reduce the power of trade unions and to make trade union leaders more accountable to their members. The philosophy behind Conservative Government policy was discussed in Chapter 4: namely, a belief in free markets and hence the need to de-regulate and to marginalise unions. The stream of legislation was described in Chapter 5. Suffice it to recall that in a series of Acts – the Employment Acts of 1980 and 1982, the Trade Union Act, 1984, the Wages Act 1986, the Employment Acts 1988, 1989 and 1990, and the Trade

Union and Employment Rights Act 1993 – trade unions' rights to take industrial action were severely constrained; secondary action and secondary picketing were made unlawful; industrial action could not be taken without a prior individual postal secret ballot; unofficial strikers could be selectively dismissed; union chief officers and national executives were made subject to secret individual postal ballots and to obligatory re-election; the closed shop was made unlawful and unenforceable; and unions, as organisations, were made subject to financial penalties and their funds subject to sequestration, so that potentially they could be made ineffective and indeed bankrupt. The nature and extent of restrictive legislation has been such that the ILO has ruled that it *prima facie* amounts to a breach of the ILO's conventions on freedom of association, to which the UK is a signatory.

Has the legislation since 1979 been successful in achieving the Conservative Government's objectives of weakening trade union power and making union leaders more answerable to their membership? The answer must be in the affirmative. The incidence of strikes and working days lost through strikes diminished substantially, as the strike statistics in Chapter 11 show. However, as that chapter also shows, most other leading industrial countries experienced a similar decline in strikes without the introduction of a series of restrictive Acts. The use of ballots before the taking of official industrial action has been universally adopted by unions, except in local flare-ups. Unions have accepted that their leading officials and national executive committees have to be elected and subject to re-election by individual secret ballots, and their rule books have been altered accordingly. They had also, by the end of the 1980s, largely accepted significant restrictions on secondary action and secondary pickets, not necessarily because they agreed with such restrictions but because earlier attempts to defy the law had proved disastrous for the unions concerned: for example, the NGA in the *Stockport Messenger* dispute, SOGAT in the Wapping dispute, the NUS in the P&O Ferries dispute and the NUM in the miners' strike. In each of these cases, union funds had been sequestered.

Some caveats must, however, be recorded to this apparent success story. It assumes that the law is of prime importance to the conduct of industrial relations. Our evidence from many major British companies suggests that this is not the case. While not denying that the law must be observed and that it was an important background factor, they considered that other factors were far more important to the way they conducted their industrial relations. By the end of the period unions had found ways of mitigating the effects of some of the new restrictions. One particular and important example is the way in which ballots prior to industrial action have often been turned to the advantage of unions. A successful ballot for industrial action is a powerful bargaining factor for the union to argue for, and employers concede, an improvement on their earlier offer: also a successful ballot legitimises the proposed action in a way that a show of hands or a decision by an executive committee cannot.

As Lewis (1991, p. 60) says:

> Formal legal rules and procedures may of course impinge significantly on the employment relationship, but their precise role and impact are likely to be affected if not determined by social attitudes, economic circumstances and the balance of industrial power. The complexity of this interaction makes it difficult to measure or even identify law as an independent factor in the conduct of industrial relations.

Moreover, the work of Brown and Wadhwani (1990) and Brown, Deakin and Ryan (1997), as does our own (see Chapter 11), concludes that the effect of the legal changes on the movement in strike statistics is highly questionable, and that the legislation alone had not produced the economic effects (for example, in limiting wage increases) anticipated by free market theorists.

In considering the future of legislation it is first necessary to accept that the legal position of trade unions prior to 1980 could hardly be described as satisfactory, as a number of leading cases showed. Moreover, as a former senior trade union official argued, although legal changes cannot easily be imposed on people who do not want them, many trade unionists (not to mention non-unionists) wanted a number of the changes which have been made.

Lewis (1991) argues that there are three main approaches to labour law. The first is a return to 'collective *laissez-faire*', where unions would have maximum autonomy within a non-interventionist legal framework. This he firmly rules out, for it fails adequately to recognise that the state's responsibility for tackling economic problems includes establishing a structure of labour law that strikes a balance between the interests of the parties and the public interest in industrial peace and an efficient economy. The second is the Conservative Party's approach, based on 'free market' beliefs which we have discussed at length in Chapter 4. The third is the Labour Party's approach, based on a 'reformist' strategy which endorses the legitimacy of trade unionism but which aims to ensure that the power of unions (and also of employers) is exercised responsibly. He further argues that Labour's approach goes with the grain of European social policy and is in marked contrast to the completely free market approach of the Conservatives.

The new Labour Government, elected in 1997, as outlined in Chapter 5, is committed to:

(a)   ending the opt-out of the Social Chapter;
(b)   the introduction of a NMW;
(c)   the restoration of trade union rights at GCHQ;

(steps were taken in the summer of 1997 with regard to the above three);

(d)   the introduction of a mechanism for statutory union recognition when a majority of employees so desire;

(e)   the ending of the three-yearly renewal of the check-off;
(f)   some protection for lawful strikers against unfair dismissal.

These are not insignificant measures, but there are no other commitments to amending the Conservative legislation, although some may be forthcoming in a Government White Paper expected in May 1998. There does seem to be a new broad consensus on much of the existing legislation (for example, on ballots before industrial action, the end of the closed shop and on secondary action).

With regard to the future, there can therefore be no doubt that the law will have an important part to play in regulating industrial relations. Collective employment law will continue to provide constraints, as well as provide certain rights. Many individual rights will also continue to be provided by law. Developments in the EU (discussed later) will add to this process. Below some of the key legal and procedural matters are considered in more detail.

Recognition

The UK, with its long voluntarist tradition in industrial relations, has been virtually unique among advanced industrial countries in not having (except for a very short period in the 1970s) a legal mechanism whereby employees could seek peacefully to obtain union recognition. Neither did the trade unions seek such a mechanism. On the whole, they felt strong enough to do without legal assistance. Moreover, the unions feared that legal intervention would open the door to legal intervention in other areas, not least in providing a mechanism for de-recognition.

The experience of the 1970s was held by many not to have been very successful, and it was ended by the Conservatives' 1980 Act. (See S. Kessler, 1995; S. Kessler with Palmer, 1996; Wood, 1997). Since then there has been no statutory mechanism. The issue, however, re-emerged with the publication of the TUC's policy document *Your Voice at Work* (TUC, 1995) which advocated:

(a)   a universal right to individual representation;
(b)   consultative rights where 10 per cent of employees are in union membership;
(c)   full trade union recognition for collective bargaining where there is majority support of those voting in a secret ballot.

The TUC proposed that there should be a new Representative Agency to consider claims on these matters.

The new Labour Government is committed to introducing proposals on statutory recognition rights, and it is expected that these will be contained in the Government's White Paper in May 1998. In the meanwhile, the Government has asked the CBI and the TUC to see if they can reach an agreement which the Government will support by legislation.

This will not be easy because the CBI is opposed in principle to statutory recognition rights, arguing that recognition should not be forced on unwilling employers even if a majority of their employees want it, and asking how could such a system work if one party were opposed to the process. There are also other difficult issues to be solved: for example, regarding the appropriate bargaining unit, the appropriate agency to carry out enquiries (possibly ACAS and the CAC), and the appropriate legal remedy if an employer refuses to abide by a recognition award.

Under the defunct ss. 11–16 of the EPA, a refusal to recognise at the end of the procedure meant that the union could resort to unilateral arbitration of matters of dispute.

A statutory mechanism would not result in a massive increase in union membership, but would right some injustices. It would not absolve unions from the hard job of recruiting members and getting majority support.

It may be in the future that more employee influence will be exercised through the extension of works council/consultative mechanisms, whether these emanate from within the UK or through the EU.

The closed shop

By stages the law was changed to making the closed shop illegal. Under the 1980 Act new closed shops needed 80 per cent support in a ballot, and under the 1982 Act existing closed shops needed an 85 per cent majority every five years. In practice few ballots were held. The 1988 Act made industrial action to enforce a closed shop unlawful, and the 1990 Act made pre-entry closed shops unlawful. According to the DE, the coverage of closed shops halved from 5.2 million to 2.65 million between 1978 and 1988, when it was said to be approximately half-and-half pre-entry and post-entry. (*Removing Barriers to Employment*, 1989). The estimate of such a large number in pre-entry closed shops, however, was highly dubious and flew in the face of all previous knowledge. By 1990, according to WIRS 3, the number covered by all closed shops was only 0.5 million.

The decline in coverage had a number of origins, mostly similar to those connected with the general decline of union membership. Places of work where the closed shop was in operation have fallen in number as steel, coal and manufacturing have contracted and the number of large establishments has fallen. Technological change has broken down old skills, and new establishments are set up away from old centres of employment. In the public sector, the Conservative Government expected management to end closed shop agreements (for example, in the Post Office and on the railways), which they did.

There have not been claims that the law on the closed shop has itself caused large losses of trade union membership, although it has happened in some cases, or that it has weakened the authority of collective agreements. It is another aspect of the legal changes which have been absorbed into the negotiators' strategies. The Labour Party's decision (taken some years ago) not to repeal this part of the Conservative legislation is in line with practical experience and its decision to support the Social Chapter in its entirety.

The closed shop, which was an important part of industrial relations history and practice, is thus now unlawful and in formal terms has ended. This does not mean that in places where unions are still strong there is not informal pressure on employees to join the union, or that some employers do not still encourage union membership. If unions are recognised it was usually considered in the employers' interest that they should be representative of the workforce, and high membership was therefore important.

Wright (1996) examined the presence of compulsory unionism in 50 large highly unionised companies between 1979 and 1991. He found that mandatory unionism among white-collar workers had collapsed, but that among manual (and particularly craft) workers, informal agreements and unofficial understandings were common. In some cases, then, the informal has taken over from the formal.

The check-off

The check-off bears the hallmark of the 1980s. The unions have come to depend extensively on employers to collect their members' subscriptions. But the provision of the 1993 Act requiring individual union members to give fresh approval every three years made a significant difference. It is the equivalent of insisting that unions recruit again their entire membership at three-yearly intervals. With the check-off the unions are plugged into the administration of the pay packet and receive regular and steady income via the employers. The employers like it because it makes the unions dependent on them. They know who is in the union and who is not. They no longer have shop stewards regularly asking members to pay up and enquiring what grievances they have, a way of doing it which unions used to believe was essential to keeping in touch with the members.

There is a great inertia in the check-off. It is extremely popular with unions and most employers are happy with it. The longer it is in operation the greater the unions' dependence on it, because an alternative becomes more and more difficult to organise. There are not many union activists where the check-off operates who remember how subscriptions used to be collected in the workplace or at the branch meeting. The alternative of union members almost universally paying their subscriptions by direct debit from their bank accounts lies some long way in the future although a number of unions, particularly white-collar unions (for example, BIFU and the RCN), have moved in this direction.

The first renewals under the 1993 Act had to be completed by August 1994. While the easier places of work were successfully covered early in the process it was only to be expected that, where employers were uncooperative and union representatives were few, the renewals would not all be secured and some of the membership would be lost, although no precise figures are available. The three-year renewal is a built-in barrier to the maintenance of union membership. The process had to be repeated in 1997. Understandably it was not popular with either unions or employers. The Labour Government is pledged to abolish the three-year renewal.

The employers know that they can exert pressure by threatening to end the check-off, especially if industrial action is contemplated, on the grounds that it would be illogical for them to collect money which could be used to pay strike benefit. The longer the check-off operates and the more extensive its use, the greater is the possibility that it will act as a restraint on unions' actions.

The selective strikes in the engineering industry for a shorter working week in 1989 and 1990 were, from the unions' viewpoint, one of the most sustained disputes of the period. The AEU ran a highly successful special levy to pay for strike benefit. The significant fact was that the employers affected considered ending the check-off, as was to be expected, but decided not to do so on the grounds that it would sour future relations with the unions. This was evidence that the threat to end the check-off if strikes are called is not always to be believed, and that unions can still raise money by asking members to put their hands in their pockets where their subscriptions are deducted from their pay packets. On the other hand, British Rail ended the check-off agreement with the RMT in July 1993 because it had taken strike action, and a year later the union's membership had fallen very substantially.

The popularity of the check-off operates strongly against certain proposals for a long-term reform of the place of the individual member in the union. John Edmonds, the leader of the GMB, proposes that membership should transcend job mobility, and that is incompatible with the check-off. His proposal is that the individual would join, pay his/her subscription by direct debit and the union would protect and advise him/her wherever he/she worked and in all circumstances. But the check-off is limited to the member's current employer. Payment of the subscription stops when the member leaves the job, and is usually only resumed in another job where there is a check-off and perhaps in another union. The idea of long-term membership was, of course, universal 20 years ago. Now the check-off stands in the way of restoring it. The 1993 Act led many unions to try to persuade their members to pay by standing order or direct debit, and this attempt is likely to continue in the future. Yet the check-off remains the preferred method among most unions and employers.

Strikes

Since 1979 there has been a continuous decline in the number of strikes, so that by the mid-1990s strike activity reached its lowest level since records began in the 1880s. The annual average number of strikes in 1994–6 was 228, and 30 working days were lost per 1000 employees; in 1980–2 those averages had been 1410 and 321.

In the 1980s there were a number of large strikes in the public sector, of which that in coal-mining in 1984/5 was the largest since the General Strike of 1926; more than half the days lost in the 1980s were lost in five public sector strikes. In the first half of the 1990s large strikes hardly ever occurred; in 1994–6 there were a mere nine strikes in which more than 50 000 days were lost. Strikes lasting less than one day declined in number but more slowly than all strikes, and by the mid-1990s they formed over half of all strikes. There was a similar decline in strike activity in other countries.

This dramatic change in the significance of strikes brought about a reversal of opinions. Twenty years ago it was said that strikes were part of 'the British disease', the touchstone of the inefficiency of industry, and a barrier to inward investment. Now it is a common view that the peaceful state of industrial relations indicates that change is accepted, and that foreign investors are assured of the cooperation of employees.

The reasons for the change are to be found in the general state of industrial relations because strikes are not independent occurrences. The balance of power has swung to the employers; unions are weaker, and only a minority of employees is covered by collective bargaining. But even in sectors where union density is still high, as in the public services and privatised firms, strikes hardly ever occur. Where negotiations between employers and unions continue to be the norm, the relationship is usually more cooperative than confrontational. The very low level of conflict reflects the quiescent state of industrial relations.

In general, those we interviewed did not believe that the law had exercised an independent influence on the amount of strike activity. The extensive legal changes affecting strikes are for the most part widely accepted as virtually permanent. The explanation is partly that the legal changes have been absorbed into the methods and procedures of negotiations, as in the case of strike ballots, and partly because the unions see no possibility of major political change.

As for the future, the main sectors where the possibility of large strikes remains are in the public services (local government, the health service and education), where central agreements remain, trade union density is still high, and where public expenditure restraints have worsened relative pay. It has yet to be seen whether the Labour Government can continue to avoid conflict in these sectors despite its commitment to its predecessor's public expenditure plans for 1997/8 and 1998/9.

In the minority of the private sector where collective bargaining operates, it is unlikely that strikes will again become a serious problem, although there could be exceptions. Managers are firmly in control, union density continues to decline, negotiations are decentralised, and employment practices generate feelings of insecurity. Even if the labour market tightens to the point where labour shortages begin to appear, it is likely that the Government will deflate rather than allow the emergence of wage inflation, stemming in part from the increased bargaining power of trade unions accompanied by real threats of industrial action.

The agenda for collective bargaining

In the 1980s and the early 1990s, in many ways the trade union agenda for collective bargaining did not change greatly. There were some changes in the mid-1990s. The unions pursued their traditional aims of higher pay and improved terms and conditions. On pay we have seen that significant increases in real pay were achieved in the 1980s, but we have also argued that this was largely management's doing. Ingram (1991b, p. 103), in his analysis of manufacturing settlements in the CBI data bank, shows that in the years between 1979 and 1989 the threat of industrial action as an upward pressure on settlements only occurred in 2–3 per cent of cases. He further shows that in every year bar one, the average settlement percentage increase for non-bargainers was higher than that for bargainers.

As has been shown, during the period there was a very substantial widening of differentials, particularly those of top and senior management and those between white-collar and manual workers: these were certainly management-led. On hours and holidays, the only significant break-through, despite the TUC's objective of a 35-hour week, was the result of the engineering strike in 1979 and the eventual settlement which led to the 39-hour week for manual workers and the phased introduction of five weeks' holiday. These union gains spread to other industries in the early 1980s. No other major changes occurred during the rest of the decade until the end of the 1980s, when there was another break-through by the engineering unions which achieved the introduction of the 37-hour week in most large federated engineering companies. These gains apart, the unions were essentially on the defensive and were on the receiving end of events and management initiatives. On reductions in manpower, unions could do no more than try to get the best redundancy terms possible. On the introduction of technological change, TUC and individual union attempts to attain technological agreements were a resounding failure. In a number of individual companies there were moves towards harmonisation of the terms and conditions of manual and white-collar workers, but these were mainly on the initiative of management, although a major landmark was the 1997 Local Government Agreement. Incoming Japanese and American companies usually had harmonisation as a matter of company policy.

The collective bargaining agenda was thus firmly set by management. This agenda for much of the period included first, the reduction in the size of the labour force, changes in working methods and increased efficiency and flexibility; and second, revised pay structures (for example, fewer grades and more integrated structures, and revised payment systems, in particular the spread of PRP). Also management set the agenda through the introduction of 'something for something' bargaining. Ingram (1991a, p. 4) again using the CBI data bank, found that in the 1980s the working practices of three-quarters of manufacturing employees covered by agreements between unions and employers were altered during the 1980s. More than half of all bargaining groups experienced more than one wage settlement involving changes in working practices, while nearly a third of annual wage settlements throughout the decade included changes in working practices. WIRS 3 indicated that in 1990 a smaller proportion of pay settlements included specific changes in working practices. It may be that employers were by then strong enough to get what they wanted under general understandings that changes would take place, without stating them specifically in each pay agreement. Certainly many employers believe that there is widespread acceptance that changes in working practices and increases in pay are complementary.

In the mid-1990s there was change in that the TUC, with the full backing of individual unions, launched its campaign for New Unionism and for Social Partnership. The objective is where possible to leave behind adversarialism and stress the value of union cooperation with management to increase efficiency, and to achieve an economy which competes on the basis of high skills, high pay and high productivity. High on the union agenda is the development of training and skills. Unions should be laying a claim to joint action on the grounds that the individuals' needs may often be at odds with the employer's short-term requirements. Unless the union is in a position to bargain for what individuals want, the employer is likely to fail to do other than offer only what is in the company's immediate or preconceived interest. Firms should recognise that what the employees want can be as important an ingredient as what the firm wants.

Another development has been for unions to seek greater security of employment in return for greater flexibility, moderation in pay claims and cooperation in achieving higher efficiency. This may sound difficult in a flexible labour market and a competitive product market, but there have been a number of such agreements: for example, at Rover, Blue Circle and United Distillers. The work of bodies such as the Involvement and Participation Association has been valuable in showing what the best British companies are doing.

The flexible labour market is not going to go away, but more could be done to make it advantageous to individuals as well as to employers. One possibility is wider choice of the mix of work and leisure, with time off being taken in more varied forms to match changing family circumstances. The greater provision of crèche facilities, extended leave for mothers of young children, and school-term employment contracts would all be valuable.

Unions are seeking to show that they are valuable for employers in providing 'a union voice' and in cooperating in the management of change. Unions' own attitude surveys have often shown that individual members rate highly job security, the provision of training and opportunities for development, a degree of participation (particularly in work-related matters), and representative rights to help ensure fair treatment.

Thus, unions need to develop the bargaining agenda in ways which have an appeal to individuals.

The European Union

Two aspects of the EU are especially relevant to British industrial relations. The first is the economic effects of '1992', and the second is EU law including the Social Chapter and its Action Programme.

On economic effects, the Single Market has meant the removal of remaining barriers to the free flow of goods and services; in other words more competitive product markets. It has also meant the removal of remaining restrictions on the movement of labour, and hence freer and more competitive labour markets. The first effect is of major importance and this combined with the free movement of capital, significantly affects the economic environment in which industrial relations takes place. On the other hand it should not be exaggerated, for Britain has already faced for many years highly competitive product markets with a relatively open economy. Developments with regard to the Euro will also be of great significance in the near future. By contrast, the effects of the free movement of labour are likely to develop slowly. The social barriers to the mobility of labour within Britain are well known, and these barriers will be all the greater across national boundaries. This is not to say that in certain parts of the labour market there will not be greater movement and competitiveness, but it will be gradual.

The direct legal effects of the EU have been discussed in Chapter 5. Of considerable importance have been Directives on Equal Pay and Equal Treatment, on Collective Redundancies and on Employment Rights on Transfer of Undertakings. More recently there has been the Working-Time Directive and the agreement of the rights of part-time workers. Decisions by the ECJ have also had a marked effect, particularly on certain individual rights of employees, and of growing importance has been a number of directives on health and safety.

The adoption of the Social Charter in 1989, with only the UK in dissent, was an event of great significance, as was the adoption of the Social Action Programme to give effect to the Social Charter. (The Charter itself did not have any binding force but was a declaration of intent.) In 1993 the UK opted out of the Social Chapter as a condition of signing the Maastricht Treaty, but this did not mean that the UK was not affected by some of the decisions taken.

The New Labour Government has ended the opt-out from the Social Chapter so that in future the UK will be fully affected by decisions taken. The EU has been a major source of improvements in individual rights and is likely to continue to be so in the future. It has also been a source of improvements in institutional rights: for example, through the Directive on EWCs, on consultation regarding collective redundancies and TUPE, and possibly in the future on national works councils. Encouraging the Social Partners to reach agreements could also be of great significance. It could be that UK employees' rights – both substantive and procedural – will in the future be very dependent on measures taken by the EU.

Conclusion

The main feature of industrial relations since 1979 is that managers are firmly in charge. This happened because of the economic necessity to increase productivity and efficiency under pressure from domestic and (above all) international competition. It also happened because the unions were weakened, and that occurred mainly because of the periods of extensive redundancies and high levels of unemployment in most years. Management sought greater cost effectiveness through the use of new technology, through increased labour flexibility – both numerical and functional – and through changing reward systems and changing contracts of employment.

Millward (1994, p. 133) concludes his analysis of WIRS 3 by stating that:

British industry and commerce appear to be moving towards the situation in which non-managerial employees are treated as a 'factor of production'. Britain is approaching the position where few employees have any mechanism through which they can contribute to the operation of their workplace in a broader context than that of their own job. There is no sign that the shrinkage in the extent of trade union representation is being offset by a growth in other methods of representing non-managerial employees' interests or view. There has been no spontaneous emergence of an alternative model of employee representation that could channel and attenuate conflicts between employers and employees.

He further concludes that 'the "high trust" practice associated with HRM had become less common, not more common, during the 1980s' (p. 129); that 'where "fragments of HRM" were found they were as commonly or more commonly found in workplaces with recognised trade unions, not those without them' (p. 129); and that 'there was no support for the notion that HRM practices and non-unionism were associated. Broadly speaking we could find little evidence that the very substantial growth in non-unionism [was] accompanied by growth in HRM or more "progressive" management practices' (p. 130).

Sisson (1994, p. 41) supports this view and concludes that:

Significant changes are taking place in personnel management in Britain: it may even be appropriate to talk in terms of a transformation. In only a small number of cases, however, is this transformation in the direction of HRM . . . Rather it appears to be taking the form of the substitution of individualism for collectivism, a reduction in standards, and an assertion of management freedom from constraints.

Things, however, did not turn out in the 1980s entirely as expected in two main ways. In the private sector where the redundancies and falling union membership were mainly concentrated, management's accession of power was at its most pronounced but it was not used to achieve what might have been expected. As the initiative passed to managers most of them did not seek to end collective bargaining by de-recognising unions or by taking deliberate action to weaken them further. Unions found it difficult to gain further recognition, and their role was cut back in numerous ways but there was no outright concerted policy of scrapping negotiations with unions. Indeed, many employers sustained unions and protected them against further falls in membership: for example, by extending the check-off.

Neither did managers make reductions in earnings an objective in a period of union weakness. In many firms managers were highly successful at proposing and securing improvements in labour utilisation: labour flexibility was a successful policy. But that was often accompanied by increases in pay which left many firms with unit labour costs rising at rates still out of line with those of foreign competitors.

There are two contrasting interpretations of these events. The first is that employers allowed the short term to dominate their thinking, and as a result they missed an opportunity to make a long-term improvement in their competitive position. On that view they should have used the increases in productivity mainly to reduce unit labour costs by settling for lower increases in pay. As it was, weaker trade unions found their members' real incomes rising faster than in the 1970s when they had been stronger. The productivity improvement was in part used to increase dividends and managerial pay, and in part distributed among the remaining workers. Other firms often followed such pay increases without achieving the same productivity gains.

The Conservative Government must have felt that private employers were letting it down by offering such large pay increases when the unions were not capable of extracting them. But the expression of that criticism was muted because ministers were committed to believing that managers were the best judges of their firms' interests. So because the government believed in the paramountcy of free markets, it could not tell employers that they were shooting themselves in the foot and that there were benefits to be gained by all of them if they put external gains above internal ones and cooperated in restraining the rate at which pay increased.

The other interpretation is that the short-term views of managers fitted in with long-term internal labour market considerations. If managers in large establishments and companies wanted to make changes they looked at ways of doing so within the existing arrangements; and, if those could produce the goods, they used them. Because managers found that the unions did not stand in their way they saw no reason for getting rid of them. Indeed, continuity with the past and the knowledge that they had to continue to live with them in the future provided an acceptable basis for getting the flexibility they wanted using the existing institutional framework. Once this approach was found to work, it was reinforced by the desire to hold together the labour force remaining after redundancies and ensure their cooperation by avoiding confrontations over pay. Managers who wanted to pay up to make sure they avoided a confrontation, even if they knew they could win, had a powerful argument. The unions' acquiescence received its reward because resistance by them would be costly to employers, even if employers were certain they would prevail in the end. That approach has meant that there has not been a fracture in the system of collective bargaining in the private sector. It may be that an opportunity to reduce unit labour costs was missed, but the achievement of labour flexibility on management's initiative and terms has been peacefully negotiated.

The second thing which did not turn out as expected concerns the public sector. Here it was the opposite of the private sector. The Conservative Government used its power to defeat the unions in strikes, yet the unions are still present and the public employers have to deal with them or find ways round them. Consider three groups. The civil service unions were defeated in the strikes over pay in 1981 and GCHQ in 1984; following the lead given in the Megaw Report, agreements covering all civil servants were made in 1987 and 1988 which depended heavily on comparability to which the Government had previously been opposed. However, this was followed in 1994 by agencies and departments being made responsible for negotiating pay and the end of service-wide agreements. In the NHS, after the 1982 dispute where again the unions were defeated, nurses' pay determination was passed to a Review Body so that now over half of the staff of the NHS have their pay determined by the findings of Review Bodies. The teachers took prolonged industrial action in 1985 and 1986 only to have their negotiating machinery abolished, yet they too were offered a Review Body in 1991.

Of course, a series of other changes, such as the contracting-out of services, cash limits, local management of schools and restructuring of the NHS, have all tended to reduce the ability of unions to protect the interests of their members. The unions have been weakened but, hard as the Conservative Government tried, it was not able to push them completely aside. Union membership continues to be high in the public service. The negotiating machinery is still there and is relied upon by managers.

A degree of continuity is an important factor which has been at work. Despite the Conservative Government's victories over the unions in strikes, the basic nature of the public services has not changed. The pay of their staff has to be settled according to some principle, and that of comparability cannot be entirely avoided. The government is responsible for the services to the electorate in the end. The services have to be kept going, and the voters can choose a government according to how well the services perform. In that sense the Conservative Government won Pyrrhic victories in strikes. Governments still have to find a basis for managing and paying the staff.

There were many exceptions to these generalisations but two were notable. In the private sector two companies in newspaper printing – the Stockport Messenger Group and News International – chose to take on the unions and they beat them. From having closed shops in the News International papers, NGA and SOGAT ceased even to be recognised. The individual employers – Eddie Shah and Rupert Murdoch – were both outsiders compared with most corporate managers because they had a big enough personal stake in the firms to make the key decisions, and they wanted to get their hands on the gains which would flow from defeating the unions. The law helped them considerably, as did the police, so the Government's action and support contributed to the demise of the unions in those newspapers. What was left unsaid was that what happened there could have been made to happen elsewhere if other employers had taken a similar line. Of course, newspaper printing was waiting for a technological revolution to take place and so the prospective gains were large. Moreover, the unions had had it their own way for a long time. It was said by many, including some trade unionists, that the newspaper unions had it coming to them. But newspaper printing did not set a precedent.

In the public sector the exception was coal. The 1984/5 strike not only broke the power of the NUM but it was the prelude to the dismantling of the industry and its eventual privatisation. The previous consensus had been that coal was essential; the Government's response to the strike and its aftermath was based on the belief that the country could manage without it. Both sides were intransigent. The Government knew that if it defeated the miners it could defeat any other group. The miners believed that they had brought down the previous Conservative Government in 1974 and they failed to read the signs that the foundation of their conviction that they were invincible had crumbled. They so managed the strike that their ranks were divided, and some worked while others were on strike.

So these exceptions support the generalisations. Had the unions in the private sector chosen to be less quiescent they would probably have been completely defeated, like the newspaper printers. In the public sector, by learning to live with defeat rather than going down fighting like the miners, the unions have survived.

What of the influence of the legislation, the Conservative Government's chosen way of taming the trade union tiger? Here too matters turned out differently from what was expected. The legal changes were extensive. Though they were always opposed by the unions and many employers were sceptical about their efficacy, they are now, for the most part, accepted as a permanent part of the legal framework of industrial relations. This about-turn occurred for two main reasons. On the union side the changes were absorbed into their operations, including the abolition of the closed shop. On the employers' side their use of the law was mainly defensive. They have not often used it to prevent unions taking action, although there have been many occasions when they could have done so successfully, most notably in the miners' strike when the Government itself prevented the NCB and other public employers from using the law against the NUM. The employers know that the law is now tipped in their favour, but they are disinclined to use it. So although the law is now vastly different from what it was in 1979, its direct effect on industrial relations behaviour has been relatively small. However, its potential importance in the background should not be under-estimated.

The Government reacted to these developments by giving individuals the power to take proceedings against unions, as they did in the miners' strike, and a Commissioner was appointed with funds to pay for their court actions. But it was a forlorn hope that individuals would make good the employers' reluctance to take legal proceedings. For the most part aggrieved union members look for other opportunities to earn their living rather than spend their time caught up in the tentacles of the law.

In the three years since Millward and Sisson drew the conclusions set out on p. 296, with which we agree, the same tendencies have prevailed. In our interviews the usual response to our questions about the recent past was that the positions adopted by employers and unions in the 1980s have been consolidated.

The employers have continued to make changes driven mainly by their product markets, redundancies have been carried out to plan, pay settlements have been adjusted to the economic performance of bargaining units (although on average earnings in the private sector have kept ahead of price increases); and there has been no lessening of the strong resistance of employers to the recognition of unions where they are not already recognised.

The unions have continued to retreat with the erosion of membership continuing (albeit somewhat more slowly). The area covered by collective bargaining has contracted further, partly as a result of the fall in the number of large establishments, the prevalence of job insecurity, changing employment patterns, and the fact that the growing areas of employment were in unorganised sectors like catering and distribution.

The question hanging over industrial relations, as over many other activities, was would things be different under a Labour Government? The question had been made irrelevant in 1992 by the fourth Conservative victory. But it was treated as a practical one from about 1995 with the arrival of Tony Blair as the Labour Party's leader and the development of a programme for the general election. With the election of a Labour Government the question became real.

In one sense the election of a Labour Government marked a turning point in that the absolute hostility of the previous government to trade unions was ended. But New Labour created different expectations from those which existed in 1992. Broadly, by 1997 the Labour Party was courting the support of leaders of the private sector and showed that it intended to incorporate the participation of senior managers into the process of government; while accepting that trade unions had a role to play which had been denied to them by the Conservative Government. The Labour manifesto contained fewer commitments to the aspirations of the unions than they had argued for.

The arrival of a Labour Government heralded little change in the balance of power in the workplace where unions are recognised. The legitimacy of managerial supremacy is not likely to be altered by Government actions, and neither will the pressures on unions be relieved. The Government's commitment to measures which have union support does not meet strong employer hostility, with one exception dealt with below; the Social Chapter is less interventionist than it looks, although not without considerable significance (employers supported the Conservative opt-out): the new NMW will affect mainly small and medium sized employers in the service sector where a floor to wages will help the competitive position of firms which already pay more, and most employers will be glad to see the end of the three-yearly renewal of the check-off.

The main exception is the Government's commitment to the statutory enforcement of union recognition. It is a good illustration of the supremely pragmatic approach of the Government which takes its stand on the proposition that if a majority of employees belong to a union, the employer can no longer refuse recognition (a form of democratic majority rule). It was left to the Archbishop of Canterbury at the 1997 TUC to assert the employees' moral right to be represented by a trade union. Otherwise, the argument that in a democracy citizens should have the right to challenge the employers' greater power by collective action hardly got a hearing. The employers' position, as set out by the Director General of the CBI, Adair Turner (also at the 1997 TUC), is that workplaces belong to firms whose managers have sole control over whether unions should be recognised, however many employees are union members.

The Government would prefer the employers and unions to agree on what the legal rules on recognition should be. There are difficult questions about the definition of the area to which the majority applies, the form of compulsion to be applied to employers, and the rules on de-recognition. If there is no agreement, as seems likely, and the Government goes ahead on its own, it is probable that the law will have only a limited effect on the extent of recognition for several reasons.

First, the Government's 50 per cent plus one as a requirement for recognition is a high hurdle because it is difficult to build up a majority in the face of employer hostility. Second, unions have shown in recent times little ability to recruit and hold members without recognition, so there is legitimate doubt as to whether the prospect of recognition will transform their abilities, particularly when so many employees are part-time. Third, implacable hostility from employers is difficult to overcome even when legal penalties are available since bargaining involves participation in a joint process. If legal recognition is to be effective in extending widely the coverage of collective bargaining, the law needs to be firmly slanted in favour of unions, and most employers must be willing to accept unions if they reach the legal threshold of support. It seems that the Government is inclined to stand back and introduce minimum intervention rather than do what is necessary to ensure that the law makes recognition the norm.

The expectation is therefore that industrial relations may well stabilise around the present balance of forces. There is certainly no reason to suppose that either economic circumstances or Government action will produce a major accretion of union power. The unions may retreat no further, but employers will remain firmly in the ascendancy.

If that prediction is plausible, it has implications for the significance of industrial relations in the economic life of the country. Industrial relations, defined in a narrow sense, are that part of employee relations which is governed by negotiations and other procedures between employers and trade unions. It has become a minority activity except in the public services, most privatised firms and some other (mostly large) private employers. If the sectors covered by industrial relations are free of conflict, except possibly in the public services, with employers firmly in control and unions in a cooperative mode generally facilitating the changes initiated by management, they will not require the special attention they have had in the past to the same extent. The majority interest will be in managing employees free of union participation.

At the margins there will be moves between the two areas. Moreover, there will always be a need for comparisons to establish their relative efficiency. It may well be the case that union participation can provide a deeper commitment by employees to a firm's objectives than can be obtained from a labour force composed of unorganised individuals with no capacity for collective action. On the other hand, it may be shown that in firms without unions, managers can relate incentives to opportunities in ways which secure the cooperation of individuals motivated only by self-interest and unimpeded by the opinions of organised employees.

Unions for their part will be seeking in a more favourable political climate (although not to the extent that they may have hoped), to broaden their appeal through New Unionism and Social Partnership, through an agenda which addresses individual needs as well as collective ones, and through opportunities in the EU which may well prove a major way forward.

Even so, if our assessment of the likely course of events in the next five to ten years turns out to be broadly true, industrial relations may cease to be a major source of concern, and become no more than a sub-section of employee relations. However, unbridled control of workplaces by managers will mean that the tone of relations between employers and employees will change: employees will be isolated individuals facing powerful and confident managers. If that happens, the lessons of the value of industrial relations between employers and trade unions may have to be re-learned.

General elections and governments 1945–97

General election	Government	Prime Minister	Government overall majority in the House of Commons
1945	Labour	C. R. Attlee	146
1950	Labour	C. R. Attlee	5
1951	Conservative	W. Churchill	17
		A. Eden (April 1955)	
1955	Conservative	A. Eden	60
		H. Macmillan (Jan. 1957)	
1959	Conservative	H. Macmillan	100
		A. Douglas-Home (Oct. 1963)	
1964	Labour	H. Wilson	4
1966	Labour	H. Wilson	96
1970	Conservative	E. Heath	30
1974 (Feb.)	Labour	H. Wilson	−33
1974 (Oct.)	Labour	H. Wilson	3
		J. Callaghan (April 1976)	
1979	Conservative	M. Thatcher	43
1983	Conservative	M. Thatcher	144
1987	Conservative	M. Thatcher	100
		J. Major (Nov. 1990)	
1992	Conservative	J. Major	21
1997	Labour	T. Blair	189

The Social Charter

The Social Charter was adopted by all Member States, except the UK, in December 1989. The Social Charter is not a legal text. It is a statement of principles by which governments agree to abide. They will be required each year to present a report on how they are implementing the Charter. Its aim is to highlight the importance of the Social Dimension of the Single Market in achieving social as well as economic cohesion in the EC.

Summary of the rights set out in the Social Charter:

1. Freedom of movement throughout the Community with equal treatment in access to employment, working conditions and social protection.
2. Freedom to choose and engage in an occupation, which shall be fairly remunerated.
3. Improvement of living and working conditions, especially for part-time and temporary workers, and rights to weekly rest periods and annual paid leave.
4. Right to adequate social protection.
5. Right to freedom of association and collective bargaining.
6. Right to access to lifelong vocational training, without discrimination on grounds of nationality.
7. Right of equal treatment of men and women, especially in access to employment, pay, working conditions, education and training and career development.
8. Right to information, consultation and participation for employees, particularly in conditions of technological change, restructuring, redundancies, land for transfrontier workers.
9. Right to health protection and safety at the workplace including training, information, consultation and participation for employees.
10. Rights of children and adolescents, including a minimum working age.
11. Right for the elderly to have a decent standard of living on retirement.
12. Right of people with disabilities to programmes to help them in social and professional life.

The preamble of the Social Charter gives added weight to other international obligations, such as ILO conventions. The preamble also includes a commitment to combat every form of discrimination, including discrimination on grounds of sex, colour, race, opinions and beliefs.

The Social Action Programme

The Social Action Programme is a set of legal proposals from the Commission. The Commission sees them as ways of enforcing some principles in the Social Charter. Most of the major proposals are for legal instruments which, once adopted, will be applicable in all member states. Other proposals are for studies or communications which may then lead to legislative proposals.

The Social Action Programme: main proposals

- a Directive on special employment relationships (part-time and temporary work) (introduced June 1990)
- a Directive on working time laying down certain minimum requirements about rest periods, holidays, night work, weekend work, and systematic overtime (introduced July 1990)
- the revision of the 1975 Directive on collective redundancies (introduced mid-1991)
- a Directive on the protection of pregnant women and women who have recently given birth (introduced November 1990)
- a third equal opportunities action programme (introduced 1990)
- a Directive on the protection of young people at work (introduced 1991)
- a Recommendation on financial participation of workers (introduced early 1991)
- a Directive on the establishment of European company councils for information and consultation of workers in 'European-scale enterprises' (introduced December 1990)
- an instrument on access to vocational training
- a range of Directives on health and safety issues
- an Opinion on the criteria for an equitable wage
- a Communication on the development of collective bargaining, including collective agreements at European level.

The Protocol on Social Policy

Article 1

The Community and the Member States shall have as their objectives the promotion of employment, improved living and working conditions, proper social protection, dialogue between management and labour, the development of human resources with a view to lasting high employment and the combatting of exclusion. To this end the Community and the Member States shall implement measures which take account of the diverse forms of national practices, in particular in the field of contractual relations, and the need to maintain the competitiveness of the Community economy.

Article 2

1. With a view to achieving the objectives of Article 1, the community shall support and complement the activities of the member States in the following fields:
   - improvement in particular of the working environment to protect workers' health and safety;
   - working conditions;
   - the information and consultation of workers;
   - equality between men and women with regard to labour market opportunities and treatment at work;
   - the integration of persons excluded from the labour market, without prejudice to Article 127 of the Treaty establishing the European Community (hereinafter referred to as 'the Treaty').
2. To this end, the Council may adopt, by means of directives, minimum requirements for gradual implementation, having regard to the conditions and technical rules obtaining in each of the Member States.

Such directives shall avoid imposing administrative, financial and legal constraints in a way which would hold back the creation and development of small and medium-sized undertakings.

The Council shall act in accordance with the procedure referred to in Article 189c of the Treaty after consulting the Economic and Social Committee.

3. However, the council shall act unanimously on a proposal from the Commission, after consulting the European parliament and the Economic and Social committee, in the following areas:
   - social security and social protection of workers;
   - protection of workers where their employment contract is terminated;
   - representation and collective defence of the interests of workers and employers, including co-determination, subject to paragraph 6;
   - conditions of employment for third-country nationals legally residing in Community territory;
   - financial contributions for promotion of employment and job-creation, without prejudice to the provisions relating to the Social Fund.

4. A Member State may entrust management and labour, at their joint request, with the implementation of directives adopted pursuant to paragraphs 2 and 3.

   In this case, it shall ensure that, no later than the date on which a directive must be transposed in accordance with Article 189, management and labour have introduced the necessary measures by agreement, the Member State concerned being required to take any necessary measure enabling it at any time to be in a position to guarantee the results imposed by that directive.

5. The provisions adopted pursuant to this Article shall not prevent any Member State from maintaining or introducing more stringent preventive measures compatible with the Treaty.

6. The provisions of this Article shall not apply to pay, the right of association, the right to strike or the right to impose lock-outs.

Article 3

1. The commission shall have the task of promoting the consultation of management and labour at Community level and shall take any relevant measure to facilitate their dialogue by ensuring balanced support for the parties.

2. To this end, before submitting proposals in the social policy field, the Commission shall consult management and labour on the possible direction of Community action.

3. If, after such consultation, the Commission considers Community action advisable, it shall consult management and labour on the content of the envisaged proposal. Management and labour shall forward to the Commission an opinion or, where appropriate, a recommendation.

4. On the occasion of such consultation, management and labour may inform the Commission of their wish to initiate the process provided for in Article 4. The duration of the procedure shall not exceed nine months, unless the management and labour concerned and the Commission decide jointly to extend it.

Article 4

1. Should management and labour so desire, the dialogue between them at Community level may lead to contractual relations, including agreements.
2. Agreements concluded at Community level shall be implemented either in accordance with the procedures and practices specific to management and labour and the Member States or, in matters covered by Article 2, at the joint request of the signatory parties, by a Council decision on a proposal from the Commission.

   The Council shall act by qualified majority, except where the agreement in question contains one or more provisions relating to one of the areas referred to in Article 2(3), in which case it shall act unanimously.

Article 5

With a view to achieving the objectives of Article 1 and without prejudice to the other provisions of the Treaty, the Commission shall encourage cooperation between the Member States and facilitate the coordination of their action in all social policy fields under this Agreement.

Article 6

1. Each Member State shall ensure that the principle of equal pay for male and female workers for equal work is applied.
2. For the purpose of this Article, 'pay' means the ordinary basic or minimum wage or salary and any other consideration, whether in cash or in kind, which the worker receives directly or indirectly, in respect of his employment, from his employer. Equal pay without discrimination based on sex means:
   (a) that pay for the same work at piece rates shall be calculated on the basis of the same unit of measurement;
   (b) that pay of work at time rates shall be the same for the same job.

3. This Article shall not prevent any Member State from maintaining or adopting measures providing for specific advantages in order to make it easier for women to pursue a vocational activity or to prevent or compensate for disadvantages in their professional careers.

Article 7

The Commission shall draw up a report each year or progress in achieving the objectives of Article 1, including the demographic situation in the Community. It shall forward the report to the European Parliament, the Council and the Economic and Social Committee.

The European Parliament may invite the Commission to draw up reports on particular problems concerning the social situation.

References*

Abbreviations: BJIR – *British Journal of Industrial Relations*
                 IRJ – *Industrial Relations Journal*
                 JMS – *Journal of Management Studies*

ACAS (1980a) *Annual Report 1979* (London: HMSO).
ACAS (1980b) *Industrial Relations Handbook* (London: HMSO).
ACAS (1987) *Annual Report 1986* (London: HMSO).
ACAS (1993) *Promoting the Improvement of Industrial Relations* (London: HMSO).
ACAS (1996) *Annual Report 1995* (London: ACAS).
ACAS (1997) *Annual Report 1996* (London: ACAS).
Adeney, M. and Lloyd, J. (1986) *The Miners', Strike 1984–5: Loss Without Limit* (London: Routledge & Kegan Paul).
Ahlstrand B. W. (1990) *The Quest for Productivity: A Case Study of Fawley after Flanders* (Cambridge: Cambridge University Press).
Atkinson, J. (1984) 'Manpower strategies for the flexible firm', *Personnel Management*, August.
Atkinson, J. and Meager, N. (1986) 'Is Flexibility Just a Flash in the Pan?', *Personnel Management*, September.
Bailey, R. (1996) 'Public Sector Industrial Relations', in Beardwell, I., *Contemporary Industrial Relations* (Oxford: Oxford University Press).
Bailey, R. and Kelly, J. (1990) 'An Index Measure of British Trade Union Density', *BJIR*, Vol. 28, No. 2.
Bailey, R. and Trinder, C. (1989) *Public Service Pay over Two Decades* (London: Public Service Foundation).
Bain, G. (1971) 'Management and White Collar Unionism', in Kessler, S. and Weekes, B. (1971) *Conflict at Work* (London: BBC Publications).
Bain, G. and Price, R. (1983) 'Union Growth: Dimensions, Determinants and Density', in Bain, G. (ed.), *Industrial Relations in Britain* (Oxford Basil Blackwell).
Bassett, P. (1986) *Strike Free* (London: Macmillan)

---

* Books, articles and official papers to which reference is made.

311

Batstone, E. (1984) *Working Order: Workplace Industrial Relations over Two Decades* (Oxford: Basil Blackwell).

Batstone, E., Ferner, A. and Terry, M. (1983) *Unions on the Board: An Experiment in Industrial Democracy* (Oxford: Basil Blackwell).

Beaumont P. B. (1987) *The Decline of Trade Union Organisation* (London: Croom Helm).

Benson, E. (1993) 'Employment Protection', in Gold, M. (ed.), *The Social Dimension: Employment Policy in the European Community* (London: Macmillan).

BJIR (1968) *The Royal Commission on Trade Unions and Employers', Associations 1965–68*, Vol. VI, No. 3 November.

Blackwell, R. and Lloyd, P. (1989) 'New Managerialism in the Civil Service: industrial relations under the Thatcher Administrations 1979–86', in Mailly, Dimmock and Sethi (1989b) *Industrial Relations in the Public Services* (London: Routledge).

Brewster, C. and Connock, S. (1985) *Industrial Relations: Cost Effective Strategies* (London: Hutchinson).

Britton, A. (1997) 'Full Employment in a Market Economy', in Philpott, J. (ed.), *Working for Full Employment* (London: Employment Policy Institute).

Brown, W. (1986) 'The Changing Role of Trade Unions in the Management of Labour', *BJIR*, Vol. XXIV, No. 2, July.

Brown, W. (1989) *The Evolution of Regionally Differentiated Pay* (London: Public Finance Foundation, Discussion Paper, No. 24).

Brown, W. (1993) 'The Contraction of Collective Bargaining in Britain', *BJIR*, Vol. 31, No. 2.

Brown, W., Deakin, S. and Ryan, P. (1997) 'The Effects of British Industrial Relations Legislation 1979–97', *National Institute for Economic and Social Research Economic Review*, No. 161, July.

Brown, W. and Rowthorn, B. (1990) *A Public Service Pay Policy*, Fabian Tract 542 (London: Fabian Society).

Brown, W. and Wadhwani, S. (1990) 'The Economic Effects of Industrial Relations Legislation since 1979', *National Institute for Economic and Social Research Economic Review*, February.

Brown, W. and Walsh, J. (1991) 'Pay Determination in Britain in the 1980s: The anatomy of decentralisation', *Oxford Review of Economic Policy*, Vol. 7, No. 1, February.

Bullock Report (1977) See Committee of Inquiry (1977).

CAB (1993) *Job Insecurity* (London: CAB).

CAB (1997) *Flexibility Abused* (London: CAB).

CAC (1976) *Annual Report 1976* (London: CAC).

CAC (1977) *Annual Report 1977* (London: CAC).

CAC (1978) *Annual Report 1978* (London: CAC).

CBI (1989) *Pay and Performance 1989–1990* (London: CBI).

Certification Officer (1977) *First Annual Report 1976* (London: HMSO).

CIR (1969a) Report No. 1, *Associated Octel Company Ltd*, Cmnd 4246 (London: HMSO).

CIR (1969b) Report No. 2, *General Accident Fire and Life Assurance Company Ltd*, Cmnd 4247 (London: HMSO).

CIR (1970a) Report No. 4, *Birmid Qualcast*, Cmnd 4269 (London: HMSO).

CIR (1970b) Report No. 9, *First General Report*, Cmnd 4417 (London: HMSO).

CIR (1971a) Report No. 17, *Facilities Afforded to Shop Stewards*, Cmnd 4668 (London: HMSO).

CIR (1971b) Report No. 22, *Shipbuilding and Repairing*, Cmnd 4756 (London: HMSO).

CIR (1971c) Report No. 23, *The Hotel and Catering Industry Part, I. Hotels and Restaurants*, Cmnd 4789 (London: HMSO).

CIR (1972a) Report No. 30, *Approved Closed Shop Agreement British Shipping Federation: National Union of Seamen* (London: HMSO).

CIR (1972b) Report No. 31, *Disclosure of Information* (London: HMSO).

CIR (1973a) Report No. 37, *Annual Report for 1972* (London: HMSO).

CIR (1973b) Report No. 40, *Approved Closed Shop in Theatre, Independent Television and Film* (London: HMSO).

CIR (1973c) Report No. 53, *Con Mech (Engineers)* (London: HMSO).

Clarke, K. (1987) Lecture at City University Business School (unpublished).

Claydon, T. (1989) 'Union Derecognition in Britain in the 1980s', *BJIR*, Vol. XXVII, No. 2, July.

Claydon, T. (1996): 'Union De-recognition: a re-examination', in Beardwell, I. (ed.), *Contemporary Industrial Relations: A Critical Analysis* (Oxford: Oxford University Press).

Clegg H. A. (1979) *The Changing System of Industrial Relations in Great Britain* (Oxford: Basil Blackwell).

Clegg, H. A. (1980) See Standing Commission (1980).

Committee of Inquiry (1977) *Report on Industrial Democracy* (Bullock Report) Cmnd 6706 (London: HMSO).

Conyon, M. and Gregg, P. (1994) 'Pay at the Top: A Study of the Sensitivity of Top Director Remuneration to Company Specific Shocks', *National Institute for Economic and Social Research Economic Review*, No. 149, August 1994.

Court of Inquiry (1972) *Report into a Dispute between the National Coal Board and the National Union of Mineworkers*, Cmnd 4903 (London: HMSO).

Cox, S. (1993) 'Equal Opportunities', in Gold, M. (ed.) *The Social Dimension: Employment Policy in the European Union* (London: Macmillan).

Cross, M. (1988) 'Changes in Working Practices in UK Manufacturing 1981–1988', *Industrial Relations Review and Report* 415, May.

DE (1991) *Code of Practice – Trade Union Ballots on Industrial Action* (London: DE).

DE (1992) White Paper, *People, Jobs and Opportunity* (London: HMSO).

Dickerson, A. P. and Stewart, M. H. (1993) 'Is the Public Sector Strike Prone?', *Oxford Bulletin of Economics and Statistics*, Vol. 55, No. 3.

Disney, R. (1990) 'Explanations of the Decline in Trade Union Density in Britain: an appraisal', *BJIR*, Vol. 28, No. 2, July.

Disney, R., Gosling, A. and Machin, S. (1994) 'British Unions in Decline: an examination of the 1990s fall in trade union recognition', *Institute of Fiscal Studies*, Working Paper Series No. WP4/4, London.

Donovan Report (1968) See Royal Commission (1968).

Dunn, S. and Metcalf, D. (1996) *Strikes in Essential Services* (London: Employment Policy Institute).

Edmund Davies, Lord (1978) *Committee of Inquiry on the Police: Report on Negotiating Machinery and Pay*, Cmnd 2837 (London: HMSO).

Edwards, P. (1987) *Managing the Factory* (Oxford: Basil Blackwell).

Elgar, J. and Simpson, B. (1993) 'The Impact of the Law on Industrial Disputes in the 1980s', in Metcalf, D. and Milner, S. (eds), *New Perspectives on Industrial Disputes* (London: Routledge).

Employment Policy (1944) Cmnd 6527 (London: HMSO).

Employment Policy Institute (1996) *After the Jobs Ministry – Options for Running Labour Market Policy* (London: Employment Policy Institute).

Evans, S. (1987) 'The Use of Injunctions in Industrial Disputes May 1984–April 1987', *BJIR*, Vol. XXV, No. 3, November.

Fells, A. (1972) *The British Prices and Incomes Board* (Cambridge: Cambridge University Press).

Ferner, A. (1989) 'Ten Years of Thatcherism: changed industrial relations in public enterprises', Warwick Papers in Industrial Relations, No. 27 University of Warwick.

Flanders, A. (1964) *The Fawley Productivity Agreements* (London: Faber).

Flanders, A. (1967) *Collective Bargaining: Prescription for Change* (London: Faber).

Fox, A. (1974) *Beyond Contract: Work, Power and Trust Relations* (London: Faber).

Freeman, R. and Pelletier, J. (1990) 'The Impact of Industrial Relations on British Union Density', *BJIR*, Vol. 28, No. 2, July.

Gall, G. and McKay, S. (1994) 'Trade Union De-recognition in Britain 1989–94', *BJIR*, Vol. 32, No. 3, September.

Gall, G. and McKay, S. (1996) 'Injunctions as a legal weapon in industrial disputes', *BJIR*, Vol. 34, No. 4, December.

Geroski, P., Gregg, P. and Desjonqueres, T. (1994) 'Did the Retreat of UK Trade Unionism Accelerate during the 1990–93 Recession?', London: National Institute for Economic and Social Research, Discussion Paper, No. 57.

Gospel, H. (1992) *Markets, Firms and the Management of Labour* (Cambridge: Cambridge University Press).

Green Paper (1996) *Industrial Action and Trade Unions* (Cmnd 3470) (London: HMSO).

Gregg, P. and Yates, A. (1991) 'Changes in Wage-Setting Arrangements and Trade Union Presence in the 1980s', *BJIR*, Vol. 29, No. 3, September.

Gregg, P., Machin, S. and Szymanski, S. (1993) 'The Disappearing Relationship between Directors' Pay and Corporate Performance', *BJIR*, Vol. 31, No. 1, March.

Griffiths, R. (1983) *NHS Management Inquiry. Report* (London: DHSS).

Guest, D. (1987) 'Human Resource Management and Industrial Relations', *JMS*, Vol. 24, No. 5, September.

Guest, D. (1989) 'Human Resource Management: its implications for industrial relations and trade unions', in Storey (1989).

Halsbury, J. (1974) *Report of Committee of Inquiry into Pay and Related Terms and Conditions of Service of Nurses and Midwives* (London: HMSO).

Heery, E. (1996) 'The New Unionism', in Beardwell, I. (ed.), *The New Unionism* (Oxford: Oxford University Press).

Himmelweit, H. T., Humphreys, P. and Jaeger, M. (1985) *How Voters Decide: A Model of Vote Choice Based on a Special Longitudinal Study Extending over Fifteen Years and the British Election Surveys of 1970–1983* (Milton Keynes: Open University Press).

Houghton, D. (1974) *Report of the Committee of Inquiry into the Pay of Non-University Teachers*, Cmnd 5848 (London: HMSO).

Hunter, L. C., and MacInnes, J. L. (1991) 'Employer Labour Use Strategies: Case Studies', *Employment Department Research Paper 83*.

Ibbs, R. (1988) *Improving Management in Government: The Next Steps* (London: HMSO).

In Place of Strife (1969) Cmnd 3888 (London: HMSO).

Incomes Policy: The Next Step (1962) Cmnd 1662 (London: HMSO).

Industrial Democracy (1978) Cmnd 7231 (London: HMSO).

Ingram, P. (1991a) 'Changes in Working Practices in British Manufacturing Industry in the 1980s', *BJIR*, Vol. 29, No. 1, March.

Ingram, P. (1991b) 'Ten Years of Manufacturing Wage Settlements 1979–89', *Oxford Review of Economic Policy*, Vol. 7, No. 1, February.

Inns of Court Conservative and Unionist Society (1958) *A Giant's Strength* (London).

Institute of Personnel Management/Involvement and Participation Association (1990) *Employee Involvement and Participation in the UK* (London: IPM/IPA).

Jenkins, P. (1970) *The Battle of Downing Street* (London: Charles Knight).

Kelly, J. and Bailey, R. (1989) 'British Trade Union Membership Density and Decline in the 1980s', *IRJ*, Vol. 20, No. 1, Spring.

Kelly, J. and Heery, E. (1989) 'Full-time Officers and Trade Union Recruitment', *BJIR*, Vol. XXVII, No. 2, July.

Kessler, I. (1989) 'Bargaining Strategies in Local Government' in Mailly, Dimmock and Sethi (1989b).

Kessler, I. (1990) 'Flexibility and Comparability in Pay Determination for Professional Civil Servants', *IRJ*, Vol. 21, No. 3, Autumn.

Kessler, I. (1994) 'Performance Pay', ch. 14 in Sisson, K. *Personnel Management*, 2nd edn (Oxford: Basil Blackwell).

Kessler, I. and Purcell, J. (1994) 'Joint Problem Solving and the Role of Third Parties: An Evaluation of the ACAS Advisory Work', *Human Resource Management Journal*, Vol. 4, No. 2, January.

Kessler, I. and Purcell, J. (1995) 'Individualism and Collectivism in Theory and Practice: Management Style and the Design of Pay Systems', in Edwards, P. (ed.), *Industrial Relations* (Oxford: Basil Blackwell).

Kessler, I. and Purcell, J. (1996) 'Strategic Choice and New Forms of Employee Relations in the Public Service Sector: developing an analytical framework', *Journal of International HRM*, Vol. 7, No. 1, February.

Kessler, I. and Undy, R. (1995) 'The New Employment Relationship: Examining the Psychological Contract', *Issues in People Management, No. 12* (London: Institute of Personnel and Development).

Kessler, S. (1983) 'Comparability', in Robinson, D. and Mayhew, K. (eds), *Pay Policies for the Future* (Oxford: Oxford University Press).

Kessler, S. (1987) 'Pendulum Arbitration', *Personnel Management*, December.

Kessler, S. (1995) 'Trade Union Recognition: CIR and ACAS Experience', *Employee Relations*, Vol. 17, No. 6.

Kessler, S. and Weekes, B. (1971) *Conflict at Work* (London: BBC Publications).

Kessler, S. with Palmer, G. (1996) 'The Commission on Industrial Relations in Britain 1969–74: a retrospective and prospective evaluation', *Employee Relations*, Vol. 18, No. 4.

Kinnie, N. (1987) 'Bargaining within the Enterprise: Centralised or Decentralised?', *JMS*, Vol. 24, No. 5.

Labour Party (1976) *Report of the 70th Annual Conference* (London: Labour Party).

Leopold, J.W. (1988) 'Moving the Status Quo: the growth of trade union political funds', *IRJ*, Vol. 19, No. 4, Winter.

Leopold, J.W. (1997) 'Trade Unions, Political Fund Ballots and the Labour Party', *BJIR*, Vol. 35, No. 1, March.

Lewis, R. (1991) 'Reforming Industrial Relations: Law, Politics and Power', *Oxford Review of Economic Policy*, Vol. 7, No. 1, February.

Local Government Management Board (1994) *Single Status Employment: Towards a New Employer Strategy* (London: LGMB).

Lodge, D. (1987) 'Working Equality into Manual Job Evaluation', *Personnel Management*, September.

Machin, S. and Manning, A. (1993) 'The Effects of Minimum Wages on Wage Dispersion: evidence from UK Wages Councils', *Industrial and Labour Relations Review*, Vol. 47, No. 2.

Machinery of Prices and Incomes Policy (1965) Cmnd 2577 (London: HMSO).

Mackay, L. and Torrington, D. (1986) *The Changing Nature of Personnel Management* (London: Institute of Personnel Management).

Mailly, R., Dimmock, S. J. and Sethi, A. S. (1989a) 'Industrial Relations in the NHS since 1979', in Mailly, Dimmock and Sethi (1989b).

Mailly, R., Dimmock, S. J. and Sethi, A. S. (1989b) *Industrial Relations in the Public Services* (London: Routledge).

Main, P. (1986) *Committee of Inquiry Report into the Pay and Conditions of Service of School Teachers in Scotland*, Cmnd 9893 (London: HMSO).

Marchington, M. (1989) 'Joint Consultation in Practice', in Sisson, K. (ed.), *Personnel Management in Britain* (Oxford: Basil Blackwell).

Marginson, P., Armstrong, P., Edwards, P. and Purcell, J. (1993) 'The Control of Industrial Relations in Large Companies: an initial analysis of the second company industrial relations survey', *Warwick Papers in Industrial Relations*, No. 45.

Marginson, P., Edwards, P., Martin, R., Purcell, J. and Sisson, K. (1988) *Beyond the Workplace* (Oxford: Basil Blackwell).

Mayhew, K. (1991) 'The Assessment: The UK Labour Market in the 1980s', *Oxford Review of Economic Policy*, Vol. 17, No. 1, February.

McCarthy W. E. J. (1966) *The Role of Shop Stewards in British Industrial Relations*, Royal Commission on Trade Unions and Employers' Associations, Research Paper, No. 1 (London: HMSO).

McCarthy W. E. J. (1971) 'Changing Bargaining Structures', in Kessler and Weekes (1971).

McCarthy, W. E. J. (1992) 'The Rise and Fall of Collectivist Laissez-Faire', in McCarthy, W. E. J. (ed.), *Legal Intervention in Industrial Relations: Gain and Losses* (Oxford: Basil Blackwell).

McCarthy W. E. J. (1993) 'From Donovan until now: Britain's Twenty-five years of incomes policy', *Employee Relations*, Vol. 15, No. 6.

McCarthy, W. E. J. and Ellis, N. D. (1973) *Management by Agreement* (London: Hutchinson).

McGregor, A. and Sproull, A. C. (1991) 'Employer Labour Use Strategies: Analysis of a National Survey', *Employment Department Research Paper 83*.

McInnes, J. (1987) *Thatcherism at Work* (Milton Keynes: Open University Press).

Megaw Report (1982) *Inquiry into Civil Service Pay*, Cmnd 8590 (London: HMSO).

Metcalf, D. (1990a) 'Industrial Relations and the "Productivity Miracle" in British Manufacturing Industry in the 1980s', *Australian Bulletin of Labour*, Vol. 16, No. 2, June.

Metcalf, D. (1990b) 'Water Notes Dry Up: The Impact of the Donovan Reform Proposals and Thatcherism at Work on Labour Productivity in British Manufacturing Industry', *BJIR*, Vol. 27, No. 1, March.

Metcalf, D. (1991) 'British Unions: Disolution or Resurgence?', *Oxford Review of Economic Policy*, Vol. 17, No. 1, February.

Millward, N. (1994) *The New Industrial Relations?* (London: Policy Studies Institute).

Millward, N. and Stevens, M. (1986) *British Workplace Industrial Relations 1980–1984* (Aldershot: Gower).

Millward, N., Stevens, M., Smart, D. and Hawes, W. R. (1992) *Workplace Industrial Relations in Transition* (Dartmouth: Aldershot).

Milner, S. (1993) 'Final-offer Arbitration in the UK', London: Department of Employment Research Series, No. 7, Ch. 1.

Milner, S. and Metcalf, D. (1993) 'Appendix: A Century of UK Strike Activity: an alternative perspective', in Metcalf, D. and Milner, S. (eds), *New Perspectives on Industrial Disputes* (London: Routledge).

Mitchell, J. (1972) *The NBPI* (London: Secker & Warburg).

NBPI (1966a) Report No. 16, *Pay and Conditions of Busmen*, Cmnd 3012 (London: HMSO).

NBPI (1966b) Report No. 23, *Productivity and Pay during the Period of Severe Restraint*, Cmnd 3167 (London: HMSO).

NBPI (1967a) Report No. 29, *The Pay and Conditions of Manual Workers in Local Authorities, the National Health Service, Gas and Water Supply*, Cmnd 3230 (London: HMSO).

NBPI (1967b) Report No. 36, *Productivity Agreements*, Cmnd 3311 (London: HMSO).

NBPI (1968a) Report No. 65, *Payment by Results*, Cmnd 3627 (London: HMSO).

NBPI (1968b) Report No. 83, *Job Evaluation*, Cmnd 3772 (London: HMSO).

NBPI (1969) Report No. 161, *Hours of Work, Overtime and Shiftworking*, Cmnd 4554 (London: HMSO).

NEDO (1986) *Changing Working Patterns – How Companies Achieve Flexibility to Meet New Needs* (London: NEDO).

Next Step Agencies in Government (1993) *Review*, Cmnd 2430 (London: HMSO).

Nolan, P. and Marginson, P. (1990) 'Skating on Thin Ice? David Metcalf on Trade Unions and Productivity', *BJIR*, Vol. 18, No. 2, July.

Pendleton, A. and Winterton, J. (eds) (1993) *Public Enterprise in Transition: Industrial Relations in State and Privatised Corporations* (London: Routledge).

Period of Severe Restraint (1966) Cmnd 3150 (London: HMSO).

Personal Incomes, Costs and Prices (1948) Cmd 7321 (London: HMSO).

Phelps Brown, H. (1990) 'The Counter-Revolution of Our Time', *Industrial Relations*, Vol. 29, No. 1, Winter.

Pollert, A. (1987) 'The Flexible Firm', *Warwick Papers in Industrial Relations*, No. 19, University of Warwick.

Poole, M. and Mansfield, R. (1993) 'Patterns of Continuity and Change in Managerial Attitudes and Behaviour in Industrial Relations 1980–1990', *BJIR*, Vol. 31, No. 1, March.

Price, R. and Bain, G. S. (1983) 'Union Growth in Britain: Retrospect and Prospects', *BJIR*, Vol. XXI, No. 1, March.

Prices and Incomes Policy (1965) Cmnd 2639 (London: HMSO).

Prices and Incomes Policy after 30 June 1967, Cmnd 3235 (London: HMSO).

Prices and Incomes Policy: An Early Warning System (1965) Cmnd 2808 (London: HMSO).

Prices and Incomes Standstill (1966) Cmnd 3073 (London: HMSO).

Priestley (1955) See Royal Commission (1955).

Prior, J. (1986) *A Balance of Power* (London: Hamilton).

Productivity, Prices and Incomes in 1968 and 1969 (1968) Cmnd 3590 (London: HMSO).

Productivity, Prices and Incomes after 1969 (1969) Cmnd 4237 (London: HMSO).

Purcell, J. (1987) 'Mapping Management Styles in Employee Relations', *JMS*, Vol. 24, No. 5, September.

Purcell, J. and Ahlstrand, B. (1994) *Human Resource Management in the Multi-Divisional Firm* (Oxford: Oxford University Press).

Purcell, J. and Sisson, K. (1983) 'Strategies and Practice in the Management of Industrial Relations', in Bain, G. (ed.), *Industrial Relations in Britain* (Oxford: Basil Blackwell).

Removing Barriers to Employment (1989) Cmnd 655 (London: HMSO).

Roberts, B. C. (1987) *Mr Hammond's Cherry Tree: The Morphology of Union Survival*, Occasional Paper, No. 76 (London: Institute of Economic Affairs).

Robinson, D. (1986) *Monetarism and the Labour Market* (Oxford: Clarendon Press).

Rose, R. and McAllister, I. (1986) *Voters Begin to Choose: from Closed-Class to Open Elections in Britain* (London: Sage).

Ross A. M. and Hartman, P. T. (1960) *Changing Patterns of Industrial Conflict* (New York: Wiley).

Royal Commission on the Civil Service 1953–1955, *Report* (Priestley) (1955) Cmnd 9613 (London: HMSO).

Royal Commission on Trade Unions and Employers' Associations, *Report* (Donovan) (1968) Cmnd 3623 (London: HMSO).

Scamp Sir Jack (1968) *Report on the Motor Industry Joint Council* (London).

Scott, B. (1981) *Committee into the Value of Pensions*, Cmnd 8147 (London: HMSO).

Seifert, R. V. (1989) 'Industrial Relations in the School Sector', in Mailly, Dimmock and Sethi (1989b).

Sisson, K. (1994) 'Personnel Management: Paradigms, Practice and Prospects', in Sisson, K. (ed.), *Personnel Management*, 2nd edn (Oxford: Basil Blackwell), Ch. 1.

Sisson, K. and Marginson, P. (1995) 'Management Systems, Structures and Strategy', in Edwards, P. *Industrial Relations* (Oxford: Basil Blackwell).

Smith, P. and Morton, G. (1993) 'Union Exclusion and the Decollectivisation of Industrial Relations in Contemporary Britain', *BJIR*, Vol. 31, No. 1, March.

Standing Commission on Pay Comparability (1980) Report, No. 9, *General Report*, Cmnd 7995 (London: HMSO).

Stevens, M. and Wareing, A. (1990) 'Union Density and Workforce Composition: Preliminary Results from the 1989 Labour Force Survey', *Employment Gazette*, August.

Storey, J. (1992) *Developments in the Management of Human Resources* (Oxford: Basil Blackwell).

Storey, J. (ed.) (1989) *New Perspectives on Human Resource Management* (London: Routledge).

Storey, J. and Bacon, N. (1993) 'Individualism and Collectivism: into the 1990s', *International Journal of Human Resource Management*, Vol. 4, No. 3.

Sweeney, K. and Davies, J. (1996) 'Labour Disputes in 1995', *Labour Market Trends*, June.

Taylor, R. (1994) *The Future of the Trade Unions* (London: André Deutsch).

Tebbit, N. (1988) *Upwardly Mobile: An Autobiography* (London: Weidenfeld & Nicolson).

Terry, M. (1995) 'Trade Unions: Shop Stewards and the Workplace', in Edwards, P. (ed.), *Industrial Relations* (Oxford: Basil Blackwell).

The Attack on Inflation (1975) Cmnd 6151 (London: HMSO).

The Attack on Inflation after 31 July 1977 (1977) Cmnd 6882 (London: HMSO).

The Attack on Inflation after 31 July 1978 (1978) Cmnd 7293 (London: HMSO).

The Attack on Inflation: The Second Year (1976) Cmnd 6507 (London: HMSO).

The Economic Implications of Full Employment (1956) Cmnd 9725 (London: HMSO).

Thompson, M. (1992) 'Pay and Performance: The Employer Experience', Institute of Manpower Studies, Report 218, University of Sussex.

Thompson, M. (1993) 'Pay and Performance: The Employee Experience', Institute of Manpower Studies, Report 258, University of Sussex.

TUC (1980) *The Organisation, Structure and Services of the TUC* (London: TUC).

TUC (1984) *TUC Strategy: A TUC Consultative Document* (London: TUC).

TUC (1988a) *Europe 1992: Maximising the Benefits, Minimising the Costs* (London: TUC).

TUC (1988b) *Special Review Body Report* (London: TUC).

TUC (1989) *Special Review Body Report* (London: TUC).

TUC (1990) *Special Review Body Report* (London: TUC).

TUC (1991a) *Collective Bargaining Strategy for the 1990s* (London: TUC).

TUC (1991b) *Towards 2000* (London: TUC).

TUC (1991c) *Unions in Europe in the 1990s* (London: TUC).

TUC (1993) *The Next Phase in Europe* (London: TUC).

TUC (1994a) *Campaigning for Change: A New Era for the TUC* (London: TUC).

TUC (1994b) *General Council's Annual Report* (London: TUC).

TUC (1995) *Your Voice at Work* (London: TUC).

TUC (1996a) *Partners for Progress* (London: TUC).

TUC (1996b) *Your Stake at Work* (London: TUC).

TUC (1997a) *Britain and Europe – Next Steps* (London: TUC).

TUC (1997b) *European Works Councils* (London: TUC).

Undy, R. and Martin, R. (1984) *Ballots and Trade Union Democracy* (Oxford: Basil Blackwell).

Undy, R., Fosh, P., Morris, H., Smith, P., Martin, R. (1996) *Managing the Unions* (Oxford: Clarendon Press).

Weekes, B., Melish, M., Dickens, L. and Lloyd, J. (1975) *Industrial Relations and the Limits of the Law* (Oxford: Basil Blackwell).

White Paper (1994) *The Civil Service: Continuity and Change* (London: HMSO).

Wilberforce Report (1972) See Court of Inquiry (1972).

Willman, P. (1984) 'The Reform of Collective Bargaining and Strike Activity in BL Cars 1976–82', *IRJ*, Vol. 15, No. 2.

Willman, P. (1989) 'The Logic of Market-Share Unionism', *IRJ*, Vol. 20, No. 4.

Willman, P. (1990) 'The Financial Status and Performance of British Trade Unions 1950–88', *BJIR*, Vol. 28, No. 3, November.

Willman, P. and Morris, T. (1988) *The Finances of British Trade Unions 1975–85*, DE Research Paper, No. 62 (London: DE).

Winchester, D. and Bach, S. (1995) 'The State: The Public Sector', in Edwards, P. (ed.), *Industrial Relations* (Oxford: Basil Blackwell).

Wood, S. (1997) *Statutory Union Recognition* (London: Institute of Personnel and Development).

Wright, M. (1996) 'The Collapse of Compulsory Unionism? Collective Organisation in Highly Unionised British Companies 1979–1991', *BJIR*, Vol. 34, No. 4, December.

Index

320